Katherine Anne Porter:

A Sense of the Times

Minds of the New South

Robert F. Martin
Howard Kester and the Struggle for Social Justice in the South, 1904–77

Janis P. Stout
Katherine Anne Porter: A Sense of the Times

Katherine Anne Porter

A Sense of the Times

Janis P. Stout

University Press of Virginia

Charlottesville & London

THE UNIVERSITY PRESS OF VIRGINIA

First published 1995

Except where otherwise noted, all photographs have been used by the kind permission of the McKeldin Library, University of Maryland.

Portions of chapter 3 were originally published in 1993 in the *South Central Review,* and portions of chapter 10 in 1994 in *American Literature*. They are reprinted with permission of the editors.

Library of Congress Cataloging-in-Publication Data

Stout, Janis P.
Katherine Anne Porter : a sense of the times / Janis P. Stout.
p. cm. — (Minds of the new South)
Includes bibliographical references and index.
ISBN 0-8139-1568-6 (cloth)
1. Porter, Katherine Anne, 1890–1980. 2. Women authors, American—20th century—Biography. 3. Women and literature—Southern States—History—20th century. 4. Southern States—In literature. I. Title. II. Series.
PS3531.0752Z815 1995
813′.52—dc20
[B] 94-42285
CIP

Printed in the United States of America

❧ To my colleague,
friend, and husband,
Loren Daniel Lutes,
sine quo non

Any sketch of her character or account of her life would have to start with or start from statements of her own about herself.

—Glenway Wescott, Journal entry, April 4, 1940

Her historical and social sense is like a fine antenna, and certain pieces shimmer with the ominous presence of history. She has been haunted by the times.

—Joseph Featherstone, "Katherine Anne Porter's Stories," 1965

CONTENTS

	List of Illustrations	xi
	List of Abbreviations and Author's Note	xiii
	Preface and Acknowledgments	xv
ONE	A Career as Big as Texas	1
TWO	Establishing an Identity	18
THREE	Politics and Art in the Radical Twenties	38
FOUR	The Harvest of Mexico	68
FIVE	"between two wars in a falling world"	92
SIX	Among the Agrarians	115
SEVEN	From Radical to Moderate: Pulling Back to the Center	142
EIGHT	The Issue of Gender	167
NINE	*Ship of Fools* and the Problem of Genre	196
TEN	Porter as Reader and as Critic	219
ELEVEN	Artistry and Achievement	248
TWELVE	"a free, intransigent, dissenting mind"	265
	Notes	293
	Bibliography	353
	Index	367

ILLUSTRATIONS

The grave of Porter's mother at Indian Creek, Texas

Porter's first passport photograph, December 1920

Caricature of Gertrude Stein drawn by Porter, published in the *New York Herald Tribune,* January 16, 1927

Josephine Herbst and John Herrmann in the spring of 1928 on the front porch of their house at Erwinna, Pennsylvania, shortly after moving in

View from the veranda of Hilgrove, the house in Bermuda that Porter rented for four months in 1929

Porter with Eugene Pressly in Mexico, 1930 or 1931

Porter and Hart Crane, Mexico, 1931

On board the *Werra,* September 1931

Ford Madox Ford, a photograph taken by Porter

Barbara Harrison Wescott, 1934, in Davos, Switzerland

Porter and her father beside a road in Texas, during her visit in 1936

Porter in her Paris apartment, the night before she returned to the United States

Allen Tate, looking literary, at night at Benfolly, his home in Tennessee

Porter with Nancy Tate and kittens, at Benfolly

Albert Erskine in 1937 or 1938, in a photograph taken by Porter

Photograph of Porter taken by George Platt Lynes in May 1939

Eudora Welty in 1941, the year in which her book of short stories *A Curtain of Green* appeared with an introduction by Porter

South Hill, the house that Porter renovated in 1941 and lived in for less than a year

Porter on a balcony with George Platt Lynes below

Porter's nephew, Paul Porter

Porter at her desk with her typewriter, 1946, with the Buddha figure given her by her brother

With novelist William Goyen, 1951

Being hoisted onto a tank by Colonel Glover Johns, Jr., the son of her childhood friend Erna Schlemmer Johns, 1959

E. Barrett Prettyman and Robert Penn Warren at Porter's Twelfth Night Party in 1969

Glenway Wescott and Monroe Wheeler with Porter, May 15, 1965, her seventy-fifth birthday

The gracious lady of literature, wearing the famous emerald ring she bought after *Ship of Fools* and a long string of pearls she bought while teaching in Michigan

Dressed for a reading

Joan Givner standing in front of the portrait painted by Marcella Comès Winslow

ABBREVIATIONS AND AUTHOR'S NOTE

CE	*The Collected Essays and Occasional Writings of Katherine Anne Porter.* Boston: Houghton Mifflin/Seymour Lawrence, 1970.
CS	*The Collected Stories of Katherine Anne Porter.* New York: Harcourt Brace Jovanovich, 1972.
Letters	*Letters of Katherine Anne Porter,* edited by Isabel Bayley. New York: Atlantic Monthly Press, 1990. Because letters in this volume are not always complete, I have sometimes referred to the holograph even when the same letter, in edited form, appears in Bayley's edition.
Beinecke	The Beinecke Rare Book and Manuscript Library of Yale University.
Hargrett	The Hargrett Rare Book and Manuscript Library of the University of Georgia.
HRC	The Harry Ransom Humanities Research Center of the University of Texas.
McKeldin	The McKeldin Library of the University of Maryland, College Park. When "McKeldin" appears alone it designates the Katherine Anne Porter Collection. When it is followed by initials it indicates other collections at McKeldin as follows: MLD: The Mary Louis Doherty Collection PP: The Paul Porter Collection TFW: The Thomas F. Walsh Collection

NOTE: In quotations from Porter's unpublished papers, I have standardized her use of multiple ellipses within sentences (which often appear in long clusters such as: . . . .) and ellipses at the end of sentences. To prevent confusion, I have avoided adding ellipses of my own in material quoted from Porter.

I have silently corrected peculiarities that appear to be obvious typographical errors. I have retained, however, her customary spelling of contractions without the apostrophe and her erratic capitalization of words such as *South*. All references to Porter's marginal annotations refer to her personal library, now located in the Katherine Anne Porter Room of McKeldin Library, University of Maryland.

PREFACE AND ACKNOWLEDGMENTS

Katherine Anne Porter once said of herself, "You know I am an artist and I am really not an intellectual."[1] It is probably an accurate assessment. Yet her intellectual growth, her opinions and cast of mind—her sensibility—are well worth studying. Why? In part because of her artistry, which is generally considered one of the stellar achievements of modernism. But an additional reason lies in the nature of her relation to her historic moment. She had an extraordinary breadth of acquaintance with the events and the people who contributed in varied and sometimes decisive ways to the growth of what might be called the twentieth-century mind, and she responded to them with intensity and sometimes, at least, with insight. The shifting multiplicity of her interests and allegiances makes her all too vulnerable to the charge of dilettantism, but she did develop a keen sense of her times, particularly with respect to the arts and politics and the complex intersections of the two.

Porter's historic moment was a long one. Her life and career encompassed a huge stretch of the twentieth century, and her ramblings took her to a great number of places. Born in 1890 (though she sometimes had it 1894), she lived until 1980—almost a century. Beginning her adult life in Texas, a Southerner, growing into rebellion against all things Texan, she became a cosmopolitan who yearned not only after fixity, but after the South.

Not that she came full circle. She did not come home again, but died in a suburb of Washington, D.C., a far piece from the banks of Indian Creek, a branch of the Rio Blanco, where she had begun. She died, too, possessed of something like wealth, or at least a level of prosperity a far sight from the poverty in which she had lived her early years. Even so, the South—and Texas, her Texas, *was* the South, or at least its fraying edge—remained at the center of her allegiances and her social affections. The South was the anchor to which she was tethered and around which she ranged.

And she did range: in her early years, to Chicago and Denver and New

York and Connecticut and Bermuda and Mexico City; in her middle years, to Berlin, Paris, Madrid, Basel, New Orleans, Houston, Baton Rouge, Palo Alto; to the University of Virginia, the University of Texas, the University of Michigan, Stanford, Cornell, Auburn, Purdue, the University of Maryland, Hollins College; in her later years, to Washington and Paris and Belgium and Italy and back to Washington. And these are only indicators; the complete list of her travels, if anyone could compile it, would be extensive. Her life vibrated between a consuming restlessness and a homing instinct that was never fully satisfied.

Porter's incessant rambling brought her into acquaintance with a great range of literary and public figures and located her at the periphery of events that are the stuff of twentieth-century history. She had a knack for being where things were happening, from the World War I flu epidemic to the protest marches preceding the execution of Nicola Sacco and Bartolomeo Vanzetti, from the Obregón revolution in Mexico to the rise of Hitler's Nazi party in Berlin (and a date with Hermann Goering), from a public stand against McCarthysim in the fifties to the launching of a moon shot at Cape Canaveral in the seventies.[2] She met Ernest Hemingway at Sylvia Beach's book shop in Paris, was probably snubbed by Gertrude Stein in the same city, and was lifted and held aloft, as if a kind of effigy, by Dylan Thomas at a party in New York. She smuggled in booze for her friends during Prohibition, after a stay in Bermuda, and enjoyed the White House hospitality of Lyndon Johnson. Hubert Humphrey wrote to congratulate her on winning a National Book Award.[3] She knew Hart Crane, Malcolm and Peggy Cowley, Glenway Wescott, Ford Madox Ford, Eudora Welty, Cleanth Brooks, Allen Tate and Caroline Gordon, Josephine Herbst and John Herrmann, Robert Penn Warren and Eleanor Clark—and sooner or later quarreled with most of them or savaged them behind their backs.

She was not only a voluminous letter writer, but a writer of marvelous letters. Indeed, Malcolm Cowley once remarked that her letters were her real masterpiece. She was bitterly offended. (But she later said much the same thing, though less tactfully, about her friend Josephine Herbst: "She was ever so much better a letter writer than she ever was novelist.")[4] Her letters are remarkably interesting in their own right, as well as for their illumination of her work. Lively, chatty, worldly, at times deeply engaged with ideas and events and at times deeply engaged only with herself, they are alternately revealing and defensive, and at times both at once. One of her closest friends during the latter half of her life, Glenway Wescott, wrote in his journal a rather mixed tribute: "Of course Katherine Anne's despairing letters are superior to any novel she could have written. Her concentration on fiction, fiction, fiction has been not only because it seemed to offer greatest remuneration but because she always wants to disseminate *un*truth, which seems easiest to do in the novel form. She doesn't stop to consider the fact that her letters are fictitious."[5] It is a cogent comment on her pervasive disingenuousness.

Porter's correspondence is of significance, as well, in explaining the spareness of her literary productivity. Writing letters to her numerous friends and acquaintances and relatives gave her an all too convenient alternative to the considerably more strenuous desk work required by the writing of fiction and essays. In a moment of rare insight into her own nature, she once said to Josephine Herbst—in a letter, of course—"Well, well, a little solitude and a job I ought to be at, and I become the world's champion letter writer." Similarly, she confessed to another of her friends, "I used to write enormous quantities of letters, and the truth was, that I did not do anything else."[6]

In writing about Porter, there is a temptation, as she said in her essay on Ezra Pound, "to get down to individual letters, to quote endlessly." But perhaps it is forgivable to quote *almost* endlessly from a person who was called, by at least two persons of well-educated taste, "the best living letter-writer."[7] To trace the life and career of this small, strikingly beautiful woman from Texas who became a writer's writer, a model of style in the literary as well as the fashion sense, is also to touch on a wide sweep of the literary and intellectual and political life of the century. If Katherine Anne Porter was not actually at the center of things—and for the most part she was not—she was usually close to it.

❧ Among the joys of an extended project of research and writing is the enrichment of one's acquaintance and cooperative interchange with others of like interests. I am fortunate in being able to acknowledge debts of gratitude to many individuals and organizations who have provided assistance, often very substantial assistance, on this project. The list is extensive: first, the University of Maryland, for permission to use its splendid holdings of Porter's letters and other memorabilia, and Barbara Thompson Davis, Porter's literary executor, for permission to quote from unpublished materials there; the staff of the McKeldin Library at Maryland, especially Dr. Blanche Ebeling-Koning, who until 1993 was the curator of the Katherine Anne Porter Collection, and Lauren Brown, curator of archives and manuscripts, for their numerous instances of kindness and help; Jordon Pecile, for permission to use his correspondence with Porter, housed at Maryland but not generally available; the Beinecke Rare Book and Manuscript Library at Yale University, for permission to quote from materials in the Josephine Herbst Collection and the Robert Penn Warren Collection, and especially Patricia Willis for her assistance; Reginald Gibbons, literary executor and editor of the papers of William Goyen, housed at the Harry Ransom Humanities Research Center of the University of Texas; the HRC itself and its remarkable staff, especially Cathy Henderson; the Hargrett Rare Book and Manuscript Library at the University of Georgia Library, for permission to quote from materials in the Donald Windham Collection; Marquette University for permission to quote from a letter in the Dorothy Day–Catholic Worker Collection; Dean Daniel Fallon, of Texas A & M University, and Dean Gordon C. Bond, of Auburn University, for their encouragement; the National Endowment for the Humanities, for a Travel to Collections Grant; Professor Robert Calvert of the Department of History at Texas A & M University, for assistance with various matters relating to Texas history, especially for referring me to Professor Worth Robert Miller of Southwest Missouri State University, who shared his valuable data on precinct voting records in Texas; Professor Larry D. Hill, who answered questions and steered me past many shoals; Professors Henry Schmidt of Texas A & M University and Donathon Olliff of Auburn University, for assistance with other historical questions; Mr. George Thomas Parsons III of Houston, who allowed me to quote from materials in his private collection; George Garrett, of the University of Virginia, Richard Dillard, of Hollins College, Nancy Tate Wood, Phyllis Rifield, and Frances Cheney, who shared their personal knowledge of Porter; Dr. Leah Atkins and Dr. Jerry Brown of Auburn University, for sharing their knowledge of the Agrarians and southern history; Joan Givner, whose generosity at every turn has been of inestimable value; Richard Holway, history and social sciences editor at the University Press of Virginia, who maintained his belief in this book even when the manuscript kept growing; and Dr. Ruth Moore Alvarez, for sharing with me not only her own expertise and her librarianship but her knowledge and her friendship as well. And there are others.

Katherine Anne Porter:

A Sense of the Times

CHAPTER ONE

A Career as Big as Texas

> Those early readings began in Texas, just before World War I, before ever I left home; they ended in Paris, twenty years later, after the longest kind of journey.
>
> —Porter, "Reflections on Willa Cather"

The biography of Katherine Anne Porter is a classic story of the rise from obscurity. The child of a subsistence farmer who in fact lost or gave up his land and took refuge with his mother when his second daughter—actually named Callie Russell, not Katherine Anne—was two years old, she lived through years of hard work and pinched finances to become the grande dame of American letters. It was a status she greatly enjoyed. Claiming to have her roots in a more aristocratic social class than she actually did, she adopted a style of life to go with her claims whenever finances would permit. After years when nothing but her own wit and beauty stood between her and penury, when she often did not have enough money even to eat adequately, she achieved, late in life, a material success comparable to the artistic success she had attained long before. With the proceeds from her long-awaited novel *Ship of Fools,* published in 1962, she bought a knockout emerald (twenty-one carats) to go with the designer dresses she had long affected. Her friends were a remarkable assortment of the famous and gifted, and she enjoyed, in the latter third of her life, a degree of fame that comes to few serious writers. Her career was long, varied, and celebrated.

Yet the very terms that define her life so well oversimplify it. Her biography veers off sharply from the paradigm of the rags-to-riches story into byways that seem not merely unlikely but at times inexplicable. To study Porter's life and career is to explore a tangle of contradictions, some of which may be unraveled, many of which can only be puzzled over. These include her shifting politics and her sense of gender, as well as her deeply conflicted sense of regional and class identity. It is these puzzles and contradictions that shaped her life, and they will shape her intellectual biography as it is presented here.

One of the great puzzles of her career—or perhaps it is one of the wonders of her career—is her intellectual stature as a person of letters, occupying a position very near the center of twentieth-century political and intellectual crosscurrents. Her formal education was scant, a sound enough basic schooling that ended when she was fourteen and had been intermittent even before. Such acquaintance with literature and history and religion as she had she gained for herself, by her own efforts. How she developed the desire, let alone the ability to pursue such a stunning project of self-education, from what combination of inner resources and external stimuli or challenges, is a mystery. Yet the evidence is abundant that she did so. Her personal library, preserved more or less intact, is extensive, and the abundance of markings and annotations demonstrates her attentive reading. These annotations, as well as her essays, letters, and fiction, are evidence of the quality of her intellect.

❧ Porter was for many years regarded as a representative of an aristocratic Southern society of fine manners and gentle customs. This belief derived from her own statements about her early life. She was fond of calling herself a member of the "white-pillar crowd," by which she meant the southern plantation-owning class.[1] She enjoyed telling friends about the faithful servants who had tended her in childhood and the extensive library that had graced her family home, much like the standard library belonging to members of the southern aristocracy, which has been described as "volumes of Shakespeare, Scott, George Eliot, Johnson, Goldsmith, Greek and Latin classics."[2] Her acounts of this extensive family library, as well as her tales of an ample home life in other respects, are now generally conceded to have been fantasy. While visiting Texas in 1936, however, for the first time in many years, she wrote to her husband, Eugene Pressly, to whom she would by then have had little reason to misrepresent her background, "I don't know what became of Dad's collection of books. Scattered and gone."[3] This remark, I believe, should be weighed rather heavily as evidence that her representations of the library were not totally without basis in fact. Her father probably did have some good books, and she apparently read in them in her early years.

Some of her accounts, though, bore little relation to the truth. To fellow novelist Josephine Herbst, one of her closest friends, she wrote that "at the plantation" servants brought hot and cold bath water to her room and "we dined in state, being fairly washed, in a room full of panelling copied from the older house for which panelling had been brought from England." To critic and sometime friend Malcolm Cowley she wrote similarly that she was "brought up in the 1852 style, a house full of sweet and friendly black people, a nurse who used to come and sleep in the same bed with me when I had nightmares."[4]

Her paternal grandmother had indeed sprung from prosperous landowners in Kentucky and had been given as a wedding present a slave whom she brought with her to Texas when she and her husband, Asbury Porter, migrated to Hays County, near Austin. A former slave woman, known as Aunt Jane, did occasionally visit the family when Porter and her brother and sisters were living in their grandmother's home in Kyle, following their mother's death in 1892. But Porter's accounts were considerably exaggerated. There were no great numbers of loyal former slaves, and the house was not of noble proportions, nor was it luxuriously fitted out with libraries and fine porcelain. The family had had land at one time, but by the end of the nineteenth century, like many others, were land-poor, lacking the liquid assets to farm on a profitable scale and maintain a comfortable way of life. Furthermore, their landholdings themselves had greatly shrunk as a result of peculiar mismanagement. When Porter acknowledged to friends that her family's fortunes had been severely reduced after the Civil War, owing in part to the unequal rail freight rates that afflicted southern farmers, she was mitigating the picture considerably.

She had been born in a log cabin in Indian Creek, Texas, a rural community near the town of Brownwood, on May 15, 1890, the fourth child of Harrison Boone Porter, a farmer, and his wife Mary Alice. One of the earlier children, a boy, had died before Katherine Anne was born. Her mother, a former schoolteacher, was apparently a woman of extraordinary sweetness and strong religious convictions; her father, a tall, fine-looking man somewhat given to adventure and to melancholy. By the time he married Mary Alice Jones, in 1883, at age twenty-six, he had already been to Mexico in a railroad-building venture and, according to his own moody statement, had considered staying there. He wrote Mary Alice in 1882, "Were it possible I would blot from my memory the knowledge of my mother tongue, and link my name, my future to [the] rising star of Castillo." He mentioned that he admired the pretty girls in Mexico and enjoyed dancing with them, but hastened to add that he "was not dancing with the class of Mexicans as seen in our country."[5] As his famous daughter would later, he had or wished to have a sense of his proper position.

Both parents were better educated than their lot in life might suggest. Joan Givner has commented at some length, in her biography of Porter, on the literary proclivities evident in the letters written by the two prior to their marriage.[6] Mary Alice, in particular, wrote in a shapely hand and a rather elevated style. She was inclined to insert into her letters small essays or set pieces such as she had produced at school. Indeed, one of her little school essays survives in the file of their correspondence. Harrison Porter wrote in a somewhat more slapdash manner, both as to script and as to prose style, but his letters, too, were grammatical and at times somewhat bookish. He seems to have enjoyed creating a slightly rakish persona. After commenting that he was studying the Bible, for example—to please Mary Alice, one suspects—he expressed questions of such heterodoxy as to evoke, in her reply, a long and painstakingly worked out scriptural refutation of the views he had hinted at. The two entered their marriage, then, in a state of intellectual or at least theological debate. That debate would prolong itself in Harrison Porter's later, more aggressive challenges to orthodoxy and in Katherine Anne's vacillation on matters of religion.

In 1892, shortly after the birth of a fifth child, another girl, Mary Alice Porter died, leaving the little Callie with a sense of deprivation that would never be entirely dispelled. Her bereft father plunged into a prolonged grief and despondency that struck her, as she later recalled it, as being essentially selfish. He seemed to her to have disregarded his children's grief entirely, counting only his own loss as being important. He moved his young family—Gay, Paul, Callie, and infant Mary Alice—to his mother's home in the little town of Kyle, Texas, a few miles south of Austin, and lapsed into ineffectuality.

Catherine Porter, the children's grandmother, known as Aunt Cat, was advanced in years and in frail health, but she seems to have coped with the demands of receiving her gloomy son and his four small children with admirable pluck and determination. Providing a measure of stability in the children's lives whose value can scarcely be overestimated, she set about rearing them in an orderly, respectable, though perhaps overly strict way. They were sent to school and taken to church as part of the visible family of a woman highly respected in her community. Yet Porter would later recall her life in Kyle as one of deprivation and gloom. Looking back on that period, she wrote to Cora Posey, a friend of her mother's in Indian Creek who had given her some of her father's letters, that "the gloom and darkness of his nature darkened the very air around us. I noticed that in these letters [written soon after his wife's death] he did not once mention the children: we early learned not to speak of our mother, his grief and regret belonged to him, we could neither share nor lighten it. I know that he loved us, and did what he could for us, but I always felt we were an immense and bitter burden to him, on his heart and in just the daily life of trying to care for us." To her third husband-to-be (by the usual count), Albert Erskine, she described her father as "quite indifferent to my fate or my living" during the "very critical years of my life." She later wrote to her sister Gay that she had heard their brother used to say "his one fear about his children was that he might make them as unhappy as our father had made us."[7] In a sense, then, Porter lost her father when she lost her mother. Givner attributes to this lack of fatherly attention and care Porter's manifest difficulties in relations with men and her "insatiable hunger for masculine admiration."[8] It is a plausible guess.

The home in Kyle to which Harrison Porter brought his orphaned children in 1892 seems to have been plain and somewhat cramped, though probably not "unbearably" so, as Givner describes it. The family was severely reduced in circumstances from its earlier economic status, to the point that the children sometimes wore cast-off clothes donated by neighbors. Again, however, that does not necessarily, as Givner believes, indicate "squalid" or "degrading" poverty.[9] Such a practice would not have been unusual in a small town where the struggling grandmother was known and respected by neighbors who wished to help. But Porter's pride was stung by the memory of such acts of charity. She envied her prosperous friend Erna Schlemmer, and in later years the circumstances of her childhood in Kyle did not accord with her myth of herself.

The conflict between Porter's actual economic origins and her sense of the social class to which she rightfully belonged were probably derived from her grandmother, whose pictures show her erect, stern, dressed in ladylike mourning, a proud figure. In 1947, after reading a statement that novelist Willa Cather "knew what it meant to be raised in the hinterland of privation and harsh necessities," she wrote in the margin of the book, "How touching I should write sometime about what it means to be brought up in the idea of superiority in spite of poverty, privation, which took no note of the reality of such things."[10] The reference would seem to be to her grandmother, who became the dominant figure in Porter's fictions set in some version of her Texas home. Porter's imagination, that is, centered on a foremother who represented the possibility of claiming a patrician heritage and to whom she was linked through her father. It is a provocative obverse of her later friend, Allen Tate, who selected as the primary ancestors of his imagination his mother's family and represented it in a novel, *The Fathers*.[11]

The conflict between family pride and actual circumstances can be seen very clearly in Porter's celebrated story "The Grave," where Miranda and Paul—two of the three fictional children who regularly represent Porter and her brother and older sister; she always omitted her younger sister, Mary Alice, called Baby, from fictional representations of the family—encounter a poor white family of former sharecroppers who have gained possession of land formerly belonging to the Rae family, including the family burial ground. The uneasiness of the confrontation and the children's sense of displacement are clear and are powerfully, tersely conveyed. The conflict can be seen, as well, in "Noon Wine," where the Thompsons (drawn from unacknowledged poor white cousins of Porter's) drive about the countryside, explaining Mr. Thompson's innocence of the murder of which he has been accused. After making such calls, they feel that they have abased themselves before their inferiors. It is easy to suppose that Porter herself came to know early on what it was to have such feelings.

Despite her inculcated sense of superior social class, she would at times express a support of the working classes that rings of theoretical, if not actual, solidarity. In some of her writings about Mexico, notably the essay "The Fiesta of Guadalupe" (1920), one sees a sincerity of sympathy with the downtrodden that can scarcely be doubted.[12] In letters to her older sister, Gay Porter Holloway, she more than once espoused the cause of the working classes, and indeed of organized labor. She urged Gay, who worked in county offices in Houston, to recognize the benefits of a "strong union" that would protect her and her fellow workers from exploitative practices. "The employers stand together," she wrote, "and they work all the time to make division and hostility among the workers." She predicted that the time would come when such employers would have to "pay decent wages out of their profits, which are always too high," and added, "Well! The unions are not perfect, but they look like angels to me when I think of what people suffered before they came." She disapproved of her nephew Breck's being in the State Patrol on the grounds that he would be repressing the poorer classes and "helping to break strikes." Yet she could also write to Gay, with peculiar emphasis, "There is nothing more coarsening and cheapening than social familiarity with one's inferiors." Again, the shaping tension, the puzzle.[13]

In 1901 a second major bereavement in Porter's life occurred when Aunt Cat, her grandmother and surrogate mother, also died. At this time the Porter family's life fell into real disorder, to the point that the record of their movements is somewhat uncertain. They lived for a time in San Antonio, where Katherine Anne, still known as Callie, received the last of her scant formal education. Curiously enough, when she was awarded her first Guggenheim Fellowship she listed her home as San Antonio, although she had apparently not lived there since this brief period in late childhood.[14] Soon they moved to Victoria, Texas, where the record of Porter's endeavors begins—efforts to make her own way that would not have alerted even the keenest observer to the prospect of her future literary achievement. In 1905, at the age of fifteen, she was announced in a Victoria newspaper, along with her sister Gay, as a teacher of "music, physical culture, and dramatic reading."[15] Photographs from the period show her to be already of extraordinary beauty and to have a keen, even theatrical, sense of style.

She had already discarded her natal first name, the simple and perhaps countrified Callie, and replaced it with a version of her grandmother's Catherine, going by either Katherine or K. R. Her marriage license in 1906 showed her as K. R. Porter. Later she would claim that Callie was only an "infant nickname," and her full given name was actually Katherine Anne Maria Veronica Callista Russell Porter. She was not consistent, however, claiming on another occasion that her "true, natural-born name" was Katherine Anne Porter. On yet another occasion she said that her "real name was Callista Russell, for a girlhood friend of my mother." She added that when she reached "the age of accountability" she "named" herself for her grandmother and "had it legally changed."[16]

She must have been very unhappy during this period. At age sixteen, after moving to Lufkin in far east Texas, she married a young man named John Henry Koontz whom she had met in Victoria, the younger son of a well-established ranching family there but himself a railroad employee living in Lafayette, Louisiana. The couple would later, in 1908, move to Houston, where he worked for a wholesale grocery firm, and, in 1912, to Corpus Christi, where she renewed her friendship with Erna Schlemmer, now married to an automobile dealer named Glover Johns. It was at this time that she began her reading of modern literature.[17]

Porter's motivation for marrying so young seems to have been at least in part to escape from her birth family to a situation that she must have supposed would be more stable. But whatever expectations she had were disappointed. The marriage was turbulent, marked by her husband's and his family's frequent dissatisfaction with her spending habits and occasionally scarred by physical violence. It would not be formally dissolved, however, until nine years later. Porter subsequently wrote to her father that recovery from the "shock" of her marriage to Koontz, in which she had been "criminally wronged," took years.[18] No children were born of this or her later marriages, and her childlessness, too, was sometimes a tormenting grief to her.

In 1914, having left Koontz, she went to Chicago to try her luck in movies, though she would later say that she had had no desire to be in movies but had been recruited for bit parts while doing newspaper work about a filmmaker. Before the end of the same year she was back in Louisiana, caring for her sister Gay and Gay's two small children, and earning a living for all of them by performing songs, dances, and recitations on the Lyceum circuit. Neither her interest nor her physical stamina was adequate to the life of touring entertainer, however, and in 1915, having quarreled with Gay, she went to Dallas to cast about for some other means of earning a livelihood. By the end of the year she had fallen ill with tuberculosis.

In those years, tuberculosis was the most dreaded of diseases, causing an estimated one-eighth of all deaths worldwide in 1920. The human body is not normally a receptive ground for tuberculosis, however, unless weakened by exhaustion, inadequate diet, chronic illness, alcoholism, or similar debilitation.[19] The fact that Porter suffered the disease, then, is consistent with other evidence that her life in the preceding years had been one of hardship and privation. When her illness was first diagnosed, she had no choice but to enter a charity "pest house" in Dallas, a type of facility common in those years and often wretchedly operated, as was this one. By the spring of 1916, with financial help from her brother, she was able to go to a well-run sanitarium in Carlsbad, Texas, near San Angelo. Here she met a newspaperwoman from Fort Worth, Kitty Barry Crawford, also a patient at the sanitarium. She completed her recovery at the Woodlawn Hospital in Dallas, where she was employed to help care for and teach tubercular children. In September 1917, sufficiently recovered to leave Woodlawn, she embarked on a newspaper career with the Crawfords in Fort Worth.[20]

The details of Porter's early newspaper work are not clearly known. She had apparently already done some newspaper work in Dallas. It is clear, at any rate, that in 1918 she went to Colorado and, after a few months of additional recuperation along with Kitty Barry Crawford, began work as a reporter and columnist on the *Rocky Mountain News*. The pattern is important: When she left her first husband, John Henry Koontz, she also left Texas, going to Chicago to work; when she again tried in earnest to launch a career, she again left her home state, which she would later say was strangling her. From the time she went to Colorado and became a newspaper writer until the end of her life, she never again made her home in Texas for any extended period. Indeed, she would say that there was "something about Texas I just can't go," and if she tried to live there she would "die of melancholy in a place that reminded me every day of all that I wish to forget."[21]

While in Denver, Porter contracted influenza and came so near death that her family began to make plans for her burial. The experience of near-death, combined with the wartime atmosphere of enforced patriotism, was to prove the germ of one of her most celebrated short novels, "Pale Horse, Pale Rider." Despite her illness, however, and the death in 1919 of Gay's little daughter, on whom Porter had doted, she found her life in Denver stimulating. She wrote her younger sister that she was "doing more, and meeting cleverer people" than she ever had before. Significantly, these included artists: "famous painters and musicians, and singers and writers." "If my luck holds at all," she concluded, "I should be in New York by August or September, and in Europe by early spring."[22]

Her luck did not hold so firmly as to get her to Europe at that time. She would later, in fact, say that she had never even wanted to go until 1931, the year she actually went. But she did get to New York. By January 1920 she was writing to her family from 17 Grove Street, New York City.

It was only in late 1919, when she went to Greenwich Village with the express intention of making her way as a writer, that Porter's real vocation and her real ambition manifested themselves. At that time she was still involved in journalism, as well as, again, in the movie industry. But she had a clear sense of working toward something more significant. She wrote her family, "I am as usual doing a dozen things, but this time all the things are productive, and leading to the same end. I have been transferred to the Select studio, publicity manager out there, which means that I spend three hours a day on subways, ferries, and street cars getting over into New Jersey to the studio. Once there, I live around on the stage, watching the players work, and write all the news of the picture making for the publicity office down town. It is a ghastly job, full of detail, a sort of sublimated reporter's work, but I shall keep it for so long as I need it." It is not clear what she means by "transferred," but it is clear that she was working purposefully toward the literary career she wanted. On New Year's Eve, she reported, she visited a "dear pair of artists" who were to illustrate a set of children's stories she was writing for *Everyland* magazine, with plans for book publication afterward. She had a contract, she said, for twelve fairy stories based on "authentic legends of far countries," and the first two were already written. Apparently only three of the stories were ever completed, however, and the book did not materialize.[23]

It would be three years before Porter's first story to be included in the acknowledged canon, "Maria Concepción," would be written and published, but she was at last living in the company of writers and artists, with sufficient experience and self-confidence to pursue her own goals, and with sufficient time to begin a real literary apprenticeship. Thereafter, although her career was slow to develop, largely because of her own frustrating unproductiveness, it was always clear that her vocation was writing. She did various kinds of work in order to support herself, including magazine work of various sorts, reviewing, and the ghostwriting of a novel, *My Chinese Marriage,* but always she was trying to write serious fiction and nonfiction. Even in those early years she was recognized by her numerous acquaintances as a serious and gifted writer, though she published less than others of her set, such as Josephine Herbst and John Herrmann.

During the early years of her writing career, spent mainly in New York but with periods of residence in Mexico, Boston, and Connecticut and a sojourn in Bermuda in 1929, Porter was building the huge acquaintance that formed one of the more interesting aspects of her life and constitutes one of the reasons why she is so significant a figure in the study of twentieth-century American culture. She seemed to know or at least to have met everyone: Mexican artists Adolfo Best-Maugard and Diego Rivera, caricaturist Miguel Covarrubias, revolutionists Manuel Gamio and Luis Morones, journalist-critic Malcolm Cowley and his wife Peggy, poets

Genevieve Taggard and Hart Crane (not one of her happier acquaintanceships), Carl Van Doren, Ford Madox Ford—the list goes on and on. In 1944 she became acquainted with journalist and revolutionist Agnes Smedley and discovered that their "early careers had been shaped by an overlapping Greenwich Village period" and that they had known some of the same women there.[24] Meeting Dylan Thomas at a party in 1949, she was seized by the drunken bard, lifted above his head, and held there (in the words of Karl Shapiro's poem "Emily Dickinson and Katherine Anne Porter")

> While everybody wondered what it meant
> To toast the lady with her own body
> Or to hold her to the light like a plucked flower.[25]

And so it went as her long career developed. A tireless letter writer, she built up a huge store of personal papers, most of them now housed at the University of Maryland. Not only does the Porter Collection there provide material for biographical study of her life and achievement, but it offers quite tangible evidence why such biographical study is worthwhile. Her correspondence with so many of the people who made the cultural and literary history of the century in the United States is both the evidence and the medium of her place in their ranks. Novelist Glenway Wescott found his correspondence with Porter so stimulating that he pondered, in his journal, what topic to strike up next.

The fact that Porter wrote so many splendidly readable letters to so many interesting people is significant, too, in explaining the shape of her career. It served her as an escape from one of the worst cases of prolonged writer's block on record. Her published works are surprisingly spare—both individually and in the aggregate. The acknowledged publications include only twenty-seven stories, four of them ("Old Mortality," "Pale Horse, Pale Rider," "Noon Wine," and "The Leaning Tower") more properly called short novels or novellas (a term she despised); one long novel, *Ship of Fools,* the writing of which occupied her intermittently for well over twenty years; a brief memoir; and a fair number of essays and occasional pieces. Despite her indignation when Malcolm Cowley remarked that her genius was manifested in her letters, it seems clear that she did at least use letter writing as a means of avoiding both the sustained effort that was necessary to produce the quality of work she was willing to publish and recognize and the fact that for long periods she was not producing that work.[26]

Porter's fitful work habits and temperamental personality were a major irritant not only to friends and family but to editors and publishers. She was forever promising to complete work soon and either delaying interminably or failing to deliver at all. Such was the case with her projected and widely discussed book on Cotton Mather. She accepted contributions from friends in order to retire to Bermuda in 1929 to complete it (and also to regain her health); she said variously that it was nearly done, she was "on the last lap," it would go into the mail right away, it would actually be published in three or four months; at least one friend was reported to have seen the completed manuscript. In 1933 she told the Guggenheim Foundation, as a part of her required year-end report, that she was "now completing the Devil and Cotton Mather." Friends continued to ask about the work. As late as December 1935 she said it would be out in April. But the book on Mather was never finished.[27] The same was almost true of *Ship of Fools*. If Seymour Lawrence, then an editor with Little, Brown, had not intervened and periodically placed her in seclusion, virtually holding her hand while coaxing the book out of her, her big success would never have come to pass.

Her problem, more basically than writer's block, was a pernicious volatility of spirits that would torment her and all who cared for her throughout her life. At times she was buoyantly cheerful, expansive, manically talkative (a quality emphasized by her fellow Texan and fellow novelist William Goyen in his unpublished portrait "At Lady A's"), the best of companions. Then her spirits would drop into gloom. Friends have spoken of her shutting herself up in her house, refusing to answer the doorbell or the telephone, refusing all communication. At many points in her life she fell into deep depressions or emotional breakdowns. There were times at which she apparently contemplated suicide. Like her father, who was given to complaining about his bad luck, she tended to cast herself as either victim or nemesis, bemoaning her fate in a variety of aspects. Her most recurrent themes were poor health, money problems, bad luck in love, and mysterious persecutions by those near her. At such times she would lash out at the most emotionally convenient target, preferably a current romantic interest. Goyen, for one, with whom she had a stormy affair in 1951, found out what it was like to be her scapegoat and the target of her fury, as did husbands Eugene Pressly and Albert Erskine and various others. Typically she then accused them of keeping her from her work or causing her to be so emotionally debilitated that she could not accomplish what she otherwise would have.

This pattern, too, emerged early, in her discontents with her family and her complaints about her first marriage, although at that time she had no real commitment to art. She linked the two, emotional state of mind and literary productivity, in an amusing letter to her father probably written in 1927: "Authors, dear Poppa, are subject to vapors. They get low in their minds and that means they're starting to get ready to begin to commence work. Then they get lower and lower in their minds as they get toward the middle of the job. Then comes a period when they get so low they feel they can only burn the manuscript and shoot themselves, and thats a sign they're getting into the home stretch. Then as they wind up, their spirits rise and rise, and they get almost human. I am now approaching that blessed state." Her tone here is light, but the substance is accurate enough except for one detail: Her own low spirits did not so much signal the imminence of successful work as herald an inability to work at all.[28]

From the heritage of her less-than-aristocratic birth in an out-of-the-way corner of rural Texas, Porter rose, almost solely by her own wits, to the status of celebrity as a writer and as a commentator on the contemporary scene. More important, perhaps—though it would be hard to say which was more important to her, for she delighted in her fame—she became recognized as a writer's writer, admired for her style and her sense of form. Her *Collected Stories,* published in 1965, won the National Book Award and the Pulitzer Prize. Moreover, numbering among her friends and acquaintances a great many literary figures of prominence and influence, she moved in circles where much of the cultural history of the century was being written. Yet the road by which she arrived at this eminence was long and difficult, and it is scarcely surprising that, even in her maturity, her attitudes and her intellectual sophistication would betray gaps and unevenness.

When one considers the paucity of her formal education, Porter's range of mind and her evident familiarity with literature, music, and philosophy are remarkable. Joan Givner points out that she enjoyed boasting that she had never set foot inside a university until she was invited to lecture at one. That she had not is probably not in itself remarkable. College attendance was by no means so common then as it is now. Education did not necessarily mean formal education. But the matter goes beyond setting foot inside a university. Porter did not even have a thorough secondary education. So far as the record shows, besides attending grammar school in Kyle, Texas, she had only about half a year at the Thomas School, a sound secondary school in San Antonio, when she was about fourteen. She would later recall "going to concerts and theatres with the crowd at Thomas School," but that, she pointed out, was as much outside school as in it. Likening herself to Willa Cather, who read Greek with a storekeeper in Red Cloud, Nebraska, she asserted confidently—and with good cause—that she "still" thought she was "a good example of what home education can do." She seems to have soaked in learning as a blotter does ink whenever she did have an opportunity, and it is clear that she was, all her life, a voracious and an intelligent reader. It was through her own reading, encouraged early on by her grandmother, and through her sensitivity and alertness to the cultural and conversational environment in which she moved, that she gained a not inconsiderable education, though probably never so polished an education as she herself believed.[29]

There will be ample occasion, throughout this study, to consider and assess the quality of Porter's mind. That is, indeed, the overarching purpose here. Clearly, she was sometimes not so deep in her understandings or her judgments as she thought she was. Even so, to have achieved such learning and intellectual discernment, when building on so paltry a base, is more than improbable; it is astonishing. In essays like "St. Augustine and the Bullfight" (1955) she displays an intellectual poise and range that bespeak real, if not formal, education and the suppleness of a great natural intellect.

As in so much of her writing, both fiction and nonfiction, her method in "St. Augustine and the Bullfight" is to link her reading of an acknowledged literary masterpiece with her own keenly felt and sharply reported experience. Just as the young Augustine's friend from the provinces morally despised the gladiatorial combats until he took his first long look, at which point he became "more bloodthirsty than any," so, Porter says, she deplored the cruelty of bullfighting and pitied "the splendid black and white bull" until he entered the ring, whereupon she "stood straining on tiptoe to see everything, yet almost blinded with excitement."[30] It is her act of self-knowledge, achieved by casting her memory of the bullfight into a framework of literature, that, in the terms of the essay, turns it from a mere adventure into an experience. But to mediate on the distinction between adventure and experience she does not merely reason through a series of abstractions or cite literary or philosophical precedent; she recreates the personal moment. Her characteristic mode, here as in her fiction, is a highly indirect, deeply mediated autobiography.

Porter's intellectual achievement and her influence, or perhaps one should say her participation, in a circle of intellectuals, when placed against the bald facts of her insecure early life and her limited formal education, present only one of several major puzzles of her life and career. Another is her relationship to her regional origins, which she alternately denounced and idealized. This relationship, along with other aspects of her formation of an adult identity, will be considered in chapter 2.

Another puzzle, or at least inconsistency, equally dramatic and perhaps even more elusive, is the fact of Porter's early political radicalism and the vehemence of her later hostility to leftist politics. For about a decade and a half, from about 1920 to the mid-1930s, she expressed in her private letters a revolutionary sense of justice and a strong attraction to communism—so warm an attraction, in fact, that she at times referred to herself as a fellow traveler and avowed an intention of going to Russia to receive instruction in the real thing. Many of her friends were communists of some stripe, and at least one, John Herrmann, a party member. By the outbreak of World War II, however, Porter's politics had shifted to an avowedly anticommunist stance, even as she adopted, at the same time, an emphatically antifascist stance. This progression of conflicting views would make for a truly vertiginous reading experience if one did not keep in mind the similar shifts that were being made by numerous others. Some version of Porter's inconsistency, a political move, basically, from left to right, was enacted by many of America's literati. In her later life, Porter's political views can best be styled liberal cum libertarian (with a small *l*). She supported the Democratic party and maintained a staunchly prolabor position in writing to her sister and others.[31]

At the same time, indeed throughout her adult life, she expressed unmistakable aristocratic yearnings, identifying herself with the "white-pillar crowd" of Southerners, boasting about her family's servants, and favoring a tone of opulence in her style of life. Her class allegiance was indeed blurred. Here Porter's biographer cannot avoid, even if she would, psychological complications and psychological explanations. During her radical years, in the 1920s and early 1930s, Porter was, as a matter of course, an avowed supporter of the common people. And it is easy to see, in her writings about Mexico, at any rate, that her sympathy and support were more than mere lip service. Moreover, it is not in the Mexican nonfiction writings alone that she expresses an identification with workers and an angry sympathy with the exploited as against the exploiter. At the same time, she portrayed herself as a daughter of the aristocracy, albeit a somewhat impoverished aristocracy, and it is obvious that an opulent life and possessions were important to her. Porter's shifting political views, the origins of her radicalism, and some possible reasons for its demise will be explored in chapters 3 and 7.

Porter enjoyed her occasional latter-day involvement in politics, and especially enjoyed issuing pronouncements on the foolishness of others' politics. Even more, she enjoyed assuming the role of the belle or grande dame, the aristocratic southern woman whose life was shaped by a combination of extraordinary physical beauty and highly developed social graces. Her beauty was of great importance to her, apparently from her earliest years. Givner relates this concern with appearance to her anxiety regarding her father, whose love was far from reliable and apparently was often based on his sense of whether his daughters were pretty and appealingly dressed. Predictably enough, perhaps, given such an emphasis on physical beauty, she was an incorrigible flirt. Throughout her life, she went from one infatuation to another, one affair to another, though there is ample reason to believe that her chief pleasure in these affairs was derived from attracting men who would desire her. After about 1935, as both age and the circumstances of her wardrobe allowed, she came increasingly to merge the belle into the grande dame, the handsome and opulent, stylish older woman at the center of social attention.[32] At the same time, she produced stories such as "Old Mortality" and "Pale Horse, Pale Rider" that convey a keen awareness of the weight of conventionalized expectations borne by women of ability and intelligence. Her correspondence, as well, indicates that she chafed against the control and assumed superiority of men. To her friend Herbst she wrote resentfully of the unfair treatment of the woman writer. The tension between this incipient feminism and the traditionally feminine role Porter more often assumed, especially in her later years, will be explored in chapter 8.

Chapter 9 examines the creative struggle that went into the writing of the book Porter conceived as her crowning literary achievement, *Ship of Fools,* published in 1962. The novel is the node of a complex set of tensions between her artistic standards and her ambition to achieve a wide public audience; between her genius for an art of compression and the felt mandate to produce an art of mass in order to secure her reputation in a literary establishment that had come to validate the novel as the genre of choice, the test of a writer's ability to handle the big challenge.

The sequence of chapters 1 through 9 is at once thematic and roughly chronological. In chapters 10 through 12, the principle of organization shifts to that of summary and assessment of Porter's achievement and stature as an intellectual, as a barometer of deep social and historical changes, and as an artist. Chapter 10 examines Porter's reading and her direct responses to her reading, both in the form of annotation in her books and in the form of critical commentary in letters and in reviews and essays. Chapter 11 considers, in a more focused and unified way than its appearance throughout this study, the nature of Porter's artistry and her achievement as a writer. The concluding chapter develops a summary view of the nature of her mind and thought, especially her religious thought, and sketches the development of the critical response to Porter's work and the vexed state of Porter studies today.

Because her opinions and her sense of herself were so varying and conflicted, Katherine Anne Porter cannot be considered in any sense an ideologue. One would be hard pressed indeed to present a summary statement as to what position or theory she espoused on the whole. Her outward life and her mental life were as full of contrasts and contradictions as Texas itself: southern yet not southern, radical yet conservative, populist yet aristocratic, conspicuously and traditionally feminine yet steadfastly, though sometimes indirectly, feminist. She might well have claimed for her own Ralph Waldo Emerson's derisive comment on a foolish consistency: It was a hobgoblin that did not much trouble her.

Porter's intellectual biography, then, must be written more in terms of conflicts and inconsistencies than of unifying themes. Even so, one overriding view of her life can be maintained, throughout the shifting patterns of contrasts: Once she established her toehold in the literary world, she was always near the center of things, always involved in the tensions that were themselves the defining attributes of the twentieth-century artistic and intellectual world.

CHAPTER TWO

Establishing an Identity

For a self that goes on changing is a self that goes on living.

—Virginia Woolf, "The Humane Art," in *The Death of the Moth and Other Essays*

All serious writing is based profoundly on the writer's experience, and this experience is no less real if it takes place only in the imagination than if based on an actual occurrence.

—Porter to a student, March 31, 1951

Porter regarded the problem of identity as one of life's major challenges, "about all the problem there was."[1] Her own identity as an artist but also as a person torn by inner conflicts was forged in the first thirty years of her life, largely in reaction to two pervasively important factors in her early experience: family and region. These two forces played powerful roles in shaping her consciousness, both as influences and as counterforces against which she struggled, resisting any shaping but her own. Both, as well, evoked warm expressions of allegiance and identification, even as they evoked her resistance.

Certainly Porter recognized the power of these dual influences in the shaping of her identity. After years of absence from Texas, she told Josephine Herbst that she felt a need to go back to the country where she was born, "where after all, everything that makes me myself has already happened to me."[2] Some of what that was is available to us from factual documents and from family correspondence. In addition, a great deal can be inferred from her stories involving the character Miranda, who has long and correctly been read as a representation of Porter herself.

Naturally, one must exercise great caution in reading imaginative literature autobiographically, that is, both as the result of known biographical facts and as the material from which to learn about the author's life. In the case of the Miranda stories or the stories set in Mexico involving the character Laura, a version of Miranda, it would be reductive and simply incorrect to take every incident and every detail as a recording of fact. But the autobiographical basis of the Miranda/Laura character is clear. Besides the abundant internal evidence, we have external evidence that this is true. One of Porter's lovers, Francisco Aguilera, a Chilean poet studying and teaching at Harvard when she knew him, referred to her as Miranda in two telegrams and a poem, "*Rapsodia chilena* a Katherine Anne Porter." These are among her papers. Also among her papers is a letter from her childhood friend Erna Schlemmer Johns stating that when she read "Old Mortality" "little Miranda at once became Callie, that dearest friend of my childhood."[3] But the autobiographical nature of "Old Mortality" and other Miranda stories—and indeed of Porter's fiction in general—is deeper than simple reference to actual events or details. Her work, fiction and nonfiction as well, constitutes a complex act of self-examination and self-representation. It is not confessional in nature, but is rather the mediating structure through which she at once validated and interpreted her sense of self and her understanding of her historical moment.

By 1920, when she had located herself in New York and begun her literary apprenticeship with a newfound seriousness and single-mindedness, Porter had already defined herself both as an artist and as a political freethinker. Writing to her family on January 3 from 17 Grove Street, she mentioned her flurry of activities and exulted in the prospect that everything was "leading to the same end," the establishment of a literary career. Later that year she wrote, in terms that recall the flaming persona of an Edna St. Vincent Millay, "The money I make from my artist work would not keep me in shoe latchets, yet I live by it! It is bread, and air, and sleep and joy. The rest of the show is just a gray background to flame against!" She continued exultantly, "All my life has been a hideous blind mad struggle to break my shell and achieve to [*sic*] my destiny, and I am just now beginning to see that I was right, that I was not deceived by that inner conviction. I am an artist." Art was, she would later say, the "solid ground" she had to stand on; it was what "gave meaning and hope to everything."[4] She would write to her father in 1931, some eleven years after her arrival in New York and her first clear assertions of her sense of identity, a statement that summed up her self-conception at the time as well as any brief statement probably could: "I don't imagine I'll ever be a popular writer, but I don't think of popularity or unpopularity. I simply want to be free to say what I feel and think as exactly as I am able—leave my testament, if you like, offer my evidence of what I found in this life, and how it seemed to me, and what I was able to make of it. . . . I have never wanted more than this."[5] Except for its omission of her desire for monetary reward and the recognition of her literary peers, this statement might have been made with equal accuracy in 1920—she had already, when she came to New York, reached that clear an understanding of what she was about—though indeed, at the age of thirty, she had not been fast in coming to it.

❧ Among the keys to Porter's sense of self is her sense of her father and her relationship to him. The idea of a father, of what it could mean to a person to have a devoted father and of all that her own father had failed to provide in her life, was of enormous importance to her. Her letters to Harrison Porter, irregular as they were for most of her life, generally profess great tenderness; she addresses him as "honey" or as "daddy darling" and claims to be hoping earnestly to see him soon or to send him a nice present. She almost never turned that avowed hope into action. But it was not her father alone who was of great emotional significance to her. Her family as a whole, but even more the concept of family, would remain of extreme importance to her throughout her life. During her first period of residence in New York, facing recurrent loneliness, she wrote to her younger sister, "Baby," that she wished they were all there. "We'd go to a concert, and then come home and broil chops over the fire, and be very snug." Finding herself "hopelessly grown up" with things not having "turned out the way we planned," she wished they could all be happy and "find a common ground of sympathy."[6]

One of Harrison Porter's most notable traits was his aggressive rationalism, signaled, as we have seen, by his debate about religion with his bride-to-be. Notes for her projected novel *Many Redeemers* include several comments on Miranda's father that can confidently be taken to represent Porter's view of her own father. A pencil segment dated 1926 begins, "She was invented, rather than reared by a father who was a consistent 18th century rationalist, and who never faltered for one moment in his [reasonableness—?] which was a fanatical faith with him. She was brought up on a marvellous array of slogans which served as members for a set of mental rules calculated to crush all intuitive knowledge of things." On another sheet, following several pages of notes that ultimately contributed to "Old Mortality," is a fragment of a scene emphasizing the father's shabbiness of appearance and his complaining temperament. The scene concludes with an exchange in which he assaults Miranda's notion of the Virgin Birth and the Immaculate Conception. All the traits depicted in these notes seem to have been taken directly from Harrison Boone Porter. More than once in letters to her sister Gay, Porter referred to their "rationalist upbringing."[7]

Porter once wrote to Kenneth Durant, in reference to her father, "I like him best now because he gave me the Philosophical Dictionary, the Memoirs of Prince Kropotkin, and the Decline and Fall of the Roman Empire to read, never dreaming, or at least not hinting, that they might be beyond my capacities, when I was fourteen years old. He merely expressed the urgent hope that this sort of reading might knock some of the nonsense out of me." She told her father on one occasion that she knew she had gotten her "philosophy and literary bent" from him. Gay agreed that Katherine Anne had their father's "mentality."[8] One must be cautious, of course, about accepting such comments as fact. Still, the weight of consistency in her comments about her father seems to indicate that he was a fairly bookish man who especially took an interest in rationalistic logic-chopping. Various statements in his own letters to family members bear this out.

In addition to her continual concern over her relation to her father and the rest of her immediate family, Porter was inordinately eager to identify ancestors, often claiming on the basis of scant evidence persons she heard of or read of who happened to share one of the family last names and whose distinctions she wished to appropriate. The strong figure of her grandmother looms large both in her fiction and in her correspondence. Among her siblings, her older sister, Gay, was clearly her favorite and one of the main personages in her life from about 1940 until Gay's death in 1969. Her brother, Harrison Paul, and her younger sister were not so close, but she maintained her bonds with them as well, at first directly in letters written to them individually or as a group (with many complaints that Paul did not write back), and later indirectly, by means of her frequent correspondence with Gay.

Believing that one's identity was very closely related to one's earliest memories of childhood, Porter once advised novelist William Goyen not to dwell on unhappy memories but to "leave your childhood where it belongs, and come away with your identity established and your history safely alive in your memory." She had done that herself, she said. She had "gone back through all the rooms to the very first one, and touched the very hearth where the fire was that warmed me first in this world."[9] She meant by this specifically her return to the Indian Creek cemetery where her mother was buried. But she also meant it, it would seem, in a more abstract sense. Unfortunately, after going back through those rooms she was not able to follow her own advice and leave there what she had found. The negative impact of family, as well as the positive, was intimately bound up with her sense of self.

She often saw her family as a power structure that had sought to restrict or confine her. After escaping the restrictions of their presence, she did not care to subject herself to it again by returning, but avoided for long years at a time the reunions she claimed to want so fervently. In 1928, for example, she wrote to Gay, with unusual candor, that their father, "bless his heart," was "dabbl[ing] with the notion that I may come there to live," but it would be "a sort of death" for her to "settle in that part of the country." After listing places she would like to live, the East Coast or Europe or Mexico, she concluded, "Probably in the end, one must go back to one's real soil."[10] But she did not do so. Even Gay, it seems, she preferred to keep at some distance, and she was capable of the bitterest complaints about all of them. Although some of her memories of childhood were "pleasant," they were "warped by the stronger memory of physical discomfort, for simply everything hurt or irritated me in some way. I know now it was nobody's fault, but that does not change my remembrance of life in childhood as being just about damned near unbearable from one day to the next." Childhood unhappiness and her home state itself were inseparably intertwined. "In fact," she said, "my life until I got out of Texas was unbearable altogether."[11]

Porter casts her family in differing lights at different times, sometimes as a fine old traditional southern clan, sometimes as an unappreciative, unenlightened lot who made her life miserable. She wrote to her sister in 1930 that she didn't really think any of the family were "completely indifferent" to her welfare, but added, "I know well, my dear, if I had depended on the love of any of you I should have been good and dead by now." In particular, she expressed a keen sense of the inadequacy of her father's love, and urged

Gay, "When you tell me Dad lives and prospers for me, Swittie, control yourself!" Her own "practical experience of paternal affection," she said, "has been very disconcerting, to say the least." (The use of sarcastic endearments such as "Swittie," for Sweetie, is a reliable clue to hostile intent in Porter's letters.) She closed bitterly that she felt she had been "so far as natural human relations go, without a family." On quite another note, she once told Cleanth Brooks's wife, Tinkum, that she had *not* been "badly treated" at all but "was very much loved and petted—spoiled, perhaps."[12] The weight of her testimony, however, is to the contrary.

In later life Porter was given to lamenting the burden that her family had been to her, both financially and emotionally, and in moments of anger would complain bitterly about their enmity to her freedom and happiness. To her nephew Paul, normally a great favorite but occasionally a source of equally great irritation, she wrote, "I wanted you for a friend and an ally, I had hoped that even the family bond might have guided your feelings (why, I don't know, my family have been consistently my worst enemy since the day I was born!) and I have never really lost hope that you were going to grow up and take hold of your life and be at least one member of the family that I could believe in and respect."[13] The letter goes on to accuse him of betraying her private business to strangers and of performing comical mimicry of her at parties. Yet it was clear that when she was not overcome by irritation or by her own emotional turmoil she doted on Paul and on her niece Ann, Gay's daughter, who also relied on Aunt Katherine's help.

Her relationship with Gay was one of great devotion. Their correspondence was voluminous. They sent each other small gifts, sometimes for special occasions and sometimes for no occasion at all, told each other about particularly good meals they had cooked and enjoyed and about especially beautiful flowers blooming in their gardens, and in general shared their joys and irritations. After the income from *Ship of Fools* started coming in, Porter provided Gay with a regular stipend. Letters written late in their lives show how they retained their affection for each other even as both were becoming invalided. It is surprising, then, to find Porter complaining to her other sister, Mary Alice, or "Baby," that Gay "just took everything she could wangle and expected more." This extraordinarily spiteful outburst, however, seems actually to have been motivated chiefly by irritation at Mary Alice, who was asking for assistance with Gay's final expenses. For the most part, she demonstrated real, albeit long-distance, devotion to Gay.[14]

An especially heartwarming sequence of letters occurred in April 1963. First Gay wrote an unusual tribute to Katherine Anne couched as a commentary on a picture she had cut out and sent in observance of Easter:

> To my little Sister—Katherine Anne Porter—Easter Greetings:
> 1. The rose means—I love you.
> 2. The lighted candle—That your dear little feet may see the path clearly.
> 3. A strong upright candleholder, signifying that a strong arm will uphold your spirit of inspiration—
> 4. And always—May the window of your sweet soul reflect the glorious blue and gold of the sky—
>
> I wish for The Little One—Love—clear sightedness, inspiration and *Freedom.*

Porter replied, "Sister darling, your lovely Easter incantation came this morning, and was the letter that made the rest of my burden of mail bearable."[15]

Yet despite the warmth of their relationship, and despite her ability to travel to a great many other places, Porter refrained from visiting Gay in person. She insisted that she was longing to go see her, but she did not go. She seems to have been fearful that she would be disappointed in the love she had come to believe was so special, or else that she would somehow be reduced to the status she remembered from childhood, that of the inadequately appreciated talented child.

She apparently thought of herself from an early age as an artist and became convinced that the family was squelching her artistic impulse. She once wrote Gay that she had been "a prodigious child, thin and nervous and with a mixture of undirected talents," who was "alternately encouraged to be a little show-off about things that didn't matter, and squelched and given an inferiority complex about things that were important to the growth of my character." She complained bitterly that "the important thing would have been, for me, to have had even one word of encouragement from any source," and added, "It is possible I am the only artist this family will ever produce." The artist, it seems, should be able to count on family support of a special kind. Several years later, she struck the same note in writing to her cherished nephew Paul, "Nobody in my family who ever tried to do anything real, intelligent or constructive ever got anything but discouragement of a very malignant kind from the rest."[16]

Porter's first independent work, when at age fifteen she set herself up (or was set up by her father) to earn money by giving lessons, was of a kind that might loosely be called artistic, the teaching of the performance arts of music and dramatic reading.[17] The first time she left Texas was as an aspiring actress, and when she returned and lived in Louisiana, trying to support Gay, it was natural for her to try making money as a performer, singing and giving literary readings. Yet she was unable to do so consistently or successfully, or to pursue the literary art that would be her life, until she had separated herself from the forces she felt were holding her back. In order to reach a clear understanding of herself and her goals, and to establish herself as an artist and an independent person, she had to leave both her family and her Texas home. But the separation was never complete or consistent.

❧ As she struggled to develop the career that was so slow in coming, Porter was no more willing to align herself consistently with her regional origins than with her family and the poor but landowning farm class from which she had sprung. To be from Texas and identified as a Texas writer was to be branded as a subliterary storyteller, a practitioner in a genre of frontier tales that, at the time she was establishing herself, had admitted little artistry.[18] Moreover, the category "Texas writer" almost necessarily meant "male writer." Texas was identified, in the popular and the critical imagination alike, with the frontier West of cowboys and wide-open spaces, hard riding and shooting. That the state was by no means all of a piece culturally, but was rather a collection of distinct regional patterns, was simply not acknowledged in the literary world or, for the most part, in popular awareness. Yet Porter's impulse in fiction lay in an entirely different direction from the stereotypical western: the direction of inward, quiet stories, never highly plotted, told in a quiet and certainly literate style. Thus the label "Texas writer," though in a literal sense it described her accurately enough, was misleadingly constrictive in its connotations. Many years later, when she read Flannery O'Connor's statement that "the woods are full of regional writers, and it is the great horror of every serious Southern writer that he will become one of them," she marked the passage with lines in the margins and underscored it.[19]

Since the Texas Porter knew in her growing years was more southern than western, the southern quality of her autobiographical fiction is not necessarily a matter of disingenuousness. With the South as a whole, her relationship was not so conflicted as it was with Texas specifically. For years she fostered the belief that she had been born, not in Texas, but in Louisiana, and had been educated in a New Orleans convent school. She claimed as her own the southern heritage of an Allen Tate or a Caroline Gordon or a Robert Penn Warren. Like them, she tended to regard Texas—or at any rate the cotton-growing regions of eastern Texas, extending into her own Hays County—as a part of the newer South. In 1943, for example, she conflated the two in a letter to Texas writer and professor George Sessions Perry: "It is quite all right to regard me as a southern, specifically a Texas, writer. I know that Texas is south*west,* but my origins were really southern, I do not think my family have been in Texas more than seventy odd years."[20]

Clearly, however, she accentuated the southernness of her Texas settings. To say as much is not necessarily, as one critic would have it, a matter of her having determined to lay claim to the "distinct advantages" of "being identified" as a southern, rather than a Texan, writer. Her imagination, reaching back in time, naturally reached eastward toward her family origins prior to their migration to Texas. At the same time, turning away from Texas in her settings and in her self-identification was a means of distancing herself from the early life she had found so stifling. Although much of her best work is set in a home place that either resembles or is explicitly designated as Texas, the home place is, in numerous small ways, reconstituted or resituated so as to evoke the Old South. It does not simply replicate the place where Porter grew up. As Don Graham points out, "She made her part of Texas seem more lush, more redolent of the deep South than it might otherwise be envisioned." In a postscript to her 1943 letter to Perry claiming to be "really southern," she said that "Noon Wine," "Old Mortality," and "He" were all set between San Marcos and Austin, Texas. Yet a case can easily be made that "Old Mortality," at any rate, conveys a sense of being located considerably farther east, toward or beyond the Louisiana line—that is, toward the Old South.[21]

Her departure from Texas in 1918, following a series of hardships culminating in her bout with tuberculosis, initiated a series of rapid steps toward her establishment as a serious writer. Kitty Barry Crawford, the relatively successful journalist from Fort Worth whom she had met at the Carlsbad sanitarium, and her husband provided Porter with work in Fort Worth on the newspaper they had founded and also provided her a place to stay, in their own home. The Crawfords would again come to her rescue several years later when she needed money to leave Mexico and a place in which to take refuge. In 1918, after Porter had moved to Fort Worth, Kitty Crawford went to Colorado for reasons of health. There she settled into a house shared with an adventurous journalist friend of hers, Jane Anderson (later tried for treason during World War II). What appear to have been strangely intense emotional complications occurred when a lover of Anderson's, Gilbert Seldes, moved in with the two women. Anderson twice wrote to Porter urging her to join them in Colorado Springs, where, it seems, Kitty was not happy. She urged Porter to realize that Kitty needed close companionship and that she, Jane, could not supply that need.[22] Porter spent several weeks with the ménage before getting a job at the end of the summer as a reporter for the *Rocky Mountain News* in Denver.

Several profoundly formative experiences occurred during her stay of a little more than a year in Denver: serious newspaper work, her near-fatal bout with the flu, and the death of her beloved little niece. All these elements of the Denver interval left their mark in ways that would issue later in her life, most dramatically in the sick world of "Pale Horse, Pale Rider."

In later years Porter would often claim to have been a pacifist all her adult life. If so, there were times during World War II when she fell away from her pacifist principles. During World War I, however, it appears that she did indeed dissent from the war fever that swept the country as virulently as the flu itself. She would claim many years later that in 1914 she had "wondered why the USA interfered in the European war—only another war such as they had been having for two thousand years."[23] Dangerous as it is to accept at face value Porter's retrospective comments on her own opinions, her report here is plausible, since "Pale Horse, Pale Rider" itself expresses, more powerfully than any direct statement she could make, dissent from the war effort. The work catches in a definitive way the atmosphere of the late war as perceived by a brooding, dissenting mind, alienated from the crassness and moral shabbiness of the surrounding world.

"Pale Horse, Pale Rider" is one of the clearest expressions, too, of Porter's recurrent female hero caught up in the pressures of a torturous world. The autobiographical Miranda as seen here has struck most readers as an admirable and appealing character, all the more sympathetic for being so tautly restrained. Allen Tate, somewhat surprisingly, found her overly precious, a heroine whose "emotions are commonplace but whose personality is handled with a solemnity that comes very near being sentimentality." Writing to fellow poet John Peale Bishop, who had expressed admiration for some of Porter's comments on "problems of the craft," Tate added, "This quality is a distinct defect in K. A.'s work."[24] The more usual response has been to see the story as an expression of stoicism, a Hemingwayesque dance on the edge of a grave at once personal and collective. Although Miranda survives at the end, it is clear that she will live on in a state of subdued hopelessness. Indeed, the atmosphere of the story as a whole is one of doom. Porter said the title was taken from an "old negro song" about the pale rider of death who "done taken my sweetheart away." "It goes on like that until practically the whole family connection is wiped out. . . . But my story has to do only with the Pale Horse and the rider who carries away a whole period and with it the first half of my life." The remark, which at first seems so explanatory, is finally enigmatic, but it is clear that Porter saw her own life as being caught up in a general destruction. Indeed, she would frequently, throughout her life, express a sense of hopelessness or doom not easy to account for.[25]

For the Miranda of "Pale Horse, Pale Rider" the prospect of romantic love is an elusive dream, as golden and as impossible as the "tawny" Adam himself. In this respect as in others, Miranda is an all-too-accurate representation of Porter herself, who had already experienced the souring of love and for the rest of her life would move from one idealized and ultimately disappointing lover to another, never able to find and maintain a love adequate to her need. She sometimes claimed that Adam, the young soldier Miranda loves and loses to the "pale rider" death, was based on a real person with whom she was in love in Denver, who was indeed the great love of her life. Like so many of Porter's interesting stories about herself, however, this one is based on only the flimsiest rag of fact. A letter to her father, written before she had achieved great fame and begun to develop her myth of self, recalls that when she was "so desperately sick" with the flu a "young boy twenty one years old" had taken care of her for three days. She explicitly dispels the romantic interest of the situation by noting that he was someone "whom I did not know at all, who happened to be living in the same house with me."[26] This version of the story is probably the accurate one. It seems unlikely that she would have felt any need to understate her involvement with the kind young man, whereas on those occasions when she claimed that he had been the love of her life she would clearly have been serving her recurrent need to depict her life in dramatically romantic terms. It is clear that there was an original for the character of Adam, then, in the sense that her fictional creation was prompted by her impressions of an actual person, but he was only a slight acquaintance on the basis of whom she erected her imaginative structure. The recreation of this acquaintance as Miranda's beloved Adam is an illustrative example of her mode of self-representation in fiction.

The illness depicted in "Pale Horse, Pale Rider" was, however, real enough. Porter had been working for the *Rocky Mountain News* for only a few weeks when, in October, she fell ill with the Spanish influenza that was sweeping the country and would kill some 300,000 in the United States alone in the course of its brief epidemic.[27] It must have been a deeply despairing time for her. She later told her sister "Baby" that when she was lying near death she felt "sorry I had been born because I hadn't been strong enough to work out my dreams."[28] When she came to use the experience in fiction, she depicted with striking vividness and accuracy the disease itself and the way in which it swamped the health care system. The story has been called "the most accurate depiction of American society in the fall of 1918 in literature."[29] Beyond its literal accuracy, moreover, she developed the atmosphere of epidemic into a metaphor for spiritual illness associated with the nation's aggressively patriotic entry into the war. Not only physically, but emotionally and in its art and in its very language, American society in the World War I days is seen as a sick and corrupted one.

The general atmosphere of the story, compounded of the pervasive menace of the flu epidemic, the overtaxed medical resources, the belligerent chauvinism of the war years, and the public celebration of the end of the war, represents quite accurately the social atmosphere of the period. The rampant superpatriotism surrounding America's entry into the Great War is clearly established by the details and language of the story. As Miranda observes to her doomed lover Adam (who believes, however, that he could not live with himself if he did not go fight), "the worst of the war" was "the fear and suspicion" it created among American citizens and, for dissenters, "the skulking about, and the lying."[30]

Miranda says that she lives in fear. Her fear—and, we can presume, Porter's own—was well founded. In part it was economic; Miranda's counting up of her few dollars as against the cost of necessities, in the opening scene of the story, is an accurate enough representation of the economic pressures faced by Americans during the rapid inflation (nearly 100 percent) that occurred from 1916 to 1920.[31] A woman working as a beginning newspaper reporter would surely have had trouble making ends meet. Equally pervasive is Miranda's sense of personal insecurity lest she be accused of disloyalty to the United States. She hates the war, and she hates the atmosphere of intolerance it has created.

It was indeed a dark period in the nation's history for tolerance and civil liberties. By the end of the war, volunteer spies for the American Protective League numbered about 250,000, their menace solidly based on the Sedition Act, passed May 16, 1918, which allowed the U.S. attorney general to prosecute persons for "disloyal utterances."[32] Indeed, the fact that Miranda dares to share her dissent with Adam is a mark of the depth of personal trust they have quickly established. When they go to the theater and have to sit through an exhortation by a Liberty Bond salesman whose speech is salted with cant terms like *the Boche* and *our noble boys,* they share their wish that he would shut up so the show could go on and Miranda could write her review. Only after that is done can they have time for themselves. Even Adam, however, does not despise the bigoted speaker as Miranda does. She associates the speaker, with his recourse to the language of jingoism and his blatant pressure to buy bonds, with the veiled threats of the government representatives who had earlier visited her office and pointed out that they knew she was not buying bonds.

The pressure to buy bonds is another accurate representation of the times. The term *Liberty Bonds* had been coined by Secretary of the Treasury William McAdoo, whose purpose, in his own words, was to "capitaliz[e] the profound impulse called patriotism." To do so, he employed such hard-sell methods as "Four-Minute Men" who appeared at movies, on stages, at lodges, and elsewhere, "fervently urging" people to buy bonds. Failure to do so could be interpreted as lack of patriotism. McAdoo himself labeled anyone who did not buy bonds " 'a friend of Germany.' "[33]

It is important to recognize that specific aspects of the political stance Porter attributes to Miranda, and thus to her earlier self, were tenets of the Socialist party during those years. Socialists actively opposed armament and preparedness as well as the subsequent entry of the United States into the war. According to David M. Kennedy, in his study of the wartime domestic scene, by the spring of 1917 the Socialist party was "the largest center of organized opposition to American participation in the war" and was "among the first groups to feel the whip of official wrath" under the Espionage Act of 1917. Socialist pacifism was linked, as well, to a belief that U.S. entry into the war was motivated by a desire to benefit Wall Street bankers and big industrialists.[34] The government spokesmen who appear in "Pale Horse, Pale Rider" and those who jump onto the militaristic bandwagon do not speak of these things, but mouth a prefabricated language of big, empty exhortations.

The issue of language as a measure of honesty and honor is one of the major themes of the story, though certainly a less obvious one than the theme of doomed love in a cruel world. The two idealized lovers, Miranda and Adam, define themselves in opposition to the atmosphere of warmongering and shallowness all around them by means of a severely restrained and ironic language. They converse, and Miranda even dreams, in the epitome of Porter's own compressed style, which takes on a symbolic power. Their speech shows, by contrast, that the language of patriotism is formulaic and specious, and shows up the slack garrulousness of others for what it is, a symbol of their slack moral state. Only Miranda and Adam maintain their honest resistance to the war mania.[35] Adam, to be sure, has succumbed to the masculine ethos of maintaining honor by fighting. Even so, he sees through the false rhetoric of the superpatriots who are enjoying their opportunity to be important.

Miranda not only sees through them but rails against them. Bitterly mocking, in thought, their inflated and misleading rhetoric, she demands, "Coal, oil, iron, gold, international finance, why don't you tell us about them, you little liar?"[36] Her list recalls a list of invidious forces Porter had already associated with the American presence in Mexico, in her early essay "Where Presidents Have No Friends." The rhetorical style shared by Miranda and Adam both establishes their honesty with each other and measures the dishonesty and inauthenticity of those around them. That is, their rhetoric is a symbolic ethical standard. Its style is compressed, understated, and witty—the conversational equivalent of Porter's own mature style. Thus Porter associates her time in Denver, which was a time both of political dissent and of the beginnings of her career as a writer, with a commitment to honesty and authenticity in language. The link between politics and art was firmly established in her mind at this early date.

In later life Porter would resent being referred to as a newspaperwoman. She had only done newspaper work, she said, to buy time while she developed as a serious writer. She wrote testily to Malcolm Cowley, for example, after he had referred to her in print as a newspaperwoman, "I was never a 'newspaper woman.' I went to Denver with my insipient [*sic*] bronchitis and asthma looking for climate and had to have some kind of job to subsist. Like many romantic young women who 'want to write,' I was a victim to the idea that a newspaper job was the place to learn one's craft.

It isn't so, of course, and it only took me about eight months to discover this fact of life."[37] At times she flatly denied that she had engaged in newspaper work anywhere except Denver. She wrote to one inquisitive student that she "never worked a day on the Dallas News" and to another that she "never did newspaper work either in Dallas or Fort Worth." Yet she had in fact worked on the *Fort Worth Star Telegram* and had at least aspired to work on the *Dallas Morning News*. An old acquaintance, apparently a onetime roommate in one of the tuberculosis sanitariums, recalled in 1951, "I remember how you used to take pencil and paper to bed with you, and write stories for the Dallas News. I sent some of them to my little girls."[38] The reminiscence not only has the ring of truth, but is corroborated by one of Porter's own letters to her family, written in 1916. The Dallas News, she wrote, had published a "little story" for which they paid her $8 and had also promised her "a good job" when she got out of the hospital. Since an official of the *Houston Chronicle*, Marcellus E. Foster, promised in 1918 to write her a letter of recommendation to the Red Cross and assured her he would be glad to vouch that she was "the best woman reporter in the United States," one wonders if she had worked on newspapers in other Texas cities as well, perhaps during the brief period immediately preceding her departure for Colorado, when she had to resign her job in Fort Worth and take refuge with family in southeast Texas because of illness. It is hard to imagine Foster's making this offer if he did not know her work directly.[39]

Porter's eagerness to deny what appears to be plain fact, and certainly no discredit, is puzzling. Perhaps she felt that her commitment to serious literature would be impugned if people identified her with mere journalists, a group she depicted (in "Pale Horse, Pale Rider" and elsewhere) as being for the most part a shallow and hardboiled lot. Though Miranda, in that story, relies on a few of her newspaper friends for emotional sustenance, she is primarily a person set apart who scarcely even speaks the language of her fellow reporters. Whatever her later misgivings, however, in Denver at least Porter regarded her newspaper work seriously. As Joan Givner points out, her drama reviews at that time took on a tone of "moral earnestness," and she began to condemn performances that did not exhibit a high level of art. We recall that in "Pale Horse, Pale Rider" Miranda resists pressure to praise the performance of a theatrical has-been when she does not believe praise is deserved. Both Porter's aesthetic standards and her vision of good and evil were becoming defined.[40]

The brush with death that Porter experienced so soon after her illness with tuberculosis seems to have galvanized her determination to address herself to serious issues, especially to art. Although she did not write about that close call or about other aspects of her life in Denver until many years later, it is clear that the experiences recreated in "Pale Horse, Pale Rider" were profoundly important ones in establishing her sense of self. When she went to New York shortly thereafter she would associate with persons seriously concerned with social issues such as the position of women and would make energetic, if sometimes diffuse, efforts to establish herself in a literary career. Her ambition to be a great writer was formed, though its fulfillment would long remain in doubt. As late as 1960 she would still be wondering. When she encountered, in a book of interviews, an expression of doubt that women could ever be "great geniuses," she underscored the question and posed one of her own: "Lets wait and see—maybe even K. A. P.?"[41]

❧ The death of her beloved niece, Gay's daughter Mary Alice (named after their mother and their younger sister), soon after Porter's near-fatal bout with the flu was another scarring deprivation. Givner writes that Porter "never quite got over the loss" of her niece and "all her life tried, without much success, to write a significant literary memorial" to her.[42] Although she did not return home for the funeral, she grieved intensely. Four years later she wrote Gay that her love for "that adorable tender and innocent baby" was "the one genuine lasting affection in me, for it outwears everything else." But her grief for the child was compounded, as she realized, with other griefs. "I buried my own childhood with her, and I feel sometimes that when I cry for her, I am crying over all the other lost things in my life, too."[43] She wrote at least one poem (unpublished) on the child's death, observed her birthday for years, and forty years later published an account of their Christmas shopping expedition in December of 1918, called "A Christmas Story."[44] In time her grief would be compounded by grief over the death of her own child, stillborn in December 1924—if that event actually occurred. If, as some of the evidence indicates, it was a fictitious loss, it remains true that her grief was expressed in her need to create the story of a pregnancy and a stillborn child. It is not at all clear which was the case. But in any event, the loss of Gay's little daughter was a bitter one. Even thirty years after the event she was still recalling the child in letters to her sister, quoting remembered sayings and treasuring the knowledge that little Mary Alice had prayed for her when she had the flu.

In her correspondence with Gay over the loss, Porter cast herself as the rationalist in contrast to her sister's lapse into self-accusation and spiritualist gropings after the dead child. "You must *not* think of her death as punishment for anything you have done or left undone," she urged Gay. "It is simply this, that [h]er little body was not strong enough to resist the disease that attacked it, and death is just that—the defeat of the flesh. . . . But no power destroyed your innocent baby in order to avenge itself upon you." She acknowledged that she too had some direct acquaintance with spiritualism—"I have gone about a bit here, and have seen one or two of the best"—and that she had also at times sensed that the child had "come back" to be with her. "I find it difficult to believe now that we do not have some sort of conscious spiritual existance [*sic*] after death," she admitted. Her conclusion, however, was a rationalistic one, as she conceded that "of course this sense of her presence might possibly be only my own mind filling the gap left by her going." Spiritualism she regarded as "a superstition for darkened minds . . . not for enlightened people, or thinkers."[45]

Porter's avowal of a rationalistic perspective positions her, within the family, alongside her father, who had played the role of rationalist opposite his wife's and his mother's roles of staunch believers. Throughout his life he liked to espouse rationalist ideas; letters written in his later years regularly go off into long seriocomic evolutionary diatribes. It is scarcely to be supposed that Porter realized at the time how much she was sounding like him, yet the tone of her remarks is one more bit of evidence of the way in which her ambivalence toward her father pervaded her life and thought. In a 1928 letter to Gay she deplored Gay's "occultism," and urged her "to take the visible world, and your little lamp of reason as guides." She attributed this belief to "Dad's eighteenth century rationalism" which only she and Paul of the four children "soaked" up. Gay, too, remembered their father as a person interested in intellectual matters who "forced" on them books like "Wells History of the World." She commented, "Told him would read it when I was old, so I am." Gay also recalled seeing their father "reading Mark Twain and chuckling now and then."[46] From reading his preserved letters and the comments in his children's letters, one can well believe that Twain would have been one of Harrison Porter's favorites.

❧ Throughout her life Porter would remain in a state of intermittent rebellion against her Texas origins and all they meant to her. But her disaffection was more encompassing than simply an alienation from family. Especially after the misunderstanding over the naming of the Humanities

Research Center at the University of Texas, which she thought was to be named in her honor though such was apparently never the plan, she would feel great bitterness against the state as a whole and its literary establishment in particular. Even before that unfortunate business, she would speak of the university with harsh sarcasm: "Oh yes," she wrote to her nephew Paul (the son of her brother, also named Paul), "and the Library of Texas recently asked me please to contribute another manuscript to their collection. Pore lil ole thaings. But I haven't got one handy. Filthy little bastards, the lot of them." Much later, finding her name in a list of writers of the "Lone Star mystique," she wrote in the margin, "Include me out, please."[47]

Yet she would also, throughout her life, keep turning back toward those roots, never fully returning to them but continuing to ponder their significance. She said that she could not consider living in Texas and that the place recalled the bitterest sort of memories for her, yet she wrote of her early regional home with great warmth in "'Noon Wine': The Sources" and elsewhere, and she spoke of the South as "my own place . . . the native land of my heart."[48] Her feelings toward her native place are curiously conflicted—almost as conflicted, perhaps, as her feelings toward her family. Indeed, the two are inextricably intertwined. They emerge in her continual search for a home and loving relationships and her continual inability to settle into either.

Texas as a whole, as well as her own family in particular, did not, in her view at any rate, provide a congenial ground in which an artist might grow. That view of the cultural environment in Texas can be and has been challenged, but it has also been supported. So respected a regional authority as John Graves has acknowledged that the "Texas Mystique" could be "pretty rough in some of its effects on people who care about the arts, or about thought, or about unfrontiersmanly, often uneconomic views of inquiry and interest."[49] Porter held to such a view strongly and with something like consistency throughout her life. She wrote to her friend Josephine Herbst, "I left the south because the atmosphere was too close for me, I could not breathe easily there," but conceded, sensibly enough, "But didn't you leave Iowa for the same reason?"[50]

After settling in Paris, in 1932, Porter characterized her life there in terms of personal freedom: "I can live and work here without question, see the people I like, arrange my life as I want it without the terrible drain on spirit and energy that it costs almost anywhere else." The implication is that her life at home, either in Texas specifically or in the United States generally, had not been a life of freedom, but one of constraint or lack of congeniality. Writing to John Herrmann only a few months later, explaining why she had pulled back from the Communist party, she referred to past repressions and a sense of being at odds with her society: "I left one way of life, a way very strictly marked out and ordered with only one end in view, because I was unable to accept it all without reservations and so live and act freely within that boundary."[51] Here she may have been referring to her departure from Catholicism, to which she had converted at the time of her first marriage, but she may have been again referring to the way of life in Texas, or to both. The point, in any case, is that her act of departure was made for the sake of freedom.

Much later in life, Porter wrote to fellow Texan William Humphrey, when he was just beginning his career as a writer, "I never had any real regional patriotism, in fact I got out of Texas like a bat out of hell at the earliest possible moment and stayed away cheerfully half a life-time."[52] It was true. Yet at one point she considered writing a history of the state (on the promise of a $2,500 advance) and she retained a suspicion that native roots were important in their own right. In 1932 she fretted, "I think it is bad to cut away from your roots, I have no wish to do this."[53]

The question of roots, regional as well as familial, was a major thread in Porter's thought and in her self-awareness throughout her life. If in her early years she manifested that thread more by avoidance than by identification, it was, nevertheless, a major impetus toward the self and the career she constructed for herself. Avoid her family as she did, she remained in correspondence with them throughout her life, mainly with Gay and with her nephew Paul, but also with others in the family. Though she might often complain, in later years, that she was exploited by her family and financially drained by the insatiable needs of Paul and of Gay's daughter Ann, she nonetheless continued to center her emotional life on those relationships, and she continued to stress, in her theoretical pronouncements about the formation of character, the importance of a good family upbringing—the kind that her grandmother tried to give her for a few years, but that otherwise she never knew for herself.

Porter's identity as a serious aspiring writer concerned with political issues but determined to retain her intellectual autonomy was firmly established by 1920, when she went to New York to commit herself to her career. But her identity as a woman who enjoyed projecting herself in terms of feminine allure was also well established, as was her tendency to vacillate and to cover her tracks. During the 1920s all these aspects of her complex character would manifest themselves more and more forcefully. She would move from place to place and from love affair to love affair. She would express a comprehensive dissent from capitalist America, culminating in a murky set of political intrigues in Mexico in the early years of the decade and participation in the protest marches in behalf of Sacco and Vanzetti in 1927. Throughout these turbulent years, however, she would cling fast to the essence of her sense of self: her commitment to her art; and she would so advance in her development as an artist that by 1929 she would produce "Flowering Judas."

CHAPTER THREE

Politics and Art in the Radical Twenties

With a feeling that this was no place for me, I would work up some kind of paying errand, and go back to Mexico.

—Porter, "Notes on the Twenties"

Mexico is not really a place to visit any more, or to live in.

—Porter, Review of Stuart Chase's *Mexico: A Study of Two Americas*

Katherine Anne Porter's political views and affiliations over the course of her long career form a shifting kaleidoscope that does not always settle into a very coherent pattern. Hailing from a region known (not entirely correctly) for its conservatism, Porter became associated with communist circles by 1920, when she was living in New York after her stint as a newspaperwoman in Denver. It was not an unusual political stance among artists and intellectuals at the time, though not so common as it would become in the early thirties, when artists and intellectuals in great numbers, searching for a set of viable social values, identified themselves with the politics of the left, and specifically with the Communist party. Porter was somewhat ahead of the trend. Throughout the twenties and into the thirties she was what might best be called a communist sympathizer. She referred to herself in various letters as a fellow traveler. By 1931, the year of the great surge to the left among U.S. intellectuals, the firmness of her radical convictions would have been shaken by a potent combination of disillusionments, but she would not yet, as she later claimed, have flown completely off the Marxist-Leninist locomotive.[1]

Elinor Langer, the biographer of Porter's friend and fellow novelist Josephine Herbst, has judged that although Porter "has something of a reputation of a radical" in the 1920s, "her radicalism does not run very deep."[2] That assessment, though unduly dismissive, is probably accurate. She liked to fancy herself as involved, committed, in on things. There is evidence that for a time she even enjoyed the excitements of political intrigue. But her involvement was at least in part a strategem to avoid the discipline demanded by her one real, overriding commitment: to literature, to writing. She later made light of her own involvement in various causes: "Being a child of my time, naturally I was to be found protesting."[3] Yet if she was not so deeply committed in her radicalism as was her friend Herbst, her life in the 1920s and early 1930s did run along courses set by those who were. Then as later, she knew a great many people who were themselves deeply involved in the political (as well as the artistic) currents of the time.

The precise degree of Porter's commitment to communism in the twenties and thirties remains unclear. Probably she was never a member of the Communist party, unless it was for a brief time in Mexico. Her longtime friend Cleanth Brooks and his wife heard her say "several times" in the late thirties that she had been a card-carrying member in Mexico but had been "thrown out because she failed to keep party discipline." Frances N. Cheney, one of the group with whom Porter shared a house in early 1944 and a longtime friend, states positively that she was a party member in Mexico.[4] More likely, Cheney simply believed Porter's exaggerated statements about her ties to communists there. But whatever the degree of her commitment, it was not one she would retain. She became disillusioned with the party and during World War II adopted a centrist America-first position in which world communism was paired with fascism as one of the two primary threats to the republic. This shift seems to have resulted from a growing perception that the Communist party, or indeed any strongly unitary political party, was inimical to a set of individualistic values among which freedom of artistic expression—Porter's primary value commitment throughout her life—was the chief. But the question of party membership was a difficult one for her that became the node of a complex set of conflicting values. The difficulty it posed was a conflict between her urge to act upon her political beliefs and her urge to maintain her convictions about the autonomy of the artist and artistic creativity. Party discipline, she feared, meant an inevitable encroachment on her "free, intransigent, dissenting mind"—and that was the very essence of her defection from Texas and family.[5]

Mary Doherty, Porter's much-abused friend from her Mexican days and one of her most faithful correspondents, would recall years later that "most of the little group of artists—pseudo artists" they had known "in the early days" became communists. "I used to tell a N.Y. friend who would come here," she wrote in 1963, "a rabid SOCIALIST, when she would wonder why one happened to know so many Communists that one would not speak to anyone in Mexico if one didn't speak to a Communist." In fact, however, membership in the Communist Party of Mexico (the PCM) remained small throughout the decade.[6] A number of their friends were indeed communist in principle, though not so many as were socialist or vaguely leftist. But in Mexico, especially, the distinctions among such groups were shifting and unclear. A recent historian has pointed out that "there have been several Mexican Communisms," not all of them identified with the PCM, and implies that in Mexico until the 1960s to be "on the socialist left" meant "automatically" being "part of the Communist tradition and its parties." Indeed, the label *communist* has been seen as being rather insignificant among intellectuals in the United States as well: "To be a 'communist' or 'socialist' in these years meant very little. One was simply a 'radical,' more or less influenced by Marx."[7]

Another feature of Porter's life during the 1920s was her advocacy of feminist causes. She had earlier been, by her own testimony, "badly upset over the fact that women enjoyed no suffrage at the ballot box."[8] Her friends in New York and even before included women who were living untraditional lives and were active in the agitation for women's rights. Even then Porter rejected the word *feminism*, choosing instead the word *modern* as an approximate equivalent.[9] Several of her reviews in the twenties were of books taking an advanced view of the gender issue, and she herself, in her review of a symposium on the woman question edited by Freda Kirchwey, espoused sexual freedom for women and used the occasion to voice something like an anarchist position, that "organized society" seems to be "a unified expression of hatred and protest against life itself."[10] The early 1920s were Porter's most aggressively feminist period, from which she would retreat to a position of avowed femininity even while asserting her right to fair treatment as an artist and a professional.

Even if, as Elinor Langer says, Porter was only a shallow radical, her life in these years was more politically involved than it would be at any subsequent period. In the end she could make her stand on no other ground than the free intransigence of her solitary mind and her art. But the portion of the political spectrum in which she most nearly found her home for well over a decade was that of the left.

❧ Virtually nothing is known of Porter's political views prior to her arrival in New York in 1919, but according to her own comments her interest in communism dated from the late teens. To Herbst she said that she had first "wanted to go to Russia" to "go through the course of training they give you" in 1917. (Herbst and her husband John Herrmann did go to Russia, in 1930, with the help of Mike Gold, editor of the *New Masses*.) She told Caroline Gordon, another fellow-novelist friend and the wife of poet Allen Tate, that when she "first went to New York, 1919 to 1920," she "fell in with a crowd just back from Russia" and heard continually that "the Revolution was not merely just around the corner" but right on their doorsteps. The mocking tone evident here is typical of Porter's detached stance but also reflects the reorientation of political convictions she was undergoing in the mid- to late 1930s, when she wrote it. Another indication of the beginning point of her alignment with the left is given in a letter written to her father from Mexico on June 26, 1931, in which she says that she has had "for twelve years a sympathy for Russia."[11] This would agree with her statement to Gordon, that the origin of her communist sympathies was about 1919, the year she went to New York from Denver. Before that time, her journalism, though it had taken on an increasingly serious tone in the course of her newspaper work in Denver, provides little clue.

Comments on Porter's radical politics after she went to New York have usually cited her literary and radical acquaintances there.[12] Indeed, she did fall in with a set of radical friends in New York, but these appear to have reinforced, rather than initiated, her leftist political leanings. Her association with friends on the left was strengthened in Mexico City, where she went in November 1920, in time to witness and help celebrate the inauguration of revolutionist Alvaro Obregón as president. Whether she would have espoused communist sympathies in any case is, of course, impossible to say. Probably she would not have become so fervent in her radicalism or so outspoken in avowing it if she had not had the friendships she did. In her early days in New York these included writer Ernestine Evans; poet/editor Genevieve Taggard, fresh from socialist circles in the San Francisco area; and Mexican artists sympathetic with the aims of the Revolution, such as Adolfo Best-Maugard and musician Tata Nacho (Ignacio Fernández Esperón). Even so, there is good reason to believe that Porter's political radicalism may have sprung in part from Texas soil, through exposure to socialist ferment there.[13]

The political climate in Texas during Porter's early life was not at all one of unchallenged conservative hegemony, but rather a lively ferment in which a noisy radicalism flourished. In central Texas, the area of her birth and early childhood, populism had been a turbulent and powerful political force in the 1890s, appealing chiefly to the small-scale indebted farmer class to which her father belonged. The Populist vote in Brown County, the county of her birth, was strong throughout the decade. It was less so in Hays County, where she lived in her grandmother's home in Kyle from 1892 to 1902 or 1903; Kyle was mainly a railroad town, and populism was not generally strong in such communities; but it was not negligible there, nor was the later Socialist vote. In both areas political talk accompanying these grass-roots surges of radicalism must have been widespread.

After the turn of the century, populism joined with an infusion of radicalism from the late-nineteenth-century labor movement to form a lively Socialist campaign lasting well into the second decade. The resulting debate was widespread, occupying a great many Texans during the period that would have included Porter's formative years.[14] She reached the age of ten in 1900 and remained in Texas until 1918—the full span of significant Socialist party activity. The Socialist party in Texas drew its chief strength from two areas: the south-central region, where Porter spent her childhood (including San Antonio, where Harrison Porter moved his children in 1904), and the lumbering region of east Texas, an area including the town of Lufkin, where Porter and her family were living at the time she married John Henry Koontz in 1906.[15] The young couple would spend their early married years, from 1906 to 1908, in nearby western Louisiana, a hotbed of labor organization and violent disputes. Socialist and IWW organizers were active among the lumber workers in eastern Texas and western Louisiana in 1910 and 1911. Because of Koontz's family home near Victoria, the two would also frequent the south-central region of Texas during the years of Socialist party agitation.

In addition to whatever political discussions went on in the neighborhoods where Porter grew up and where she lived as a young adult, a vigorous and highly partisan journalistic debate was conducted at the time throughout the Southwest. The center of Socialist journalism in Texas was in the town of Hallettsville, some seventy miles southeast of Kyle and forty-four miles north of Victoria. The *New Era*, a "Socialist-oriented" paper, was published in Hallettsville by E. R. Meintzen beginning about 1904, and the *Rebel* was also published there by Meintzen's father, E. O. Meintzen, from 1911 to 1917. By 1912 the *Rebel* had a circulation of 18,000, and the Socialist press overall, including numerous relatively short-lived papers in Texas and Oklahoma, is estimated to have reached at least one hundred thousand readers in the Southwest. It is inconceivable that an alert person—as Porter assuredly was—and a person so interested in journalism could have grown to maturity in the area without being aware of the socialist debate. Socialist agitation in the Southwest propounded a Marxist ideology of class struggle and, in the pages of the *Rebel*, linked exploitation of the rural poor in Texas to exploitation of "the peons of Mexico," a group for which Porter would be keenly concerned in the years ahead. She may well have known of the Texas Socialists' defense of the "class-conscious revolutionists" Emiliano Zapata and Pancho Villa in 1914 and the *Rebel*'s refusal to abandon its admiration of Villa even after other Socialist papers condemned him for his raid on Columbus, New Mexico. She herself would later speak of Villa admiringly as a "perfectly good revolutionist . . . paying his workers a living wage, and establishing schools for their children."[16]

Whether an acquaintance with radical politics from newspapers and general public talk was reinforced by political conversations at home is impossible to say with any certainty. Porter's father seems always to have been a talkative person and one who enjoyed debate. Granting these traits, we can guess that daily conversation in the Porter household during the earlier years of the century would have covered the political scene, which included a strong ferment of radicalism. There is plenty of evidence in letters from 1930 on that Harrison Porter took a keen interest in politics. A letter of Katherine Anne's indicates that he may have been present at the 1928 Democratic convention when Al Smith was nominated. In 1932 he rejoiced at the election of a Democratic president as a kind of "miracle."[17] Among the few political references in his own letters is an indication in 1934 that he had voted for Tom Hunter in the gubernatorial primary and would "vote for him again when the opportunity presents itself." Since Hunter was regarded as the most liberal candidate in the field and was defeated by a candidate (James Allred) who is still considered by many historians the most liberal governor Texas has ever had, this means that the elder Porter's political views were probably somewhat left of center.[18]

Another piece of evidence about Harrison Porter's political views suggests that he may have been considerably more conservative when social issues or the integrity of the South was involved. When in 1938 he referred to the election of Governor Richard Coke as "the first ray of hope to arise above the horizon of our beloved state for many years," he was looking back to 1874, when the election of a Democrat, Coke, put an end to Reconstruction in Texas. Clearly, Harrison Porter had welcomed that event. In another document filed with his letters in the Porter Collection, an undated sheet labeled "Early reminiscences," he wrote bitterly of Reconstruction: "After the Civil War came Carpet baggers and negro troops. The whole South was flooded with debts the south did not honestly owe. Negro soldiers walked in contempt of the rights of citizens where they were stationed."[19] In the 1870s Harrison Porter had been a member of the Travis Rifles, a group avowedly ready to take up their rifles again in rebellion against the victorious North if the provocations of Reconstruction became too great to bear. We can conjecture that on social issues such as race the elder Porter may not have been as far to the left as the leading voices in the socialist debate were.

Exposure to such a ferment in her childhood and youth would not necessarily have inclined Katherine Anne to radicalism in adulthood. But we can see, at any rate, that she would have had ample opportunity to become acquainted with socialist views. Socialist candidates in the early years of the century did not draw a large portion of the votes cast, but neither did they represent an isolated fringe. In Texas, the party's high point was reached in the election of 1912, when, after a noisy campaign, Eugene V. Debs drew one-twelfth of the votes cast in the state and one-sixth in Oklahoma—but more than one-fifth in the south-central Texas county of Lavaca, home of the *Rebel*. Although one-twelfth may not seem to be a very strong proportion, it actually reflected a large Socialist vote, three times the vote Debs had drawn in 1908, an increase of over 10,000. The percentage of the total was depressed by the year's unprecedented turnout of Democratic voters for Woodrow Wilson. In a year of ordinary voter turnout, the same Socialist vote would have formed a much larger percentage.[20]

At some time during the surge in Debs's popularity, Porter apparently heard him speak. She told Kenneth Durant, director of the ROSTA (later TASS) bureau in New York, that her father had taken her to hear Debs when she was fourteen. It is hard to be sure which year she meant, since she habitually misrepresented her age and Debs made several speaking tours in Texas, including 1904 (when she was in fact fourteen), 1908 (fourteen years after the birth date she often claimed), and 1912 and 1913. She recalled that "the southern newspapers were still referring to him as a raging, blood thirsty monster of revolution, and describing his famous 'tiger crouch,' when speaking." Her own impression was of a "tall, pale colored thin man who did lean over as near as he could get to his hearers," who "talked very urgently but gently" and said "mild and reasonable" things.[21]

Southwestern socialism did not represent a simple resurgence of populism. Indeed, one well-recognized historian of the two phenomena argues that they "represented significantly different constituencies on the basis of rather different ideologies." Still, there was considerable overlapping between the two. "Leftover Populists" were among the "virtual circus" of groups making up the Socialist party of America. A "labor paper" in New Orleans, the *Issue,* urged Populist farmers to consider affiliating with the Socialists. The platform of the Texas Socialist Party in 1912 appealed to rural as well as to industrial groups, declaring that the two had interests in common in that "capitalism divided rural society as well as industrial society into 'warring groups and classes based on material interest.' "[22]

The spirit of unity would founder, however, on two issues: race and nationalism. With the outbreak of war fever after 1914, and with the Socialist party taking a strong antiwar position, public reaction turned against socialism. Mob scenes occurred, the state secretary of the Socialist party in Texas was arrested, longtime radical leader Tom Hickey was kidnapped, and on June 9, 1917, the U.S. postmaster general banned the *Rebel* from the mails under the not-yet-signed Espionage Act.[23] On issues of race, too, the rank and file would fall away. Socialists had long recruited supporters without regard to color, but racial sentiments continued to run strong among the small farmers and tenants who had supposedly been recruited to the socialist program. A statement in the Oklahoma paper *Harlow's Weekly,* of July 3, 1915, demonstrates how economic radicalism was combined with social conservatism where racial issues were concerned: "A very large percentage of the recent growth of this party has been among the small farmers in the southern part of the state, who, before they became Socialists—and since—were white men, who upon such an issue will be more influenced by their racial feelings, inherited through generations of southern ancestors than by the highly theoretic considerations which influence the leaders of the Party."[24] In 1910, two-thirds of all Texans were "native whites of native parents," by far the greater number of them born either in Texas or elsewhere in the South. According to a contemporary observer, so many

Texans had come out of the South that the state was "predominantly Southern in thought and feeling."[25] Porter herself would later display a similar combination of radical economic politics and conservative racial views.

In summary, Porter's regional roots were set during years of radical ferment. Long before she left her native state, she was exposed to a lively political and journalistic debate in which radical voices were strong. Moreover, if we can take "Pale Horse, Pale Rider" as direct testimony, when she arrived in New York she was fresh from the scene of another powerful experience in dissent, her demurral from war hysteria in Denver. The circumstantial evidence is strong, then, that she would not have arrived as a political tabula rasa, to be written on by radicals in Greenwich Village, but would have brought with her an awareness of radical positions, even a leaning in that direction, that was pushed into alignment by the influence of her new set.

❧ Among Porter's new friends in New York were several Mexican artists, among them Adolfo Best-Maugard, with whom Porter collaborated early in 1920 on a ballet for the great dancer Pavlova. Although, as Thomas F. Walsh has said, he was "nobody's idea of a revolutionary," Best-Maugard was sympathetic to the goals of the Revolution and was then developing theories of the primitive origins and patterns of art that were consistent with those goals.[26] It was he who arranged letters of introduction paving the way for Porter's first trip to Mexico.

Porter's interest in Mexico was one she shared with a great many Americans of the day who, in the aftermath of World War I, felt a disaffection from "capitalist civilization" that spurred an "extraordinary interest in folk cultures, agrarian communities, and peasant life."[27] Europe, it seemed, was "spiritually and intellectually bankrupt." People turned their attention to Latin America instead, their particular interest in Mexico fueled by the Revolution and its image of concern for indigenous groups. Mexico became a "haven for the flotsam of alienation" who wished to escape technological, capitalist society and "dreamed of a fusion of art and politics."[28]

Arriving in Mexico City on November 6, 1920, Porter quickly established contact with two socialist activists, Thorberg Haberman, editor of the English-language section of *El Heraldo de México,* and her husband, Robert, who served as a liaison between labor groups in Mexico and both the American Federation of Labor and the Socialist party of America—an interesting combination in that the AFL was ardently anti-socialist.[29] Roberto, regarded by José Vasconcelos, Obregón's minister of education, as a "professional atheist," would become an adviser to the socialist and anticlerical governor of the state of Yucatán, Felipe Carillo Puerto.[30] Through the Habermans Porter became acquainted with a number of people involved in the Obregón government and others of leftist political inclinations. These included Carillo Puerto, the important revolutionist intellectual leader Manuel Gamio, labor leader Luis Morones, and a somewhat mysterious foreigner present in Mexico City at the time, Polish intriguer J. H. Retinger, whom she met either at the inaugural festivities for Obregón shortly after her arrival or at the Habermans' that Christmas. She was quickly drawn into both a romantic relationship with Retinger and a swirl of idealistic radical activity, including occasional work for Morones. She would later regard Morones as the fourth-strongest man in Mexico—probably an underestimation of his power.[31]

Almost immediately upon her arrival Porter became a contributing writer for *El Heraldo,* publishing her first article there, a review of *Mexico in Revolution* by V. Blasco Ibáñez, on November 22. By the end of the year she had published in *El Heraldo* a second review and two other articles—a brief but forceful account of the funeral of General Benjamín Hill and a lengthy anticlerical essay, "The Fiesta of Guadalupe," in addition to writing a regular column that she had taken over from Thorberg Haberman. The connection with *El Heraldo* is in itself one more piece of evidence of her radical political affiliations in those years, even though she also worked for a publication backed by conservative American bankers, the *Magazine of Mexico*.[32] At the time Porter began her association with *El Heraldo* it was owned by Salvador Alvarado, a noted anticlericist and a member of Obregón's cabinet who had been chosen by Venustiano Carranza, Obregón's predecessor, to put down counterrevolution in the Yucatán in 1914–15 and had taken the region further to the left than any other part of Mexico controlled by the Constitutionalists, to the distress of American business interests. The editor from 1915 through 1918, Charles Phillips, had attended the Second Congress of the Comintern as a delegate of the Communist Party of Mexico and would be deported in May 1921, when Obregón attempted to rid Mexico of Bolshevik agitators. Under Thorberg Haberman's editorship, the English-language page of the paper had a distinctly radical cast.[33]

Shortly after her arrival Porter wrote to her family that she was teaching dancing and primary ballet in a socialist institute and along with "two radicals here," that is, the Habermans, was to "write a revolutionary text book of English for use in our Institute." The textbook apparently never materialized, but as early as January 1921 she published a heavily propagandist article coauthored with Robert Haberman in the socialist *New York Call* (where another acquaintance of Porter's, Dorothy Day, had worked as a reporter), and in March an essay, "The New Man and the New Order," in the *Magazine of Mexico*. The new man of the essay's title is, of course, Obregón; indeed, the entire first issue of the magazine is given to praising him and his cohorts, one of whom is celebrated for riding his "native mountains for seven years with a copy of Karl Marx and another of the Bible in his pocket." Some of Porter's activities during this first stay in Mexico, however, she did not mention to her family. She would later say in an interview that she had been "like the girl who took messages to people living in dark alleys" in "Flowering Judas."[34]

Luis Morones, one of the organizers, in 1918, of the Confederación Regional Obrera Mexicana (CROM), was influential in the Obregón government and served as minister of industry, commerce, and labor under Obregón's successor, President Plutarco Elías Calles. He has been regarded by at least one historian as "the most powerful man in Mexico" in 1924 except for Calles himself. This was the height of Morones's influence and power; he would never attain the presidency, the goal toward which he was working and which Porter thought would assure "the salvation of Mexico."[35] Though not identified with the Communist Party of Mexico per se, Morones was considered both by the U.S. government and by Porter to be a Bolshevik (a "perfectly good" one, she called him). He was one of the main leaders of the labor movement demanding "economic and social justice for the workers at the expense of the American-owned oil companies."[36] Despite his having opposed the creation of a communist party out of the Congreso Socialista in 1919, Morones was certainly given to Marxist rhetoric at times, declaring in a speech on September 27, 1920, that his "one purpose" was "the destruction of the capitalistic system." That had been the aim, as well, of the anarcho-syndicalists of the Casa del Obrero Mundial, founded in 1912, with which Morones had been associated prior to its suppression (and his jailing) by Carranza in 1916.[37] The Obregón regime of which Morones was a part might best be described as socialist and nativist, but despite its "apparent commitment" to land distribution and the position of labor, which alarmed conservatives, its policies were those of "moderation and pragmatism."[38]

Porter became closely associated with CROM and with Morones. Although he was condemned by members of the far left for what they perceived as a sellout to the American Federation of Labor in November 1918, when he cooperated with Samuel Gompers in forming the Pan American Federation of Labor (PAFL), Porter does not seem to have objected when she first knew him. Then as later, she simply did not understand the complex currents of Mexican politics in general and the Mexican labor movement in particular. Later in the decade she would comment to her father that Morones "had done badly, I think, selling out to the American Federation of Labor, a gang of thugs if ever I saw one." Her view of the AFL may have been colored by memories of its members' heckling of Eugene V. Debs during his speaking stops in Texas. In January 1921, however, she seems to have supported the PAFL. She appears in a large group picture with Morones, Gompers, her friend Mary Doherty, the Habermans, and others attending a PAFL meeting in Mexico City.[39]

Porter's involvement with Morones extended considerably further than the "odd jobs" Walsh attributes to her and the comments that appear in her papers. In the spring of 1921, after Retinger was arrested and jailed in the United States while on an obscure mission in behalf of Morones, she was sent by Morones to Laredo to try to get him released. It is by no means clear what was going on, beyond the fact that the U.S. government considered Retinger and his mission, ostensibly the buying of saddles, undesirable. One member of the circle of acquaintances involved in the business, Paul Hanna (a correspondent for the *New York Call* and the *London Daily Herald,* who later published a series of articles on Mexico in the *Nation*), told Porter that the source of the problem was a feud between Morones and the American consul at Nuevo Laredo. The consul, he said, had told him Morones was a Bolshevik. In a letter dated April 2, 1921, Hanna outlined a story about Retinger's having earlier been sent to Mexico by parties in New York, who demanded a guarantee that he not return. One of these parties was Gilbert Seldes, who had been involved with Jane Anderson, the dashing journalist, in Colorado. What it was that had prompted such an action the letter does not spell out. Porter drafted a response, which she may not have mailed, saying that she had known "a great deal" about the matter for several years and had met Seldes in Colorado. In one of her several drafts of this puzzling letter she alludes to a woman who was the "central figure in all this," who had "spoiled her own life and half a dozen others."[40] She was referring to Anderson, with whom Retinger had been and perhaps still was passionately in love.

What is clear about all this, amid much that is not clear, is that Porter was living in a densely conspiratorial atmosphere. Her attempts to use that atmosphere in fiction are evident in crumbling fragments dated 1921, found among her papers. She made at least two starts on a story involving a character called De Ret, who speaks in a "Polish voice." The female protagonist, called Miranda in one of the fragments, says, "It was a bad show. . . . But I think now I have come to a worse one." What "it" was is not explained.

Retinger would later, in 1926, publish a book on Morones. Reprinted in 1976 as *The Rise of the Mexican Labor Movement,* the book was evidently in preparation early in 1921, and sounds several notes that are heard also in Porter's letters and other writings about Mexico dating from the same period. She may indeed have assisted him in writing it. She had published an article on Morones in April 1921, in which Morones himself probably had a hand, as he probably did in Retinger's biography. Retinger instructed her in March 1921 to "take the greatest care about his biography . . . and before printing submit it to Luis," and mentioned the article as a separate item to be cleared.[41] Retinger's book is forcefully pro-labor. It is clear that he as well as other acquaintances Porter made during her first stay in Mexico would have fortified her concern for the poorest of the oppressed Mexican people, the Indian. It was this concern, as much as her theoretical interest in Marxism and the great Russian experiment, that motivated her political involvements in Mexico. She shared the hopes of her friends who were actively involved in working toward political change on behalf of the Indian and other economically oppressed people. In writing to her family, her tone in referring to these social initiatives was exultant: "Life here is a continual marvel to the eye, and to the emotions. . . . Nobody seems to realize elsewhere that a full fledged revolutionary government is in full swing here, with everybody from the President down a seething radical." She notes having had Christmas dinner in 1920 at the home of "the one genuine Bolshevik in Mexico who is really helping to run things."[42] This was Haberman, her link to Morones and Retinger.

In his book on Morones, Retinger states plainly that the Mexican laboring masses had been "cruelly persecuted" before President Madero came to power in 1910 and advocates international labor solidarity to fight capitalist "exploitation," a theme Porter would also develop. Although Retinger is identified in the editors' preface to the 1976 edition as a "British Marxist" having "close ties with both the British Communist Party as well as with the Comintern then functioning from Moscow," any definition of his politics is in fact elusive. His obituary in the *New York Times* indicates that he was an exile from Communist Poland and worked for the unification of non-Communist Europe, but the period referred to there is post-World War II; his views might well have shifted by then. In 1982, Mary Doherty remembered him as an anticommunist, but again, it is hard to know how much credence to give to a statement made more than fifty years after the fact. U.S. Intelligence termed his views "obscure."[43] At any rate, in his book on Morones he writes as a gradualist, advocating cooperation between labor and Mexican owners in order to rid the country of foreign capitalists. The principle of capitalism itself should be accepted during this transitional period, he says, in order to advance the cause of Mexican nationalism.

Porter's political involvements were sufficiently serious that for a time in 1921 she feared arrest or deportation. She wrote to Retinger, "I wonder, with a faint grimace of curiosity, what they would do with me after they had me? What on earth could they charge me with?" The question was at least partly bravado. She had played a part—a minor part, apparently, and a very obscure one, involving the surreptitious copying of letters addressed to anthropologist William Niven—in the intrigue that would lead to the death of rebel general Sidronio Méndez on June 24, 1921.[44] In late August, with the help of her Fort Worth friend Kitty Barry Crawford, Porter left the country. She had flirted with danger and counterrevolutionary intrigue, and her name had become known to U.S. government intelligence. It was indeed time for her to retreat.[45] With money sent by the Crawfords, she went to Fort Worth and again stayed in their home and did newspaper work, as well as some abortive fiction writing. In addition, she acted in local theater. She reported to her sister "Baby" that she was in a play that had been "an immense success" and if the family read "the oil Journal here" they would see her stories "featured in big type all over the place." When she returned to Mexico the following spring, she must still have felt somewhat apprehensive. Mary Doherty warned her to "watch out" because "there were a few enemies about loose when I left Mexico, do not let them jail you."[46]

Her return, however, was made at the invitation of the Mexican government. On March 24, 1922, Retinger conveyed to her by telegram a commission to write the catalog for a major exhibition of Mexican folk art. Although much of the collection had been shown the previous year with a catalog by the noted artist Dr. Atl (Gerardo Murillo), it was being greatly expanded. Numerous artists, government officials, and anthropologists were involved in the effort, or at any rate were thanked in Porter's preface, including José Vasconcelos; Vincente Lombardo Toledano, director of the Preparatory School of the National University; Jorge Enciso, of the National Museum, "collector and restorer of examples of early Colonial art, connoisseur of Mexican jade and Aztec design"; Ramón Mena and "his associate" William Niven, "the indefatigable digger who has brought out of the earth an extraordinary volume of relics from buried cities." Others who are thanked include Retinger, Diego Rivera, Adolfo Best-Maugard, and painter Xavier Guerrero. It is clear that Porter was pleased by her role, not only for the sake of her fee but because of the subject and the association with this group. In July she proudly told her family that she was "writing for half a dozen magazines and newspapers at once" and had just written the "official monograph" for President Obregón's Exhibition of Mexican Popular Arts.[47]

In the monograph she prepared as a catalog for the exhibit, Porter gave careful thought, probably for the first time, to a coherent theory of art. In particular, she argued a view of artistic authenticity that emphasized a sense of place and of indigenous folkways. The emphasis on folk art was partly, of course, dictated by the governmental plan under which the exhibit was assembled. But her development of the history of native Mexican art and the rationale for the exhibit also demonstrates that she at least entertained, whether or not she entirely accepted, theories of art comparable to those that would be enunciated that fall in the manifesto of the newly organized Union of Technical Workers, Painters, and Sculptors. Formed by David Alfaro Siqueiros, Rivera, Guerrero, and others, with the support of José Clemente Orozco (who would later depict himself as having been apolitical), the union repudiated "the so-called easel painting and all the art of ultra-intellectual circles" in favor of art as a "public possession."[48] Porter's glorification of the art of the people in contrast to an effete aristocratic art was also very much in keeping with the views of Best-Maugard, whose book *A Method for Creative Design* she would prepare for English-language publication in 1926. Best-Maugard states, for example, "All popular expressions of art are the fruit of a collective ideal."[49]

Best-Maugard's aesthetic theories were, of course, highly political in their implications. Democratization of art and liberation from the dominance of European styles had been official policy in Mexico as early as 1914, as a part of a general assertion of the pre-Columbian roots of Mexican national identity. A public art expressive of the concerns of the workers was being encouraged at the time, specifically in the form of the mural movement, by José Vasconcelos, the intensely political minister of education under Obregón.[50] Thus Porter's emphasis was not new in the context of Mexican art, but it was well argued for the new audience, the American public, that the 1922 exhibition was designed to reach. Seven years later, in reviewing *Idols Behind Altars,* by Anita Brenner, Porter would praise the artists she had known in Mexico for restoring not only the ancient art of the Indian but "the Indian himself, a perpetual exile in his own land."[51]

Photographs included in the monograph, as well as comments by Porter and others, show that the exhibition was indeed a rich and beautiful one, including fine examples of Mexican crafts. Ultimately, however, the project did not reach its intended goals. Although the fate of the exhibit is not entirely clear, what is clear is that it was not an entirely happy one. As an amateur in the field, Porter had difficulty arranging for major exhibit sites. Then, on its way to be shown in California, the collection was halted at the U.S. border, possibly on grounds of being political propaganda, and sat there for some weeks on a railroad siding. It was finally exhibited in Los Angeles in November 1922 to enthusiastic crowds before being sold off piecemeal.[52] Xavier Guerrero wrote Porter on January 1, 1923, that although he did not personally approve of selling any part of the collection, he had been instructed to do so and had followed instructions. He apparently sent her, as a souvenir, five hundred copies of the exhibition booklet. Interestingly enough, Guerrero's letter lamenting the sale provides corroboration of the U.S. government's judgment that the exhibit might be considered propaganda. He had given away rather than sold most of the booklets, he said, for the purpose of aiding the propaganda effort on behalf of the Mexican government. (Guerrero was a member of the executive committee of the PCM and, in 1922, with Siqueiros and Rivera, a "founding member" of the Syndicate newspaper *El Machete,* which first appeared in March 1924 and in October of the same year became the Communist party organ.) The monograph, however, is of much greater value than the label *propaganda* would indicate.[53]

Porter often bemoaned the fact that her beautiful exhibit was not more widely shown and thus her work of many months failed to reach as large an audience as she had hoped. (She would later claim that she had come across her exhibition, every piece of it and more, on display in Paris in 1952. It is safe to assume that the claim reflects some degree of hyperbole.)

Despite the disappointment, however, her role in preparing the exhibition brochure was a valuable experience. Not only did it give her the opportunity to view what was apparently a splendid collection of beautifully crafted objects, but she was led to think more seriously and systematically about art than she ever had before. The effects of her residence in Mexico, her involvement with Mexican political leaders, and her work on behalf of the exhibition would extend far into her literary career.

During this second stay in Mexico, in 1922, Porter became well acquainted with Diego Rivera, whom she had probably not known during her first stay, since he was out of the country until July 1921, shortly before she left. Rivera and his views on socially responsible art were influential in her experience and thought for several years. She attempted, without success, to sell some of his work in the United States before he was known outside Mexico, and she would speak of him for a time, before turning against him, as the greatest artist of his age. It would not be long, however, before caricatures of Rivera appeared in her fiction emphasizing his obesity, his lugubrious self-importance, and his tumultuous relationship with Guadalupe Marín, who served as a model for him and became his wife. Porter had observed the two in action. They provided her with the originals for Ruben and Isabel in her story "The Martyr" (published in 1923).

By mid-1922 she was back in New York, sharing an apartment with actress Liza Allen (later Dallett, later Monk), even though by this time, if Porter's retrospective dating of the letters is correct, Liza had written to say that she too had fallen in love with Retinger. Her first widely and lastingly noted story, "María Concepción," using observations she had gathered during her first stay in Mexico, appeared in December of that year in the *Century* magazine. As Givner says, after this story Porter was "launched."[54]

In 1923 Porter again returned to Mexico, this time engaged in a piece of work that strikingly links a number of her undertakings of these years in its political themes and its view of art. This was the editing and in part the writing of a special issue of the magazine *Survey Graphic*. During her earlier visits she had delighted in frequent excursions to Xochimilco, where Mary Doherty taught school, and to Teotihuacán, where Manuel Gamio was conducting archaeological work. Now she continued her explorations, visiting Cuernevaca and Xochicalco in company with Robert Haberman.[55] She also spent considerable time viewing the murals being painted by Diego Rivera and others. Her awareness of the lively controversy over the murals in the popular press can only have increased her sense of the complex tensions between political spokesperson and artist, private expression and public communication, especially when all of these issues were brought together in a single entity.

It was probably during this stay that Porter met another of her many radical/artistic friends, the strikingly beautiful Italian-American Tina Modotti. Now well known as a photographer, Modotti was a sometime movie actress when she first went to Mexico from California in March 1922. She brought with her some of Edward Weston's photographs, which were exhibited at the Academia de Bellas Artes and quickly attracted the interest of Rivera and others. When Modotti returned to Mexico in August 1923, Weston came as well. The two were quickly received into Rivera's circle of politically radical artists and by October were well acquainted with Best-Maugard.[56] Given Porter's familiarity with the Rivera circle (a "circle of artists and intellectuals who were close to the Communist party")[57] and the fact that she spent considerable time observing Rivera's work in 1923, it would have been natural for her to become acquainted with Modotti during her stay.

Weston, who taught Modotti photography, was active during this time in both portrait and scenic photography as well as urban landscape and was experimenting with extreme close-ups, especially, surprisingly enough, of toilets and of the glossy, rounded or elongated shapes of peppers. His portraits and nudes of Modotti are remarkably powerful, as are his portraits of Rivera and his boldly featured wife, Lupe Marín. We can wish that he had photographed Porter, but if he did so, or if he ever really knew her, there is no record. Both Rivera and Pablo O'Higgins, who joined Rivera as an assistant on the Secretaría de Educación Pública murals in December 1924 after becoming acquainted with his work in California, painted Modotti.

Tina Modotti was not a member of the Communist party when Porter first knew her, but joined the party in 1927. Like Porter, she demonstrated against the execution of Sacco and Vanzetti in that year—not in Boston, however, but in Mexico.[58] Many years later, after her own politics had shifted considerably, along with those of many other liberals, Mary Doherty would describe Modotti as "a raving noisy Communist" and would resurrect a piece of manufactured hearsay to the effect that she had conspired in having a man murdered on the street in Mexico City for political reasons.[59] The murder victim, Julio Antonio Mella, Modotti's lover at the time, was in Mexico as a "refugee" from Cuba. (Rivera called him "a Cuban revolutionary leader who had fled the dictatorship of President Gerardo Machado.") William Spratling, in his autobiography, judged that Mella was "of such political importance to Machado, that the Cuban government set agents on his trail." He was shot on January 10, 1929, while walking with Modotti, apparently by Cuban agents. In reporting that Modotti was involved in the killing, Doherty was retailing the slurs of the reactionary press at the time.[60]

Though cleared of Mella's murder, Modotti was deported from Mexico in 1930 after being accused of plotting the assassination of the president. Refused entry by both the United States and the Netherlands and not daring to enter her native Italy, which sought her return, she went to Berlin (where Porter would go less than a year later) and then to Moscow. Pablo O'Higgins also passed through Berlin, seeing Porter there in late 1931, on his way to Moscow. Soon Porter reported to Eugene Pressly that she had received a letter from O'Higgins, from Moscow, saying, "Very cold: this wonderful new world. New forms of living very interesting and VERY energetic. Is happy with new friends and comrades. Tina well and cheerful. Doesn't do photography because there isn't enough light." Porter regarded Modotti as "one of the best photographers" she had known, and praised her "masterly" work in a 1943 review of Anita Brenner's *The Wind That Swept Mexico*.[61]

The May 1924 issue of *Survey Graphic,* the occasion of Porter's 1923 trip, was devoted entirely to Mexico. It included a number of decorations by Adolfo Best-Maugard, whose book on design Porter was editing. As she did in the 1922 exhibit catalog, she here develops a theory of art that validates the direct expressions of indigenous peoples. Besides pieces on art, the issue includes articles on the educational aspirations of the Revolution, a subject in which Porter had already demonstrated her interest. With its glorification of the populist educational efforts of the Obregón revolution and its emphasis on class struggle—political themes evident in her essays and other writings from these years—the magazine is a production in which socialist and Marxist ideas are evident.

A signed article by Porter entitled "Corridos" describes the topical folk songs or printed ballads, often illustrated with sketches and caricatures and recounting political events or lurid crimes, that were sold on the streets of Mexico. Both the *corrido* and the art of caricature, a highly developed tradition in Mexico, would be of importance in Porter's fiction (for instance, in "Flowering Judas"). Mentioning a *corrido* about the "bandit general" Emiliano Zapata, Porter praises Zapata for being "one of the first Mexicans to apprehend the principles of soviet government." In seemingly attributing to Zapata both a theoretical basis of action and a large-scale organizational design for the country, however, Porter's view was inaccurate. Zapata was in essence a leader devoted to a single region, his home state of Morelos, and a single idea, the restoration of land to small farmers. He was "the chief of Morelos." Only gradually did he move beyond thinking locally and in terms of "patchwork remedies" to entertain, reluctantly, a vision for all of Mexico.[62]

Both in her article "Corridos" and in an article called "The Guild Spirit in Mexican Art," attributed to Diego Rivera "as told to Katherine Anne Porter," she celebrates the untutored folk art so warmly praised in the Best-Maugard book on design, where it is argued that the great value in folk art is its expression of the group sense of a people. In the article on the "guild spirit," Rivera/Porter describes the young artists of Mexico as a "robust" group of "workers" drawing on their "apostolic energy" in working toward the goal of a revolutionized society. It is the group mission, not the particularity of the individual's art, that is most highly valued.[63]

One wonders how comfortable Porter could have been with the arguments she helped to voice in favor of artists' subordinating their expressive urges to the purposes of a "syndicate." She had already seen, or at least believed she had seen, politics interfere with art in the delay of the folk art exhibit, and she would later break with Communist interests over precisely this issue, accusing the party of squelching free expression.

Only a few years after her work on the *Survey Graphic* issue, Porter would turn against Rivera, calling him "the fraud of frauds, with his syndication of painters, and his false Communism," a reference, perhaps, to his acceptance of lucrative private commissions and possibly also to his 1929 expulsion from the Communist party.[64] It is a tangled story and an uncertain one. Rivera's work in the United States had, in the words of one commentator, "created a conflict between his artistic goals and his political convictions" in that the opportunities he pursued for creating public art, an "art for the proletariat," had been made possible by "capitalist patrons."[65] Rivera's relationship to the party was turbulent. After years of active membership, he resigned in 1925 on the grounds that he would be "better able to devote himself to Marxism through his art" than through "militant activities." He was readmitted in 1926 but expelled in September

1929, apparently because he refused to join with the party in denouncing the Mexican government and in fact accepted a governmental appointment as director of the Academy of San Carlos. In his own version, however, the reason was a dispute over aesthetic judgment. In 1932 he was denounced in the *New Masses*.[66] In 1955, however, he was readmitted to the party on what he said was his third application.

By 1924 Porter was having misgivings about communist politics as she saw it in action, though not about communist ideology. If she had earlier been a party member at all, she had already retreated. The distinction is perhaps not of great significance, but it seems to have mattered a great deal to Porter. She wrote to Peggy Cowley in 1932 that she had been "a Communist twelve years ago" but "couldn't go on with it." The reason she gave was the conflict between commitment to the party and commitment to art: "First [the intellectuals] were so busy being artists they couldn't be Communists and now they're so busy being Communists they can't be artists any more." In the same year she made a torturously qualified statement to Herbst: "I still may go to Russia, and I still go hoping, and if I do go, I want really to see and learn, and if I could believe in what is being done there—or rather, the way it is being done—I would still be a Communist." She qualified her avowal still further by pointing out that "the situation of the artist there is very dubious."[67] But she would have other reasons for pulling away from communism besides her sense of its repressive attitude toward the arts. In particular, her disillusionment with the Mexican Revolution and her sense that it had betrayed the indigenous lower class of Mexico, the Indians, would contribute to her disaffection from leftist politics.

❧ Porter's concern for the Indian laboring masses of Mexico and the note of keen-edged social criticism that accompanied it, especially criticism of foreign capitalists, are clearly evident in three early essays that are included in her *Collected Essays and Occasional Writings:* "The Fiesta of Guadalupe," first published in 1920; "The Mexican Trinity," published in 1921; and "Where Presidents Have No Friends," 1922.[68] In all three she expresses characteristically Marxian ideas of class antagonism along with socialist agrarian convictions.

In these early essays on Mexico, Porter berates capitalists as oppressors of the poor, specifically of the Indian population, and ridicules the bourgeoisie who, "much resembling the bourgeoisie elsewhere," ally themselves with foreign capitalists in opposition to "all idea of revolution" and mindlessly "chant," " 'We want peace, and more business.' " A letter to her family dated December 31, 1920, strikes the note of anticapitalism in berating the "frightful set of rich American rankers" (apparently meaning bankers) backing the *Magazine of Mexico,* for which she was then working. These rich Americans, she writes, "love oil and silver and coal and gold—love the very sound of those unctuous words, and can think of nothing else by day or by night, drunk or sober."[69] The trinity of oppressors she denounces in her 1921 essay is made up of landowners, oil interests, and the Church. In particular she singles out, in "Where Presidents Have No Friends," the "Guffey interests." (The Guffey Petroleum Company was the ancestor of the Gulf Oil Company, which has now been assimilated into Chevron, demonstrating Karl Marx's observation that capitalism tends to agglomerate assets.) Mexico's capitalist enemies are sanctioned in their rapacity, she says, by their governments, which are members of a "cynical freemasonry of finance, diplomacy, and war" for purposes of "organized pillage." Her attitude toward capitalists who came to Mexico to strip the country of its wealth would be restated forcefully in a 1927 review of two books about Mexico and its history, where she ended, "The thundering racket you hear outside is Mexico getting her pockets picked by her foreign investors."[70]

In the same essay, "Where Presidents Have No Friends," she sounds a theme that she seems to have derived in part from Blasco Ibáñez's *Mexico in Revolution,* which she reviewed in 1920.[71] The idea is that Mexican history discouragingly repeats itself. But the differences in artistic control between Porter's work and Blasco Ibáñez's are as evident as are their superficial similarities. She shared his avowed sympathy for the Mexican people, "the eternal victim of a tragi-comedy that never ends," but it is doubtful that she would have called the people of Mexico, as he did, "the everlasting dupe." Certainly she would not have complained that the country as a whole "deifies the Indian, despite all his cannibalistic and heart-eating traditions, endows him with a whole set of historic virtues and reviles the Spaniard who first planted on the country's soil the standard of Christian civilization." As Walsh points out, however, though scorning Blasco Ibáñez's "patronizing" racism and his claim to be an expert on Mexico on the strength of a six weeks' stay, she borrowed his "theme, tone, and [anecdotal] form" and by 1922 had come to share his skeptical view of the outlook for political stability and lasting social change.[72]

Although she produced effective polemical writing in these essays, she achieved a more lasting effect in the earliest, "The Fiesta of Guadalupe," where her tone is more sorrowful than aggressive. Here she writes simply and directly of the Indian people she is just coming to know, letting the tormented humanity of her subject carry the argument. Through clearly visualized details such as their "brown and work-stained hands" she makes real for the reader the patient endurance and the credulity of the long-suffering Indians. She makes real, too, her caring for these people. Although her vision here is powerfully pessimistic, as she depicts the harshness of the Indians' lives, it does not represent disillusionment with the Revolution; as Walsh points out, its early publication date scarcely allows for that.[73] Indeed, Porter maintains, with great poignancy, her support of the principles of the Revolution and the cause of the oppressed classes. Only at the end, with her expression of hope that "men do not live in a deathly dream forever," does she convey indirectly what she states directly in "The Mexican Trinity," her support for the agrarian "revolutionists" of Mexico who have been "working toward civilized alleviations of present distresses pending the coming of the perfect State."[74]

It is a support she makes clearer yet in a 1926 essay, "La Conquistadora," where she mocks a wealthy landowner and adventurer, Rosalie Evans, who "was ruled by a single-minded love of money and power" and "thought the Indians made good servants." With heavy sarcasm, she writes that Evans—who was popular in the United States for her nervy defense of her estate from expropriation—died "as a martyr" to a "holy cause," the "sacred principles of private ownership of property." Her own commitment to democratic principles is evident in her complaint that Evans never showed a "single glimmer of understanding of the causes of revolution or the rights of the people involved." She emphasizes her scorn through repetition: Evans died "in a grotesque cause"—that is, the cause of private property.[75]

These essays on Mexico form an illuminating context for the major story (her first acknowledged fiction) Porter published in 1922, "María Concepción." "Where Presidents Have No Friends" had been accepted for the *Century* magazine for July of that year. Recognizing that the piece, though nonfiction, had a fictionlike quality, Carl Van Doren, the literary editor of the *Century,* provided encouragement that proved to be the catalyst of a decisive recognition: Porter realized that what she most wanted to write was short fiction. "María Concepción" was published in the *Century* in December. Drawing on the powers of observation that had driven her previous work, she here realizes the Mexican setting with an immediacy that brings it before the reader's eyes in all its heat and harshness. The battered feet and ragged toenails of the Indians, like their work-hardened hands in "The Fiesta of Guadalupe," serve to objectify the harshness of their lives. Tina Modotti would similarly emphasize the hands of workers in several of her photographs.

The theme of class antagonism and exploitation that Porter first developed in her early essays on Mexico would subsequently appear in other short stories such as "He" (published in late 1927) and "Magic" (1928). "He," set in the South, perhaps Texas, emphasizes the scantiness of the resources available to the poor for coping with devastating adversity, here the presence of a severely handicapped child. "Magic," set in New Orleans, concerns the absolute domination exercised by a small-scale business owner over a worker—that is, by a "madam" over a prostitute—ostensibly by the use of magic, but actually by the power of hunger and utter economic dependence. In "He" especially, the situation rendered so simply is actually so complex in human emotion and so daunting in its impossibility of successful resolution that the reader's sympathies are enlisted for all members of the hard-pressed family, and easy judgment is impossible.

At about the same time she wrote these stories, Porter again linked the theme of class struggle to conditions in Mexico in a review entitled "Paternalism and the Mexican Problem," where she included an excursus on social problems in the United States, including bread lines, strikes, and the seemingly inextricable linkage between the enjoyment of bourgeois comforts and the exploitation of laborers.[76] Clearly, issues of social injustice were much on her mind throughout the decade, and she associated them with her experiences in Mexico.

❧ Porter spent the remainder of the decade, except for a few months in 1929, in the United States. For the most part, she was in New York, where she earned an uncertain living by such quasi-literary efforts as reviewing, ghostwriting, and editorial work. She spent some time in Salem doing research on Cotton Mather and lived for various periods in Connecticut, partly with friends and partly with her second (or third) husband, a would-be artist named Ernest Stock, who was sometimes referred to, in joking references among Porter and her friends, as Deadly Ernest. In 1929, with the assistance of friends, she went to Bermuda to recover her health and supposedly to finish the Mather book. Her life during these years was characterized by fitful motion, dissipated efforts, and scattered emotional alliances.

She did remain politically active on at least one important occasion, however, by participating in the last-minute protest against the execution of Sacco and Vanzetti in 1927. She marched, carried signs, was arrested and released, and helped in the office of the organizers. It does not by any means appear to be true that, as the biographers of Agnes Smedley write, the case "absorbed her energies off and on" for seven years. Will Brantley is more accurate in terming her involvement "limited" and "ancillary." She was not a leader or organizer of the protest, then or at any other time. The real importance of Porter's connection with the Sacco-Vanzetti case was its lasting impact on her as an emblem of totalitarian oppression.[77]

Porter's political activism on behalf of the two condemned anarchists, probably her most conspicuous act of overt political dissent, can well be explained, as she herself explains it in *The Never-Ending Wrong,* published fifty years later, by reference to her convictions about freedom of expression. Resistance to power groups that tended to suppress such freedom was a theme in her political thought that would persist to the end. Furthermore, she was always attracted to stories of persecuted innocence. But the Sacco and Vanzetti case was also a cause in which the Communist party played a significant role. The speakers' slate at a mass meeting held on Boston's south side on Sunday, August 21, the day before the execution, was, in one writer's summation, "dominated by Communists."[78]

The extent to which Porter's participation was orchestrated with that of the party is difficult to say. Her later statement that she had "worked with Communists for quite a while, in Mexico, and a little in New York" and had witnessed things that gave her sinkings in the pit of the stomach is probably a reference as well to her close-up observation of Communist organizers during the Sacco-Vanzetti protests.[79] She claimed to have heard Rosa Barron, one of the party organizers, say that the two anarchists were worth more to the party dead than alive. David Felix implicitly corroborates Porter's statement when he writes that the Communists were glad to "dissociate themselves from a defeat" in the case and then "claim the martyrdom of Sacco and Vanzetti for the world proletariat." (But Felix must be interpreted in the light of his clearly evident anticommunist ideology.) Whatever sinkings Porter felt must not have been very severe at the time, however, because her associations, to the extent that they were political, remained with communist and other leftist groups throughout the twenties and into the thirties, not only in New York and Mexico but also in Europe, during the earlier years of her residence there.

In addition to her other scattered endeavors during the mid-1920s, Porter apparently did occasional work for the *New Masses,* with which she was well acquainted from its inception. Three of her friends—Michael Gold, Helen Black, and Freda Kirchwey—were on the editorial staff when the journal began publishing in May 1926.[80] Porter indicated to Genevieve Taggard in that year that she was expecting to do some drawings for them and told Taggard that she considered the second issue of the *New Masses* "better than the first maybe, but yet none so good." The remark has been taken to indicate her dissatisfaction with the corruption of good writing by politics, and indeed she does complain of the contributors' writing "so very badly," but she also complains that they are "radical in the manner of the petty bourgeoisie convicted of the commonplace." Her point, which presumably would have been clear to her friend, was more likely a complaint about the compromise between radicals and liberals in place at the journal's founding. Daniel Aaron points out that although the *New Masses* supported workers' rights from the beginning, it did not "explicitly declare itself an organ of proletarian literature" until 1928, when most of the "liberal contingent" had departed.[81] It was there that "He," with its strong sense of the hardships of the poorer classes, was published in 1927.

Porter also seems to have worked for a while as assistant to the editor of the Russian news agency in America, ROSTA, the predecessor of TASS. Her claim to have done so, in *The Never-Ending Wrong* and in correspondence, has been questioned by Walsh, who comments that he was unable to find evidence of such employment. A letter to her from Kenneth Durant, however, seems to provide confirmation. While she was living in Paris, Durant, who would have been her boss there, sent "greetings to an old member of the TASS staff." Written in the margin, in the same hand and the same brown ink as the signature, is the note, " 'Rosta' to you."[82]

Despite her continuing associations with radical individuals and causes, Porter was developing, in the late twenties, an "aristocratic view."[83] For years she had been preoccupied by a chimerical sense of her family's significant forebears. While nominally doing research on Mather, for example, she spent time in the library looking up possible ancestors. In Bermuda, her residence in a stately home onto which she could transfer her fantasies about her familial past in the South nourished that aristocratic view. The incipient clash with the political values she had held for a decade is obvious.

❧ Back in New York in 1928 Porter obtained work as a part-time editor for Macauley. It was there, in September, that she met the dadaist critic and man of letters Matthew Josephson. By that time she had published (besides miscellaneous journalism, reviews, a handful of poems, four children's stories, and eight fine essays about Mexico) "María Concepción," "The Martyr," "Virgin Violeta," and "He." "Magic" was published in *transition* that year, possibly with Josephson's help, and also "Rope," in *The Second American Caravan,* a Macauley publication. She had also compiled and written, under the pseudonym Hamblen Sears, the introduction to a book of excerpts on marriage—an example, apparently more significant than most, of the kind of hackwork she was doing to support herself.[84] Josephson, whose massive book *Zola and His Time* was just coming out, seems to have thought her gifted and down on her luck. He played a role in attracting the interest of Harcourt Brace in publishing *Flowering Judas,* which appeared in a small edition in 1930. (Robert McAlmon, whom she met in 1929, was "outraged by the pitiful size of the edition of her book," only 600 copies.) The two, Porter and Josephson, became lovers for a period of months in 1928 to 1929, during Josephson's wife's pregnancy. Porter's retreat to Bermuda in 1929 was in part an occasion for recovering from the end of that affair after Josephson "sought to transform" it into "a platonic friendship" following the birth of his son.[85]

In the spring of 1930 Porter again went to Mexico, this time for a stay of sixteen months that proved to be disappointing and disheartening. Her health had once again been poor, and again she was going at the behest of friends who had raised funds for her. Besides her bronchitis, which may actually have been a recurrence of tuberculosis, she was also depressed. Despite the publication in 1929 of "The Jilting of Granny Weatherall," one of her most enduring achievements, and the completion of "Flowering Judas," she was keenly aware of the paucity of her production, especially when compared to the expansiveness of her ambitions and commitments and the opportunities she had had for sustained work, largely through the generosity of friends. She hoped that Mexico would again, as it had nearly a decade before, release her creative energy so that she could take up notes made earlier and work them into a novel. But instead of concentrating on her work she pursued distractions of various sorts and blamed her lack of productivity on Mexico itself and on the friends and acquaintances who came to visit her there, some sharing expenses. Her creativity was stymied. Rather than escaping her depression and irritability, she fueled them. By midsummer she was writing friends that she was sorry she had returned.[86]

A sense of uselessness, meaning inability to live in a productive way the life of commitment to art, haunted this last period of residence in Mexico. Perhaps it is for this reason that she reacted so violently to the presence of Hart Crane and the series of incidents in which he was involved in 1931.

Crane came to Mexico in April 1931 and stayed with Porter, Eugene Pressly, and Mary Doherty for about two weeks before moving to a house nearby. There was tension right away. She wrote to her then best friend Josie Herbst that to say Crane and Pressly did not like each other was "putting it mildly!" "Gene hates melodrama and scenes, Hart lives by them." The scenes persisted and got worse. Crane was drinking heavily and getting more and more blatant about picking up young men and picking quarrels, behaviors which landed him in jail. By the same token, Porter provoked him by her unreliability, setting off the final quarrel by promising to come to dinner and then going into the city and not returning until late, after his dinner was long since ruined. His resultant screaming and name-calling in front of her door must indeed have been upsetting, especially to someone who preferred to get her vengeance more deviously and in writing rather than face to face. She described the incident in letter after letter, dwelling even a year later on the misery the episode had caused her and claiming it had brought on, or nearly brought on, a nervous breakdown. Her bitterness was such that after hearing of Crane's suicide she wrote Mary Doherty, "No, I do not regret his death. I think it was well done."[87]

In view of this great bitterness, it is curious that her first letter to Herbst after leaving Mexico, a long letter at that, does not so much as mention Crane. Her bitterness toward him and her sense that she had been victimized seems to have grown during her first year in Europe, under the pressure of her tensions there, to the point that she was writing long diatribes against him months after he had killed himself. Her bitterness and her fixation on it seem excessive.

The real source of her misery at the time was quite another matter—her continuing inability to produce works for which she had made commitments and received publishers' advances. Throughout her career Porter was tormented by financial problems, sometimes of her own making. Partly as a result of these problems, she was also tormented, perhaps as severely as anyone has ever been, by the phenomenon of writer's block. Subject to extreme mood swings, so that she suffered repeated spells of near-suicidal depression and nervous debility, she was further driven to despair by recurrent periods when she could not produce work that met her high standards. The Crane episode became entangled in this snarl of tensions in two ways. It was, first, simply an out, a means of avoidance, something she could blame. If he had driven her nearly to madness, then was it any wonder that she could not complete her projected works? And, second, it was an enlargement or exaggeration of her feelings toward herself when she was caught in the toils of writer's block. This view—that Crane showed her herself, wasting her great abilities, living in a debased and self-destructive way when she might be creating literature, and that her response was to fix on him her own self-loathing—was actually formulated as early as five years after the events themselves by an early biographer of Crane, Philip Horton: "It was not so much this violence, however, nor even the shocking sordidness of his sexual life, that appalled his neighbor, as it was the terrible spectacle of a great talent, an essentially noble spirit, caught in the grip of a slow, inexorable disintegration."[88]

Not that the sordidness of Crane's sexual life was irrelevant; Porter's lifelong prejudice against homosexuals intensified during those years, and she could scarcely avoid recognizing Crane's bent in this respect. Their great quarrel arose in part over his attempted seduction of her fourteen-year-old houseboy. His resumption of heterosexual relations (with Peggy Cowley) after she and Pressly left for Europe did not cause her to abate her view of his debauchery, but rather inspired her to turn more sharply against Peggy.[89] But the primary reason, as Horton perceived, was that in other respects Crane showed her herself, writ large.

Given this combination of pressures and anxieties, it is little wonder that she became disillusioned with Mexico and everything associated with it. She complained that the Mexican government was "in the hands of the most appalling set of grafters" and was "simply rotten from top to bottom." Indeed, she was correct in realizing that the Revolution had by then "ebbed."[90] It had ebbed, in fact, in the view of many historians, a good many years before, as vaunted hopes for land redistribution were sacrificed to moderates' concern for process and ultimately their support for the *hacendados,* leaving the rural poor as poor and almost as landless as before; as the assertive labor movement was co-opted by governmental authority, with the founding and gradual quasi-legitimizing of CROM; as ambitious educational reforms fell prey to deficient funds and the resistance of conservatives; and as foreign wealth continued to exploit Mexico's resources. The Revolution produced reform, but its more transformative aims were a "faltering pledge" that delivered a "meager harvest." "Practice," in the view of many who have assessed the revolutionary gains of the first thirty years of the century in Mexico, "did not match rhetoric." One of the most tangible results following Obregón's years in power, when the gains of the Revolution were supposedly being consolidated, was a "proliferation of politicians," who, to Mexico's villagers, were "about as welcome as a visitation of locusts."[91] Porter's view accorded with this gloomy verdict.

During Porter's last year in Mexico, 1931, culminating a period of more than a decade during which she had come and gone, she became acquainted with the great, controversial Russian filmmaker Sergei Eisenstein, then filming his huge and ultimately frustrated opus *Qué Viva México!*. Eisenstein and his assistants apparently came to a dinner party at her house at least once, and in the summer she went to the Hacienda Tetlapayac to watch the filming of the segment that would later be made into the film *Thunder over Mexico*.[92] This experience fused with other aspects of her disillusionment with Mexico so that when she left for Europe in August, having received a Guggenheim Fellowship, she was ready to take another major step in her career, the writing of "Hacienda."

CHAPTER FOUR

The Harvest of Mexico

> My time in Mexico and Europe . . . gave me back my past and my own house and my own people—the native land of my heart.
>
> —Porter, " 'Noon Wine': The Sources"

In notes for her projected novel "Many Redeemers," probably made in the early 1930s, Porter called "the Mexican interval" a "tangent for Miranda, the complete negation of all she has known, a derailment." We can infer that she was feeling at the time that her Mexican years had been a derailment for herself, both professionally and emotionally. But her experiences in Mexico would ultimately have a far more positive impact on her art than these notes suggest.

Precisely what Mexico meant to Porter's intellectual development and to her personal independence is difficult to assess, but its importance can scarcely be overestimated. In part it was a pervasive sense of renewal. She referred to her initial period in Mexico as a time when she looked at things as if she were "newly created in a new world." [1] More specifically, her social and political thought was profoundly affected by her experience of Mexican politics. Arriving at a moment when revolutionary hopes were being implemented, with the inauguration of President Obregón, and when revolutionary thinkers were able to express and to apply their ideas in more radical ways than ever before, she developed both a keen sympathy with such aspirations and, in only a short time, an equally keen sense of disillusionment as it became clear that the hopes of the Revolution were not being realized in the lives of the poorest and most oppressed members of society. Darlene Harbour Unrue observes astutely that "the failed Mexican revolution and the Sacco-Vanzetti affair coalesced in Porter's mind as the annihilation of her idealistic faith in organized political movements." Yet her hope and her affiliation with revolutionary thinkers would remain with her in subdued form for many years. In her 1943 review of Anita Brenner's *The Wind That Swept Mexico,* she concluded that one has only to compare Tina Modotti's print of a photograph of Emiliano Zapata (reproduced in the book) to a picture of Bishop Pascual Díaz, expelled by President Calles in 1927 for plotting against the government, or a photograph of William Randolph Hearst to one of Alvaro Obregón, to know "at once which side one is on, now and forever."[2]

The tension between idealism and disillusionment is evident, however, in a variety of published and unpublished statements. In her 1929 review of Brenner's *Idols Behind Altars,* for instance, she acknowledged the "disturbing" nature of Mexico in that the contradictions "in this land of miracles, of Messiahs, of venal politicians, of dedicated scholars, of sober artists and extravagant dreams" were "too violent."[3] Among the dreamers she singles out for praise is artist Xavier Guerrero, who "articulate[d]" his "faith" by editing a "Communist periodical, in itself a work of art." Her awareness of these disturbing contradictions and the disappointment of the "extravagant dreams" of idealists such as Guerrero would be manifest in the major work she produced shortly after leaving Mexico, "Hacienda." Many years later, after the 1943 review that reaffirmed her allegiance to the revolutionary cause, she would express the extent of her disillusionment with her earlier Marxist hopes by means of the bitterly mocking marginal comments she made on her papers, now on deposit at the University of Maryland.

Mexico provided Porter an immersion in political "effervescence" and turmoil, testing and ultimately overwhelming the intensity and coherence of her commitment to radical politics.[4] Beyond this sociopolitical legacy, it provided her with an enormous aesthetic legacy. She found in Mexico the elements of a direct, highly visual style and a milieu that encouraged her to conceive of herself as a working artist. Her acquaintance with the Mexican muralists and their work is of far-reaching importance in the maturation of her art and can be traced in very specific ways.[5] Most important, perhaps, Mexico challenged her to find herself by finding a world as different from her childhood society as New York was, but without what she saw as the hectic "aimlessness" of life in New York and the defensiveness it evoked.

A great deal of the influence of Mexico on Porter's thought and work came in the form simply of subject matter. Though she derided "ignorant and provincial" people who went "looking for material," she both looked for and found material for her writing in Mexico.[6] She first went on a commission to look for material for magazine articles, and when she began to write successful stories she naturally drew on the subjects she had been using for her journalism. Her years in Mexico provided the material for much of her best work, especially her crucial early work. Besides the early political essays and a number of reviews, only a few of which are included in her acknowledged canon, this includes the stories "María Concepción," "Virgin Violeta," "The Martyr," "That Tree," "Flowering Judas," and "Hacienda." In addition, the late essay/story "St. Augustine and the Bullfight" (praised by Glenway Wescott as a wonderful and innovative "hybrid of essay and tale")[7] as well as the early scenes of *Ship of Fools* sprang from her experiences in Mexico.

Porter claimed that Mexico was not exotic to her, but was a "familiar country" she could call her own. But her various statements that her father had taken her there when she was ten years old or earlier appear to be false. There is no evidence that she ever went to Mexico as a child, unless she "crossed the border for an afternoon as we all do," as Givner has guessed, when she was visiting her uncle in the El Paso area.[8] She claimed, too, that the atmosphere of San Antonio (where she and her brother and sisters lived with their father for about a year) provided an early acquaintance with Mexican culture and scenes. But it does not seem plausible that this picturesque Texas city, Hispanic in culture though it was and is, could have been sufficiently Mexican to have done so. South and south-central Texas enjoyed a significant Mexican presence, but it was not Mexico.[9] Her claims of early familiarity with Mexico seem to have been based on very slight experience and to have been made in an effort to evade possible charges of shallow adventurism.

Porter's father had indeed been to Mexico, however, and had indulged in melancholic fantasies of staying there and forgetting his life north of the border. Porter may well have heard stories of the country and its people from him. This, together with her familiarity with San Antonio, would have given her an indirect acquaintance with Mexico. In addition, her sister Gay refers in a 1931 letter to having spent a year in Mexico "20 or 25 years ago." But it appears that when Porter went there in 1920 she went essentially as a stranger and that, despite her avowed scorn for writers who went abroad for adventure, she went at least in part for precisely such a reason, seeking at once retreat and adventure, a radical change from life in New York and from her own state of emotional depression. Indeed, in retrospect she would exaggerate the adventurousness of the trip, claiming that armed soldiers rode on top of the train and revolutionary banners greeted the travelers at every town. Walsh corrects this claim, pointing out that armed guards were not riding the trains in Mexico at the time.[10]

She would go to Europe in 1931 in much the same way, seeking both adventure and escape from her troubles and dramatizing the adventure she found. If she later made of her travels in foreign countries and her years of residence abroad not an adventure but an experience—to use the distinction posed in "St. Augustine and the Bullfight"—that was a result of the prolonged attention of her alert intellect, not the fulfillment of her initial motive.

There was also a more practical motive for going to Mexico in 1920: an opportunity to earn some money. Shortly before, she had worked with Adolfo Best-Maugard on a Mexican ballet intended for the great dancer Pavlova. As an outgrowth of their collaboration, he arranged for Porter to be offered a job with the *Magazine of Mexico*. Her life until that time, subsequent to her departure from Texas, had been lived on the fringes of the literary, publishing, and newspaper worlds, in a state of continual emotional and financial turmoil. Now, besides paid employment, she was offered the kind of situation that she would so often elect, a venture involving real risk and the appearance of danger, but with a margin of security provided by some other party. Ernestine Evans, features editor of the *Christian Science Monitor,* linked the two, adventure and expectation of material gain, in a note about the prospective trip: "I hear that you are going on a great adventure, down to Mexico. Are you going to do all magazine work or will there be some chance of our getting an occasional rambling sketch from you for the Monitor?" At least one other editor, Ethel R. Peyser of *Everyland,* also wrote to say that she had heard Porter was going to Mexico and hoped she would remember to seek out material on Mexico appropriate for a children's audience.[11]

When she had been in Mexico only a short time, Porter expressed a zestful sense that her experience there had already contributed enormously to her personal development: "My own life is a welter, so far as experiences are concerned, but I can not tell you how far I have come."[12] During the next ten years, as she shifted her home base between Mexico and the United States, mainly New York, she would continue her mental and emotional journey, broadening her set of acquaintances to include a great variety of artistic and political types while also becoming familiar with the repressed Indian populace of Mexico who so moved her sympathies. She developed a keen and ultimately transformative interest in Mexican folk art, leading to her production of the booklet *Outline of Mexican Arts and Crafts* in 1922. She would not, however, produce the quantities of work that she expected and promised to produce during her periods of residence in Mexico. Ultimately it would be that fact, together with the emotional pressures of her tumultuous acquaintance with Hart Crane, whom she had known in New York but whom she came to know much better when he lived either with or next door to her in Mixcoac, that would spoil her Mexican retreat and make her glad to go on to other international adventures.

One of the most notable tangible results of Porter's acquaintance with Mexico and its people is the early story "María Concepción," published in 1922. Coming as it did at a time when she had never before produced a work of fiction that either she or we would consider eligible to be placed in the canon of her characteristic works, the story is startling and almost inexplicable in its artistry. Its detached narrative perspective and visual clarity, developed in part through her admiration of such modernist masters as Henry James and James Joyce but also from her acquaintance with Mexican genre painting, crafts, and caricature, seem to "spring full-blown into life," unsignaled by any of her apprentice work.[13] At the same time, the story continues a number of motifs and themes evident in the journalistic work Porter had been producing since her arrival in Mexico two years before. As she had in her essays and reviews, she here attributes to her Indian characters a set of traits that may strike some readers as being stereotypical or reductive, but which were assuredly intended as a sympathetic presentation.[14] Committed to the idea that the Indian population of Mexico constituted the real Mexican identity but that it had been exploited and mistreated, she presents her Indian characters as being strong and somewhat enigmatic, and she stresses their harsh lives. If the battered dignity and the profound superstitiousness of the Indian characters in "María Concepción" come close to implying a condescending stereotype of the primitive, her sympathetic respect for her subjects is nevertheless clear. Moreover, her insistence on the absolute contrast between whites and Indians can be attributed, in part, to the intellectual currents of the time in Mexico. A revisionist view of Mexican identity emphasizing the Indian's native authenticity, repressed by a foreign and utterly uncomprehending

Spanish power, was deeply implicated in the thinking and the appeal of the revolutionary party after about 1910.

The title character is depicted as a strong, independent woman and, in a strange and surprising way, the center of her community. Although the plot chronicles the desperate jealousy of a woman for her man, and thus would seem to place her in a role of abject need, it is not the male who is elevated in the story but the female. She is a canny but also intense woman capable of managing her own affairs and exacting her own vengeance, and it is her power that gives the story its motive force. Structurally, she is validated by the reaction of the community to her murder of her husband's lover, María Rosa, shortly after the birth of their child. When gendarmes come to take her for questioning, she maintains her self-control and outfaces them. Symbolically, she defeats the instrument of an alien and exploitive culture, casting them out of the restored social order of which she is the center. But she could not have done so alone. Her victory is attained with and through the complicity of the townspeople, all of whom, even the godmother of the dead woman, vouch for her, leaving the gendarmes no basis for pursuing their suspicions. She is acknowledged as the symbolic center of the village, the powerful agent whose continued presence is worth maintaining even by lying.[15]

Very specifically, that center is a maternal one. After her act of murder and her vindication by the townspeople, María Concepción takes the child home and sits against the wall of her house with the baby "cradled in the hollow of her crossed legs," feeling the pulse of the earth through her body, a "limitless, unhurried, benign breathing." She is at one with nature and with her people—a primitive matriarch.[16] The unacknowledged children's stories Porter had published prior to 1922 had also developed a theme of a clever woman who outwits her rival. It is the woman who grants absolution to her lover if she chooses. In "María Concepción," the female hero makes her own living through the sale of fowl, imposes not only her vindictive wrath but her very will on the village, and receives her amazed male on her own terms by resisting when he would have beaten her to reassert his authority. To be sure, toward the end of the story she adopts the behaviors of the subservient woman, walking behind her man and serving him food, but it is nevertheless true that she has impelled the course of events and it is she who, at the end, enjoys satisfaction, while he sleeps exhaustedly.

Like Porter's early essays and her later major work on Mexico, "Hacienda," though less overtly, "María Concepción" conveys a sense of social class and class struggle and manifests her sympathy with the oppressed. The theme of class struggle and in particular the oppression of the Indians was her primary preoccupation during her early years in Mexico. Her disillusionment with the revolution that failed to achieve justice for the repressed Indians would be a preoccupation during her later period of residence there, a motive force driving her from Mexico to Berlin almost as compelling as her long-standing wish to go to Europe. That disillusionment would be expressed most powerfully in "Hacienda." In "María Concepción" the traces of class struggle are evident in the harshness of the Indians' lives and in their subjugation to both white and mixed-blood groups. They are employed by the Anglo archaeologist Givens on a project to dig up their own past, and there is a silent hostility evident between them and the representatives of social authority, the gendarmes. They successfully resist the gendarmes' authority. If the theme of class struggle is not obvious or intrusive, it is because Porter had learned the distinction between politically committed art and propaganda. She had written some of the latter, as well. Ruth Moore Alvarez appropriately labels her magazine article "Striking the Lyric Note in Mexico," published January 16, 1921, as a "propagandistic piece."[17] Its idealized depiction of a cheerful labor strike in Mexico, juxtaposed with a brutally suppressed strike in the United States, is extreme and obvious in its contrast of good and bad. In "María Concepción" the point of view is not so simplistic. The reader is hard-pressed to label María and Juan good; yet, because of the subtle balancing of narrative detachment and narrative sympathy, their lives are clearly valued and they are affirmed as representative characters. María Concepción, in particular, is shown to possess an impressive dignity.

Even more forceful than the theme of class struggle, but related to it, is the theme of religious conflict between the old, indigenous ways and the new ways of Catholicism brought by the Spanish. María Concepción is, most emphatically, a Catholic. Unlike other women in the village, she has insisted on being married by the priest, and she regularly practices penance, kneeling "for hours" with her arms stretched out in the form of a cross and crawling on her knees to the shrine at Guadalupe. Specific incidents or tableaux in the story can be read as approximations of incidents in the story of Christ that were often represented pictorially in Mexican churches. Thus, as she holds the baby, María Concepción resembles the Madonna, and the many wounds in María Rosa's body are reminiscent of the gory figures of the wounded Christ in many Mexican churches.[18] Not incidentally, the *pulquería* where Juan celebrates is the Death and Resurrection Pulque Shop. Yet it is not her Christianity that restores María Concepción to her proper and satisfying role in life, but her bloody vengeance against María Rosa and her courage in outfacing the gendarmes and the villagers. It is through blood "sacrifice," recalling the sacrifices practiced in Aztec religion, that she gains a kind of resurrection. Thus, as she does in her early articles, Porter argues the exploitative nature of the Catholic presence in Mexico and the pervasive survival of an earlier and presumably more authentic Indian ethos. As we have seen, this argument was promoted by the policy of the Mexican government.

❧ The pictorial presentation and the clarity that characterize the style of "María Concepción," as well as the story's social values, can be traced in large part to Porter's acquaintance with Mexican art and artists. That acquaintance originated with her work on the Mexican ballet with Best-Maugard in 1919 and was quickened by her delight in the pottery and other crafts she saw and purchased in the Mexican markets as she made her residential quarters livable, as well as by her acquaintance with artists and anthropologists knowledgeable about pre-Hispanic art. During her several visits to Mexico in the early twenties, Porter became well acquainted with the excavations of pre-Columbian artifacts being carried out by William Niven, visiting the excavation site and personally assisting in his work. Moreover, she was keenly aware of the murals then being fostered through government commissions. The effects of her acquaintance with the muralists' productions are directly recognizable in some of her work—for example, her awareness of Rivera's "Creation" mural at the Escuela Nacional Preparatoria appears in quite specific ways in "The Martyr"—and are indirectly important throughout. The muralists combined portraiture with genre scenes in a way that Porter herself would sometimes adopt.[19]

The fresco movement in Mexico may have been fueled by a desire to emulate European frescoes, but it was also to some degree an outgrowth of the *pulquería* folk art that was very common, which Porter would also have known. The decoration of pulque shops with frescos was not a new phenomenon at that time, as has sometimes been asserted. (José Clemente Orozco, for example, never reluctant to assert his views, writes that "the humbug of pulque-shop painting arose" between 1924 and 1926.) Xavier Guerrero had worked on such decorations before becoming involved with the muralists in Mexico City in 1921, as had his family before him. Numerous *pulquerías* in Mexico City and elsewhere bore on their walls decorations painted by working-class artists. In the 1920s, however, these paintings "attracted the attention of painters and photographers" including Edward Weston.[20]

Porter's familiarity with Mexican art was developed in the course of her preparation of the catalog to accompany the 1922 exhibition of Mexican folk art. She spent at least two months of that year, from April to June, on the project, reading a large number of authoritative sources, including Dr. Atl's catalog to the folk art exhibit of 1921. She quoted from many of these in her monograph, even while developing her own characteristic tone and the rudiments of a personal aesthetic. Her notes on the exhibition comprise a fifty-six page booklet, including several pages of excellent photographs of pottery, needlework, weaving, ornate saddles, and other objects. The work reflects careful attention and effort and can well be taken as a statement of aesthetic principles. Her emphasis throughout is on genuineness, painstaking craft, and individual expression. Stressing a concept of indigenous art, she goes into considerable detail on the particular kind of product—pottery, leather work, or whatever—that is made in specific towns or areas. Not that she proposes a theory of a spirit of place working itself out in art; she shows no interest in that sort of connection. Rather, her emphasis on location conveys a notion of authenticity or appropriateness as a standard of judgment.

It is clear in the monograph that Porter had absorbed the theories of some of her influential Mexican fellow artists. Best-Maugard's theories about recurrent motifs in primitive art and in the art of children appear in Part One, on pre-Hispanic art. Rivera's enthusiasm for the Indian past is reflected in the pervasive emphasis on the persistence of a Mayan-Aztec-Nahuan (Porter wrote "Nahoan") cultural sense that enabled Mexican artisans to adapt European styles by filtering them through their "magnificent traditions" and their own understandings and everyday idioms. In this way, while "translating" alien styles, the native artisan makes them "his own" and "absolutely individual."[21]

Her celebration of the indigenous and of the artistry of everyday objects made for use should not be taken to mean that Porter was an enthusiast of aesthetic primitivism. A cultivated primitive style she would condemn as heartily as she did the imposition of alien high-art styles on the native artisan. Nearly a decade later, when she undertook to write an updated article on developments in Mexican art (which she did not complete), she promised a "firm but I hope gentle remonstrance against the fashionable adoration of peasant and 'primitive' art, which I believe is a sign of debased judgment and pernicious esthetic anemia." She did not mean, she explained, that genuine early and peasant art should not be "valued for its self" in its "own right" but that the "easy and indiscriminate hurrah for every thing peasant and primitive," the "imitation," the "snobbery" of "artificial simplicity," was a debasement of honesty in art. Significantly, she links that debasement with Diego Rivera.[22]

That linkage represents a notable change from the admiration she had earlier expressed for Rivera. In 1922, while she was working on the exhibition monograph, she had called Rivera "simple and splendid," "one of the great artists of the world," who "paints like a god in a mood of repentance for the hurts he has given his creatures." In the preface to the *Outline of Mexican Arts and Crafts* Rivera's role is that of a major influence helping her to establish her own point of view and "sympathies." That the point of view expressed is indeed her own is manifest not only in the straightforwardness of the prose style, or voice, recognizably Porter's own (in contrast to some of the sensational and melodramatic fiction she was trying to write at the time, fragments of which exist among her papers), but also in her emphasis. Adopting Rivera's interest in communal work by artistic groups or guilds, expressed in the *Survey Graphic* article on people's art on which she collaborated with him, she emphasizes the leadership of such guilds by master workmen who are supplanted in that role of individual authority when their craft is surpassed by that of one of their "disciples." The highest art, then, remains individual. She stresses another of her chief interests, the position of women, in praising the ancient Indian cultures of Mexico. "Every evidence," she says, is that in the Nahuan culture women "enjoyed a cleanly human equality in society utterly foreign to the ideals that governed the relations between men and women of the European and Asiatic races."[23]

As this comment indicates, Porter's affinity for Mexico may have been motivated in part by its association with a mythology that elevated women to a position of social prominence and power.[24] A more decisive motivation, however, was her hope to find in Mexico both a place of intense sociopolitical reality and, paradoxically, a retreat. Cowley would later write in *Exile's Return* that Mexico City was Porter's Paris and Taxco her South of France—that is, that she had gone to Mexico in the way that Stein, Hemingway, Fitzgerald, and others went to Paris. It was a statement she would bitterly resent, telling him that she had not gone to Mexico as an exile at all and that she obviously had no "true place" in his "charming" book. She insisted that she went to Mexico because she was familiar with it and was going exactly where she wanted to go; she "was not running from anything" and had no desire to go to Europe, but went to Mexico simply because it seemed "natural."[25] Clearly, however, her disclaimer of a desire to go to Europe was to a great extent sour grapes. Her correspondence demonstrates that she had long wanted to go to Europe but had been unable to do so and that she went to Mexico for much the same reason that other expatriates of the twenties were going to France—to gain a respite from the pressures of life in the United States, to develop perspective on their own experience, and to find both the stimulation and the low cost of living they needed in order to get on with their writing.

For Porter, that retreat was both successful and unsuccessful. During her early visits she experienced a rush of creative energy. Her involvement in politics stimulated her to produce articles and later fiction in which the hardships of a disadvantaged people are depicted clearly and compellingly, in the beautifully compressed prose style that was already becoming her own. These powerful short works established her among a small number of discerning readers as a real literary presence and, more important, gave her the assurance that she was in fact the writer she had long hoped to be. She was also, by a remarkably fortuitous convergence of events, provided the opportunity to develop a theoretical basis for her emerging art at the same time that she was beginning to produce it. It is safe to say that she might never have become a productive and recognized artist if she had not, with the financial assistance of friends and a generous sponsor, gone to Mexico.[26]

Even so, she was not able to work there as she hoped. After the initial burst of stories drawn from her Mexican years, especially "María Concepción," her productivity declined. For several years she struggled to complete uncongenial and ill-advised projects, notably her sardonic study of Cotton Mather and a novel or pair of novels about Mexico, while earning her living by writing reviews and doing other literary piecework. When she returned to Mexico in 1930, after years of frustration and comparative creative barrenness which had finally, however, yielded two of her best stories, she must have expected to experience another outburst of productivity like that of the early years of the decade. Once again, however, she allowed a tangle of involvements, parties, and a hard-drinking style of living to interfere with her work. Her notes from the period reveal a series of false starts. While telling her friends that she was making progress on a novel or novels whose structural schemes she sketched out for them, she in fact produced only these scattered fragments.[27] Among them are the jottings that would later develop into some of her major works, including "Old Mortality" and "Noon Wine"—belying her claims that those works were entirely written in brief bursts of creativity.[28] But at the time it must have seemed scant comfort to be producing such fragments rather than the work she needed to produce if she was to capitalize on her successes of recent years and satisfy the publisher who had paid her an advance for a novel.[29]

Her despair during this period is evident in her correspondence. She was again having severe financial difficulties; in letters to and from Becky Crawford, in New York, and Yvor Winters, in California, references are made to assistance that both are trying to provide her. In late June, two weeks after Porter's arrival in Mexico, Crawford sent assurances that "for Jesus, or Moses, or Mohammed's sake," whichever she preferred, she should not worry about her debts until she got well. It would appear that Porter was using references to ill health, even a tubercular hemorrhage during her journey to Mexico, as an excuse for not writing and also for not paying back money she owed the Crawfords. Even so, to regard her simply as a manipulator would be unjust. She felt the pressure of her situation, and she paid the price, in anxiety and emotional instability and at times in physical illness as well. By midwinter her state of mind was at another low, and she was complaining that Mexico was a "dreadful place," a "God-forsaken spot." To Peggy Cowley—then, apparently, a good friend, though Porter would later revile her—she wrote, in February 1931, "I wonder why I sometimes am so gloomy and useless."[30]

❧ In a sense, it is difficult to understand how she could feel herself to be useless. Less than a year before writing that lament she had published what has often been praised as one of the great treasures of the modernist aesthetic, "Flowering Judas." Despite its ambiguity (a rich and provocative ambiguity, as the great volume of interpretive criticism attests), "Flowering Judas" shows no trace of the uncertainty of purpose that has sometimes been seen in "María Concepción." The intrinsic uncertainty of the situation, the mingling of idealistic hope with cynical disillusion that characterized the political scene in Mexico, which Porter knew so well, is realized in a way that seems at once detached, because of its clearly visualized details, and intensely personal, because of the sense of dread and guilt that permeates the narrative tone.

The characters are a harvest of her associations during her first three trips to the country, but not in a simple or reductive way. Rather, they are resonant compound figures, at once representing her acquaintances and reflecting her own early associations and emotions. Laura, the quietly rigid young woman who sits through Braggioni's serenade and rejects not only his but other men's advances, was identified by Porter as a representation of Mary Doherty, who, she said, had endured just such a serenade. At the same time, Laura is Porter herself, lonely, disappointed, guilt-ridden. Braggioni is a composite of Luis Morones and Samuel Yúdico, the man who in fact serenaded Doherty and whose wife cried and washed his feet (according to notes Porter jotted in 1921) when he went home after philandering.[31] Both were active in Mexican labor politics, both were very close to President Obregón and involved in the atmosphere of plotting and menace that surrounded him, and both were notably corpulent, fitting the description of Braggioni. Caricatures published in Mexican newspapers in the early 1920s used Morones's girth as his identifying trait, just as they used Obregón's stump from the amputation of his arm.[32] The quality of sexual corruption that pervades the characterization of Braggioni reflects, as well, the odor of decadence that had attached to Morones by the mid-twenties. The betrayed Eugenio, who comes to Laura in her dream and offers her the blossoms of the judas tree, is not so directly a representation of anyone Porter knew but, if Walsh is correct in his surmise, was "created" out of her "guilt" over her role in the death of General Sidronio Méndez.[33]

The pervasive menace and preoccupation with death that characterize the story were not only a fitting representation of the death-centeredness of folk customs in Mexico and of actual circumstances in Mexico during the early twenties, especially Porter's terror when in May 1921 she was warned that her name was on a list for arrest and deportation, but an expression of her own fixation on death. In notes jotted in 1921 she expressed a sense that it was not only "of no importance t[o] continue living, but ever to have lived at all seems now a futile, wasteful business. . . . I have set my sails for death." She encountered in Mexico an objectified version of the disillusion, fear, and preoccupation with death that had haunted her at least since her own near-death from the flu in 1918 and implicitly ever since her mother's death in 1892.[34]

However interesting the tracing of its elements, "Flowering Judas" is a whole that far exceeds the sum of its parts. Scene, incident, tone, and style come together as they do in few other stories, constituting a work that has persistently engaged critics. Whether biographical or symbolist, readings of the story find in it a depth of elusiveness combined with a perfection of surface which together mark it as a rare achievement.

❧ Shortly after leaving Mexico in 1931, Porter produced another of the major tangible fruits of her years there, "Hacienda." In this work, fiction in only a highly qualified sense, she drew on her observations of the Mexican political scene much as she had in "Flowering Judas," but here expressed her own judgments on that scene more explicitly.

"Hacienda," which she once contemplated calling "False Hopes," is now counted among Porter's long stories or short novels, but it was initially published in a shorter version as a nonfiction piece of what might be called interpretive journalism or an artistically rendered narrative essay. Even in this original version, though, the distinction between reportage and fiction is somewhat blurred. Porter herself said at the time that it "almost took the form of a story" though it was "not fiction" but "very exact."[35] Its account of the filming of *Qué Viva México!* and of incidents that occurred at the Hacienda Tetlapayac during her three-day visit is fairly direct, although her thematic intention is never far from the surface. References to actual persons are clear though nominally disguised by the use of initials rather than complete names. Hunter Kimbrough, the brother-in-law of Upton Sinclair, who was attempting to provide financial backing for Eisenstein's film, appears as K——. Grigori Alexandrov, the master's assistant director and "indispensable comrade,"[36] is A——. Adolfo Best-Maugard, who served as the government's cultural attaché to the enterprise and whose long-selling book on design Porter had helped edit for its 1926 publication in English, is simply the "art adviser," "full of Spanish elegance and detachment."[37] Eisenstein himself appears, however, not as E——, but merely as "the famous director." Perhaps Porter thought he was too noted a personage for her to take the risk of indicating his initial. Despite these displacements, it is not a misnomer to call the original "Hacienda" nonfiction, although nonfiction written with the full stylistic resources of fiction.[38]

The factuality of "Hacienda" is worth emphasizing to underscore its directly political intention. The story is indeed, as Porter referred to it, a "summing-up" of her view of Mexico.[39] It emphasizes the tragically deprived and "mournful" nature of the Indian people, in whose hearts foreign intruders raise "false hopes" of prosperity, even so negligible a prosperity as might come from the sale of maguey worms, which Indian women offer as they run alongside the slowly moving train (H-1, p. 556). The misled hearts of the Indians are seldom, Porter says, moved to rebellion; they are too "enslaved" for that, economically, too dependent on the owners of the great haciendas for their "sixty centavos a day and a half pound of corn" (H-1, p. 565). The Indian "is stabled worse than his own burro," she writes, "but he eats his corn and cannot be persuaded away from it. For who would give him corn but the master?" (H-1, 566). This statement of her doubt as to the ultimate efficacy of the Revolution, one of the most directly political assertions in the piece, would be removed from the later, more highly fictionalized version.

Even more than the misery of the Indian, Porter emphasizes the injustice and the arrogance of the landed aristocracy and the imperceptiveness of foreigners who come to Mexico to exploit what they see as its picturesqueness and drama. These exploiters, well represented by "washed, shaven, clipped, pressed, polished" K——, fail to see the humanitarian issues before them because they are preoccupied with superficialities such as their own need for creature comforts. K——, for instance, can talk of little else than the local deficiencies of hygiene and social order. What Porter has given in her characterization of K—— is, in fact, an accurate sketch of Hunter Kimbrough, who "had a natural suspicion of strangers and foreigners" and "disliked the smell of the highly-seasoned Mexican food" while the lack of modern sanitation "made him dread disease."[40] Partway through Eisenstein's protracted filming, Kimbrough was called back to California for consultation with Sinclair and returned bringing chocolate bars and oranges, just as K—— in "Hacienda" has done at the beginning of the story. He is shown very much as the ugly American, the man with a "loud voice and commanding stride" (H-1, p. 558).

This invading capitalist is leagued with the landowners and the Church (the "chief enemies" of the Mexican people, as Porter called them in her essay "Where Presidents Have No Friends") in exploitation of the Indian. Porter makes very clear her judgment of the wealthy few who oppress the many both through violence and through dependence and then refer to them derisively as "animals" (H-1, p. 569). Although some may think economic reform has changed these age-old patterns, it appears that in fact "nothing has changed at all" (H-1, p. 567). Despite the coming of Obregón, the peons are still weary and hungry and the wealthy still find the system "beautiful."

When Harrison of Paris, the fine edition press run by Barbara Harrison and Monroe Wheeler, published the expanded version of "Hacienda" in 1934 as a small book, it contained a disclaimer of any reference to real persons or events. Wheeler told Porter that the press's attorneys had advised them to include this statement "to protect you and ourselves from any denouncement from 'Kennerly' in case he should recognize himself." In a letter to her family shortly after she received the first copies, she said that the disclaimer represented only the publisher's desire to avoid a libel suit—implying that it did not mean that the story did not in fact refer to real persons and events. Even so, the differences from the first version are real and significant.[41]

A comparison of the two versions provides evidence of Porter's social and economic concerns during and immediately following her years in Mexico. The overtly fictional "Hacienda," published some two years after the original, was considerably expanded (much beyond the "twice as long" Givner allows it) and its political import rendered both more indirect and more fully dramatized. The later version is less concerned with Eisenstein and more concerned with the Eisenstein episode as a complex symbol. Thus one might well read Porter's disavowal of topical reference ("all characters and situations in this story are entirely fictional and do not portray an actual person") not only as an effort to "focus on the artistic themes of the story," as Unrue has it, but as an effort to establish its larger and directly political social implications.[42]

In both versions Porter conveys her own political interpretations both through overt commentary and satiric tone and through a series of symbolic actions. For example, seeing a jack rabbit pursued by dogs, she sides with the weaker, the oppressed, exhorting the rabbit to run; but when she later sees a dog chasing a "little fat-bottomed soldier" she does not take sides. Another example is her objectification of her detachment from the decadent atmosphere of the hacienda by depicting herself wrapped in a blanket and sitting apart on the balcony (H-1, p. 566).[43] The expanded version not only maintains an emphasis on the invading American but strengthens it, as the opening "we" of the original, referring to the group of train passengers on their way to the hacienda, is exchanged for a view of Kennerly (the K—— of the original) as he "take[s] possession of the railway train among a dark inferior people" (H-2, p. 135). The narrator herself is distanced from

Kennerly, the ludicrously imperceptive exploiter, by a buried metaphor of theatergoing: It was "worth the price of a ticket" to see him in action. The Indian women who pursue the train in an effort to sell their pulque worms are now more fully individualized through the addition of details about their blue clothing and their hope for trade. The narrator's stance is particularized, as well, and rendered complex by an added excursus on cleanliness, which shows that she shares Kennerly's values to some degree while nevertheless judging that he had "overdone it" (H-2, p. 139). Unlike Kennerly, however, she associates cleanliness with the Indians.

The cast of characters at the hacienda is also more fully developed through characterizing details and a series of incidents centering on a theme of exploitation and class conflict. Best-Maugard is now given a name, Betancourt, which accords well with his actual French blood and French education, newly acknowledged in the story; and he moves nearer the center of the action, representing an aestheticized view that drains experience of its political realities. Eisenstein, now called Uspensky, takes on a greater grotesqueness than in the original, with his "striped overalls" now becoming a "monkey-suit of striped overalls" and his face "like a superhumanly enlightened monkey's" (H-2, p. 153). (Photographs show that Eisenstein's face did have a simian quality.) The director's taste for bawdy performances is introduced, and the character of Doña Julia, also grotesque in her Chinese-style satin pajamas, is elaborated.[44] The concluding focus on the Indian's wistful anticipation of there being "enough to eat again" (H-1, 569; H-2, 170) is more fully prepared for by attention to the shooting of the peon girl, the jailing of her brother, and Don Genaro's negotiations over the price of his release because it is, after all, "his peon." The peons going about their work are contrasted more directly with Genaro's impulsive joyriding in his car and on fast horses. After this well-dramatized series of contrasts between the exploited and the exploiting classes, the story ends with the message given the narrator directly by an impoverished Indian who looks forward, with a touching simplicity, to the time of year when there will be enough to eat.

This concluding message of hunger and constricted hope at the end of "Hacienda" both prepares for and justifies the coming of a revolution that will move beyond the supposedly reformed conditions Porter witnessed in Mexico. That is, she does not so much emphasize class conflict as the need for class conflict and the justness of an agrarian revolt. But hope that such a revolution will actually materialize and improve the lot of the Indian remains dim.

As critics have often commented, "Hacienda" betrays Porter's disillusionment with the Revolution. She had been expressing such disillusionment in letters for at least two years. To her father, for example, she commented on the "Mexican business": "One by one I see all my friends there die before the firing squad, or driven out of the country. My friend Felipe Carillo, governor of Yucatan, was killed with all his cabinet during the de la Huerta counter-revolution. And men that I thought good revolutionists turn against the government and try to get into power, and are executed over night."[45] In a letter to Herbst written a few months before she left Mexico for Europe she lamented, "If the leaders had taken away the lands from the rich to give to the Indian, as they said they were doing, it would have been indeed a revolution. But when you see the Indian poorer, more desolate than ever, and every political official and every general in the country now in possession of the beautiful properties they murdered and banished the owners to get, you can hardly control yourself when they point out a few little under-nourished country schools, a few orphan asylums, a few stretches of land actually given to a village in common, but run, after all, by a 'revolutionary' leader."[46]

❧ Porter left Mexico having developed a theory of artistic integrity, of the paradoxical nature of art as an expression at once of localized specificity and universal commonality, and of the artist's role both in and outside of social experience. She had developed, as well, a measure of detachment toward her native region, an artistic distance that would prove invaluable in the years ahead as she turned back toward childhood and home as subjects evoking emotional intensity submitted to clear analysis. Perhaps most important of all, she had developed a style that combined compression and visual impact in a distinctive way—a style clear-edged, simplified, and often related to the art of caricature she knew well from her close acquaintance with Mexican caricaturists and her own production of caricature drawings. She had built up a fund of jottings and notes on which she drew in the years ahead as she produced the major works on which her reputation rests. And she had, in fact, already written several of these, the most important being "María Concepción" and "Flowering Judas." She would soon complete "Hacienda." She had in hand Eugene Pressly's translation of *The Itching Parrot,* most of the work on which was completed and which would be published in 1942 with her revisions and substantial introduction.

The importance of her Mexican years to Porter's distinctive style can scarcely be overestimated. To be sure, she might have picked up the art of caricature and her minimal style elsewhere, but in fact both caricature and a boldly simplified style conveying strong emotional presence were particularly identified with the Mexican artists who were then active. The flowering of caricature, which Porter praised for its ability to reveal inner truth by exaggerating and simplifying external features, was evident as well in the highly contrasted style of the politically committed murals being painted at the time, which often utilized a combination of portrait and genre scene, and in the folk art of the pulque shops. Many of the pulque shop paintings were sentimental in idiom, but at times they adopted a satirical style such as Porter used in stories like "Rope" and "The Martyr."

Porter was well acquainted with the work of noted caricaturist Miguel Covarrubias (and with the artist himself). In reviewing his *The Prince of Wales and Other Famous Americans* in the *New Republic* in 1925, she noted the "lacerating gift" of fine caricature that is a "well seasoned tradition" in Mexico.[47] Her style in the review is itself a kind of enactment of the art of caricature—defined as exposure of "the very outer appearance of a sitter that is the clue to an inner quality the sitter has spent most of his life trying to hide, or disguise"—with its depiction of Covarrubias's devotion to a seemingly "innocent pastime" that was in fact, she says, a kind of "murder."

Porter, too, practiced an art that was at times murderous. She sometimes, in fact, drew quite competent sketches and caricatures herself—of her lover Luis Hidalgo, who was himself a caricaturist, of John Herrmann, Gertrude Stein, and others. Several were published along with her book reviews.[48] More significant, however, are the deft verbal caricatures she drew in her fiction—of Diego Rivera and Lupe Marín in "The Martyr," of her husband Ernest Stock in "Rope," of Hunter Kimbrough in "Hacienda." Even when her characterizations cannot be labeled caricatures, they are often rendered with a similar abbreviated deftness in which a minimally detailed appearance reveals an uncomfortable inner truth. Her familiarity with caricature as practiced by her acquaintances in Mexico (and others who drew for the *corridos* she discussed knowledgeably in her *Survey Graphic* article on the genre) was an element in the fullness of her techniques of characterization.

It is conjectural but plausible to relate Porter's famous style to another aspect of Mexico: its strong sunlight. The idea is implied in Robert Penn Warren's praise of the "essential austerity" of her style and its "devotion to the fact drenched in God's direct daylight."[49] One has only to study the photographs of Edward Weston, Tina Modotti, and Sergei Eisenstein's assistant director, Alexandrov—three photographic artists whose work Porter knew well—to realize the intensity of the Mexican sunlight and the strong contrasts and clear outlines it creates. Porter, too, drenched herself in this light, and she can well be said to have achieved in words the kind of effects that were achieved in visual images by these photographers, all of them stirred and educated by Mexico. The visual images in her work took on a notable clarity as she "saw more outwardly."[50]

Her achievement in the vein of the restrained, clear style can be seen in any of the stories that have been mentioned here. But it would be more useful, perhaps, to consider the stylistic features, along with the Mexican subject matter, of two somewhat less familiar works: her review of D. H. Lawrence's *The Plumed Serpent,* published in 1926, and her narrative essay "St. Augustine and the Bullfight," published in 1955.

Despite an overwhelming dislike for Lawrence, she praised him, in her 1926 review, for having created an "immense and prodigal feeling" for the panoramic scenes in which his novel of Mexico is set. His picture of the "visible Mexico" does not "omit a leaf, a hanging fruit, an animal, a cloud, a mood." The statement might seem to imply that she found the novel cluttered, yet she does not seem to mean that. Rather, she was identifying a quality very much like that of the sense of place in her own Mexican works. Without indulging in extensive description through a "laborious building up of local color," Lawrence achieves clarity of impression, capturing an emotional tone related to place and creating an impression of detailed specificity. Moreover—and this is of great importance to Porter—he does so in "a prose flexible as a whiplash." The phrase conveys deftness, leanness, accuracy: qualities that are customarily singled out in Porter's own style.[51] In what might be called the content of Lawrence's novel she found less to praise. In her view, he did not understand his subject. The mysteries of the Mexican psyche remained just that, mysteries, however insistently he tried to claim that he had penetrated them. This failing, she implies, derives from fear, from bravado, and from a failure of humanity. Finding Mexico "cruel," Lawrence recoiled. Seeing the death-centeredness, the acceptance of death, in Mexican folk customs (such as the Festival of the Dead, which so fascinated Sergei Eisenstein), Lawrence was not moved but stricken with "terror."[52] It is interesting that Porter would single out for comment Lawrence's recoil from the Mexican focus on death, since she herself, as Walsh has demonstrated, was obsessively fearful of death.

Porter saw Lawrence as having gone to Mexico for reasons of exoticism, a motivation she generally regarded as shallow and frivolous. He tried to "touch the darkly burning Indian mystery," but instead merely projected upon the Indians his own troubled identity. Moreover, in doing so, he became guilty of a great "pretentiousness" and, perhaps most culpably, showed himself as having "contempt for the revolution and the poor." In her view, then, Lawrence had violated the principles that were of highest importance in her own social vision during the twenties. Reading, by comparison, one of her denunciations of the exploitation of Mexico by "Land, Oil, and the Church" or her sympathetic account of the suffering Indian populace in "The Fiesta of Guadalupe," we can see that she too achieved a "whiplash" style, but she achieved, as well, sympathetic understanding of her subject.[53]

Late in her career, at the age of sixty-five, Porter returned to her Mexican material from the 1920s in "St. Augustine and the Bullfight," a work that has been increasingly admired. She begins the piece with the single word "adventure"—a cryptic and suggestive opening, since she was always eager to deny that motives of adventure had led her to Mexico and the essay itself rejects adventure in favor of "experience." That is, it rejects an unstructured reveling in events and sensations as an unworthy mode of life in comparison to the gradual ripening that enables one to grasp the significance of one's experiences. That act of purposeful ordering, of the grasping of significance, is a kind of yelding to "the truth that finally overtakes you." Being overtaken by that truth (a curiously passive state) is equivalent to fulfilling the writer's purpose, which is described not in passive terms at all, but in very active ones: "to try to wangle the sprawling mess of our existence in this bloody world into some kind of shape."[54]

To illustrate and develop the contrast between adventure and real experience, Porter adduces several personal experiences, especially that of attending a bullfight and discovering her own complicity in the cruelty occurring in the ring. Her initial reasons for going to Mexico sound curiously like adventure-seeking: She was there "for the express purpose of attending a Revolution." The phrase has her characteristic lightness; "attending" conveys ease and routineness—one attends school or attends a play, not a revolution. The interplay between the two words produces the kind of deft irony for which Porter is known. While there, she says, she had "Revolutionist friends and artist friends, and they were gay and easy and poor as I was." Again, the counterpoising of "Revolutionist" with "artist" and of "poor" with "gay" and "easy" achieves keen irony with a light touch. Short, simple adjectives, words that do not ponderously obtrude themselves, they nevertheless encompass a great tension, something like Hemingway's grace under pressure, but in miniature.

For all its grace and seeming ease, the essay centers on death and cruelty, much like her earlier review of Lawrence. Again the "whiplash" style hits its ironic mark, with the goaded bull's blood furnishing "an interesting design" on his coat, giving the whole a "highly aesthetic effect." But rather than recoil from the sport which she at first found so appalling that she could not look, she (either Porter or a fictionalized first-person central character and central consciousness) became "drunk on it." She reveled in it, going to bullfight after bullfight because it "had death in it, and it was the death in it that I loved." She became, for the time, a seeker of "pure sensation," like Augustine's young friend who, perversely, came to love the gladiatorial games. Her life became, in short, committed to adventure.[55] But thinking and writing about it turned the adventure into experience.

Porter's acquaintance with Mexico, bullfights and all, proved to be of enormous value to her. If it was mere sensationalism at the time, enhanced by the dangerous political ambience, it did, after all, help her to find herself. Mexico provided her the occasion for discovering the truth of her own nature, her complicity in cruelty. By so doing it provided her the means and the material for later looking back at herself and her world and pulling them together into a statement of meaning. It provided her the key to wangling the sprawling mess of her existence in the bloody world into a significant shape. "St. Augustine and the Bullfight" is not a journalistic piece or even an essay about Mexico. It is a work that uses qualities of Mexico and of the outsider's experience there to reach tentative conclusions about the self which may be generalized into hypotheses about humankind. Mexico constitutes, not the stage center, but the background that gives the whole its tone. Through a very few details Porter achieves a sense of place, as she had said some thirty years before that Lawrence did. Against that background are poised a few isolated tableaux resonant with meaning. Rather than assert her meanings, she brings them alive in a series of narrative moments.

Mexico did that for Porter herself. It provided a distinctive background, keenly realized and incorporated into her writing, against which she lived the moments that helped her to realize herself. Finally and paradoxically, the harvest of Mexico was reaped in her turning to her own experience and her own place. She said in " 'Noon Wine': The Sources" that her time in Mexico and in Europe "gave me back my past and my own house and my own people—the native land of my heart."[56] Since she believed that the "main occupation" of the writer must be "endless remembering," this function of her ventures into the wider world must be accounted very important indeed. She had to get away from the South in order to remember the South most effectively. Her most enduring artistic achievements, more fully achieved even than her stories and essays of Mexico, are those works in which she recaptures and uses her childhood experiences in her own family and the region she knew so well. In part, this embrace of her own native material can be seen as a result of her having gained the perspective that distance affords.

But the embrace of her native material was a legacy of Mexico in another and more direct sense. Through her acquaintance with the art of Diego Rivera and other Mexican artists, she gained not only a ripely developed sense of integrity in style but a perception of the achievements that could be made by people who addressed themselves to their own experience—and their own past. Rivera painted scenes of Mexico, devoting his primary attention to the indigenous people of his own country. The same might be said of Guerrero and other members of their circle. Just as they depicted their own personal and racial experience in their art, she came to understand that she needed to draw on her personal and regional past. In the mid-twenties, even as she was continuing to develop her Mexican writings, she began to turn to a depiction of the places and people she knew from childhood, even to the extent of drawing on her personal memories and family photographs. She completed then most of the work that would be published, long afterward, as "Holiday," using techniques of portraiture and genre scenes that characterized the work of the Mexican artists she knew so well and the death-centered sensibility pervasive in Mexican culture.[57] In 1927 she published "He," a story of the common people of the South. With these stories she struck what might be considered her authentic material and voice, which would blossom in what is probably her finest work, "Noon Wine."

Although Porter's admiration for Diego Rivera soured rather drastically in the thirties, she retained her esteem for the Indian artist Xavier Guerrero. A 1930 exhibit of Mexican art at the Wadsworth Atheneum in Hartford, Connecticut, included three drawings by Guerrero on loan for the occasion from Porter's personal collection. After the exhibition the director wrote to her expressing the gratitude of the trustees for her "kindness and generosity in permitting us to show your Mexican works of art." He went on to say that the exhibition was "one of the most successful we have had in the museum and aroused a great deal of interest." In reply, she expressed once again her sense of the power and authenticity of the art produced during what is usually called the Mexican Renaissance: "I believe that Mexican painting, even with its prodigious faults, may be praised before any other for its energy and integrity. . . . I should like to see some one write a severe and balanced estimate of the really important work being done here."[58] Her fiction provides, if not an estimate, at any rate the evidence of that important work.

CHAPTER FIVE

"between two wars in a falling world"

I intend to travel again as soon as I get free of this present load on my mind, and visit London, Paris, Rome, Dublin, Edinburgh, Stockholm, Oslo, Madrid, and see everything and go everywhere, and then come back and find myself a house in a deep lovely country somewhere.

—Porter to Ann Holloway Heintze, February 15, 1957

My life has been a long history of my attempts to take root in a *place*.

—Porter to Glenway Wescott, January 23, 1941

After leaving Mexico for Europe in 1931, Porter would never again live in the country she sometimes spoke of as the place of her heart. In 1925, among some scattered notes on the Mexican materials she hoped to make into a novel, she had recorded, in terms that evoke a sense of sacrality in her wish for an idyllic home: "I shall come back some day to live in Amecameca, at the foot of the Volcano, in a house of adobe with an adobe wall around it, and mottled, copper green moss will cover it over within a year. There shall be a tiled fountain in the garden, with ducks, and ferns and figs and pomegran[a]tes growing along the walls. There shall be a tiled fireplace in the room where I keep my books, and the designs shall be made by Adolfo Best Maugard. A silence will be all over the place, so enormous [that] any spoken word shall sound quite unnecessary. . . . This, no matter what end is prepared for me in its stead, is my dream." At the time of her departure she did not regard Mexico that way. Disillusioned in her political hopes, tired, frustrated by her failure to produce a novel, her nerves frayed to the point of breakdown, she was in no mood to idealize the scenes of the past few months' experiences. She wrote to Josephine Herbst, shortly before leaving, that Mexico was "a terrible place."[1]

As we have seen, this was not her settled opinion. Mexico had provided her a rich harvest of experience and of artistic maturation. It had provided her, too, a wider perspective from which to view her own native place and culture. Her Mexican years were indeed second only to her childhood years in Texas in their importance to the development of her art.[2]

In sailing for Europe, Porter was embarking on an adventure in a wider internationalism that would enrich her sensibility, her intellectual frame of reference, and her circle of acquaintances perhaps as richly as Mexico had. She was establishing that cosmopolitan outlook (and, paradoxically, its limits) that would combine so resonantly with her southern regionalism, giving much of her work, fiction and nonfiction alike, a distinctive tone of focused clarity within a wide and mature perspective. It is this quality in her work, as much as its stylistic finesse, that accounts for its effects of limpid depth and, ultimately, of worthwhileness. If her acquaintance with Europe would also, at times, give her a false sense of her own political expertise, it was nevertheless valuable and important in her development as a thinker and artist. For the rest of her life she would be able to view events in the United States within the context of the events she had witnessed both in Mexico and in Europe, especially the rise of Hitler and the Nazis. During World War II, for example, she wrote to Freda Kirchwey, in an attempt to explain her political position, "I am Anti-Nazi and have been since I was in Germany ten years ago and saw the beginnings of that party in power."[3]

To what extent her claim to have recognized the evil of Nazism at first sight reflected hindsight rather than actuality is difficult to say. The record of her dislike of Berlin is clear enough, but the timing of her political insight is less clear, and the reasons for it, whenever it developed, are even less so. She came to Berlin in a state of emotional irritability or debilitation that was quickly exacerbated by financial insecurity, tensions between herself and Eugene Pressly, discomfort from the cold weather and inadequate diet, and depression. Porter was highly impressionistic and always tended to link her impressions with her opinions. It was natural that the dislike of Germany that emerged, in part, as a function of her personal unhappiness would readily accommodate itself to an emerging realization of the larger significance of events witnessed there, convincing her that she had known it from the first.

To the complex of emotional factors that led her to find Berlin dismal and repellent was added the opportunity to witness the huge political rallies, both Nazi and Communist, then taking place in the capital. On these occasions she observed that the security measures and agendas of the Nazi meetings were tightly organized; their gatherings exhibited a high degree of control. This control of public matters, reinforced by her impression of the conventionality and repressiveness of the Germans' everyday lives, would have been enough to evoke unpleasant associations. She had spent much of her life struggling against what she perceived as repressive surroundings. She would almost certainly have recoiled from the Nazis' use of "offensive physical terror" against their Communist opponents. Moreover, the aggressive "hardness" of the Nazi system may have evoked a measure of gender anxiety. It is not clear that she was conscious of this aspect of the emergent regime—what Susan Sontag has called the "erotic surface" characteristic of right-wing movements. Hitler, Sontag writes, "regarded leadership as sexual mastery of the 'feminine' masses, as rape."[4] It *is* clear, though, that Porter was generally alert to such affective qualities of public life and that if she did become aware of it, at some level, the anxieties it evoked might have been reinforced by anxieties related to her father.

Porter's continuing friendliness with Communist sympathizers and party members would have been the most obvious impetus to a dislike of the Nazi movement in Germany. By 1931 the Comintern and the KPD (Kommunistische Partei Deutschlands) generally perceived the National Socialists as dangerous rivals for the loyalty of the working classes in the war against capitalism.[5] More specific causes of her dislike of Germany and of the right-wing regime then in power may be conjectural, but the dislike itself was undeniable.

❧ Despite Porter's claims that she had never wanted to go to Europe until the time she actually went, the record is clear that her trip in 1931 was a long-delayed wish. As early as 1919 she had told her family that she hoped to be in Europe by the following spring. She and J. H. Retinger apparently talked of going to Europe and doing collaborative work there. In 1922 or 1923, Mary Doherty was hoping that the three of them could "do Europe to-gether," and as late as 1924 Retinger was still declaring his hopes that Porter would come to Europe with him. Unfortunately, he does not seem to have offered to pay her way. Moreover, she had long distrusted Retinger and avoided cultivating a close relationship with him, to the point that he complained she had behaved "abominable." A year after the award of a Guggenheim Fellowship at last enabled her to go, she admitted, "I love it and wish I had come here first, ten years ago, when I planned to go to Spain and then to Europe and was persuaded by Adolfo Best to go to Mexico."[6] We can presume that the denials of her earlier wish to go to Europe were made out of a feeling that to admit a frustrated wish to go years before would have been to admit that she had not been successful enough to do so.

Joan Givner plausibly traces Porter's desire to visit Europe back even further: to her childhood. Her best friend in Kyle, when she was living at her grandmother's home, was Erna Schlemmer, the daughter of well-read and well-to-do German immigrants who maintained a European tone in their household and made extended visits to their home country. It is not hard to read between the lines of the record Porter's envy of her friend's lot. In later years, when the two resumed their friendship, it was with the European context looming in the background. When Erna Schlemmer Johns' son and daughter-in-law, who were living in Germany in the early 1960s, invited the by-now famous Porter to come for a visit, she responded with a reminiscence of how her old friend's European ties had affected her in childhood: "It seems so odd that not only Erna's son, but Erna herself is back in Germany, in Berlin of all places, for her family went back quite often, and I have (at home with my sister) some letters of hers, from Mannheim, Wiesbaden, Berlin itself, and then we talked when she got back, and it was all one thing—she hated it, every day of it, all parts of it, the custom [*sic*], the language, the manners, the looks of things; it was very strange to me, who would have been so happy to get *any* where out of Texas, a place I hated as consummately as she did Germany."[7] It appears that Porter called upon her friend's early dislike of Germany as a validation of her own dislike, which, because of its extremity, may have been troubling to her at a deep and unacknowledged level. She must have realized that it arose, at least in part, from her own emotional debility at the time she formed her opinions.

She left Mexico in August 1931 intending not only to fulfill the conditions of her Guggenheim Fellowship, which called for a year of writing in Europe, but perhaps to go on to Russia and study Communism at first hand. Essentially she wanted "to get *any* where" other than the place she was. Her urge to adventure and her need to escape existing problems were very much the frame of mind in which she had gone to Mexico a decade before. But she was never able to acknowledge her own escapism, which was in fact a pattern of behavior that manifested itself repeatedly—in her departure from Texas and in various retreats from New York, including her stay in Bermuda, which she considered a paradise until she became restless and longed to "earn time off for good behavior, and so get off this island!" Her departure from Mexico was another attempted escape from her own settled patterns of life as well as from external complications. She was never able to remain comfortably in any one place for long. Probably she was truthful in stating to her father, "Where I can work, there I live."[8] But it was often the case that her incurable restlessness and intermittent homesickness—for a home she never had—kept her from being able to work regardless of where she was living.

With them on the German liner *Werra* in late August, Porter and Pressly, whom she would marry in 1933, took their working papers on Lizardi's *Itching Parrot,* being translated by Pressly but ultimately published as Porter's own. The fact that they had this project in hand would have buoyed her spirits considerably; she needed the energizing focus of work in progress. After her inability to complete her long-promised book on Cotton Mather or the novel on Mexico she had begun almost a decade before, she must have enjoyed the prospect of a feasible project that could actually be delivered to a publisher. Moreover, the Lizardi project was congenial because of its subject's freethinking and untrammeled expression of opinion, qualities Porter valued highly and saw, or tried to believe she saw, in herself. It would be some years, however, before the translation, with her fine introductory essay, would be published.

She seems to have enjoyed the voyage and the opportunity it gave her to observe a variety of personalities at close quarters for a sustained period. The journal letter addressed to Caroline Gordon that she kept on the way, which became the seed of *Ship of Fools,* is generally relaxed and cheerful in tone, though it contains several barbed descriptions of fellow passengers in which one can recognize the hostile caricatures of the novel. Her initial response to German culture, as represented by the German passengers on the *Werra,* was, considering her later views, surprisingly positive. She wrote to Herbst that it was "so pleasant to hear German spoken, and see the pleasant German faces, and have life go so orderly and smooth, after all the row and nervous tension and sharpness of Mexican life" and that she was looking forward to Berlin "with happiness." The last entry in her log of the trip, written on September 24, after she and Pressly had arrived in Berlin, praised the attractive housing provided for the poor, the musical tones of people's greetings, and their gracious manners. All in all, she told Gordon, she found Berlin a relief after the "meanness of Mexico." Although she later told Doherty that she and Pressly had been "instantly bowed down" by the "tonnage of the German spirit," her statements at the time indicate that she at first "loved" Berlin. "I feel serene and steady here, what I see of the Germans pleases me." She found them "so pleasant and friendly" that she felt "at ease" with them. "I was always predisposed towards them, but I did not particularly expect it to be mutual. If it is so, if I am not deceived by my own hopes, I can be very happy here."[9]

Shortly after arriving in Berlin, however, she seems to have suffered a period of nervous debility characterized by anxiety, irritability, and gloom. She described it herself as a nervous breakdown. After the brief initial period of enthusiasm, her letters speak of depression, loneliness, and a sense that the Guggenheim was proving to be not only a waste of the foundation's money but, by placing her under obligation to produce a book, a burden. Pressly had quickly become frustrated by language problems, the money he had expected did not arrive, and, facing keen financial anxiety, the two began to argue. After only a few weeks he went on to Madrid to seek better fortunes there, leaving Porter lonely, depressed, and frightened. By November she was writing to Cowley that the Crane episode had "made her ill." She complained to Pressly, "Lord, I am tired of crying, but I can't stop," and confessed that she had been "not altogether sane."[10] The violent dislike she took to Berliners during these weeks would remain with her for the rest of her life as a fixed prejudice—only one, however, among several.

As early as December 1, Porter was writing to Pressly, in Madrid, that she had begun to doubt she could "thrive" in Berlin. She felt "hacked away at the roots from all familiar earth," she wrote, "and without language."[11] Language was, of course, the most secure anchor in her life. She was estranged from family, she had endured a series of love affairs that ended in despair and two (actually three) unsuccessful marriages, either a pregnancy ending in stillbirth or the compulsive need to claim one, and the disappointment of a powerful set of political ideals. The one anchor of her identity and the one reason she had to feel a sense of pride in her self was her writing. For the past year she had failed in that. It is easy to see that a sense of being "without language" would be profoundly disturbing. She later observed, "The really homeless, rootless lost man is the one without a mother tongue."[12]

Later in December she wrote to Pressly that she disliked "almost everything" she saw in Berlin. With unusual candor she admitted her own fault but cited, as well, the tension of German society between the wars: "They seem under a curse, I have never seen so many despairing faces as here." The lingering economic aftermath of the war oppressed her; "the misery, the distress," she wrote, were "simply horrible." It must not have helped much that at the same time Pablo O'Higgins was sending glowing reports from Moscow on Soviet progress toward a classless society and "a truly humane world." On New Year's Day, 1932, still brooding over the Hart Crane episode, she wrote to her old supporter Yvor Winters that she was on the verge of "a nervous smash-up." But she quickly dropped her own troubles to explain, more analytically than in her heavily emotional letters to Pressly, the problems she saw in Berlin. The country, she thought, had been "almost completely annihilated by its defeat and long punishment: the weight of taxes staggers them, and yet increases." There was much evidence of poverty and also—an ominous note that would recur in her correspondence for years—of the growing power of Hitler and his party, threatening another war.[13]

Only two days later she was again writing one of her long screeds to Pressly, indicting the entire German race for its "total lack of vivacity." "Life is horribly a business of having a plate and a doily under every glass and bowl, a matter of keeping the toilet bowl well scrubbed and obeying all the little verboten signs you see in every place you step." His Spain, she thought, again showing her restlessness, sounded considerably better than her Germany. She felt a sweeping dislike of Germans, in whom she saw a "respectable, unimaginative, dumb middle-class wretchedness." Her emphasis on this depressing or "oppressive" quality of life in Berlin would in retrospect become a foreboding of trouble to come, a sense of "some great—oh, *vast* beast crouching." But in claiming this sense of portentousness she was probably enhancing the keenness of her foresight.[14]

Later, from the vantage of Basel, Switzerland, where she found the people to be "simply lumpy, every creatur[e] . . . so fat it can hardly waddle," the Germans would look somewhat better. The Catholics of the Black Forest region, at any rate, where she and Pressly enjoyed walking tours, struck her (at least for the time it took to write a letter or two) as being "calm and friendly" with "perfect human dignity." But her prejudice against Germans and Germany would remain for the rest of her life. The worst barb she could hurl at Eugene Pressly, after their relationship ended, was to call him German. In the margin of a letter to her father dated March 2, 1933, in which she had announced that she would soon marry Pressly, she wrote, in May 1950, "On his mothers [side] he was German! *half-German!* and behaved like one at last."[15]

Unlike Germany, she loved France from the moment she made its acquaintance, and loved it with a consistency rare in her response to anything or anyone. Indeed, when she left Berlin in early 1932 and stopped over in Paris on her way to Madrid, where she and Pressly planned to be married, it was in large measure the spell of that beautiful city that disrupted her plans. (Givner points out, though, that the disruption was also occasioned by a flirtation.) She had been hounding Pressly for weeks to find them a place to live, and according to his progress reports he had been combing Madrid for something acceptable that they could afford. Even so, when Porter arrived in Madrid she fell into crying fits, the marriage was postponed, and she went back to Paris. Soon she was exulting to Peggy Cowley (whom she still addressed as "Peggy darling," though she would shortly be referring to her as a calamity) that she loved the city and had met such notables as Sylvia Beach, Ford Madox Ford, Caresse Crosby, and the noted anarchist Emma Goldman.[16] It seems clear that at least part of her gloom in Madrid had stemmed from the fact that Madrid was not Paris.

Later, during periods of financial distress or depression, when she was beginning to want to go back to the United States, Porter would sometimes complain about the high prices and the grayness of Paris—much as she complained of Belgium when she went there on a Fulbright in 1954. But such outbursts were rare. For the most part, she preferred Paris to any other place she knew. There were many reasons for her fondness, including the presence of interesting people and a fast social pace, but the strongest reason had to do with her sense of cultural and aesthetic depth. As an artist, she felt a sense of belonging in a city long known for its embrace of the arts. She explained her love of Paris to her brother Paul by reference to personal and intellectual freedom and a sense of community: "I do not have that feeling of being at odds with society because I am an artist."[17] In other words, what she appreciated in Paris was its difference from Texas, where she *had* felt at odds with society because she was an artist and where she was always, she felt, having to explain.

Even so, her life with Pressly in Paris was disordered and emotionally wracking. He remained bored and discontented with his job and spoke of getting a transfer to "China, or Turkey or Peru,—any place we haven't been." Although Porter sometimes seemed to think this would be a good idea, she at least as often said that she couldn't think of leaving Paris, which became "more delightful" every day. Pressly's discontent exacerbated her perennial unsteadiness of concentration on her work, and it was easy for her to blame him when the words did not flow. The less she was able to work, the more she turned on Pressly, and the more discontented he became. They were caught in a tightening coil of mutual recrimination. Letters written by both contain references to drinking bouts that ended with their passing out. When Porter in 1934 withdrew to a sanitarium for what she referred to as a nervous breakdown, she accused him of being the cause of "half of my illness" because he had refused to "*see* what was happening." She was dying, she said, "of poverty and hardship too long continued, and too many disappointments." There was "nothing to hope" for from Pressly "in the way of help in any real crisis"—and would he please get some cupboards and shelves put into their apartment so they could get rid of "those big armoires." She accused him of spite in having secretly written a novel of his own and confessed that before coming to the sanitarium she had made up her mind to commit suicide, "really made it up, I think . . . I mean, I wanted to so badly I fought the notion all the time, and could think of nothing else."[18] Her distraught state and the way in which her tensions resolved themselves into a nesting urge are obvious.

The person who paid for her treatment in the Swiss sanitarium during these weeks—because she and Pressly were again having serious financial troubles—was a friend who was to be important in her life for years to come, wealthy patron of the arts Barbara Harrison. It was through Harrison that Porter met, soon after settling in Paris in 1932, novelist Glenway Wescott, whose brother Barbara would soon marry, and art critic Monroe Wheeler, Wescott's companion. Wheeler wrote to her on February 23 inquiring whether she might be willing to translate some old French folk songs for publication by Harrison of Paris, as Ford Madox Ford had indicated to him that she might. The correspondence between Harrison and Porter began in March with letters about the songbook project. All together, the Harrison-Wescott-Wheeler files (along with the George Platt Lynes and Russell Lynes files, representing friendships that arose out of her acquaintance with Wescott et al.) are among the most voluminous in the

Porter papers. Her correspondence with Wescott, especially, is remarkable for its range, wit, and readability and provides rich insights into the thinking of two fellow writers well acquainted with the currents of twentieth-century art and literature. Many years later the two would decide to publish a selection of their letters, and Wescott would expend considerable effort in preparing them for the press, working with Porter's agent, Cyrilly Abels. The proposed volume was never completed, however, and their scintillating correspondence remains mostly unpublished.

Wescott, Wheeler, and Barbara Harrison Wescott would provide Porter with important emotional and financial support. Besides publishing the *French Song Book* and the expanded *Hacienda* and paying for her to receive treatment in Switzerland when, not once but twice during the Paris years, she had emotional and physical breakdowns, Barbara later subsidized her at the Harbor Hill Inn in Cold Spring, New York, for several months in late 1943 and early 1944 when she tried unsuccessfully to complete *Ship of Fools*. Glenway attempted during that period to take on the role of general adviser and sensor of Porter's artistic and emotional temperature.[19] He and Porter would quarrel at times, and their relationship seems to have included large portions of disingenuousness on both sides, but the friendship outlasted most, and it stood Porter in good stead. She could be thankful for her years in Paris for having provided her this human context, as well as for other reasons.

One of the subterranean tensions in her friendship with Wescott and Wheeler resulted from their homosexuality. Only a little more than two months after meeting them, and while she was working on the French songbook project that provided important financial support, she wrote to Pressly that although "W. and W." were "probably the nicest" homosexuals she knew, they were tolerable only because they were "well bred" and watched their step. For the most part, she wrote, "I don't really like homos or Lesbians, and I never shall." That was true whether they were "outright swine, like Hart Crane, or pleasant bloodless young men like these two."[20] Porter, too, must have watched her step. Even many years later, having known her relatively well, Wescott believed that her prejudice against homosexuals arose when George Platt Lynes made an overture to her nephew Paul while Porter was living in Lynes's house in California (because of finances) and, according to Wescott, "felt some inclination to marry him."[21] He was wrong. Her letters from Mexico had indicated extreme distaste for the gay and lesbian scene there, and her letters from Berlin take note of the open homosexuality she witnessed in cabarets. Her prejudice was deep-rooted, but she apparently concealed it fairly successfully from Wescott.

Politically, Paris was turbulent in the 1930s, with mass demonstrations and incidents of repression of leftist elements. Porter reported to Herbst that the "scale of political assasination [*sic*], and common murder of communists, socialists, and anybody, in fact, of the low-down classes who do the work and have the gall to ask for a living, outdoes anything I ever saw or heard of in Mexico."[22] She had earlier reported on the mass meetings of both Communists and fascists in Berlin, in the course of which the police were especially severe in their control of the Communists. All these events gave her severe forebodings of the coming ascendancy of fascism throughout the world and of the likelihood of another war. She had met Hermann Goering while in Berlin and claimed to have been approached by him sexually until she said that she was in love with another man, whereupon he kissed her hands and praised her virtue. In notes made for the purpose of using her impressions in a story (which became "The Leaning Tower"), she depicted Goering as a "gross sentimentalist and glutton" who talked compulsively about the Jews, and she credited herself with premonitions of evil. Since the notes are undated, it is hard to know whether to take her observations for prescience or hindsight. At any rate, they reflect a genuine disapproval of the fascist mentality in all its manifestations. In that she was consistent.

She was not consistent, however, in her view of Communism in Europe. Although she responded more favorably to the Communist mass meetings she attended than to the fascist popular meetings, she was torn by the ambivalence that characterizes so much of her political thinking. Already she was careful to distance herself from those who were committed to the Communist party, claiming not to know how to spell *bourgeois,* a word she had spelled quite well in the past. She ridiculed a passage in a letter from Mike Gold that she had been shown, in which he said that the party wasn't interested in "Sex Education, nor any other aspect of Sex." If a thing was once called bourgeois, she thought, "that settles it for the Communist. He'll soon be refusing to blow his nose or make pee-pee because its a B——— (you know) custom." She disliked Gold's having said (if her report of the letter is not exaggerated) that he wished Lutte Lutke, a TASS employee, "might have a dozen children at once for the revolution—with him, of course," finding that it sounded like "the Catholic idea of souls for God" or "Mussolini's idea of souls for Fascism." Here and in similar comments she was expressing ideas she would later emphasize with some consistency—that there was all too little difference between communism and fascism and that fascism and the Catholic church were linked. Her linking of communism and fascism was indeed a standard rhetorical strategy used by anti-communist, right-leaning liberals of the late thirties and forties.[23]

She advised Pressly, who was having misgivings about working for the capitalist U.S. government in consular duties, against throwing over his job and going to work for the party. "Why exchange one kind of slavery for another? They are even more exigent, more narrow, more dogmatical, more mistaken in so many things, than the Burgues they never tire of denouncing." The Communists she had known, she explained, were "base and treacherous towards their friends," playing "vile tricks" and excusing them "in the name of political expediency."[24] Even so, she continued to sympathize, in general, with communist ideals.

❧ By 1936 Porter was feeling the need to return to her own country. She had not been any place she could call home in six years and had not been back to Texas to see her family in eighteen years. She was also motivated to go back to the United States because it was a plausible excuse for getting away from Eugene Pressly, whose indecision and ineffectuality she was finding unbearably irritating. He had visited the United States in 1935, but after his return their previous bickering had resumed. Soon afterward, she left on her own visit with plans to work, meet with publishers, and see her family. During her time in Europe she had completed some of her most important work: "Hacienda," "The Grave," "The Circus," parts of "Noon Wine," and the "Old Order" story now titled "The Journey." Even more important, she was now prepared to write "Old Mortality."

She first spent some time in Boston, where she reported to Pressly that she had straightened out her papers and was ready to "dig in." Unfortunately, she was still working on the bruited Cotton Mather book and was making little progress. Realizing that she had wasted far too much time and energy on that project, she managed to attribute her own misgivings to Pressly (who probably, in fact, shared them) in a way that implied he had begrudged her her identity. "Sweet," she wrote, "you may always think we would have had an idyllic marriage if it hadn't been for Cotton Mather . . . but that is saying, I think, that we might have had an idyllic marriage if

I hadn't been a writer." As she grew more and more frustrated with the effort, her recriminations became more severe. She assured him that she loved him and had "never felt such a bond with any one" else, but even so she railed that they had "done nothing but just live dully as we might have done anywhere" during their years in Europe. "It is an unpardonable way to pass the only life we shall have, and I *will not do it any more.*" It was his fault. She had worked ahead as best she could in spite of his "fixed and unchangeable opposition" when he would never say what he wanted to do, but now he was going to have to decide. "This way we are both wasted, and it is abominable." Meanwhile, Pressly was writing encouragingly that she "must not get tied into bowknots about the time it has taken or will take to finish the Mather book." The main thing was to finish it. "I think it will be very epoch-making in your life and your literary career, the day the Mather manuscript is finished."[25]

He could not know, nor could she, that she would soon drop the project entirely and take up the long-prepared-for stories that would fix her reputation as a consummately accomplished writer for good and all. Before the end of the month, March 1936, she decided that she could not possibly finish the Mather book, but would simply drop it and go on to Texas to see her father. Shortly before leaving, however, she made a breakthrough. On April 2 she wrote Pressly that she had taken up the previously begun "Noon Wine story": "This evening while doing some little last things, I suddenly sat down and added five pages."[26] The story would not be finished until November, after she had visited Texas, gone back to France, come to the United States again intending to stay, and settled temporarily at the Water Wheel Tavern in Doylestown, Pennsylvania. But the return to this resonant material was decisive, and her visit to her home would prove to be the needed catalyst in her achievement.

She was no more enamored of Texas than she had expected to be. She reported on April 10 that she "couldn't exist" in Houston and was "dying to get away," feeling "irritated and baffled." But in the course of the visit she made a pilgrimage with her father and her younger sister to Indian Creek, her birthplace, and left on her mother's grave a draft of her poem "Anniversary in a Country Cemetery." One of her two best poems, probably the only two good poems she ever produced (the other being "After a Long Journey"), "Anniversary" opens with lines expressive of her rootlessness and her yearning for a home:

This time of year, this year of all years, brought
The homeless one home again;
To the fallen house and the drowsing dust
There to sit at the door,
Welcomed, homeless no more.[27]

Laying that poem on her mother's grave was an important experience for her, a moment of touching once more her personal roots, and it freed her to address herself to her authentic material.[28]

She returned to France telling herself that she was lonely for Pressly, but it was soon clear that a permanent change had to be made. It was essential that she complete some major work. She had failed to deliver at least two books, Cotton Mather and the Mexican novel, for which she had accepted advances from publishers, and she was finding herself unable to work in the proximity of her husband—a characteristic complaint against the men in her life. In addition, as Givner emphasizes, "Noon Wine" and "Old Mortality" were now well developed in her mind. On October 8 she and Pressly left France permanently. Shortly before her departure she wrote to Ford Madox Ford and Janice Biala Ford, "It is quite true, I believe, that everything I may do in the future depends very largely on what I do just now in my own work. And this is so important to me that I almost believe that I would divorce Gene if he got in the way. And this really desperate state of mind has grown upon me gradually, because I am slow to realise that unless I am first severe with myself, and then with everything and everybody, my time and my life will go on being completely wasted and pointless, as it seems to me to have been until now. I am quite prepared for a change, it is high time."[29] She was testing out, so to speak, the word *divorce*. A year later she would break off the marriage.

In addition to her personal reasons for making a change, she was worried about the prospect of war. She had seen clear evidence of the rise of Hitler since 1931, when she witnessed Nazi gatherings in Berlin, and 1932, when she and Pressly saw swastikas and placards for Hitler during an otherwise pleasant walking tour in the south of Germany. For all these reasons they decided to go. They returned to the United States together, agreeing that he would go to Washington to look for a job while she settled in elsewhere (in Doylestown) to write. The change quickly proved fruitful. In fairly short order she produced "Noon Wine," "Old Mortality," a decade in growing from seeds in her notes on Mexico, and, after moving on to Louisiana, “Pale Horse, Pale Rider,” which she had also worked on intermittently for some years.

While working on her stories at the Water Wheel Tavern in Doylestown she was also looking at real estate brochures and hoping to buy a house. During her first trip she had thought of the possibility of getting a house in the country if her next book sold, admitting to Pressly at one point that their letters were reminding her of the letters they had written when he was in Madrid and she in Berlin and he was struggling to find acceptable housing. On November 9 she wrote that “Noon Wine” was finished—and she had found a house. At once she turned to “Pale Horse, Pale Rider,” but found herself unable to get on with it and started “Old Mortality” instead. On November 28 she reported that she had not “been able to write a line this week” and was in “a terrible state of upset and worry,” but would be “all right again, while the work lasts.” At the top of this letter she later wrote that she had done “the actual writing of both in exactly 14 days!”—which was not precisely true, but was close enough.[30] She was ready to mail “Old Mortality” the next day.

Porter was right in stating that life in Mexico and in Europe “gave me back my past and my own house and my own people—the native land of my heart.” But it was a delayed and indirect gift that brought with it another gift, the confidence to make a definitive break with Eugene Pressly. By the end of the year she would tell him unambiguously, “*I am not going to live with you any more.*” An unkind observer might say that, having finally completed work she could confidently expect to provide her some significant income, she no longer needed to put up with him.[31]

❧ During her visit to the United States in the spring of 1936, Porter wrote to Pressly that Paris was “nothing” to her any more. Clearly this was not a settled opinion but a reflection of her fatigue with their life together and her dissatisfaction with his failure to provide her both the financial security and the separateness she needed in order to persevere in her work. By this time she wanted to end their relationship and was looking for reasons to do so.

In truth, her love for Paris remained with her to the end. In 1947, disgusted by what she saw as the ascendancy of native fascism in the United States, she told Gay, “For the first time in my life I have considered going to another country and changing my citizenship—France of course, where else?” She told Cinina Warren that she was “heading out into the world” and hoped to "make Rome headquarters, but go perhaps for a month each to Germany, France, and England," though she also had a "deep wish to go to Palestine."[32] She didn't manage it then, but in 1952, when she returned to Paris for an international writers' conference, she wrote exultantly to her niece Ann, "Paris was never so beautiful, so green and sunny and magnificent." She enjoyed running into celebrities, and especially enjoyed being one herself. John Malcolm Brinnin, she exulted, "came into Paris meaning to look for me, was quite desperate *where* to look, and there I was sitting on the sidewalk in front of the Flore with Sam Barber the composer." As it turned out, they were staying in the same hotel. "Such is Paris. All you have to do is to go to some center and sit down and anybody, everybody, it seems, will happen along." When she again returned after *Ship of Fools* had brought her the money to enjoy herself, she complained of an air of "skulduggery and malice" evident in the smart shops and restaurants of Paris, but attributed the problem to "the way the Germans are taking over."[33] It was not the first time she had said the French were avaricious, but for the most part she thought of Paris as a place that could only be spoiled by other people, not by the Parisians themselves.

At that late stage of her life, however, the country she most enjoyed was Italy. She went there on a long vacation with plenty of money to spend as a result of her success with the novel and sent back parcel after parcel of beautiful objects for her nephew to store for her until she returned. "The only trouble," she wrote, "is I am having a time persuading myself ever to come home." Curiously enough, the reason she found to explain her desire to linger in Italy was that it reminded her of Texas. In the south of Italy, she said, "all the beauty of our south seems to flourish without the various curses we had—the negroes, the vicious climate, vicious people." It was the South, but better. Restlessly, she moved on to Paris, which she could not manage to enjoy as much as she once had, although she confessed she still did not want to return to the United States. "And certainly never to Washington." In truth, she was not able to be happy anywhere, confessing in a black moment, "The average American makes me weary, but the European makes me sick!"[34] Inveterately restless, she believed or hoped that travel made a person feel more at home afterward. For her, it did not work that way. She was never really at home anywhere.

Throughout her life she kept on the move, driven by restlessness often combined with economic need and emotional distress. After her first long residence in France, she would return to Europe four more times before coming back to her home country, at age seventy-five, to stay. For a person who spent so much of her life abroad, Porter was not really well traveled. She opened an acquaintance with the world, but she did not develop that acquaintance into real intimacy. Like other famous expatriates among her fellow modernists, she focused solely (except for Mexico) on Europe. Her experience of foreign places and cultures never included South America, Africa, or any part of Asia. Although she once wrote Mary Doherty, "What I wouldn't give to go to China or Korea or Japan," it was only a momentary impulse; she seemed really to have no wish to go.[35] She regarded Asian people as distinctly inferior to Europeans and Americans of European stock and did not care to see any of their countries for herself. In a questionnaire sent by the Institute of International Education she responded to the question, "Is foreign experience valuable for the writer, or does it deprive him of his 'roots'?" by saying, in part, "I think foreign travel and experience are good for everybody—not just writers, but for writers they are an invaluable, irreplaceable education in life."[36] Her own boundaries, however, were fairly narrow. When one of her lovers, late in life, urged her to meet him in Japan for a few days, she simply did not respond. Clearly, there were limits to her internationalism.[37]

Porter's restlessness was an aspect of her personality of far-reaching, if elusive, significance. From the time she went to Chicago in 1914 to try to get into the movies, she was continually on the move. Even so detailed a chronicle as Givner's biography cannot claim to trace her movements with completeness. She was in Louisiana; she was back in Texas—in Houston, in Dallas, in Fort Worth; she was in Denver; she was in New York, Michigan, Mexico, Connecticut, New York again, Massachusetts, Bermuda, Mexico again and again, Germany, France, Spain (briefly), France again, Switzerland, New England, Pennsylvania, Louisiana, Houston, Louisiana again (two different cities), New York, Pennsylvania, Virginia, California, Washington, Belgium, Michigan again, Italy, France, Maryland. The order breaks down and becomes hopelessly incorrect, incomplete.

The homeless one longed for a home but found herself unable to feel really at home anywhere for very long. Time after time she found a place that she pronounced perfect—beautiful, quiet enough for working, accessible enough for visiting with friends, utterly congenial. Within months or even weeks she would find these same places inconvenient or lonely or frightening, in some way intolerable. Equipped with intense nesting instincts, she would expend enormous amounts of energy and time settling in, painting, slipcovering, putting in gardens; she would write to family and friends giving loving descriptions of her household arrangements and extolling the homeyness of wherever it was she had settled; then find herself miserable. She could not stay in any one place, just as she could not stay in any one relationship, for long. Her friend Cleanth Brooks called her "perpetually . . . a wanderer, a seeker, a person looking for the bluebird of happiness and the one happy valley in which she could be truly at home."[38] The only house she ever owned, celebrated in the essay "A House of My Own," she occupied for less than a year. When she left it she complained, "It was no good at all trying to run my house and be general factotum for my entire community: the more I did the more I had to do."[39]

Her internationalism was an aspect of this restlessness. Convinced that she had been almost fatally handicapped in her struggle to achieve artistic greatness by her Texas origins, that she had managed to struggle free of those origins only by heroic effort, she continued, for the rest of her life, to flee the constraints of home even while she longed for the security of at-home-ness. Traveling to foreign countries was a way of proclaiming her hard-won freedom. She enjoyed writing back to her family about life in Paris and elsewhere, knowing, surely, that her accounts would seem to them wondrously exotic but also, perhaps, irritating, compared to their stay-at-home lives, especially when she wrote during the Great Depression requesting money.[40] The niece whom she saw as a younger version of herself—beautiful, talented, limited by her environment—she urged to go to Europe as if she were urging her to seek salvation.

But if Porter's internationalism was in part an expression of her restlessness and her defiance of all that Texas meant in her memories, it was also much more than that. She was a remarkably well-read person who realized that the literary and musical and artistic riches that had come to be seen collectively as Western high culture were identified chiefly with Western Europe. Although we may now read that identification not only as an indication of her own narrowness but as a manifestation of a general narrowness in the prevailing frame of reference of literate Americans, we must also realize that it is an indication of her aesthetic astuteness. She understood that her heritage and her cultural experience were limited, and if she later made of that limitation a strength, producing an art so deeply anchored in her native region that it speaks to the entire theme of rootedness and geographic identity, she first sought to expand it.

Whatever the reason for her restlessness, she was able to use it for purposes other than escape. She made of this uncomfortable aspect of her personality a vehicle for rejecting authoritarian structures, transcending personal limitations, and gaining a significant acquaintance with a variety of European cultures. From the vantage of cultural maturity thus gained, she was able to view her own cultural origins, their patterns, and their values with new eyes. She was also able to perceive the dangers for American society as the forces of ethnic divisiveness and fascistic control that she had witnessed in Mexico and in Europe gained influence in her own country. Out of that perception came her tortured vacillation between the pacifism she had long claimed and her urge to see fascist forces eradicated in World War II. Out of that perception, too, came her uneasy middle-of-the-road position in politics, the search for an acceptable pathway between unacceptable political extremes. After the war, she refused to accede to the forces of official repression in the United States, even as she came increasingly to dislike the groups that Senator Joseph McCarthy and others sought to repress. One cannot regard Katherine Anne Porter as a great or a balanced or even an original political thinker, but she did possess a remarkable sensitivity to the politically mixed atmosphere of the twentieth century and to the exquisitely complex plight of the liberal in trying to find an ethically defensible position without oversimplifying the issues. Her travels helped her achieve this sensitivity.

Unfortunately, her acquaintance with the wider world, or at least the Western European portion of it, also developed in her a pervasive pattern of ethnic prejudice. She particularly reviled the Germans; indeed, she never broke free of the dislike she developed during her intensely unhappy months in Berlin. She held similar prejudices against Jews and at times, though less bitterly, against other groups. These prejudices, like her undeniable prejudice against African Americans, would become a blot on her thinking and a sign of increasing rigidity in her sensibility. They were, in part, at the root of the ungeniality that has so often been noted in *Ship of Fools*.

❧ "The Leaning Tower," published nine years after the stay in Berlin that marked the beginning of Porter's acquaintance with Europe, demonstrates with great clarity both the blight and the ripeness that resulted from that acquaintance. It is her only story with a European setting, since *Ship of Fools,* which follows and elaborates upon her voyage to Europe, ends at the point of debarkation.

In the opening sentence of "The Leaning Tower," Porter places the time very near the time of her own arrival in Berlin. Charles Upton, the main character, has arrived on December 21, 1931, six days before the opening of the story, nearly three months later than Porter herself actually arrived. It is interesting to speculate why she bothered to make the change at all, since it is so slight a change, and why she dated the story so precisely. The answer, I believe, lies in her desire to move the entire action fully into a winter setting. Her own impressions of Berlin were dominated by cold and gloom. In "The Leaning Tower" she emphasizes these qualities, making them into symbols of the living death of Germany between the wars, its national face set toward the absolute death of Hitler and Nazism.

Several critics have pointed out the appositeness of a poem Porter composed early in her stay in Germany, first titled "Bouquet for October" but published in 1957 in *Mademoiselle* as "After a Long Journey." The poem emphasizes, in Givner's words, "the chill which has fallen on the two lovers," representing Porter's own sense of the waning of her love for Pressly. In the poem, it is not a "timely season" for their love. Kisses "freeze in our mouths," and their arms, reaching "by habit" around each other, enclose, not warm human beings, but "talking columns of stone," hard and lifeless as if frozen.[41] The implied contrast is with an earlier time of emotional warmth, just as the implied contrast of the cold German setting is to the warmth of Mexico. Porter had declared Mexico a "terrible place," but now, from the vantage of a frozen and lonely place where she felt love waning, she recalls it with an enhanced pleasure. The imagery of coldness and hardness in the poem would constitute, a decade later, the symbolic framework of her story of the gathering menace of Nazism in prewar Germany. "After a Long Journey" also develops an important theme of the interrelation of personal and political life that would emerge both in "The Leaning Tower" and in *Ship of Fools* and, by implication, in much of her work.

"The Leaning Tower" both generalizes and intensifies the disillusionment that had overtaken Porter in Mexico. There she had seen her political hopes wane and her admiration for many of Mexico's leaders turn to distaste for their venality. Corruption in office, she believed, pervaded the Mexican system of government and made it, not the fulfillment, but the betrayal of the Revolution. In Germany, where she had hoped to see a more mature culture, alive with the ferment of a better-schooled communism, she saw much the same, a society in turmoil with the ordinary people paying the price. On New Year's Day, 1932, she wrote to Yvor Winters that she had thought Hitler was "rather a bad joke" until she got to Germany and observed matters at first hand, but now took him seriously and feared he might "turn out to be a very bad bargain."[42] Giving up, for whatever reason, her notion of going on to Russia, she settled into a fusty boardinghouse and, after Pressly went on to Madrid to find a job, tried to write. But once she had completed the first version of "Hacienda," around November 1, she found herself unable to go on. It was during this period of extreme frustration, loneliness, and gloom that she fell into the deep depression that she referred to as a nervous breakdown.

The conditions that beset Porter during these cold months of late 1931 and early 1932 are recreated in "The Leaning Tower." The atmosphere of Upton's hotel at the start of the story is "oppressive," "dark, airless, cold." When he moves to a pension, it bears a strong resemblance to the one in which Porter lived, with its "stuffy tidiness, a depressing air of constant and unremitting housewifery, a kind of repellent gentility." She complained in her letters that her landlady maintained a mournful air of impoverished gentility and drove her mad by continually bustling into the room, interrupting her work, and attempting to tidy up her desk, going so far as to move her working papers around. Just so, the Viennese landlady of "The Leaning Tower" interrupts Charles when he is at work on his drawings to complain about her life and to "take a light turn among his papers, setting up a small commotion by moving his ash tray and the India ink a few inches out of their places." For Upton as for Porter, it is impossible to pursue an artistic vocation in such surroundings.[43]

The trouble, however, is not only a matter of domestic arrangements. On the streets the people are impoverished and disheartened; misery is conspicuous and omnipresent. If Upton manages to shake off his gloomy sense of pity, he falls into a mood of hatred in which he sees the German people as grotesque animals. And so he draws them, primarily as pigs, employing techniques of caricature like those with which Porter had become familiar during her years of acquaintance with Miguel Covarrubias and other caricaturists in Mexico.

Beneath the economic misery of the people lies the incipient Nazism soon to overwhelm the entire society. At first Upton is aware of Hitler only as a grotesque, slightly comical demagogue. Getting a haircut, he has to resist the barber's desire to style him after a photograph of Hitler stuck up on the mirror. He does not see the image of the rising dictator as an exemplar, as the barber does, but as "a little shouting politician, top lock on end, wide-stretched mouth adorned by a square mustache." That is, he views him as a caricature. Later in the story, however, when Upton goes out to celebrate New Year's Eve with his fellow roomers in the pension, he comes to realize the seriousness of the demagogue's spell, which, indeed, merely focuses the underlying mentality of a people whose better qualities are distorted and perverted by their misery and resentment. In the long scene in the cabaret that forms the penultimate section of the story and serves as the occasion of its fullest realization, Upton's German comrades reveal their ethnic pride and willingness to stereotype other national groups, their militarism, and their determination to avenge themselves for their defeat in the first World War by launching a second. One of them, Hans, who is enduring the discomfort of an infected dueling scar that will become his mark of pride in the old Prussian tradition, brags that "power is the only thing of any value or importance in this world." Although the Germans were beaten in the last war, he says, they will "win in the next." Even the gentlest and most sympathetic of them, a mathematics professor named Herr Bussen, becomes sly and resentful when he finds himself beholden to anyone. He cannot stand to receive favors; however reduced his circumstances, to be given anything implies that he needs it, and his pride will not tolerate such a revelation. It is the German pride that will propel the world into another war.[44]

If the picture of this "torpid" city seems utterly negative and frightening, Porter nevertheless manages to assert, by means of the title, that it will not, in the long run, prevail. This is the story's one manifestation of hope and the one relief from its somber tone. But it is a negative hope at best. The tower of pride and resentment being so painstakingly constructed by the Germans is, after all, unstable. It leans. The object that symbolizes this concept of the shaky tower, the miniature leaning tower of Pisa that Upton's landlady keeps as a souvenir of happier times, is itself so fragile that it will not withstand a touch. Examining the rooms he is considering renting, Upton attempts to pick up the tower, only to have it crumble in his hand.[45] One might read the incident as a boastful claim as egregious as the boastfulness of the Germans: The leaning tower that is the flawed German system will crumble in the hand of the American. It is an elusively complex but convincing symbol of an entire society. Once again, as she had in "Hacienda," Porter found an aesthetically and intellectually satisfying concrete representation of a social and political whole.

"The Leaning Tower" is not generally numbered among Porter's finest works. Robert Penn Warren thought it might even be called a failure because of its excessive "topicality." More important, perhaps, the atmosphere of the story is so unrelenting that it is simply uncomfortable to read, and its perspective creates difficulties because it is obviously not one of thorough understanding but rather one of bewilderment and dawning discovery. That, of course, is the point. But the result is that the story lacks the full resonance of "Noon Wine," "Old Mortality," and Porter's other southern stories. Even so, it must be regarded as a major work, only slightly lesser than those in its polish and its total import. Certainly as a piece of political commentary it is richly suggestive. So keen a critic as Glenway Wescott regarded it as being "not only all right" but "rather godlike." After musing in a journal entry about the ways in which the story surpassed his own work and the ways in which it was not quite so good, he caught himself up and admitted that his feeling toward Porter's work was one of envy: "I envy her having written this; and I also wish I were the author of her novel and her letters and her journal; I feel practically dead with fine rivalry."[46]

Porter was not typically a patriotic zealot, but when she returned to the United States in 1936 after her stay in Europe she entered a period in which her misgivings about her own country were generally muffled. Occasionally she expressed a patriotic fervor unanticipated in her earlier years. Many years would pass before she again left the country to renew her acquaintance with the wider world, and when she did, she would not be sure she liked it.

In the course of a life of rootlessness and considerable fame, Porter traveled a great deal and developed a cosmopolitan air. She spent time in Mexico, Bermuda, Germany, France, Spain, Switzerland, Washington, D.C., Belgium—living what Givner calls a "high life *and* low life throughout all the major centers of the Western world." She was inveterately restless, and though she gave no real evidence of interest in the non-Western world, she claimed to want to establish an acquaintance with it all. She did not of course accomplish this, but her acquaintance with those parts of the world in which she had traveled did immeasurably enhance her perspective on public affairs, as well as on her own origins, and enhanced her plausibility in making public pronouncements.

The grave of Porter's mother at Indian Creek, Texas. The marker reads, "Alice, wife of Harrison Porter."

Porter's first passport photograph, December 1920.

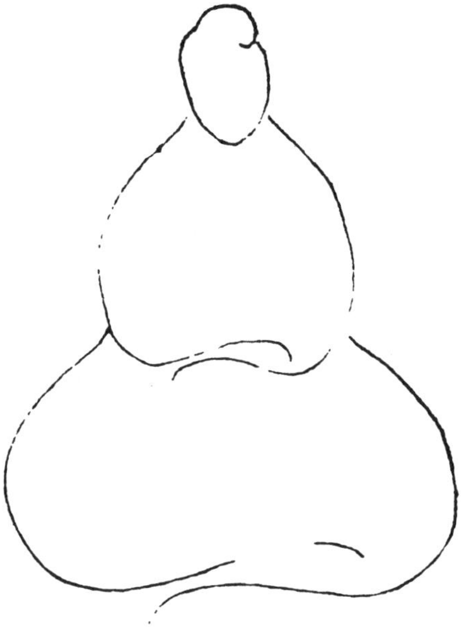

Caricature of Gertrude Stein drawn by Porter, published in the *New York Herald Tribune,* January 16, 1927.

Josephine Herbst and John Herrmann in the spring of 1928 on the front porch of their house at Erwinna, Pennsylvania, shortly after moving in. Used by courtesy of the Harry Ransom Humanities Research Center, the University of Texas.

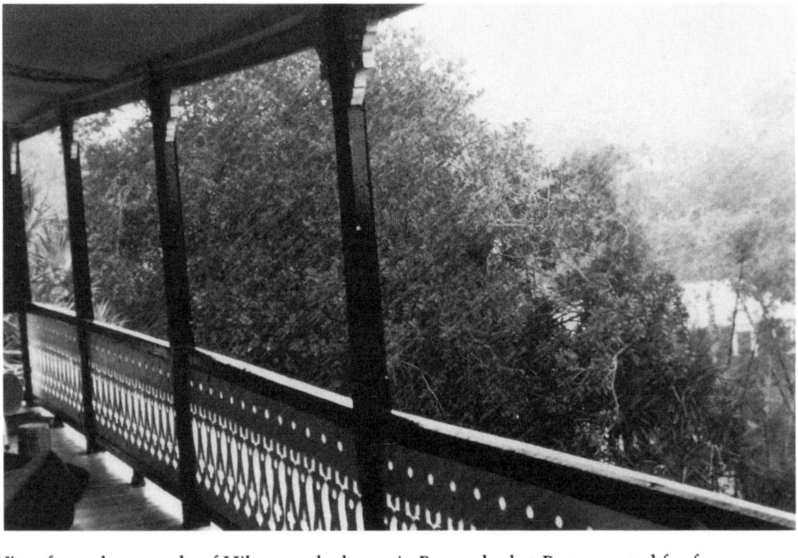

View from the veranda of Hilgrove, the house in Bermuda that Porter rented for four months in 1929. Taken in 1976 by a cousin of Joan Givner.

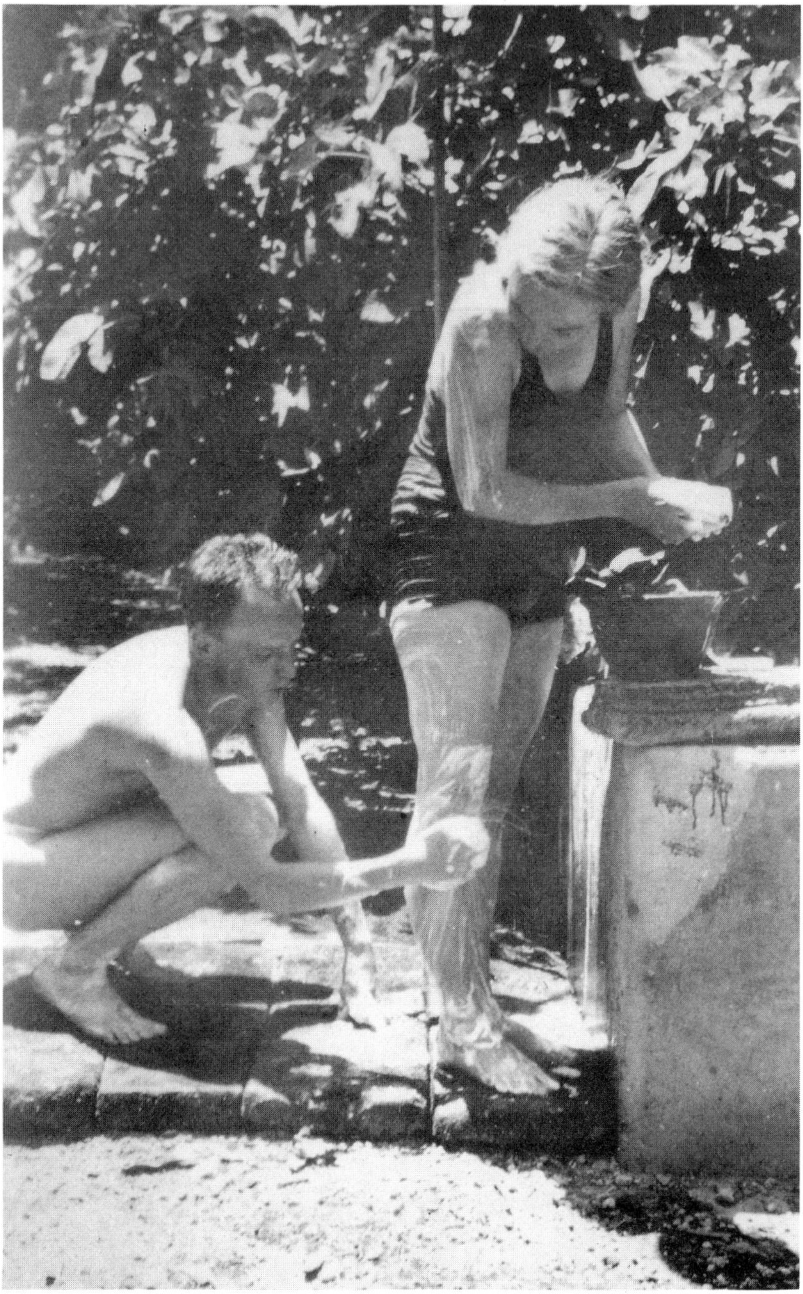

Porter and Hart Crane, Mexico, 1931.

Opposite: Porter with Eugene Pressly in Mexico, 1930 or 1931.

On board the *Werra*, September 1931.

Ford Madox Ford, a photograph taken by Porter. The inscription reads: "Natural daylight near window, midafternoon, late summer in Klein Basel, Switzerland, 1932. Overlooking the Rhine with the light from the river shining through the window. Bulb exposure, ¼ second."

Barbara Harrison Wescott, 1934, in Davos, Switzerland.

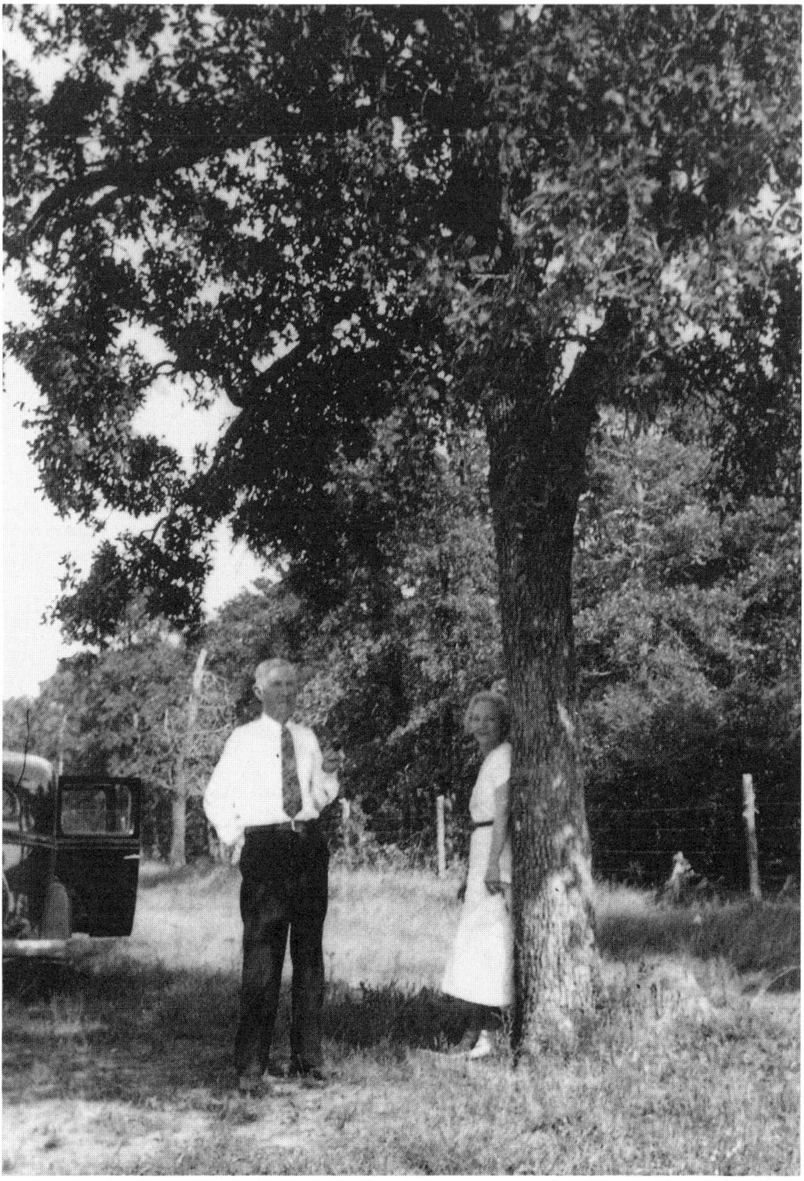

Porter and her father beside a road in Texas, during her visit in 1936.

Porter in her Paris apartment October 7, 1936, the night before she returned to the U.S.

Allen Tate, looking literary, at night at Benfolly, his home in Tennessee.

Porter with Nancy Tate and kittens, at Benfolly. An inscription on the back in Porter's hand reads: "Nancy Tate, about 12, at Benfolly, Summer 1937 with our lapful of kittens. Nancy was a dear love, my favorite child from two years until grown."

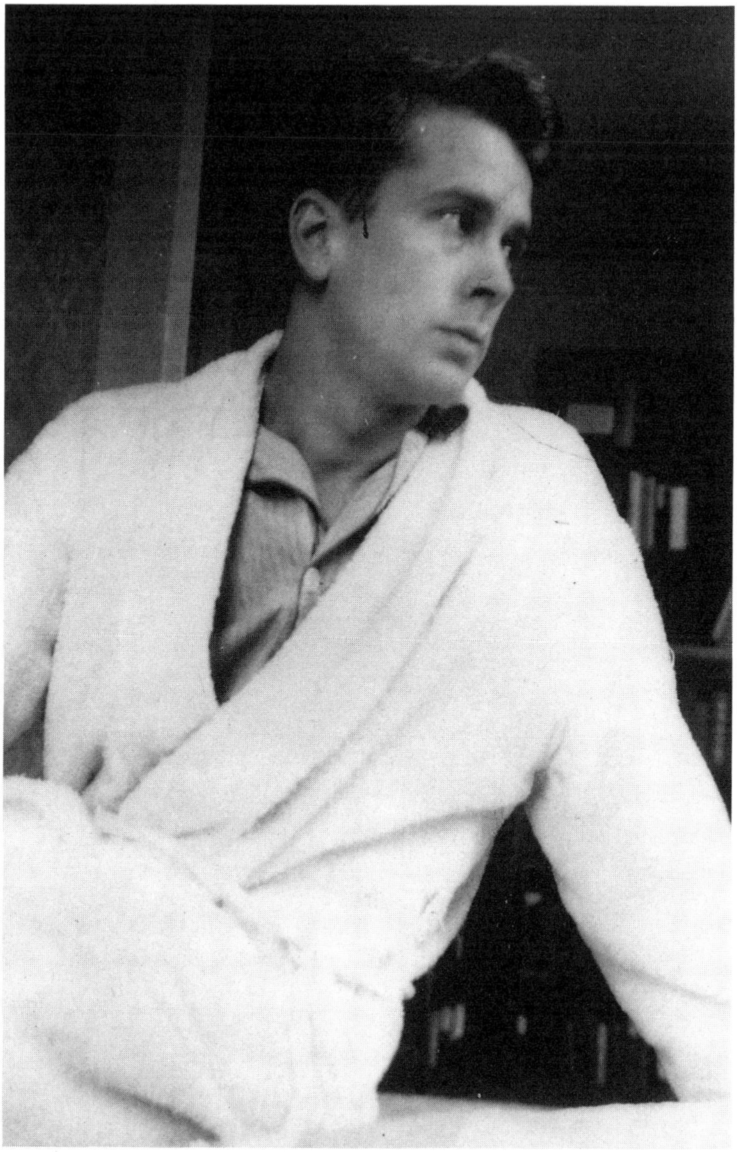

Albert Erskine in 1937 or 1938, in a photograph taken by Porter.

Photograph taken by George Platt Lynes in May 1939. Lynes made many portraits of Porter that showed her at her most glamorous.

Eudora Welty in 1941, the year in which her book of short stories *A Curtain of Green* appeared with an introduction by Porter. The inscription reads: "For Katherine Anne with love and gratitude from Eudora—as of 1941 'A Curtain of Green' (below) Introduction by KAP and 1973 now and the years in between and to come—"

South Hill, the house that Porter renovated in 1941 and lived in for less than a year.

Porter on a balcony with George Platt Lynes below. One of a series of parody Romeo and Juliet shots made one summer day at his house in Santa Monica, California.

Porter's nephew, Paul Porter.

Below: Porter at her desk with her typewriter, 1946, with the Buddha figure given her by her brother. Photo by John Engstead.

With novelist William Goyen, 1951.

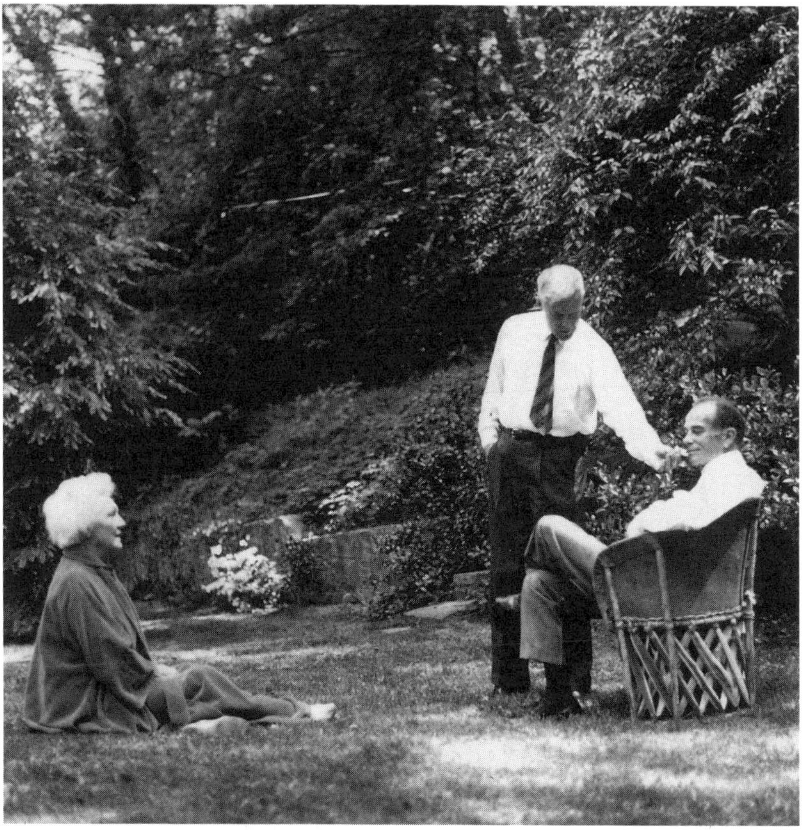

Glenway Wescott seems to be holding a flower for Monroe Wheeler to smell as Porter watches. The snapshot was taken on May 15, 1965, her seventy-fifth birthday.

Opposite, top: Being hoisted onto a tank by Colonel Glover Johns, Jr., the son of her childhood friend Erna Schlemmer Johns, 1959. The inscription on the back, in her nephew Paul's hand, reads: "*So* typical! The kind of thing about her that Givner missed—the reckless joy exuberance of letting herself be tossed up on top of a tank—'letting' indeed! she probably suggested it! I wish I knew where and when."

Opposite, bottom: E. Barrett Prettyman and Robert Penn Warren at Porter's Twelfth Night Party in 1969.

The gracious lady of literature, wearing the famous emerald ring she bought after *Ship of Fools* and a long string of pearls she bought while teaching in Michigan.

Dressed for a reading. Unfortunately, the gracious lady tried to go on being a glamour queen long after she should have.

Joan Givner standing in front of the portrait painted by Marcella Comès Winslow. An inscription on the back written by Paul Porter reads: "Joan Givner and that *godawful* painting by Marcella Winslow. Joan liked it, of course."

CHAPTER SIX

Among the Agrarians

> And all the time I was making notes on stories—stories of my own place, my South—for my part of Texas was peopled almost entirely by Southerners . . .
>
> —Porter, " 'Noon Wine': The Sources"

> Generations of Southerners have, I believe, been engaged not so much in writing about the South as in writing the South.
>
> —Richard Gray, *Writing the South*

In the late 1920s, in New York, Porter had become acquainted with Andrew Lytle, Allen Tate, and Caroline Gordon, all from the South and all developing, at that time, the reverence for the customs and the ideals of the Old South that bound them, together with a handful of others, into a group identity.[1] This group, known as the Agrarians, had grown out of the earlier Fugitives, a literary group centered at Vanderbilt University in the early 1920s composed of students and colleagues of John Crowe Ransom. Prominent among the Agrarians (often referred to by themselves simply as the Brotherhood or the Brethren) were Robert Penn Warren, Donald Davidson, Tate, and Lytle, who is described by one of Caroline Gordon's biographers, Ann Waldron, as "an unreconstructed rebel, a true believer in the Old Confederacy."[2] When Porter returned from Europe in 1936, she renewed her ties with these southern writers. The connection and its ideological underpinnings formed one of the major threads in her intellectual life and are important in tracing her political swing to the right.

How Porter moved from being a leftist radical to being an intimate of this set of rightist radicals wishing to restore traditional ways in religion, economics, and southern folk life is a complex matter, involving a set of profound feelings and anxieties relating to her home region and her early years there with her family. It was a deeply emotional linkage, which she was not alone in making. The compounding of family with region has been seen as a "strong strain in Southern thought."[3] Elizabeth Fox Genovese has observed astutely that post-Civil War southern women, in particular, "remained uncommonly concerned with the history of their region as an aspect of their own identities."[4] The issue of Porter's Texas origins and her feelings toward those origins and toward the family that she saw as having failed to supply her needs is intimately bound up with her increasing affinity with southern intellectuals and their evolving mythos of the South during the thirties.

❧ The Texas into which Porter was born was not so much a region as, at minimum, a regional duality. It still is. Part of the state was the West, a frontier place of dry grassland and a rough-and-ready style of living associated with cattle raising. This was not Porter's Texas. Another part of the state, what has been called a "plantation belt" in the eastern section,[5] was more like the South of Louisiana and Mississippi—wooded farmland populated by independent small to medium farmers plus sharecroppers, making their livelihood by agriculture and often relying on cotton as their cash crop. The idea that Texas was basically southern was emphatically argued early in the century by a member of the University of Texas faculty, Charles William Ramsdell, who insisted that Texas had "southern moorings, which made the state socially and culturally part of the South." The writers of a history of Texas intended for a more general audience, published in 1916, also asserted that Texas was "predominantly Southern in thought and feeling."[6] These characterizations, of course, suit the eastern region of the state far better than they do the areas around Abilene and Dalhart, in the Panhandle region, or El Paso, in the far west. Economically, ethnically, and in the general tone of life, these regions are utterly different. The question of whether Texas was and is more southern or more western in its traditions and culture is one that still occupies historians. Probably the most reasonable course is to declare the inadequacy of both notions: Texans "cannot place their history or their identity in the analytical framework of either the South or the West."[7] Region itself is a point at issue among revisionist southern historians, some of whom argue that there is and was no such entity as *the* South, but a collection of distinct regional entities. Still, it is important to recognize that at least in some areas, Texas was southern in character.

Porter's birthplace was in the central zone of the state where the two regions meet and overlap. What is probably more important, she was born into a family that had declined in the social and economic scale and was in the process of declining further. Hearing stories about a more prosperous and refined family past, embarrassed by present circumstances, she felt a powerful urge to transfer her family allegiances back in time, which meant transferring them eastward, toward the Kentucky from which part of the family had come. She sometimes claimed that she had been born in Louisiana or had spent her childhood there. It was not true. But her strong grandmother and her brood had apparently lived in Louisiana for a time, along the way of their migration to Texas. Moving her imagined home eastward, to Louisiana, was a way for Porter to move into the true South and at the same time into the past, to identify herself with a stage in the family history that better suited her conception of herself. It was not an unreasonable movement of self-imagining, since her Texas roots were at the edge of that part of the state that more nearly resembles the South than the West. In her teenage years she had lived for a while in the easternmost part of the state and, after her marriage, in Louisiana.

Although Porter frequently expressed some degree of bitterness toward Texas, when she wrote about the larger South, as distinct from Texas in particular, she usually (though not always) fell into a mode of celebration. In that vein she confessed to Herbst, "Its perfectly fatuous how I believe that every one would like the south if only they could see it once, gayly on a holiday." The South, she told her, was "my place, my part of the world." [8] In reconceiving her Texas background as an Old South background she also moved her political thinking into alignment with those southern men of letters (and almost all of them *were* men) known as the Agrarians.[9]

Certainly it has been common to see Porter as a southern writer, although this point, too, is debated. The distinguished historian C. Vann Woodward mentioned her in discussing writers who show what he considered a distinguishing characteristic of southern literature, an "almost obsessive concern" with the "consciousness of the past in the present." [10] Cleanth Brooks, a longtime friend and admirer of her work who also regarded her as southern, enumerated a more fully elaborated set of attributes of southern writing, all fully characteristic of Porter's fiction: "the family as a still living force," a "peculiar historical consciousness" and "sense of [the] tragic dimension" of history, "the concreteness of human relationships including the concreteness of moral problems," and "the belief that human nature is mysterious and relatively intractable."[11] Her story "He" was included by Robert Penn Warren in an anthology of short stories by southern writers published in 1937, and "The Jilting of Granny Weatherall" appears in another such anthology published in 1986—to mention only two.[12]

Reading Woodward's argument that the single most distinctive feature of the South is its sense of history, which is a history of defeat and of poverty, one recalls Porter's repeated insistence that what set the South apart was the fact that its people had grown up in a defeated land. Her essay "Portrait: Old South" (first published in 1944) opens, "I am the grandchild of a lost War, and I have blood-knowledge of what life can be in a defeated country on the bare bones of privation."[13] Certainly she came by this preoccupation honestly; her father frequently lamented the South's defeat and exploitation, and she heard her grandmother tell about hard times after the war. But in making such assertions she was also manifesting her adoption of the unitary views of southern intellectuals such as Allen Tate. Tate attributes the emergence of southern literature in the twentieth century to a powerful confluence of the local with the universal through the expansion of the southern "legend" of "defeat and heroic frustration" to the status of a "myth of the human condition."[14] This myth, with its valorization of suffering, of an honored past, and of the righteous nobility of an empowered elite, was peculiarly well suited to the conservative mood of mid-twentieth-century America.

A vision of the South's distinctiveness in defeat flatly excludes, of course, the perspective of the African American—who could scarcely have mourned the downfall of the Confederacy—and minimizes to the point of denial the voices of southern women even prior to the Civil War. Revisionist historians and literary scholars have, in Nina Baym's words, rejected the "consensus that has dominated study in American literature and history since the 1950s."[15] But it was this consensus that Porter adhered to in voicing her own version of southern identity.

During her early adult years, Porter seems not to have taken a particular interest in the history of the South or its problems except insofar as her father's insistent regional patriotism brought it to the fore. She was consciously resistant to Texas and all it meant. In those years her primary sense of regional connection was with Mexico. She liked to emphasize (or indeed, to exaggerate) the Mexican quality of her early life in south-central Texas—a quality more readily associated with the state's western aspect than with its southern aspect. At other times, however, she liked to emphasize its eastward-looking, southern quality.

She always enjoyed thinking of her forebears as being "nobly unreconstructed." Her father, in particular, she characterized as a classic gentleman of the Old South's better yeoman or small planter class, and she often mentioned that image of him in family letters. When her sister Gay read in the newspaper that a mountainside sculpture of Robert E. Lee had had its nose painted red, she was quick to share it with Katherine Anne, asking, "Wonder how Dad will take that?" It was true, of course, that Harrison Boone Porter's roots were in the South and that he shared the traditional southern gentleman's interest in literature, especially of the eighteenth century. It was true, as well, that his mother, who raised Katherine Anne (then Callie) for several years, held very strong traditional values and played the role of southern matriarch to the hilt. So Porter's claims of southern origins, at least, were well founded, though sometimes magnified. Her fervor as a Southerner was periodic; it waxed in the late twenties, reached a peak in the thirties, when her interactions with the Agrarian group were closest, and waned after that. References to the South in her letters are most numerous in the 1930s and decline sharply in the 1940s and beyond. Even so, she continued to maintain, as she did in " 'Noon Wine': The Sources," that the South was "my own place, my South."[16]

Even Josephine Herbst, who was for several years Porter's closest friend, seems to have been told and to have believed stories of Porter's life in the South that included a New Orleans rearing. She wrote to Porter in 1930, after reading a review by Tate that attributed or seemed to attribute Porter's work to her " 'southern aristocratic origin'—or words to that effect," "Now this sounds more like a Tateism than truth to me. I never think of New Orleans as the Old South to begin with." New Orleans, she continued, was "always a more European port & open to French & Spanish influences & besides you spent a lot of your childhood in Texas which is no Old South at all." Herbst's comment tells us several things: one, that she believed Porter's origins were in Louisiana rather than Texas; second, that she did not seem to question that those origins were aristocratic; and third, that she was aware of a Texas connection but did not count it as constituting southern roots. When Tate denied that he had praised *Flowering*

Judas only because of Porter's origins (having praised it, he said, because of the quality of the writing), he too seemed to leave unquestioned the notion that she was in fact an aristocrat.[17]

In her personal mythmaking, then, Porter reenacted the ambiguity of the state's identity. Probably the variance in her accounts of her roots arose from the strong duality in her work, between stories of Mexico, mostly written relatively early in her career, and stories of the Old South. She felt a need to legitimate or even to capitalize on the different groupings of work at different times, as well as a need to suit the interests of the different persons to whom she was writing. As her identification with Caroline Gordon, Allen Tate, and others of their group strengthened after her return from Europe in 1936, the griefs, the cultural heritage, and the distinctive features of the South would come to occupy a larger place in her thought and in her correspondence, and she would begin to give disquisitions on agrarian economics and the evils of northern industrialism, quite in the vein of the Agrarian group.

❧ Porter had first become acquainted with Tate and Gordon in 1927, when she lived in the same apartment building with them in New York (561 Hudson Street).[18] Ann Waldron credits them with passing on to Porter at that time the "lesson" that had recently been taught them by Ford Madox Ford, that they should not "deprecate their Southern heritage." The editors of the Tate-Lytle letters put the change in Tate's views somewhat more positively: His initial note to Andrew Lytle in 1927, before the two of them had actually met, expressed his "new-felt warmth toward the South."[19] Actually, Tate's conversations with Ford in New York did not so much initiate as reinforce his process of "reevaluating his attitude toward his rural Southern heritage." He had already, since the summer of 1926, been developing a new esteem for the South in his correspondence with John Crowe Ransom and others. That correspondence, Veronica Makowsky notes, was "the seed of the Agrarian movement," but another seed had actually come from (not been received by) Caroline Gordon, who "sang the praises of rural life" into Tate's ears in 1925 and 1926.[20] When Porter met them, the symposium that served as the Agrarian manifesto, *I'll Take My Stand,* was in its gestation period.

It was soon after her long (but not uninterrupted) friendship with Tate and Gordon began that Porter's interest in writing fiction set in the South, drawing on her memories of childhood and the stories she had heard told in her family, sharply increased. She had earlier, in 1924, written "Holiday," for which she had drawn on her retreat to an east Texas farm when her marriage to John Henry Koontz was breaking up, but because of dissatisfaction with the ending she had not attempted to publish it. Except for that attempt, her first story set in the South was "He," published in the *New Masses* in October 1927. She attended Tate's publication party for *Stonewall Jackson, the Good Soldier* in 1928 and remained on an intimate basis with the Tates for several years, maintaining her correspondence with Gordon throughout her years in Europe. It was through Tate and Gordon that she met Lytle and others in the Fugitive/Agrarian group. In fact, it would later be her friendship with Tate and Gordon that would lead to her fourth (actually fifth, counting one that was annulled) marriage, to Albert Erskine, business manager of the *Southern Review.*

The manifesto of the Agrarians, *I'll Take My Stand,* was published in 1930 and was immediately labeled curiously aberrant. In a sense, however, the Twelve Southerners who contributed to the volume were participating in the general tendency of their day among literary minds in that they were expressing their engagement with social issues and their disaffection from American society as they perceived it. After the country's precipitous plunge into the Great Depression, writers were demonstrating a pronounced turn toward criticism of the social and economic systems that had produced so appalling a spectacle of suffering and stagnation. For the most part, of course, this upsurge of social engagement was a turn toward the radical left. Daniel Aaron and Richard H. Pells, two historians of the leftist surge in American intellectual life, agree that by late 1930 there had been a "great swing leftward." In contrast with the crisis American writers witnessed in the United States and in Europe, the young Marxist-Leninist regime in Russia then seemed progressive and energetic, a "hive of happy industry," and writers in impressive numbers espoused communism as a way to set their own country on a similarly renewed path.[21] In this, of course, the Agrarians differed. They shared the leftists' perception of the ills of industrial capitalism but formulated a very different cure for those ills. Even more basically, they shared the sense of estrangement from stable traditions that was a "central concern of the modernist movement" and that powered the modernist search for order.[22] For the Agrarians, the cure for the sense of rootlessness and lack of order was not global in scope but regional and did not entail a march into a collective future but rather a return to traditional values at once individual and communitarian. It was a minority statement so far from the general trend as to be eccentric, a minority statement even by comparison with the positions of most other southern intellectual critics, who advocated a New South of industry and modernized education.[23] In only a few years, however, *I'll Take My Stand* would become one of the most discussed documents in the world of American letters. The Agrarians were the advance guard of a turn to conservatism that occurred a decade later in the wake of widespread dillusionment with the left.

As has so often been observed, the twelve essays that make up *I'll Take My Stand* vary enormously both in their literary quality and in the topics they address in formulating a prescription for the ills of the South.[24] John Gould Fletcher wrote about education, Lyle H. Lanier offered a critique of the idea of progress, and Allen Tate presented a call to traditional religion. (Yvor Winters commented that he hadn't "the vaguest idea" whether Tate was "recommending a new Civil War, an evangelical campaign, or an act of the will," but that at any rate he wished Tate "had not rushed into an agrarian manifesto . . . before getting his first crop of tobacco planted.")[25] Robert Penn Warren attempted to formulate a strategy for improving relations between the races, primarily by means of educating blacks in trades and in farming methods. Although he was firm in his insistence that blacks should have equal rights before the law, he had no desire to disrupt everything by recourse to social equality. Like the others, Warren assumed that the majority of blacks, as well as some whites, had innate limitations that restricted their role in society to rural labor. Although some few blacks might be capable of higher education, that would be, he thought, a futile undertaking, since their own society would have no place for them. He did not contemplate the mixing of the races in a single social network, but at the time accepted segregation unquestioningly.

Warren's later views on race relations in the South would be considerably different, at any rate on the issue of segregation.[26] In the mid-fifties he would "interrogate his own thought formations" in a brief monograph called *Segregation: The Inner Conflict in the South* and emerge as a gradualist—"if by gradualist you mean a person who thinks it will take time, not time as such but time for an educational process . . . I mean a process of mutual education for whites and blacks." Gradualist or not, Warren was clear in his judgment that desegregation was "just one small episode in the long effort for justice." A decade later he was even more emphatic in *Who Speaks for the Negro?* in which he proclaimed that racist evil was "implicit in the structure of the society" of the South and urged white America, North as well as South, to recognize "the justice of the Negro's demands." He prophesied that the "effect of the Negro Revolution" might prove "redemptive" for America as a whole or, more precisely, might provide the catalyst that would help Americans "redeem ourselves—by confronting honestly our own standards." Both books made Warren's rejection of racism and segregation "unambiguously clear."[27] His friend Katherine Anne Porter would never reach that position. Indeed, her marginal notations in her copies of both books emphatically reject any notion of racial equality.

Equality *within* the white race was also a concept rejected by all of the twelve who took their stand. Their conception of an agrarian society was inherently hierarchical and their tone predominantly elitist. Lytle might praise the virtues of the plain people, but he, too, accepted the idea of a natural aristocracy, regarding it as inevitable that some would become wealthier and more powerful than others because of their natural ability. That, he said, is "the common way a ruling class establishes itself." He was not uncomfortable with the resulting economic inequality, arguing that "those who accumulate great estates deserve whatever reward attends them, for they have striven mightily." The elitist foundations of the Agrarians' program were more blatantly evident in the essays by Lanier, Fletcher, and Stark Young. Young devoted his concern throughout to the "better class," envisioning a society based on a paternalistic aristocracy having "long responsibility for others" and a "habit of domination." He agreed with Fletcher that higher education was "suited to a small number only." Fletcher went to the furthest extreme, stating categorically: "The inferior, whether in life or in education, should exist only for the sake of the superior." One hears Porter echoing this, perhaps under the influence of the Agrarians, when she writes, "Eighty percent of the people of this world" are "stuff to fill graves with," and wonders what became of the onetime radical.[28]

The chief heroes of the symposium, however, were not the aristocrats of the traditional Old South, centered in Virginia, but the smaller independent farmers of the hinterland (a relocation of the true South toward Louisiana and Texas that facilitated Porter's project of linking her Texas upbringing to the Old South). Lytle took up the cause of the southern yeoman class more forcefully in his noted essay, "The Hind Tit," where he argued that the "plain people" had suffered from the destruction of the planter class, who would have provided legitimate leadership for the region. Lytle's essay was the piece that Porter singled out for praise, mingled with amusement. Little wonder: It is still marvelously readable.

Besides their shared elitist assumptions, the twelve were united in their perception that the New South movement of the late nineteenth and early twentieth centuries, with its call to modernization and industrialization, was a mistake so drastic as to constitute more a betrayal than a renewal of the South. The ordinary people of the region, Lanier claimed, would suffer if the South became industrialized, because domination by the industrial system of the North would be merely another form of slavery, "as complete and vicious as any form of outright ownership." The South should not alone, then, be tarred with the brush of slavery. The twelve were united, as well, in their belief that the cure for the South's ills entailed a return to the values and customs of a previous generation, having a culture based on an agrarian economic system and the supposedly associated agrarian ways.

Historian Frank Lawrence Owsley enunciated the central tenet of the Agrarians' cluster of beliefs in his ringing call to regional distinction, "The Irrepressible Conflict": "The fundamental and passionate ideal for which the South stood and fell was the ideal of an agrarian society." By agrarian he meant an ordered society based on a traditional, that is, not a big-business, agriculture. The other contributors to the volume supported this position in their various ways, adding to it their own particular interests and concerns, often emphasizing the contrast between the society they proposed and the Marxist system with which their colleagues to the north were becoming so enamored—despite the fact that their argument shared the Marxists' dislike of industrial capitalism. (Langdon Hammer has pointed out that Allen Tate was led to the right by the same force, "romantic anticapitalism," that led Malcolm Cowley, for example, to the left.) Herman Clarence Nixon, in a considerably drier essay than Owsley's, argued that although the South was "no longer conquered territory" it was in danger of a "conquest of the spirit" if it allowed its agrarian system to be eradicated by the forces of industrialization. He warned "Southerners in strategic or public positions" against the perils of encouraging "rapid industrialization." One of the merits of an agrarian system, Nixon argued, was the fact that agriculture had in the past "furnished the chief escape from socialism."[29]

Porter might have been expected to protest the symposium's harsh rejection of socialist principles. Interestingly enough, however, she seems to have made no forceful comments on individual essays or on the book as a whole. Lytle wrote to her on November 1, 1930, the year of publication, opening his letter with "My Dearest, and most beautiful Katherine Anne": "We have had such a fine time here [in Clarksville, Tennessee], discussing the old Confederacy and might I say its legitimate offspring, which several of your friends are serving as w[e]t nurses." He went on to promise that she would "certainly" have a copy, "all properly signed and sealed." It appears likely that she received that copy and started reading it right away, since less than two months later she commented to Herbst, accurately enough, "I think what the Nashville group hate is the industrialization of the south, which is an agrarian country, and should remain one." She went on to align herself personally with such a view, saying, "I should rather live in an agrarian community than an industrial one; I know this, but I don't think I have to be southern to feel this way. Only in the south most people do feel this way." Some seven months after Lytle's letter promising to send her a copy, she mentioned the essays in a letter to her father, adding, "Ask Gay to get you these out of the public Library. Andrew is a throw-back, and whoops her up for the Old South." Only shortly before, she had referred to her father as a "born southerner, positive product of an agrarian culture."[30] Her comment is evidence that she was making her friends' terminology her own.

Once she had, she kept it. In later years, she continued to lament that northern factory owners exploited southern labor and disrupted the agrarian way of life. In a letter to Herbst, for instance, she complained that factories in the South were "almost 100% owned by the north and the chain stores too and nearly every exploiting agency and if it is not already well known it should be." Her concern, of course, was for whites, not often for blacks, whom she, like many of the Agrarians, regarded as a burden. Throughout her life she enjoyed "darky" jokes, and she sometimes made overtly racist statements. Southern white people, she liked to say, had a natural dignity and grace. After a five-day trip to Kentucky and Tennessee in 1966, she wrote to Glenway Wescott extolling her hosts' "good manners and good voices and what an air of freedom and repose." So many Southerners, she said, lived "simply, and handsomely and generously." She could hardly bear to leave. She always did leave, of course. She enacted the critical paradigm that a Southerner "must identify his home through separation, disavowal, and contradiction," and seems to have felt a considerable measure of the "relief" and "expanding vistas" Robert Penn Warren says that a Southerner felt "when going out of the South," though not so consistently or perhaps so consciously as Warren felt it. She was very conscious of the expanding of her vistas when she left Texas in 1918, but kept persuading herself intermittently that the South was her heart's home and took pride in being regarded as one of the South's own. "I like being judged by a jury of my peers," she told Caroline Gordon. "If the southerners approve, I know its coming off properly."[31]

❧ When Porter returned to the United States from France in late 1936, she first settled in Pennsylvania and then, with Pressly, in New York. She had told her family a few years earlier that she preferred the East to the South: "I never felt at home in the south and I felt at home in the east the day I landed there." But she was again hounded by restlessness and a sense of not belonging, and she was eager to stay away from New York after Pressly returned from a job in South America because, in Tate's words, Pressly was "refus[ing] to recognize the separation and camp[ed] in the apartment like a spider awaiting her return."[32] When Tate and Gordon, who were engaged to teach at the Olivet College Writers' Conference that summer, conveniently discovered that another writing teacher was needed, they recommended Porter and she went. Afterward she joined them in a leisurely drive back to Benfolly, their Tennessee home, where they regularly entertained numbers of visitors, some of whom (such as the young poet Robert Lowell) simply dropped in. There she met Albert Erskine, with whom she seems to have become instantly infatuated, sitting up all night with him on the veranda. She was forty-seven at the time, and he was twenty-six, an even greater disparity in age than the fourteen years' difference between Porter and Pressly.

The Tates were dismayed the next spring when they discovered the matrimonial result of their hospitality. Tate reported to Lytle with wry humor:

> Katherine Anne and Albert Erskine have announced their intention of getting married in April.
>
> Let it sink in.
>
> They already have the Little House in the country, and are setting out I think it is forty trees. A year from this summer we can go down and see forty dead trees around a deserted house. Albert will say nothing. K.A. will say that she couldn't possibly foresee that Albert would develop such sinister qualities. . . . I am convinced that even this isn't the last attempt. There will be others. And they get younger all the time.[33]

While at Benfolly Porter enjoyed the country living that the Tates and their friends had been recommending. She especially delighted in making brandied peaches and elderberry wine, but found it all "too distracting" for writing. In Gordon's view, Porter "indulged" her "natural passion for domestic activity" in order to escape the rigors of writing.[34] At any rate, her interval at Benfolly led to her living once more in the South.

Earlier in the year she had made a second visit to her family in Texas, returning to Kyle, where she had lived with her grandmother in childhood. While there, she had attended the Old Settlers Reunion in San Marcos, which had so pleased her that she felt she could even contemplate living there. She may have had in mind the people she talked with in San Marcos when she reprimanded T. S. Eliot, in her essay "On a Criticism of Thomas Hardy," for forgetting that "country people were also human entities, each possessed of a soul important, however rural, to God," who have "individual dignity and importance." She left with what she described to Herbst as a feeling of "complete detachment" combined with a "pleasurable sense of possession." For once she felt herself "no alien or wanderer at all."[35]

Now the attractions of Erskine himself and the prospect, through him, of close relations with the excellent literary journal *The Southern Review,* combined with her perennial restlessness (Tate observed that she was "getting restive") and her determination to stay away from the East Coast until Pressly was safely out of the country, turned her interest to New Orleans, a city she liked to claim in her myth of herself. With $400 borrowed from Monroe Wheeler, she moved her possessions to New Orleans and took an apartment on Jackson Square, exulting to Glenway Wescott that she would be able to enjoy the city's "fine old tradition" of great music that winter. "You know," she commented, "I think people don't believe me when I tell about all the opera and the great actors I heard and saw in New Orleans when I was a child."[36]

In New Orleans she completed "Pale Horse, Pale Rider" for *The Southern Review,* notifying Wescott that she had finished the story the morning of December 3, 1937. "Nearly twenty thousand words, darling, laid neatly in rows on paper, at last. . . . But most of them were written years ago, I almost know them by heart. I began this story in Mexico, went on with it in Berlin, Basel, Paris, New York, Doylestown, and now New Orleans . . . what a history."[37] Her ability to finish the story at last may well have been stimulated by her visit to Texas, where she would once more have seen the landscape for the story's opening dream ride with death on the old family horse Graylie and the second dream's "place she had known first and loved best."[38] Almost at once she began, or returned to, work on the long-promised "Promised Land" (the material that became *Ship of Fools*). Her report to Erskine that she "wrote the first three pages of Promised Land this morning," December 7, is somewhat puzzling, however, since she had earlier mentioned working on the story while at Doylestown.[39] At any rate, it did not go far at this time. In only a few days she was expressing frustration and depression, and on Christmas Eve she left New Orleans for her sister Gay's home in Houston.

By January she had settled into an apartment on Houston's 15th Street, reporting to Erskine that although she still wanted to marry him and was finding a lawyer to handle her divorce from Pressly, she was very ill with lung problems and would not be able to return to Louisiana or undertake the rigors of a sexual relationship for some time. She apparently resumed work on "Promised Land," took on a few writing students, and projected the building of a house in the country near Baton Rouge, where she and Erskine had bought a piece of land that he worked on sporadically, clearing underbrush. Indeed, judging by her letters during the months in Houston, it would seem that her dreams centered more on the house, to be called "The Cares," than on Erskine. Marginal comments in pencil scribbled on these letters at a later date show that she suspected him of having had an affair in her absence. His own letters at the time, however, show great ardor. She imagined herself living a true rural life in the South. On April 19, 1938, in Orleans Parish, the two were married, and she began her short-lived southern idyl in an apartment in Baton Rouge. The house was never built, and it was not long before Porter had again gone north, teaching at writers' conferences and attempting to work during a period of residence at Yaddo. She separated from Erskine, so she wrote the Warrens, on May 1, 1940, but the separation had effectively occurred some time before.

Porter's temporary enthusiasm for the Louisiana setting, social as well as natural, is evident in her essay "Audubon's Happy Land," published in 1939 in *Vogue*. It was an enthusiasm that may have arisen from her reading, as well as from her relocation; she had acquired a copy of Constance Rourke's *Audubon* in late 1936, while staying at the Waterwheel Tavern, and Albert Erskine gave her Audubon's *The Birds of America* for Christmas in 1937. At any rate, in her essay she celebrates the trees and flowers of the deep South—"camellias, gardenias, crepe myrtle, fine old-fashioned roses; with simpler things, honeysuckle, dogwood, wisteria, magnolia, bridalwreath, oleander, redbud, leaving no fence or corner bare," the houses and traditions, and Audubon's birds. She celebrates, as well, the livable simplicity of the elegant old homes and their air of leisure, "the most desirable of all things we have lost." Her friends the Agrarians would have agreed perfectly; simplicity and leisure, allowing time for a life of the mind, were two of the social qualities they most prized in country living.[40]

❧ Porter's development of an affinity with the Agrarians was an emotionally useful alliance, enabling her to claim a set of values centering on stability and deep cultural roots—precisely the values she needed to compensate for her personal sense of instability. It was also an intellectual shift that helped her accommodate her earlier political radicalism to her incongruously elitist social views and her claims of descent from aristocratic forebears. In this respect, the useful aspect of the Agrarians' thought was that they rejected, at least insofar as the South was concerned, the industrial system of the North. What this meant, of course, was that they rejected the epitome of capitalism itself, precisely the target of Porter's sometime socialist and communist principles. The two ideologies, the one leftist and the other reactionary, were both critiques of the prevailing capitalist system. Moreover, one of Porter's primary emphases in even her most radical period was land reform. She came to Agrarianism, then, not only in response to some of her longest-held anxieties and familial affinities, but as a convenient progression from the communism that was becoming increasingly uncongenial to her. Her acquaintance with the Agrarian critique offered her a solution to which she could turn as her misgivings about communism deepened. Thus the drastic inconsistency in her political thought was not quite so capricious as it at first appears.[41]

Her close association with those Southerners who were then gaining influence as the celebrated New Critics—Tate, Warren, Cleanth Brooks—also reinforced Porter's existing veneration of a highly crafted literature of style. The roots of her commitment to this vision of literary art would be difficult to trace, but can be found, in part, in her urge to establish an identity that distinguished her from the crowd (in particular, from her origins) and in her need to fashion a system of values based on artifice in resistance to the perceived lack of naturally or traditionally decreed values. This was, of course, a need she shared with others of her generation such as Hemingway and Stein. The results of her commitment to such a set of literary expectations, validated by the encouragement of the New Critics, can be seen in the high standards of artistry she continued to set for herself, which conflicted with her growing desire to gain a wider audience for her work. For Tate, Warren, and Brooks, stringent standards of literary style and form became a bastion against social and intellectual decay. For Porter, they became an added impediment to the productivity she so needed.

Part of the appeal of the Agrarians was that their writings and personal attitudes catered to Porter's own deep-seated racism. The racist foundation of the Agrarians' argument in *I'll Take My Stand* is most clearly expressed in Frank Owsley's essay "The Irrepressible Conflict." Slavery, Owsley claimed, was a "red herring dragged across the trail" of the conflict between North and South; only one element in the complex differences between the two ways of life, it was too simple an explanation of that conflict. So far, so good. But Owsley's racism is apparent in the very language in which he makes his case: It is a language of infestation. He foresees "the negro race cover[ing] the North as thickly as it does the lower South." If that is not clear enough, he goes on to explain that the reason Southerners did not free their slaves at the time of the American Revolution was that by then they were so numerous and being "cannibals and barbarians" were "dangerous." "Even if no race wars occurred, there was dread of being submerged and absorbed by the black race." Obviously, he assumes his readers will agree that this is a horrible prospect.[42]

Owsley was by no means alone among the Agrarians in his views on race, though he did give the most agressive expression to those views.[43] Donald Davidson, whose essay concerned itself with the social environment necessary for the flourishing of the creative arts, would increasingly become a champion of the cause of segregation. Tate, in calling for a religion that would promote social stability, was demanding, in one scholar's words, a religion that would provide "permanent value" in support of a segregated social system. Unlike his friend Warren's, Tate's views on the subject would "show little substantive change over the course of his career."[44]

Many Southerners, of course, had long considered the "negro race" (meaning all persons of sub-Saharan African descent, with no distinctions made among different ethnic groups) not only inferior and inadmissible to white society but actually a burden to their white superiors, who had to take care of them out of a sense of humanitarian morality. Fred Hobson, in *Tell About the South*, provides a convenient summary of this particular apologetic: The well-known antebellum spokesman for slavery George Fitzhugh, author of *Sociology for the South* (1854) and *Cannibals All!*

(1857), argued that slaveowners would naturally care for slaves as "an extension of the family," thus assuming a burden instead of an asset. A governor of Virginia, Henry A. Wise, proclaimed in 1873 that slavery was "the worst curse ever brought upon the Southern people" because it entailed an "unfeasible" balance of caretaking versus profit. When Thomas Nelson Page, early in the twentieth century, presented the by-now familiar argument that slavery had been the " 'curse' of the antebellum South, beneficial for the Negro but detrimental for the Southern white," he concluded that white Southerners were a "heroic race trapped with a faulty system." The view persisted beyond the Agrarians' paternalism. In 1941, the same year anti-Agrarian W. J. Cash's *The Mind of the South* was published, William Alexander Percy, in *Lanterns on the Levee,* wrote that "if anyone suffered in the plantation system, it was the planter class," which "carried 'on its shoulders a weaker race' " and from carrying that burden lost " 'its own strength!' "[45]

Porter, too, often mouthed such views. She enjoyed citing her grandmother's statement that emancipation had freed only the slaves, not their owners. The South, she said, was a place "where your help clasps you firmly around the neck and hangs there, a dead weight of loving, childish, interested, opportunistic tyranny." As late as 1964, after having broken off her friendship with Caroline Gordon and then resumed it, she wrote to Gordon, "My grandmother remarked on hearing of the Emancipation Proclamation, 'I hope it works both ways,' but she was disappointed. The slaves were freed, more or less, but her bondage of moral, spiritual, practical, material responsibility ended only with her death; and her two old left-over slaves who refused to leave her followed her to the grave side and wept because they had lost their last true friend." This indicated a quality of the South that "these Johnny-come-latelies will never be able even to imagine." She could feel sure that in Gordon she had a sympathetic listener. As far back as 1928 Gordon had written to her from Merry Mont, in Kentucky, "My dear, you *must* come down here. You can live for next to nothing. There are still plenty of good niggers left, thank God." Gordon liked her Negroes the way she remembered them from childhood, and hoped to keep them that way: "The negroes on Merry Mont are extraordinarily uncorrupted. They still 'wrop' their hair!" She later reported to Sally Wood that Memphis had "the most wonderful niggers," meaning that one could "hail the first one that passed and get a jewel"—that is, for housework. Tate, too, blandly oblivious to the interests of the persons themselves, had expressed a hope that southern negroes could be kept in a state of backwardness until their distinctive character could be captured in literature.[46]

Porter claimed to have been "brought up in Old South ideas, but without most of the prejudices." Yet it is clear from her letters that she was deeply prejudiced and that her preoccupation with race deepened toward the end of her life. In earlier years she sometimes expressed sympathy toward blacks. For instance, when her father reported that Baby's son Breck had "killed a negro and wounded another in the longshoremen strike at Galveston while a Texas ranger," she replied that "poor negroes" were "mistreated in too many ways anyhow" and she didn't approve of his being in the State Patrol.[47] A draft of scattered notes labeled as having been intended for Glenway Wescott, possibly written in the late thirties, shows a fair degree of insight into the sources of racial prejudice by attributing it to economic anxiety: "The labor troubles," she wrote, "scare people" with the "prospect of race war and the natural violence of strikes." In the same set of notes, however, her prejudice emerges in unmistakable terms: "negro is nero in Italian and negre in French and negra in Spanish, but it's a Latin word, and we make this—and it means Black, for God's sake—if you prefer to speak English instead of Latin or French or Spanish why, go ahead but I don't see why . . . and most of them aren't black, anyhow, the disgrace of this country is that so many of them have white blood and the nearer they get to white blood the worse they are. The more bad mannered bad tempered, unreasonable—they have no right to have the things they scream for—they have done nothing to earn them and . . . they're not ready for them." At some later point, when she was going through her papers and assigned to these notes the date 1937, she wrote in above the last five words ("they're not ready for them"), "this is understatement. Speak up!"

As she grew older her racial attitudes hardened, to the point that in 1965 she could write so insensitive a comment as "no witch was ever burned in New England or anywhere else in America, and *even no Negro* except among the New England Puritans in the seventeenth century" (emphasis added).[48] She had earlier manifested similar prejudices toward other groups, but one finds less concern about Germans and other European ethnic groups as time passes. Toward blacks, however, her expressions became genuinely scurrilous, especially in her later letters to her sister Gay, where she was at her most unguarded. In a 1964 letter, after reporting on a visit she had made to the White House, she added, "I hope you are improving every day, and enjoy your life even if those worthless colored folks do, as usual, slack along on their deathless motto, *All Pay and No Work Makes Uncle Tom a Free Nigger!* I just invented that, but they can have it!" Gay had elicited this response by her own complaints about shiftless blacks. In other letters that year Porter complained of "irresponsible" colored help and "up and coming niggers." "I *cant* call them Mrs. It sticks in my throat."[49] After praising the work of a white gardener she had hired who did the work of "any four negroes I ever knew," she added, "All my help now is white—I shall never have another negro in the house, or on the place. I have put up a life time with them, but its all over now." It was a theme the two pursued in their letters until the end.

In 1968, Porter wrote perhaps her most offensive expression of racial intolerance in that it not only conveys a virulent opposition to the entire civil rights movement and to those who participated in it, calling Martin Luther King an "agitator" and his followers "a mob of thugs and hoodlums," but speaks callously of King's death. Commenting on recent riots, she told her old friend and benefactor Barbara Harrison Wescott that she was "appalled" at the paradox of King's "preaching peace and non-violence" while "methodically" doing everything necessary to cause civil violence. Part of the problem, though, had been solved: "Now he has been put out of the way." But as a result his admirers were "honoring his memory and holding memorial ceremonies, and calling [him] a martyr, etc etc, until I could upchuck."[50] It is hard to imagine a more complete failure to understand the issues, their historic context, or the significance of the changes that were then occurring.

Porter was particularly unaccepting of blacks in literature and the arts. She objected when black musicians and dancers were sent abroad as cultural emissaries and was convinced that such writers as James Baldwin attracted favorable notice only because people had been frightened into kowtowing to blacks. In planning an anthology of short stories she resolved to have "no Negros [*sic*] because of their obsessed hatred—some of them are talented, especially for men of a totally alien race who have taken on the language and some of the habits and even ways of thought of a people they consider as irreconcilab[le] enemies. All their work breathes horrible threats and insults and etc." When she was nominated for the Gold Medal of the National Institute of Arts and Letters and was enduring the suspense of waiting to see whether she would receive it, she wrote to Tate that she had been "on the list for the Nobel" since 1962 but a "Token Negro" had gotten it. (Apparently she was referring to the Nobel Prize for Peace awarded to Martin Luther King, Jr. in 1964.) "What earthly chance has [*sic*] a white southern Catholic woman of old Virginia and Kentucky families have against such a cabal as now runs things in the east? say rather a ghetto." She seemed constitutionally unable to entertain the possibility that a person of African descent might deserve such an award on the basis of merit alone. Even jazz music she was inclined to sneer at because of its link to African Americans, naming "Negro jazz" as an example of "peculiarly pointless" popular music.[51]

It would be surprising, perhaps, if a person raised in Texas at the time Porter was, living in the South through the days when racial tensions were building toward the outbreak of lynchings and labor violence that marred the early decades of the century, and then experiencing drastic changes in racial customs, were *not* infected with racial prejudice. Many Texans were intolerant of Hispanics as well. Porter seems not to have held that prejudice, but to have concentrated almost entirely on African Americans. (She occasionally made insensitive comments on Jews and American Indians as well.) One can explain it, to a degree, by her extreme personal insecurity—which is also a plausible explanation for some of the acts of backbiting she displayed toward people who were at other moments her friends. Still, after one explains away as much as one can by reference to environment and to private anxiety, much remains. It is distressing to see a person who in so many ways displayed humane perceptiveness display so inhumane a bigotry.

In another way, however, it is surprising to find these sentiments expressed in Porter's letters, because in her fiction she created black characters of dignity and complexity who would seem to imply a perspective of sensitivity and acceptance. Nannie, an important character in the "Old Order" stories "The Source," "The Journey," "The Last Leaf," and "The Fig Tree," is presented with great dignity despite the indignity of having once been called "crowbait" and a "little monkey" and sold for twenty dollars. Indeed, it is Nannie's "journey" as well as Sophia Jane's that is recounted in "The Journey," where she achieves the independence and personal authority to criticize the white judge who had once sold her, after he has unapologetically related the insult to others. " 'Look lak a jedge might had better raisin',' she said, gloomily, 'look lak he didn't keer how much he hurt a body's feelins.' " Both Grandmother Sophia Jane and the story itself accord Nannie the higher level of right and good judgment in that exchange. As for Sophia Jane, she journeys from an unquestioning acceptance of slavery and of her right to call the black child a "little monkey" and value her equally with her horse to a level of moral discernment that allows her to defy the strictures of society, voiced by her mother and her husband, and nurse Nannie's baby when Nannie "almost died of puerperal fever." Here, too, Porter's narrative voice vindicates the act, presenting it simply and naturally and attributing Sophia Jane's determination to her having developed a character "altogether just, humane, proud, and simple." The two characters journey through life to the point that each regards the other as her best friend.[52]

Only after Sophia Jane's death, however, does Nannie reach her fullest level of dignity, because only then can she discard the last vestiges of slavery, her role as "the faithful old servant Nannie, a freed slave." She becomes "an aged Bantu woman of independent means, sitting on the steps, breathing the free air."[53] In giving Nannie her proper tribal identity, rather than a racial label blurring that specificity and one that would implicitly assign to her the stigma of inferiority such labels have historically carried, Porter releases her from the social system that would limit her authentic power and dignity, now fully evident as she inhabits her own place with the impunity of independence. One would be hard-pressed to find an image of the older black woman, seen from an external vantage by a white narrator, that more fully validates her as an individual and as a social icon.

Uncle Jimbilly, as well, who appears briefly in "The Journey" and "The Last Leaf" in subservient roles, is given great power and authority in "The Witness," where he is the title character (although Miranda, too, is a "witness" in that she witnesses, in Jimbilly, the aftermath of slavery). Jimbilly is presented in somewhat comical caricature, but his witness to the inhumanity of slavery, which he describes in mythmakingly horrendous terms, is not undercut. He is the voice of a cultural memory that whites have found it all too convenient to suppress. Dicey, of "The Circus," is also presented sympathetically, as a person of formulaic and rather comical lamentation who nevertheless, in the last analysis, shows enormous patience and kindness to a child. Given the way in which Dicey's wish to see the circus is ignored and her services simply taken for granted, one might read the last line of the story—"Dicey ain't mad at nobody . . . *no*body in the whole worl"—as irony, indicating either that if Dicey is not mad it is because she isn't thinking very clearly or that she *is* mad at a deep level that will someday come to the surface. And if Porter were a different writer either of those readings would be plausible. But in Porter's hands, this line means simply that she has forgiven and is prepared to go on giving what is expected, a moral status that may be stereotyping at some level but is also a status of virtue and dignity. All of these three characters, then, are presented with far greater affirmation than Porter's personal comments on African Americans would lead one to expect, though neither Jimbilly nor Dicey achieves the level of dignity accorded to Nannie.

In addition to these published works, which address the issue of race indirectly through their portraits of black characters, an unpublished, uncompleted work tentatively titled "The Man in the Tree" addresses the issue directly.[54] Unfortunately, the manuscript is in such a state of disarray that it is difficult to be very certain of Porter's intentions. Narrative point of view shifts from one section to another, and the forty-eight-page manuscript breaks off and starts over several times. One factor, however, is constant among the different fragments. The central concern is with a lynching and the discomfiture of white characters as they attempt to maintain their accustomed relations to blacks in the wake of this horrifying event. A scholar who has thoroughly examined the rough typescript has termed the main theme a "mutual victimization of the races,"[55] but the theme of a woman's distance from her community is also sometimes emphasized, providing a note of continuity with the Miranda stories, especially "Pale Horse, Pale Rider" and "Old Mortality," and with what might be called a Laura/Miranda story, "Flowering Judas." Maria, as the central character in "The Man in the Tree" is sometimes called, thinks at one point, "It was all too mixed up, too cr[u]el and unreasonable and nobody should be asked to live in such a place and under such conditions." She is haunted by fear, not of the potentially vengeful blacks who live around her, but of the whites who have committed this crime, whom she must now regard as murderers.

At some points in the story Porter brings in her old notion that the master class is the true slave. "For they drain her life, and take all her supplies and resources, and are a horrible burden on her goods and"—significantly—"her conscience." But her notes to herself also emphasize Maria's "sense of guilt" and how she "tries to justify her self by remembering how good [a]ll her family had been to the negroes." At this point Porter asks herself, "Shall I put here Dad's always tipping his hat to the old negroes" and "Grandmother's boast that no negro had ever been formally whipped on the place?" (The supposed virtue of this absence of formal whippings is considerably vitiated by her qualifying statement, "the most was a blow with a small stick for the men or a good hearty box on the ear for the women.") Clearly, this story would have been, as the manuscript calls it, a story of the family. The lynching is a crime committed practically in the family.

The view of the South presented in "The Man in the Tree" is obviously very different from the one Porter espoused in many of her letters as well as in published essays and stories. It might reasonably be regarded as a view that she tried to keep repressed, that reflected deep-seated feelings of guilt for her participation in racial injustice and for misrepresenting both the South she knew and her own place in it. One of the beginnings of the story expresses such a sense of group guilt in its first words: "The man in the tree hangs there, a reproach to and a [w]itness against his murderers, and these are not [o]nly the men whose hands put him there, but many others who believed they were his friends. It is something I know well and remember with shame as if I had done it." The notion of group guilt is one that she would reject in connection with the persecution of Jews and other groups in Nazi Germany, when Herbst suggested in a letter that "we are all guilty . . . the world is guilty in its greed and indifference." But Porter seems to accept such an idea here.[56] At several points, she noted as a possible title for the story "The Never-Ending Wrong," the title she ultimately used for her memoir of the execution of Sacco and Vanzetti.

One would like to believe that the views expressed in this uncompleted manuscript represent, in some respects, Porter's real racial attitudes; that she understood that the system of racial prejudice and injustice evident in her sometimes-beloved South was indeed injustice and that all who participated in it, whether actively or passively, shared a real measure of guilt. Unfortunately, there is another uncompleted manuscript that makes this interpretation impossible.

Also found in the Porter Collection at Maryland is a set of drafts and notes labeled "The Negro Question." These are as forceful in their expression of racial hatred as "The Man in the Tree" notes are in their expression of grief and guilt. Bearing her typed name on their first page, the notes start out in what seems to be a fairly enlightened way. She expresses satisfaction at having seen, when she "returned for a visit to Texas and Louisiana after rather a long absence," a change for the better in the living standard among blacks. Many seemed to have better jobs than they had had when she lived there, and they shared to a greater extent in the American standard of living, for instance, driving their own cars to work. Their children were "better clothed and better fed. It was not the Millenium [*sic*], by a long shot, but it was all going in the right direction." But her satisfaction in the material progress of blacks is vitiated, even on this first page, by two endorsements of segregation: The Negroes, she notes, had "their own moving picture theatre" and, as a group, were "staying reassuringly black." What can this mean except that she, the representative of the white master class, is satisfied, "reassured," by these black people's willingness to stay in their place, not to mix carnally or in any other way with whites?[57] "I am one of those," she avows, who believe that both races are "better for not mixing at all."

One could scarcely expect Porter to have been greatly ahead of her time in her racial attitudes. Separate but equal was still the accepted standard until the Supreme Court's verdict in *Brown v. Board of Education* in 1954. But she showed little realization of how unequal separate facilities and separate standards almost always were, and her expression of limited, indeed bigoted, attitudes toward blacks is, in this set of notes, especially crude. She goes on to denounce the "fallacy of modern egalitarianism," asserting that equality "quite simply is something that exists between equals" and that the notion that "if the lower can drag the higher down to his level, that somehow gives him equality, or even superiority over the higher" is "foolish." Her terminology begs the question, of course, with its assumption that whites are inherently the "higher" and blacks the "lower." She has no patience with people who decry the African American's condition but say nothing about the American Indian, "who is much worse treated by his government and his society." This sentiment does not lead her to conclude, however, that the Indian should be treated as an equal. "He is of course a savage with no written history or literature—but so is the Negro."[58] Contrary to what is expressed in "The Man in the Tree," she here denies that she feels "one trace of guilt because my grandparents and all my known ancestors were slaveholders." All that meant, she repeats, was "their slavery to slaves."

The draft labeled "The Negro Question" begins as a roughly typed manuscript and ends in a set of scrawled notes on irregular slips. Near the end—in terms that inescapably recall the scrawled note in Joseph Conrad's "Heart of Darkness"—she drew a heavy black line and entered, before drawing another heavy black line, the following: "They were savages and all they Brought to this Count[r]y was their Savagery. Their former good manners were the manners taught them by their white masters. Sometimes with the whip." It is hard to resist the inference that the isolation of these curt sentences by those heavy black lines represents their encapsulation as her definitive statement. If so, the tortured sense of guilt she expressed in "The Man in the Tree" was well deserved.

❧ Porter often referred to herself as "homeless." At times she applied this sense of homelessness to her feelings about the South, saying she had "lost [her] birthright" by leaving and had become "a stranger in a strange land" when she returned. From Europe, for instance, she wrote to her sister, "I am having a time persuading myself ever to come home—if I can call any place there home, because the truth is I never had one—I never really felt at home anywhere, and least of all when I was a child. God, that was strange country indeed, and sometimes I think I must have dreamed it."[59] At other times, however, she enjoyed claiming that she was a true Southerner and that the South was and always had been her own true place. She was enamored of other places at other times, deciding variously that the place she found most congenial for a permanent home was Pennsylvania, or Connecticut, or California. But her enthusiasm for the South (despite her occasional complaints that she would not be able to bear living there) was more persistent than any of those.

One of her major outbursts relating to her identity as a Southerner was prompted by a comment made by her friend Eleanor Clark. Porter lamented to Albert Erskine that Clark had "manage[d] to praise me at the expense of my South" and the fact that she was southern. That was "damned embarrassing and I don't deserve it and it makes me uncomfortable." It was true, she added, that she felt "rather generally and amply southern, rather than 'regional' whatever that may mean, and I see no reason why I should not write about any kind of person or any part of the world I know enough to write about, nor why I should adopt any attitudes or sets of beliefs because some southerners have so adopted them, and in the long run I mean to think feel and write as I please, and say what I believe, the same as I have from the beginning." Her right to do so was, of course, among Porter's most strongly held principles and had been the primary sticking point that caused her to back away from the Communist party. She continued, "I am not in the least afraid of not being southern, since I am, born, bred, and for a hundred fifty years. If I am not quite according to pattern, still it remains and no one can change it that I am one kind of product of the south."[60]

Even after she left Erskine and returned north, settling in New York in the only house she would ever own, her occasional incursions into the South for speaking or teaching engagements would revive her sense that this was where she belonged. For the 1958–59 academic year she was at the University of Virginia and at Washington and Lee. She initially found Charlottesville so delightful that she spoke of making her permanent home there. Before her stint was over, she was impatient to leave. But during the time she worked there she enjoyed, as she did at most places, excellent rapport with the students. One of these, Richard Dillard, now a professor at Hollins College, recalls her as having been "gentle and sweet, very kind to a shy, overweight boy." George Garrett, now on the faculty at Virginia, met her when she came to Hollins shortly after the publication of *Ship of Fools* and found her charming. She took off her big emerald ring, told him to notice how heavy it was, and said, "That ring is *Ship of Fools.*" She had him wear it during the rest of the evening.[61] What was happening during these intervals was that she was enjoying playing one of her favorite roles, that of the southern belle.

The Agrarian movement of which Porter was a tangential part was not, in the final analysis, so eccentric a phenomenon as it at first appears. Like the surge of leftist politics among artists and intellectuals, it was a reaction against the perceived disorder and rootlessness of life in the 1920s and 1930s. Powerfully anomic social changes became blatantly evident in every country of the Western world in the wake of World War I, which contributed enormously to the acceleration of a great variety of reactive movements that had already had their beginnings before the outbreak of hostilities. Among these were the spread of political anarchism, syndicalism, and communism and the rise of aesthetic modernism. All these phenomena shared a sense that the societal accelerations witnessed in the early decades of the century were not so much changes as revelations of the corruption of the old ways. The apostles of revolution had recourse to more drastic forms of change as a means of eliminating such corruptions. The Agrarians constituted another reactive search for a way to be rid of the same ills; but they chose a different way of going about it. Rather than planning for the elimination of a defunct order, they sought to restore what they saw as a more valid order from the past. Rather than blaring forth their message in a designedly crude language signaling their allegiance to the workers (as Mike Gold called on hoboes, steelworkers, miners, and sailors to do in the pages of the *New Masses*),[62] they adopted a language of decorum signaling their allegiance to an old-fashioned aristocracy.

Whether in fact the Agrarians offered a genuine return to the past or only the embrace of a past they posited in their imaginations is a serious and by no means simple question. As historian Fred Hobson has pointed out, even Thomas Jefferson, surely the fountainhead of agrarian philosophy, had supported, as president, a "'due balance between agriculture, manufactures, and commerce.'"[63] The Agrarians' proposals may have been more radical than conservative. Perhaps this is only to say that they were, in a classical sense, reactionary. In any event, this means that they were more akin to those of their contemporaries who were proponents of leftist projects than they would appear to be.

Porter joined in this intellectual project partly by accident, through becoming acquainted with several of its leaders, and partly because of her own need to find a point of stability in the historical flux that so unsettled her life. She had tried leftist politics and had been unable to adhere to its ideological demands, particularly with respect to free expression in the arts. She had tried Roman Catholicism, but without the depth of conviction that would make her affiliation with the church a major part of her life for more than intermittent periods.[64] She had tried and would continue to try sexual adventurism, but had paid a price in self-disgust and in the loneliness that resulted from having been unable to find an accompanying steadfastness of indulgent love adequate to her need for replacing the love her father had withheld. In the 1930s she tried agrarianism, both as an ideology and for the sake of the set of friends it afforded her. We can see in her relation to the Agrarians' project of traditional southern values both an expression of her own distinctively unsettled personality and an embodiment of the uncertainties of the time and its casting about for resolutions of those uncertainties.

CHAPTER SEVEN

From Radical to Moderate: Pulling Back to the Center

I have gone here and there, looking too for understanding, trying to know something of the causes of the disasters of our times.
—Porter to Josephine Herbst, April 8, 1938

When Porter returned from Europe in 1936, she was in the process of pulling back from the left. She would still get "right out and marc[h]" with her "old friends the proletariat" on May Day, and soon after returning (or perhaps shortly before), at the urging of Kenneth Durant, she would join the Communist party–linked League of American Writers. Cyrilly Abels, later the managing editor of *Mademoiselle* and Porter's agent, was executive secretary of the League in those years. In 1938, Porter contributed to the League's *Writers Take Sides: Letters about the War in Spain,* a statement of opposition to Franco. But she dropped her membership in 1939, possibly because she realized that identification with leftist groups was getting more and more dangerous.[1] The direction of her political thinking was clearly rightward. In this she was only slightly ahead of the great turn back to the center that occurred among American writers and intellectuals at the end of the Red Decade, as she had been slightly ahead of the great number who turned to the left at the start of the decade. By late 1939 the "retreat from Moscow," in Daniel Aaron's words, "seemed to be motorized."[2]

Porter had become tired, perhaps, of hoping for the new classless society. Also, she had become comfortable in the friendship of people like Allen Tate and Caroline Gordon, enthusiasts for conservativism and orthodoxy, and Barbara Harrison Wescott, monied, cultured, and safely liberal. She was disillusioned by the Moscow trials of 1936 to 1938, after which she could no longer center her political ideals on an image of the forward-looking Soviet Union—which, Aaron points out, had had far greater influence on American writers than the actual Communist party. (The *New Republic* had what has been called an "unabashed romance" with the Soviet Union.)[3] By 1938 her disillusionment was so great that Herbst was moved to protest, "I can't believe with you that those who long for a new world and a different, want only personal power." Porter had witnessed, too, the battles among factions on the left and the insistence of the committed few that maintaining a party line was more important than freedom of artistic expression and artistic evaluation. The party in the thirties "envisioned art as a weapon in the class struggle." But for Porter art had to maintain its own values. This was one issue on which, wavering as she was, she drew the line, and she never ceased to draw it.[4]

❧ Porter's political thinking between the time she left Mexico in 1931 and her return to the United States in 1936 had continued the pattern of hope and disillusionment so evident in her Mexican years. When she went to Europe, although she doubted she could ever be a "real communist," she had still considered herself "what Trotsky defined as a 'Fellow traveller'" and had wanted to go to Russia to see for herself what was "really going on." At isolated moments at any rate, her idea of going to Russia was apparently a fairly firm intention. In a letter to Malcolm Cowley written about this time she said that Eisenstein's assistants had given her letters to friends in Berlin and Moscow and she was to buy cosmetics in Berlin to take to "sisters and such" in Moscow.[5]

In Germany she quickly made contact with Communist circles, going by TASS offices to arrange a meeting with party leader Johannes R. Becher. She reported to Herbst that she told Becher, when he asked whether she was a Communist, that she was a fellow traveler. Apparently she disagreed with Becher's estimate of Mike Gold, editor of the *New Masses;* she defended Gold as the "best worker" among the "Comrades" in New York.[6] She was taken about and "introduced to a few nice dens where the comrades gather" by Herbert Klein, a "communist sympathizer" and newspaperman. She planned to do some writing, she said, for the periodicals *Linkskurve* and *Die Rote Fahne,* which she identified as "Communist magazines." *Die Rote Fahne* was in fact the Kommunistische Partei Deutschlands daily, and

Linkskurve, which in 1929 and 1930 carried on a debate about the nature of proletarian literature that would later be replicated in the *New Masses,* the *Saturday Review of Literature,* and *Partisan Review,* was the organ of the Bund proletarisch-revolutionärer Schriftsteller. She told Cowley that she was writing two chapters "for a grammar they are getting up for the Young Communists' School here."[7] No more is heard about the plan to go to Russia, however, except from Pablo O'Higgins, who, already in Moscow, seems fully to have expected Porter and Eugene Pressly to join him there.[8] O'Higgins wrote glowing letters about the advances toward a classless society being made by the Soviets, with occasional comically rueful comments about his difficulties with the language. He advised them to bring "at least 10 grammars for morale [*sic*] support."[9] By the time she had been in Europe nearly a year, however, she was putting the idea in the past tense. In a letter to John Herrmann she wrote, "You remember, maybe, that for years I was simply on the verge of going over and trying to become a party member."[10] "Was": The verb measures the change in her intentions.

Porter's letters provide abundant evidence of her inner debate over whether to take up party membership. John Herrmann, among other friends, did. In the mid-1930s he would be involved with the Ware Group, which would play an important role in the Alger Hiss case. Eugene Pressly apparently did not. Her "Blonde Young Man," she told Herbst, was "Communist but not a party member." The question was clearly a difficult one for her. "I know where I stand," she mused, "without any argument or the shadow of hesitation. . . . But can I be a Communist? I mean by this a working party member, for I refuse to think of any kind of compromise . . . Well, can I? For I must be sure." She was quite sure, at any rate, that it was possible to be communist in one's leanings or principles without being a member of the party. As she explained, "I can't argue against something in my bones that simply is for the Revolution and dead against the other side." Party membership, though, was "another thing," a "very small item, but an important one." "Let the party members do the organizing and the managing," she argued, "and the nagging and the rule-making. That's all very necessary. And let them keep their faces shut about things they don't understand." Among those things that they did not understand was, of course, literary art. But it is clear that she considered joining the party and at times felt, as she wrote to Herbst in January 1932, that just a little more and she would be "a good Communist."[11]

The date of this statement is interesting in view of her assertion in *The*

Never-Ending Wrong that she "flew off Lenin's locomotive and his vision of history in a wide arc" shortly before the execution of Sacco and Vanzetti, in 1927. Such retrospective reconstructions of her political evolution are to be taken cautiously. The fact is that when she went to Europe in 1931 she was still, at times at least, a communist sympathizer, caught in an uncertainty so profound that it complicated her life for years. She avowed or disavowed communist leanings depending on the occasion and the identity of her correspondent, and she would continue to do so for some time. In 1932 Caroline Gordon recognized Porter's leftist political bent in a cryptically comical verse note to Andrew Lytle: "Katherine Anne is a plumb flurry of sentiment / A bas la bourgeoisie!"[12]

Within only a few years of telling Herbst that she was close to becoming "a good Communist," Porter would be drastically minimizing her earlier interest. Her correspondence from the late 1930s reveals that she was not only wavering and pulling back from her pro-communist sympathies, which had never meant support for communism as an organized political movement so much as for its political ideals, but also beginning to disavow her own earlier stands. She confessed to Pressly in 1936, "Well, its true you have been pretty Russian, and so have I, in our moments," but those moments were passing. Pressly, who seems to have waged a long private struggle between his political predilections and his State Department career, asked pensively if they shouldn't at least pay membership dues to the Civil Liberties Union so there would be at any rate "that much accomplished." Apparently in full expectation of her agreement, Monroe Wheeler could write to her, speculating about Archibald MacLeish's attitude toward the Trotskyite *Partisan Review,* that MacLeish was "not a Communist—just a Liberal, like all the rest of us," and not be contradicted. In fact, when Porter wrote back she was careful to label the *Review* communist and to distance herself both from it and from the party: "Let MacLeish help them raise the money. He is a member of their party, and I am not."[13]

Even beyond this date, however, Porter would waver in her position. By 1938, like many others, she was distinguishing between approval of communist ideas and approval of Joseph Stalin, whom she regarded with as much distaste as she felt for any dictator. She wrote to Herbst about her "change of attitude towards, not Communism, but Stalin, the Party, and the Party Line," deploring "the same old bloody murder, the same old religious persecution." She added, "If that is Communism, believe, I am not in the least a Communist. But I do not in the least believe that is Communism." Does this mean that she was still privately a fellow traveler, only lying low until the present regime passed? Perhaps. Herbst reported sadly, in a letter that must have crossed Porter's in the mail, that she felt "as dismayed as you about the Russian trials although I am much more dismayed by other conditions, which I do not understand."[14] The two also pondered the political bent of the *Partisan Review,* which Porter had earlier discussed with Wheeler. Herbst mentioned in September 1937 that she had heard the editors of the reconstituted *Partisan,* Philip Rahv and William Phillips, say they meant to write to Porter to solicit a piece. "Unfortunately," Josie commented, "they have become very Trotskyite and I am afraid that political slant is so strong it will influence everything." When Porter replied, several months later, she conceded that the *Review* was Trotskyite in a "weak-kneed" way. "I mean to say, if that's the best support he can get, God help him." She went on to clarify her position in a way that leaves it more ambiguous than ever: "Insofar as they are opposed to the present reign of terror of Stalin, I am for them. But that does not mean I am for Trotsky."[15]

In early 1938, however, she wrote to the editors of the *Partisan Review,* saying that she believed it was a "fine magazine" and she would hope to have a story in it soon. She had not been at all "disturbed," she said, by the magazine's "political tone." After citing a controversy from the January 1938 number in which it appeared that the *New Masses* had "refused to print" William Carlos Williams unless he "boycotted" the *Partisan* and had actually misrepresented certain comments of his by taking them out of context, she attempted to clarify her political position: "Let me tell you frankly, I am not a Trotskyist, but I am not a Stalinist, either. (According to the *New Masses* line of reasoning, I suppose this makes of me a Fascist, or a Hitlerite, or an advocate of lynching, or a capitalist, or an anti-Semite, or a person who beats children. Oddly enough, I am none of these things, either.) And some of the reasons for this, after all my years of intense sympathy with the Soviet regime, are given very clearly and sharply in Gide's *U.S.S.R. Reconsidered.*"[16]

Porter had acquired André Gide's book in 1936, the year of its publication. Her marginal annotations show that she read it carefully and agreed in viewing recent developments in the Soviet Union—as well as the recent behavior of Communist party members in the United States—as a betrayal of communist principles. In the January 1938 issue of *Partisan Review,* Gide published an article called "Second Thoughts on the U.S.S.R." in which he declared that the Stalinist regime had in effect turned its back on genuine Marxism. The article made it very clear that the disaffection from the Soviet Union he had announced in his book was not a matter of turning against communism. Denouncing the rise of a "new bourgeoisie," the frequent travesties of justice leading to deportations, and other iniquities, he declared that the U.S.S.R. had "betrayed our hopes."[17] By avowing her agreement with Gide's position, then, Porter was making a public statement of her continuing support of communism as a theory and an ideal as well as her disgust with the Soviet system under Stalin.

To her old radical friend Herbst, as well, she continued to avow her belief in communist principles. "Josie, you know well that the original aim of the Russian Revolution was the best thing that had happened to the mind of men as to social and governmental theory, in all the history of social theory." The Revolution, however, had been "betrayed" by demagogues and dictators. Stalin, she believed, would not rest until he had "wiped out every trace of Lenin in that revolution except the embalmed corpse in the Kremlin," and if he dared he would "have Lenin's corpse tried and shot as a traitor." Once again her answer was free expression: "This is much too much of a subject to try to settle in one evening, or even in one life time, Josie; I just mention it, to show where I stand, did stand, shall stand, in this question. I have never been thrown off for one hour by the current argument which insists, in effect, that political parties and social theories are more important than art, and that the artist owes his duty to propagandize for his side." That principle, she explained, was why she was turning back to the South, which meant to the Agrarians. The southern people "still read a poet without inquiring too deeply into his politics."[18]

As we have seen, however, her alliance with this supposedly disinterested group turned her attention to more issues than pure literature. She adopted, at least to some degree, a sociopolitical agenda of conservative elitism when she aligned herself with the Agrarians.

❧ From her earliest awareness of the growth of the Nazi party in Germany, Porter regarded fascism as the greatest danger in world politics. She felt, she said, "a contempt for Hitler that made my contempt for some Mexican politicians seem like pure affection and respect by comparison." But it was not Hitler alone she disliked on the German political scene. She found the German people generally averse to democracy, recalling some years later that when she told them the American Constitution guaranteed the freedom to criticize the government they "disliked the idea intensely, every one of them. 'That is no government,' one told me, severely."[19]

By mid-1932, as the Hitler contagion became increasingly evident, she fretted over reports that he was "about ready to demand Nazi rule."[20] Comparing the mass meetings she witnessed while in Berlin, she found similarities between the Communist rallies and the fascist rallies, but always regarded the tight organization of the fascists as a dangerous quality. Her greater sympathy with European Communists was evident in her indignation at their suppression by the police. She might deplore equally the tendency of both political machines to impose thought control as well as crowd control, but she saw the Communists as being on the side of social justice, whereas the Nazi party was utterly wicked as well as dangerous.

War quickly began to seem inevitable. Even before she left Berlin for France and Spain, in early 1932, she was worrying to Pressly that war was "just over the horizon." Pressly, while working as a translator at disarmament conferences in Geneva several months later, agreed that the prospect was alarming. The delegates, he thought, would "go home puffed up and satisfied about the nothingness covenanted," having pledged the "greatest possible reduction in the scale of world armanents," but it would all be just words. "We'll all continue to develop the possibilities of planes capable of lifting unbelievable quantities of bombs loaded with incredibly powerful explosives, deadly bacteria, horrible gases, liquid flame . . . ." The catastrophe would come.[21]

In the same year in which Pressly wrote this fearful prediction, 1932, Porter's new friend Glenway Wescott published a book he called, on its dedication page, a "troubled record and unexpected result" of a trip he had made to Germany the previous August and September with Barbara Harrison, Monroe Wheeler, and George Platt Lynes. A travel book of linked essays, *Fear and Trembling* circles continually back to the theme of impending war. "Who is not afraid? Who wants war?" Wescott asks rhetorically. The answer, it seems, is in part those who will profit from it, the munitions makers. But a larger cause, though felt, cannot be identified. Some unnamed something was "dragging them and the rest of us stupidly, nervously along in the direction of [a] war" that "everyone talks of" and "all the journalists write of." For this war, he warns ominously, the Great War was "just a good beginning." The prospect appalled him, but he regarded it as an inevitable recurrence of the "old martial rite."[22]

By 1934 Porter was writing to her family that people in Europe talked of "nothing but war." It was coming "as sure as fate," she thought. Also aware of the "old martial rite," she regretted that her "young nephews" would "crack their heels together for joy at getting a chance to be officers and wear those uniforms they have practically been brought up in." After Wescott and Wheeler went back to New York, she continued to hold on in Paris despite recognizing war in the air "like a plague germ." She and Pressly would stay until even family members in the United States were warning them of the danger.[23]

In her foreboding about the likelihood of another war, Porter shared the feelings of a great many American intellectuals and ordinary citizens of her day. A mood of isolationism had mushroomed in the United States as the Great Depression settled in, but awareness of the threat of a "foreign war" was widespread and uneasiness mounted as, after 1931, "preliminary reverberations" were felt.[24] These reverberations would grow steadily stronger. An observer even slightly alert would have seen ample reason for anxiety in Japan's invasion of China beginning in 1931, the rise of National Socialism to power in Germany in 1933, the attack on Ethiopia by Mussolini in 1935, the remilitarization of the Rhineland in 1936, the beginning of the Spanish Civil War the same year, and Germany's annexation of Austria and part of Czechoslovakia in 1938. George Orwell, Stephen Spender, and other literary figures warned of war throughout the decade. In 1933 and 1934 the U.S. ambassador to Germany, William E. Dodd, Jr., confided his anxieties about the likelihood of another war to his diary. Janet Flanner, the Paris correspondent for *The New Yorker,* who may have had the widest acquaintance of anyone among American expatriates there, was aware as early as November 1933 that the French were "frightened over the possibility of impending war." Porter's friend Robert McAlmon also felt "potential war or revolution in the air" in the Paris of 1934.[25] By the mid-thirties, the fear of war had closed in on both Americans and Europeans all across the continent and in England.

From August 1938 to January 1939, Louis MacNeice, in England, wrote an extraordinary poem about the "heavy panic" of the civilian as war neared. MacNeice's words from the opening of Canto V of "Autumn Journal" convey the uncertainty and discouragement of Britons attempting to deny what was happening even while the moment-by-moment news reports haunt their awareness:

To-day was a beautiful day, the sky was a brilliant
  Blue for the first time for weeks and weeks
But posters flapping on the railings tell the fluttered
  World that Hitler speaks, that Hitler speaks
And we cannot take it in and we go to our daily
  Jobs to the dull refrain of the caption "War"
Buzzing around us as from hidden insects
  And we think "This must be wrong, it has happened before,
Just like this before, we must be dreaming;
  It was long ago these flies
Buzzed like this, so why are they still bombarding
  The ears if not the eyes?"
And we laugh it off and go round town in the evening
  And this, we say, is on me;
Something out of the usual, a Pimm's Number One, a Picon—
  But did you see
The latest?

As the poem progresses, preparations for war become unmistakable. In Canto VIII MacNeice marks the Munich Conference, which gave the Sudetenland (Czech territory) to Germany in the hope of achieving, in Neville Chamberlain's famous words, "Peace for our time."[26]

In the United States, attention and concern were focused primarily on domestic economic problems, but alongside the prevailing isolationism there existed a widespread anxiety that war was coming. Concern over the armaments industry as a threat to peace was manifest in the Senate's May 1934 ratification of the Geneva Convention on International Trade in Arms and Ammunition and in Implements of War. By 1935 legislation to ensure American neutrality was introduced by several senators, and pacifists "began to speak freely of the likelihood of another war, and set to work to keep America out of it."[27] By 1936, when Porter visited the United States for the first time since 1930, the *New Republic,* a good barometer of left-liberal thought, was full of articles, reviews, and letters about the uncertain international scene. The National Convention of the Socialist Party endorsed a Keep America Out of War Committee in May 1937. Even in 1939, on the verge of war, public opinion clung to hopes for peace (though by then the Keep America Out of War Committee had split into factions and was "moribund"). About 60 percent of all American citizens believed the United States *could* stay out of the threatening war in Europe, but a far stronger majority (95 percent in the Gallup poll of April 9, 1939, and

84 percent on May 3, 1939) believed the United States *should* stay out. The shift to support of the war effort came quite late, only when the United States itself was directly threatened.[28]

As the political choice in Europe seemed to evolve into one between fascism and communism, Porter had found it easy to choose which side she supported. She was horrified to see traces of fascism in the United States after she returned from France and felt "amazement" and "desolation" at seeing a parade in Boston with "banners, slogans, Up Fascism, up Mussolini, with songs and marchings."[29] But by 1940 her backpeddling from communism had carried her so far that she could feel undecided which she hated worse: "We really do have a choice of evils now, conscious or unconscious. I don't choose either." In 1942, in contrast to earlier approving references to Trotsky (such as her report of having taken Trotsky's part in a conversational debate with the Communist leader Becher, in Berlin), Porter wrote to Freda Kirchwey, editor of the *Nation,* that Trotskyites were "marvellously adroit in their manipulation of human sympathy" and the "American Communists of either wing" were "treasonable." Unlike Kirchwey, Porter adopted the popular rhetoric that presented fascism and Stalinist Communism as being virtually the same.[30] On the whole she was antifascist. But when it became clear that the governmental choosing of sides meant active military involvement, when the choice had to be between supporting or opposing war, it was more difficult for her.

She had long enjoyed proclaiming herself a pacifist. Opposition to World War I had been one of the primary principles of socialist groups in America during the war, and in the immediate postwar years, if not before, she had been associated with those groups. Certainly in "Pale Horse, Pale Rider" she associated herself retrospectively with the antiwar dissenters of the Great War years. Shortly after her arrival in Berlin in 1931 she expressed her hope that "anti-imperialist[s] and all objectors to war" could "get together again[s]t the strain of the next war." Pacifism, hatred of war, was one of the qualities in Thomas Hardy that she praised, at least by implication, in her 1940 essay "On a Criticism of Thomas Hardy": "War, he believed was an abomination, but it recurred again and again, apparently an incurable ill."[31]

As long as the coming conflict remained hypothetical, she was loud in trumpeting her pacifism, announcing that she could tell her potentially martial young nephews one thing: "Aunt Katherine Anne is planning to spend the rest of her days in jail, if necessary, rather than miss a chance of saying just what she thinks about war, now and hereafter." The approach of war was a "huge and shapeless horror" that could have been avoided; that was "the almost unbearable thing." As war became a reality, though, it became more and more difficult for her to maintain this stance. An undated but clearly prewar letter written to Caroline Gordon displays her inner conflict between hatred of war, on the one hand, and the kind of simple patriotism that included hatred of democracy's enemies, on the other. "I am a pacifist in this our day and time," she avowed, but would support "a defensive war." "I am against Fascism, and against Hitlerism, and Stalinism, and I don't care much for England's Imperialistic policies, either. This country, such as it is at present, is all we have. . . . For this I would say, yes, I suppose we must fight. It certainly looks that way. Very well, up and at 'em. . . . But I still think its a waste and a horror."[32] From pacifism to reluctant support of war in a page. Clearly, she was deeply conflicted over the issue.

In the dark days of 1938, as she hung by her radio for news on Hitler's move into Austria, she continued to refer to herself as a "convinced pacifist" who viewed the war as "criminal in all its aspects."[33] But she would not maintain this position for long. Although she felt oppressed by the start of war, her hatred of Nazi Germany engendered in her a surprisingly fervent patriotic zeal. Her quick change was paralleled by an equally dramatic about-face on the part of her husband, Albert Erskine. In mid-1940 he avowed his unwillingness to kill French, German, or anyone else. Any good that might come of the war, he predicted, would be in spite of the fighting rather than because of it, and he for one would refuse to participate. He declared his firm intention of speaking out in opposition to the war effort, even if it meant going to jail. Four months later he reported that Registration Day was two days off and there was nothing to do but go register and hope for a lucky number.[34]

Porter's turn toward patriotic support of the war was powered, in part, by the fall of France in 1940. Her emotional bonds to France were strong, and she felt the surrender of Paris as a tragic event. She wrote Erskine from Yaddo, where she was trying unsuccessfully to work, "I am stunned quite literally in a way that never happened to me before. I can't sleep, I can't work, certainly I don't think except intermittently, and some things I know well are very important seem for the moment not worth even remembering." Two days later she admitted, for the first time, to a warlike impulse in that if France had crushed Germany she would have "felt the whole war well justified. Yes, that is true, that is the way I really feel. I am at that point now where I would be quite willing to die myself in the next effort to beat them." In her next letter she disavowed the "terrible things" she had said "about violence" and reasserted her pacifism: "You know what I really believe, and what I have always to come back to." And on the same page she described how the Czech cook at Yaddo waved her butcher knife and said Hitler would pay. She hoped the cook was "a good prophet."[35]

Her views on the war would continue to waver. Her longtime support for Roosevelt (one of the earliest marks of her distance from her more radical friends, many of whom resisted his appeal until late in the decade) weakened under the pressure of his aggressive pro-British policy. In the election of 1940 she preferred Roosevelt to the Republican Willkie as a matter of course, but said that she would "like best to see Norman Thomas in." Thomas, of course, was the Socialist candidate, and the Socialists had long been the party of pacifism. "What do you want to bet," she asked Erskine, "that when and if we go to war, Mr. Thomas is going to jail? Mr. Debs, Socialist candidate, did the last time, and maybe that is one tradition that won't be broken." But after the fighting began she became a hearty patriot and supported the Allied war aims. In December 1941 she wrote Warren that she was now "all for this war" and felt "patriotic and united enough to go to work in a munitions factory"—a notion she quickly discarded. A month later she told her younger sister that she was still a pacifist in the sense that she knew war "settles nothing, and could always be prevented if those in power did not stand to gain by it," but now she was for the war and wanted to see Germany "blasted off the map once for all. Japan too."[36]

One factor impelling the change in her position may have been her reading of Ambassador Dodd's *Diary,* published in 1941. Unfortunately, the date when she obtained the book is not recorded. But she did read it carefully and marked with double emphasis (that is, both with lines in the margins and by underscoring) his warning that "pacifist peoples" needed to "act courageously" in order to avert the "subordination of all Europe to Germany."[37]

As the war went on, Porter, like many others, was greatly troubled by what she saw as its death knell for all humanity, not the combatants alone. It "reache[d] in insidiously, here and there," distorting all of life. She began to feel that her entire life had been shadowed by the consciousness of war, beginning with the "disgraceful" Spanish-American War, of which she had been barely aware, and extending probably for as long as she would live. "Imagine," she wrote Donald Elder, "it has really taken me all this time to understand that recurring war, every generation, is the constant, the one thing we can depend upon in this world." She envisioned a day, long after the end of the present war, when the United States and Russia would face off.[38]

Despite her misgivings, Porter published in 1942 a patriotic piece called "Act of Faith," a rallying cry couched in tones of quiet determination. After noting that "the people who are doing the work and the fighting and the dying, and those who are doing the talking, are not at all the same people," she announces, in crisp understatement, "By natural sympathy I belong with those who are not talking much at present." She must, then, be one of those on the side of working and fighting. After this stiff-upper-lip beginning, she launches into effectively couched emotional rhetoric: "The boys by the thousands are getting off to camp, carrying their little two-by-four suitcases or bundles. I think of this war in terms of these people, who are my kind of people; the war they are fighting is my war." It is a war to save the country "for democracy," which means to "create an economy in which all the people were to be allowed access to the means and materials of life, and to share fairly in the abundance of the earth"—a definition that sounds curiously like a socialist democracy. But then this egalitarian theory of political economy also turns out to mean "the importance of the individual man and his rights in society"—a hint at a more conservative, less collective ideal than she and her left-leaning friends might have contemplated a decade or two before.[39]

The distance she had come since "Pale Horse, Pale Rider," written only six years before, can be measured by contrasting her praise in "Act of Faith" for the sturdy good people who "do their jobs and pay their taxes and buy War Savings Stamps and contribute to the Red Cross and China Relief and Bundles for Britain and all the rest" with that story's condemnation of coercion to engage in these very kinds of activities. To be sure, the war-effort rhetoric of her essay may have been only public posturing. Many writers responded to the call to patriotism by contributing their persuasive powers in wartime. In a 1945 letter to her sister she sounded more like the Porter of old, deploring "various semi-official groups" beginning to "trespass on private lives to the extent of telling them how much 'voluntary' contributions they are to make to this and that, and all such things, well, it smells like totalitarianism to me." At any rate, she did not adopt the kind of florid rhetoric Miranda had despised in the speeches of the "four-minute men" who intruded into all phases of public life during the period of U.S. participation in World War I. On that her attitude remained the same: "Blind, fanatical patriotism which shouts and weeps is no good for this war."[40]

The extremity to which Porter's patriotic support of the war effort carried her is evidenced in her attitude toward the defeated Axis powers after the war, which can only be described as one of vengeance. Toward Germany, her vengeful feelings were fueled by years of dislike. After Hitler's defeat she felt no urge to forgive the German people or to provide humanitarian aid. Her letters to Herbst in 1945 were so extreme in their castigation of the "god-damned Boches" as to evoke Herbst's protest. Complaining about how much it cost to send food packages to England (where her niece Ann was working with a dance company), Porter sounded off about being able to send "22 pounds a week of food stuff if you are sending it to a *German*. That is simply because we have millions of Germans in this country who are citizens in name only, no matter how long they have been here they are still Germans and natural Nazis. . . . Six million pounds a month of good food are sent by *private* senders to that damnable country, and the German belly is being filled as usual at everybody else's expense." She added, with astonishing spite, "I was praying we would keep them good and hungry for a few years, let them raise their own food, go to work or starve." When she again wrote to her sister several months later, she was still fixated on the thought of the Germans and their presence in the United States. She had decided that the music of Robert Schumann had "too much of the sickly German sentimentality in it, that dirty sentimentality that turns to foul brutality with too much ease." She added, "I do loathe the German mind in all its workings, and we have too much of it in this country; I can see it rising and sliming over everything in our national life."[41] The image of a track of slime is one she used repeatedly for various groups toward whom she felt an intense and moralistic dislike.

Porter's long-standing dislike was reinforced about this time by her reading of Sigrid Schultz's *Germany Will Try It Again,* which she acquired in 1944. She found there and marked denunciations of German militarism and an emphatic argument that the United States was being wrongly "saddled with a feeling of guilt." In 1945 she acquired Henry Morgenthau's *Germany Is Our Problem* and marked similar denunciations, as well as assertions that when Germany was asking for economic aid after World War I on the grounds of widespread hunger the Germans were "a great deal better off than a great many other peoples of Europe."[42] Morgenthau may have contributed to her resentment of relief efforts for Germany in the postwar years.

❧ Even while the war was going on, however, Porter began to have misgivings that the home front mobilization necessary to support the fight against fascists abroad might itself contribute to the rise of a domestic version of fascism. As early as 1942, she deplored the "virus" working in people so that "all the time they think they are fighting Nazis abroad, they can't even see what is happening to their own minds and the minds of their neighbor." While worrying about the progress of the war and her nephew Paul's safety "up there with the 9th Army near Julich," she berated the "scoundrels in our own government" who were "sabotaging every thing they are fighting for." By this she meant, in part, the U.S. policy of "keeping up friendly relations" with Franco in Spain. "You simply have to keep in mind," she told Gay, "that there is a Fascist movement here that we have to fight as we go." Ever since she returned from France, she said, she had worried about the "unconscious Nazism" in the United States. She saw people saying and doing things that were "pure Nazism" without "even know[ing] what it is really." Josie Herbst, while trying to dissuade her from condemning all Germans as a people, agreed that it was troubling to see the United States "still smiling on Franco" and "hold[ing] out the hand" to Argentina.[43]

The history of Porter's long friendship with Josephine Herbst is entangled with such political vicissitudes. Clearly, Herbst was the more committed and activist of the two, and her loyalty to communist principles outwore Porter's. Except for its timing, the trajectory of Porter's sympathies for the party followed a common arc; she admired, then espoused, and finally, slightly ahead of the great rightward stampede of 1939 and 1940, retreated from communist political ideology. In later years she took an aggressively anticommunist, America-first position, saying that the communists' "whole point" was to "keep the Western world in a state of disorder."[44] The extent to which her views shifted to the right is illustrated by the retrospective comments she added as she went through her papers late in her life. Many of these marginal comments point out that this or that organization was "a Communist Front outfit," having, she sometimes added derisively, "the usual manners and morals" of that group.[45]

Her apparent betrayal of Herbst to the FBI in 1942, first asserted by Herbst's biographer, Elinor Langer, and then acknowledged by Givner and

Walsh, reflects her rightward turn. But it reflects much more, and should not be regarded as a fully controlled, deliberate act of superpatriotism or of malice. Given the atmosphere of suspicion prevalent during the war years, and given her own history of involvement in the politics of the left, we might well add to the list of contributing motivations listed by Givner—loneliness, her liability to being charmed by an attractive male, drink, impulsiveness, and an unrecognized revulsion against Herbst's bisexuality—the motivation of fear. Indeed, Walsh conjectures that the FBI agent who interviewed Porter in Reno may have "intimidated" her by citing her record as an avowed communist sympathizer.[46]

As the war ended and the pressure for patriotic support waned, Porter's concern for civil liberties and her dislike of repressive domestic groups waxed. It was the age of McCarthy and loyalty hearings, and she felt "plagued" by "totalitarian repressiveness" on every side. "Damn it," she fretted, "one is either a democrat or not, and I am one, and I don't believe in censorship." It was for this reason that she had written a letter advocating that the governmental ban on James Farrell's book *Bernard Clare* be lifted. Farrell might be a Communist, she conceded, and if so he was "working for my extinction and the extinction of all like me," but the principle of free expression was more important. Even then, having distanced herself so far from her earlier communist sympathies that she would express distrust of someone she "knew" to have been a communist once in the past, she still preferred communism to fascism because it at least advocated economic justice. Attempting to walk a tricky middle line, and as a result sometimes adopting blurred or seemingly contradictory positions, she avowed that she was both anticommunist and antifascist. Like many other liberals, she "deplor[ed] the specific tactics of HUAC and the blacklisters while agreeing with their general aims."[47] But it was clear that she hated most the rising neofascism of the time and despised the academic world for having harbored fascists in their midst, she believed, almost until the very outbreak of the war. In a letter to the *Saturday Review* in 1949 she claimed that as late as 1939 "certain faculty members of a southern University were accepting medals and citations from Mussolini."[48]

In 1947, when the attention of the House Un-American Activities Committee was focused on the danger of Communism in the film industry, Porter did not attempt to maintain a low profile, as one might expect, but went on the offensive, publishing in the Westwood, California, *Daily* a barbed account of a so-called debate that had been broadcast on the radio.

In her account of the event she tars State Senator Jack Tenney, the leader of the red-baiters in this broadcast encounter, with the brush of authoritarianism, hence, by implication, fascism. Indeed, she likens the radio host's overorganization of the event to the behavior of "a little man with a sawed-off moustache standing before a crowd, lifting his hands for the applause to begin, slapping them down on the table for it to cease"—in other words, Hitler himself.[49] In contrast, she casts herself as a "Jeffersonian-Democrat" spurred to defiance by these manifestations of authoritarian control. Long a practiced essayist of great rhetorical adeptness, she turns on the witch-hunters the powerful weapons of ironic humor and understatement, charging them with bad manners. Senator Tenney, she says, "seized every opportunity to shout, 'Red, Communists,' into the microphone, whether in turn or out of it," while his opponents (also identified as a group of people who wanted to fight communism, "but not in the Senator's company") held to the "good American doctrine" of nondiscrimination on the basis of religious or political beliefs. The audience's support of the opponents to Tenney's steamroller tactics refreshed her faith, she says, in the American people. She ends with the resounding line, often quoted, that the HUAC's activities were "the most un-American thing I know."

The essay reveals what Joan Givner identifies as Porter's "abhorrence of such an act" as fingering one's friends, or even one's adversaries in a fair debate, as communists.[50] If it is true that she herself had committed that act only five years before, it may also be read as an expression of self-condemnation. Even more significantly, one must recognize that considering her various avowals of being a fellow traveler and her record of association with communist sympathizers and Party members,[51] she was showing considerable courage in taking this public stand. It is important to remember this stand and also her support of Elizabeth Ames, the longtime director of the Yaddo Artists' Colony, at the time she was being investigated by the FBI for supposed "Communist conspiracy," when one seeks to weigh Porter's apparent betrayal of Herbst in 1942. The circumstantial evidence in the Herbst affair is powerfully against her. It includes her own statement to Donald Elder, written from Reno, where the interview took place, that "the F.B.I. finally tracked me down to ask questions about friends."[52] Still, there were many factors operating in her actions at the time, and she did make courageous stands on other occasions.

As a liberal, rather than a reactionary, anticommunist, Porter was quite clear in her opposition to the phenomenon that has come to be known as McCarthyism (a much larger and longer-lived phenomenon than merely the career of one senator from Wisconsin). Again, she might well have opposed McCarthy and his ilk out of fear. But her lifelong political principles were antifascist and antirepressive. She feared and hated the "unconscious Fascists" of the United States and wrote to her nephew Paul that she was saying so in her lectures. "And then I try to explain that I too want to do something about the Communists AND the Fascists, but the Mundt Bill is not the way."[53] The Mundt-Nixon Bill of 1948 would have required registration of members of all communist and communist-front organizations.

She told Gay in 1947 that she was so disgusted with public events in the United States that she was thinking of emigrating. "At least in other places they don't call Fascism Democracy, and have people up before the Anti-American committee for criticising rotten Congressmen." With more than a little disingenuousness but entire sincerity as to the point at hand, she told Herbst that when she read about the "Communist-hunt in Washington" she remembered that Herbst was "one of the early victims." "You know I don't like Communists, the American Brand. But I hate to my bootsoles the Fascists," she wrote. "Every foul reactionary in the country is back in the driver's seat." Her anger waxed and waned. She wrote to Cinina Warren that she couldn't understand why anyone who was not a Communist would mind saying so directly. But in 1951 she refused a stint at the University of Colorado rather than sign a loyalty oath. "We're going to be made sorry very soon," she wrote, "for our refusal to reject unconditionally the kind of evil that disguises itself as patriotism."[54]

In the 1948 election, when Republican Thomas Dewey opposed Harry S. Truman, Porter fretted that the forces of native fascism were about to sweep all before them. (Political observers in Europe would agree, in the 1950s, that fascism seemed to have "migrated to the New World.")[55] She called Dewey a "little mean-eyed dough-faced Hitler" and said mockingly that his supporters looked to him as a "second saviour" who would "get this country out of the grip of labor and all those gangsters and Communists of Roosevelt days, and put the government back where it belongs—in the hands of business and free enterprise. . . . I'll bet he does it, too."[56] Her dislike for anything resembling fascism and her concern for her cherished principles of free speech and free artistic expression propelled her into two acts of minor heroism in the late 1940s. One was her public opposition to McCarthy and all he represented, and the other was her vote in favor of awarding the Bollingen Prize to Ezra Pound despite his having given aid to Mussolini during the war.

Porter's postwar hatred of groups she viewed as fascist took on, as well, a tinge of anti-Catholicism. Her attitude toward the Catholic church varied throughout her life, from the apparently perfunctory conversion after her first marriage to occasional periods of devoutness to skepticism and sometimes hostility. In May of 1947 she recalled to her sister Gay a time when Gay and her little girl, Mary Alice (who died while Porter was in Denver), had a mass said for her recovery from the flu at the Queen of Heaven Orphanage in Denver and the child "would not go in chapel until she had a veil for her head, like the other little girls, and how, when you came out she said very earnestly, 'Now mother, we've done everything we can, she is bound to get well." Her tone here is one of fond reminiscence, with no hint of distance from or mockery of the faith depicted. Less than two months later, however, she was associating the Church's likelihood of getting "a cut of public school taxes to support their parochial schools" with a series of reactionary or protofascist political events.[57] It was not a new idea. She had linked fascism and the Catholic church in Mexico in the 1920s.

In succeeding months of 1947 and 1948 her antagonism would intensify. She spoke of a "Fascist-Catholic combine" and charged that the Vatican had become the "center of power for fascism" as Germany had been under Hitler. Proclaiming facetiously her liability to charges of heresy "of one kind or another" (she always enjoyed thinking of herself as an independent thinker), she added, "And indeed, if I stay around much longer, with the Catholic Church on the one hand and the Communists on the other, they may get me yet." Above "Catholic Church" she wrote in "and Fascists." By the end of 1947 her linkage of the two forces had become attached to a friend of years back. In a letter to her nephew she accused Dorothy Day of having led "a life of crime no less," after which she "turned Catholic and is part of a Catholic Fascist organization which works unde[r] the aegis of the Franciscans, I believe; in a kind of mission in downtown New York. She is as evil as ever, but now cloaked in sanctity." She urged her nephew to "notice specially the connection between the rise of the power of the Catholic church in this country and the rise of Fascist power."[58]

The comment about Dorothy Day probably reflected a tangle of resentments. Zealously rightist Catholics had been conspicuous in public political discourse, especially in the mid-to-late 1930s, when Father Charles E. Coughlin in Michigan, emulated by Father Edward L. Curran in New York, had broadcast and written diatribes against, as one historian phrases it, "the twin dragons of atheism and Communism," with anti-Semitic "innuendoes" resembling the "malicious statements" of Nazi propaganda.[59] Even so, Porter's smear of her onetime friend reflected little reason. Dorothy Day had been a devout Catholic for years, but had also been an ardent socialist since her teens and had founded the leftist Catholic Worker movement. In Givner's words, she had "tried to join her religious faith to her commitment to communism." She is now regarded as a deeply spiritual person by the few admirers who knew her or know of her. Day played an indirect role in Porter's meeting Eugene Pressly and a larger role in Caroline Gordon's conversion to Catholicism. Gordon, who believed that Day had been praying for her since the mid-thirties, was baptized on November 24, 1947, but Porter regarded her conversion as a pious fraud. Gordon and Tate, she wrote to Wescott, "have singly and together the most irresponsible tongues in the world, the most slanderous minds."[60] It was not her settled opinion of them, only a temporary peeve. Her opinion that the Catholic church was linked to an insidious fascist movement was also temporary. It dropped out of her letters after the 1940s.

❧ After Porter pulled back from her earlier radical views, she adopted a generally liberal political stance, though not one of direct engagement.[61] She continued to insist that she was a pacifist and had always been, although she had deviated from her pacifism far enough to support the war effort against Hitler. Her views did not merely change over time, however; they were often self-contradictory. Her early radicalism and her later liberalism coexisted, whether easily or uneasily, with social views, particularly on matters of race, that might well be labeled reactionary. She deplored violations of civil liberties in the name of combating Communism, but "called for a tough suppression of the Fascists," which meant, in at least one scholar's view, that she herself countenanced "totalitarian methods."[62] Still, we have no reason to believe that Porter's avowed political convictions during her radical years, approximately 1919 to 1937, were not genuine enough at the time. She seems to have been entirely sincere when she wrote in 1932, to John Herrmann, "I know this, I am against what we have now." On the other hand, she seems to have been equally sincere in 1948 when she wrote to her nephew Paul, "I want to do something about the Communists."

The primary reason for the change in her attitude toward Communism was her sense that affiliation with the Communist party was inconsistent with her commitment to free expression in art. She had been uneasy, from the earliest days of her radical activism in New York and Mexico, about the monolithic nature of Communist ideology. She was especially concerned about control of free expression and the party's insistence on judging art not by the standards of art alone but by its adherence to a party line. Her emphatic convictions on this point appear in such writings as her speech before the Paris Conference of Writers in 1952, in which she announced that her purpose was to "celebrate our freedom of speech and thought in the arts as well as in government" and urged that the writer "shouldn't play the fool for a political party." Her concern with the threat to free expression posed by Communist ideology dated, however, from much earlier. She wrote to Herbst in 1932, "I cannot possibly agree with them about writing" and concluded emphatically, "If it were not for this one sole question, I should be a Communist now."[63] Her keenly polemical article "On Communism in Hollywood" is not so much about its putative topic as it is about how her own "Jeffersonian-Democrat hackles rose" when she observed "authoritarian" attempts to manage free expression.

The issue of Ezra Pound's Bollingen Prize in 1949 was more complex than her protest against Senator Tenney et al. in 1947, and also more difficult for her. Defending Pound's poetry meant seeming to condone his belief in the fascist system she hated. Essentially, though, the issues were the same. Again she took a stand for free speech and the integrity of artistic valuation, without regard to the politics of the artist. It was on this principle that she had earlier differed with the Communist Party in the United States, which insisted on a correctly proletarian art. When Pound was nominated for the Bollingen Prize, a great storm of controversy erupted because of his propaganda work for Italy during the war. Porter, despite her hatred of Mussolini, supported Pound for the prize simply because of her esteem for his poetry. To poet Muriel Rukuyser she explained that "in the long run, I consider that in voting for Ezra Pound I fought more nearly on my own side than I s[h]ould have done if I had voted against him." Her essay on Pound, written soon after the controversy, takes as its title his own words, from Canto 13, "It Is Hard to Stand in the Middle."[64]

Standing in the middle was precisely what she was attempting to do. It was the only ground that, in the wartime and postwar years, she considered honorable. She begins the essay anecdotally, recalling the time many years before when she and Hart Crane had read Pound together and decided that, tiresome as he might sometimes get, there was no other writer to equal him. Pound's undeniable anti-Semitism Porter dismisses (being undeniably anti-Semitic herself) with the modifier "so-called." She does not equally dismiss all of his heinous social and political views, but regards his "lapses" or "mistakes," which "would include his politics," as occurring "when he deals with things outside his real interest, which was always art, literature, poetry." She supported him for the prize strictly for his poetry. Her having done so is one of the signal examples of the integrity of her views on art and on freedom of expression.[65]

Although her essay perhaps minimizes unduly the extremity and the hatefulness of Pound's politics, it is clear from her correspondence that she did not simply dismiss what he had done. He had committed treason, "about the lowest crime there is—and he didn't even have sense enough to know it was treason until he was told." Furthermore, he "was prejudiced and had some ugly notions." But he was "a great poet," as great as either Robert Frost or William Carlos Williams, and he was "a critic who helped a whole generation of writers to find out what they were doing." For her, that was what mattered. "I voted for him as a poet," she recalled many years later. "If I had been on his trial jury I would have voted to hang him as a traitor; a man can be a great poet" without "necessarily being either a good man or a good patriot." She recognized quite clearly the irony of having supported Pound despite his fascism and immediately thereafter supporting Elizabeth Ames despite accusations of communist sympathies. Those were the times.[66]

The announcement of the award to Pound triggered a public debate in the pages of newspapers and literary journals. The *Partisan Review,* in its March 1949 issue, ran a "Comment" by William Barrett in which he asked, "How far is it possible, in a lyric poem, for technical embellishments to transform vicious and ugly matter into beautiful poetry?" In response, the May issue featured a seven-person symposium in which three—W. H. Auden, George Orwell (with important reservations), and a belligerent Allen Tate (who had been on the panel of judges)—stated positions favoring the prize, and Robert Gorham Davis, Clement Greenberg, Irving Howe, and Karl Shapiro were against the award to Pound. Porter's reaction is not on record. The arguments put forth in the symposium, however, were cogent and thoughtful ones that captured the complexity of the issue. In particular, several expressed reservations about an overly precious aestheticism that would attempt to sever "art" from experience and ideas. Porter could scarcely have read it (and she usually did read *Partisan*) and not felt the need to revisit her opinions. Several years later she marked Tate's defense of his vote in her copy of his *The Forlorn Demon* (1953).[67]

Porter's sense of the importance of free artistic expression sprang from the deepest emotions of her personal life, from her childhood in Texas when for whatever reason, right or wrong, she felt actively discouraged as a budding writer, even squelched. During those years she felt her emergent identity threatened, both by her family and by the general culture, to the point that she was impelled to leave, to get away. The similar threat posed by doctrinaire Communism evoked responses from deep within. Her conviction that the Communist artist was controlled or required to speak in certain ways was sufficient, despite her dissatisfaction with the existing political system as she saw it, to deter her from continuing on the road of the fellow traveler.

Like her earlier radicalism, then, the rightward readjustment of Porter's political allegiance can be traced in part to her Texas roots. The one thread of continuity in her shifting political views was the primacy of free speech. It was this, more than their anarchism, that prompted her to maintain for fifty long years her indignation over the execution of Sacco and Vanzetti. The durability of her concern with the Sacco-Vanzetti issue, which she had taken up when her identity as a politically engaged artist was already beginning to show some strain, may lead readers to impute to her political thinking a degree of consistency it did not possess. But in fact the wrong that in her view never ended was repression of free speech, not any specific political program or set of principles. Her sense of the wrong she had suffered in having been repressed and thwarted as an aspiring artist during her childhood and early adult years provided the emotional fuel for her commitment to the demands of a free and highly developed art and formed the essence of her hard-won identity, however much her overt political identity might vary.

❧ In her later years Porter remained a liberal-to-moderate Democrat, more of the libertarian than the humanitarian school of liberalism.[68] Obscuring her earlier radicalism, she took the posture of a distinguished public figure, comfortably giving endorsements and attending functions, and avowed her steadfast belief in individual liberties. In 1952 she was one of the six American writers sent by the U.S. government to attend an International Exposition of the Arts held in Paris by the Congress for Cultural Freedom. Tate, another of the six, said that the Congress was "the only international group opposed to Communism that means business." Though she occasionally expressed her support for labor, she was never again a collectivist or indeed an activist of any kind. When Diego Rivera sent her a form letter in 1957 urging her to raise her voice with "all artists and men of culture in the world" against nuclear testing, she did not reply but scrawled on the letter "*what* a spectre!"[69]

She was never again so enthusiastic about any Democratic president as she had been for Franklin Delano Roosevelt. After her lukewarm support of Harry Truman's candidacy for the presidency in 1948, she became excited about politics once more when Adlai Stevenson became the Democrats' standard-bearer, continuing for many years to regard him as "just the kind of man we need," with his "dignity" in public affairs. By comparison, John F. Kennedy and Lyndon Johnson seemed distant second bests. In 1960 she regarded both Kennedy and Richard Nixon, the Republican candidate, as "young toughs" and hoped they would listen to Stevenson—"Kennedy, anyway, Nixon is past praying for." Her nephew Paul agreed, calling Stevenson "our old darling." He could be confident that his aunt would be pleased by the phrase.[70]

With the advent of the Kennedy years, she was convinced that presidential politics had deteriorated. Despite her admiring essay "Jacqueline Kennedy," published after the President's assassination, she railed about the low standards evident in the White House at the time he was there. "The Roosevelts began inviting Negroes: being Democratic, of course; Truman liked low life so well he had nigh[t]club singers to the White House, and had real gangsters in his political machine, the first time the combination got in together; and *then* the country elects the grandson of a real honest to God law-abiding but God-awful shrewd saloon-keeper, and a ditto Ward heeler Boston Politician, and not only the gates are down, but the whole fence, and the stampede is really on." It is one of the ironies of her long life that in 1964, after decades of espousing pacifist principles (which, however, she was able to disregard during World War II), she endorsed Lyndon Johnson for president even as he was planning a great escalation of the Vietnam War. She did not do so, however, with enthusiasm but out of a sense that he was the better of an undistinguished pair of candidates. Though she publicly endorsed Johnson and was congratulated on her achievements by Johnson's vice president, Hubert Humphrey, she deplored his lack of elegance and wondered to her sister "just whose poverty our Mr. Johnson thinks he is fighting: not ours, certainly—the rich seem to get richer, and the poor are being helped all over the world: it seems to be the middle citizen who works for his living and tries to save something for his children that is feeding every damned beggar in every nasty little country in the world." She especially deplored pouring U.S. tax dollars "down the cess pool of East Asia." The remark demonstrates, once again, that her internationalism was somewhat less than encompassing.[71]

For the rest of her life, however visible her presence on the national scene, Porter felt estranged from public events. Although she went to Cape Canaveral and wrote up the launching of the moon shot for *Esquire,* she thought it was "horrible" that tax money should be spent in this way.[72] She shared, in fact, the disaffection from institutionalized political action that characterized much of the early 1970s period, when readers in great numbers flocked to the idea of "greening" America. She shared, as well, America's turn from working toward reformed governmental systems to dropping out, from activism for the poor to concern for the middle class. In a kind of "pox on both your houses" mood, she came to enjoy making pronouncements about the ineptness of public figures of all stripes, casting herself as elder stateswoman on the strength of her few years of life abroad and her many years of commenting on whatever came within her ken.

CHAPTER EIGHT

The Issue of Gender

> I shall one day wind up by a lone fire, with a cat and a line of books to my credit, and a reputation lost through flirtations. I foresee it.
>
> —Porter to Mary Alice Porter Hillendahl, probably 1921

> Woman has been symbolized almost out of existence.
>
> —Porter, "The Flower of Flowers"

After she returned from Europe at the age of forty-six, Porter moved into the role of grande dame or "Southern queen" of American letters, a figure characterized as being "busy with gracious ceremony and elegant appearances."[1] She surrounded herself with an increasingly glamorous circle of acquaintances, maintained a dazzling wardrobe, and, all in all, presented herself as a gloriously feminine public figure, something of a prima donna. In her many speaking engagements, she liked to come on stage bathed in "amber or rose" light, wearing an elaborate evening gown, with long gloves and flowers, her trademark silvery white hair beautifully coiffed. She wanted to make such occasions, she said, "festive," and was pleased when she was greeted with a "packed" house that "cheered me as if I were Billy Graham."[2] Flannery O'Connor observed slyly that her long gloves "interfered with her turning the pages." Gently ridiculing her fixation on attire, O'Connor also reported that during a visit to her home Porter had "plowed all over the yard behind me in her spike-heel shoes to see my various kinds of chickens."[3]

In short, the fixation on appearance that had been one of Porter's driving anxieties from her earliest days reached its fullest blossoming in her mature years. It went to seed in outbursts of fury if anyone dared print a photograph of her that was less than flattering. In 1961 she tried to get *Newsweek* to run another picture after it had printed one showing her wrinkles, and she admitted to having written a "ferocious letter" to another magazine that had printed a "perfectly frightful photographic caricature" of her on its cover. With her conspicuous glamour and her compulsive romances, she enacted a role of tortured and torturous femininity during the very years she was reaping the harvest of her long artistic development. With her narcissistic vanity and her promiscuousness, she recapitulated the fall of the southern belle from ideal to symbol of decay that Kathryn Lee Seidel locates in the years 1914 to 1939.[4] Moreover, her consciousness of her beauty and her willingness to be celebrated for it may well have handicapped her literary production.

By her own avowal, Porter had no use for feminists of the Betty Friedan stripe who came into influence in the late 1960s. Her reaction to Friedan's *The Feminine Mystique* was, " 'Oh, Betty, why don't you go and mix a good cocktail for your husband and yourself and forget about this business.' " She referred to Simone de Beauvoir's monumental *The Second Sex* as a "stupid performance" and marked up her copy with protests, mainly arguing a need for balance or moderation, a less "one-sided" view. An article she did for the *Woman's Home Companion* in 1956 retails, in her graceful way, conventional conservative platitudes about the genius of women consisting of loving, suffering quietly, and giving happiness to others. She advised women to make themselves charming and please their men. The very fact that she would publish in popular magazines like *Vogue*, *Woman's Home Companion*, and *Mademoiselle* reveals her need to cater to conventional ideas of femininity, a need that existed in tension with the absoluteness of her commitment to art. It also reveals her need for money and her willingness to seek it in the larger audience of the popular women's magazines. This willingness positions her in alliance with the feminine mass culture against which, according to a hypothesis argued by Andreas Huyssen and Langdon Hammer, male modernism defined itself through a "conscious strategy of exclusion, an anxiety of contamination by its other"—while at the same time she claimed a place among the modernist masters.[5]

In her work, however, as well as in various of her personal pronouncements, we can see that throughout much of her career Porter engaged the subject of gender roles in ways that can only be associated with feminist thought. In this respect, too, then, Porter was deeply engaged with the issues of her time even while she was, in her personal life, constrained by debilitating patterns of sensibility and behavior. She once told an interviewer that "everything" in her life had "had to do with being female."[6]

❧ In her youth Porter was apparently an active suffragist. She said as much in a 1925 review of *The Story of Woman,* by W. L. George, and more than fifteen years later in a letter to Donald Elder, and these claims are confirmed by a letter from her brother in 1909, in which he expostulates with her for her "unwomanly" arguments for equality and the ballot.[7] From her earliest days in New York, she was associated with women who were building their own careers and whose views on social relationships were unconventional. Ernestine Evans, whom she knew well by 1920, had been arrested in 1917 along with Peggy Baird Johns (later the wife of Malcolm Cowley) and Dorothy Day (who would later live either in the same building or across the street from Porter and Caroline Gordon) for picketing on behalf of women's rights. In 1924 Evans became an associate editor of *Equal Rights,* the organ of the National Woman's Party, working for passage of the equal rights amendment.[8] Moreover, unconventional sexual behavior by women seems to have been accepted in her set at the time.

Gender issues seem to have been important to Porter during her Mexican years as well. Among her papers are some sheets about the Mexican Femenist [*sic*] Council, including its program for "Economical Emancipation for Women." A rough list she made of Mexican leaders approvingly labels one the "only intelligent pro-feminist in Mexico." The socialist governor of Yucatán whom she so greatly admired, Felipe Carillo Puerto, was a staunch and active supporter of women's rights and of the equality of the sexes. In one of her earliest book reviews she characterized the feminist views of Mrs. Bertrand Russell as showing "abundant vigor and relevancy" and the male-supremacist vision of Anthony M. Ludovici as "Dodoism."[9] Yet she disliked the word *feminist,* calling it a "slimy" or "dirty" word and insisting that "above all" that term could not be applied to her. She preferred to "read her life" in "individualistic terms" rather than identify herself with a "general women's movement."[10]

Certainly Porter was not unaware of the inequities of the old ways. In another of her early reviews she wrote wittily of the woman who first "turned a realistic eye upon her surroundings and perceived that a man standing between her and the world represented not so much defense, protection, entertainment and nourishment as a mere shutting out of light and air." To her translator Marcelle Sibon she once lamented the "grim fact" that women "have always been, since the times that human history began, so badly treated by men." She understood clearly that male writers did not care to have women taking over any part of their literary prominence, and in her reading was attentive to sexist strains (for example, considering Leo Tolstoy's depiction of Natasha in *War and Peace* an act of "revenge" on women).[11] Her sense of the tormented plight of women in a masculinist culture is conveyed in the image of the racing filly in "Old Mortality." Run by her owner in a desperate race even though he was aware that she was not able to sustain the effort, the filly looked beautiful, vital, full of energy. She was well groomed, well trained. But she is seen after the race with blood coursing from her nostrils and stiffening the hairs about her "delicate" mouth—all to fulfill the role set for her by sentimental, feckless men. This has been seen as a representation of the beautiful southern belle who ran in the race for husbands at great cost to herself, covering until after she had won the fact that she had been struggling to stop the bleeding, to keep it hidden.[12]

The filly might equally well have served to represent Porter herself. As "an independent woman, a social activist, and a writer," in one critic's words, she assumed roles "antithetical to the subservience customarily demanded of southern women."[13] Yet her struggles with problems of gender and society's expectations of women, though often concealed, were painful ones which in some ways blighted her life and her development as a person and as a thinker. In this she participated in a pattern that has been seen among women writers of the South in general, for whom, as Anne Goodwyn Jones writes, "the very act of writing itself evoked . . . a sense of self-contradiction." The reason for such an inner conflict is linked by Jones to an inculcated sense of societal expectations, for "southern ladies were expected to defer to men's opinions, yet writing required an independent mind."[14] Porter's career illustrates the accuracy of Jones's assessment.

To understand Porter's entrapment in this conflict, we must return to her childhood and to her relations with her father. Harrison Boone Porter seems to have told his children more than once that he wished they had never been born, that if they had not been born his wife would still be alive. A troubling burden of guilt to impart to any child, male or female! But among the three girls he practiced the additional cruelty of showing favor to whichever one looked the prettiest at a particular time. It is easy to see that the sensitive Callie might well grow up with profound anxieties about her appearance and the insecurity of male love.

Porter's early photographs show her to have been unusually pretty and inclined to play up her beauty by means of costume or dramatic pose. In photographs taken during her thirties, she often appears sad, troubled, or world-weary—a genuine enough expression, probably, but again, often accentuated by costume and pose. In the 1930s, in Paris, she became acquainted with George Platt Lynes, an excellent photographer who became extremely successful in the fashion industry, heading the *Vogue* studios in California. Lynes recognized in Porter a model of extraordinary qualities. Her facial bone structure leant itself to striking effects of light and shadow, and she enjoyed posing in ways that projected great drama and inner force. As her name became more widely known, photographs of her taken by Lynes were published in fashion magazines (for example, in *Vogue* and in *Town and Country,* 1941). These contributed to her image as a sophisticated lady of the literary world. In Givner's words, Porter's "great beauty and elegant fragility made her seem more like a work of art than a working writer." Cultivating this image by posing for Lynes and others, she placed herself precisely at the point of tension between the traditional passive ideal of woman as a beautiful object and the active role of the maker of beauty. She said that no really modern woman would "assume female poses merely pleasing to the eye," yet she did so herself.[15]

Porter's nephew Paul recalls that when she first came back to Texas after her years abroad she impressed members of the family with her jewelry, her haute couture, and her makeup—including rouged earlobes. She had successfully translated herself into the persona she had been developing during her years away, that of the glamorous woman of the world cum artist. Young Paul at once fell under her spell and would remain so from that time on, writing charming and affectionate letters to her, tolerating her scoldings and instructions, accepting her gifts, borrowing money, but abundantly repaying her indulgence by serving as her general mainstay in her later years. In reminiscences published some years after her death he said that she had "a great talent for fun. She could be difficult, unreasonable, touchy, often just plain impossible . . . but she was always fascinating, and more often than not, a joy to be with."[16] A photograph taken by Paul in 1975, when she was eighty-five years old, shows her in a gracefully drooping wide-brimmed hat, her face turned at an angle to emphasize her fine profile and cheekbones, stunningly dressed and made up and bejeweled. It shows, too, in the photographer's careful, hovering angle and his attention to light and composition, the doting devotion she could inspire, especially in men.

Porter's relations with men were troubled and were troubling to her life. They have proved troublesome to biographers and literary critics as well in that they seem to convey a frivolousness or shallowness strikingly at odds with the thoughtfulness of her work. Flannery O'Connor commented, with her wry understatement, "I gather she has a way" with men. Porter was married, it is usually said, four times. Sometimes she said three. The truth has recently been established as five marriages. Between the first, to John Henry Koontz, when she was sixteen, and what is usually designated the second, to Ernest Stock, when she was thirty-five (and he was twenty-five), she had another brief marriage, apparently in name only, that was quickly annulled. Interestingly enough, she seems to have acknowledged this phantom marriage (or if not, another that is not yet known!) in a 1929 statement to Becky Crawford that she had then had *three* mothers-in-law.[17] She would not marry Eugene Pressly, usually counted as her third husband, until 1933.

She seems to have begun each of her marriages in a flush of infatuation, assuring her friends each time that this was the perfect match. Two years into her marriage to Pressly she wrote to Robert Penn Warren that she was "altogether cheerfully, comfortably and I hope permanently married" and that marriage "as an individual and private arrangement" could not be "bettered" when it was "really successful." Marriage as an institution, though, she thought "over-rated." Two essays she wrote on the subject reflect a similar view. "The Necessary Enemy," published in *Mademoiselle* in 1948 as "Love and Hate," defines a woman's emotions in marriage as a conflicting duality of the two. The marriage vows, Porter says, are a woman's "statement of honorable intention to practice as well as she is able the noble, acquired faculty of love," but love in marriage is dependent on conditions "impossible by their very nature of fulfillment." Marriage, then, is inevitably a flawed relationship. When three years later she again published an essay on marriage in *Mademoiselle,* she called it "Marriage Is Belonging," and her attitude seemed more positive. This time she was prepared to admit the possibility that a fair number of people, not just rare exceptions, were able to keep their marriage vows and build satisfying long-term relationships. The reason not only these people but others as well continue to try marriage is the universal need for belonging.[18] Porter herself keenly felt such a need, but was never able to fulfill it. Her loving relationships inevitably turned to bitter recrimination. She was no more successful at finding a person with whom she could feel a sense of belonging than she was at finding a place where she belonged.

Besides her marriages, she had numerous love affairs, some perhaps casual, but many of them passionate to an exhausting degree. She fell violently in love on short acquaintance, idolized the lover and idealized the relationship while it lasted, then fell just as violently out of love, denouncing the man as an abuser, a worthless bore, a cruel heartbreaker, a betrayer. It is impossible to know how often this happened. In the 1920s alone she had a torturous affair with dadaist Matthew Josephson and others with Sumner Williams, J. H. Retinger, Luis Hidalgo, Xavier Guerrero, Nicaraguan poet Salomón de la Selva, possibly the much younger Miguel Covarrubias, possibly Luis Morones, possibly Diego Rivera, probably Felipe Carillo Puerto, Chilean poet Francisco Aguilera, and Alvaro Hinojosa—at least. In 1964, at age seventy-four, she told Cyrilly Abels that her love affair with a Washington doctor had now ended with their becoming "the best and most faithful and merry of friends." As late as 1968, when she was seventy-eight years old, she engaged in serious flirtation, at one point apologizing to her attorney, Barrett Prettyman, for her "sudden attack of femaleness" while he was visiting at her house and assuring him two weeks later, "I shall love you until I die. God help you."[19] It is by no means clear what to make of the seemingly amorous tone of these letters to Prettyman. He resented and vehemently denied Joan Givner's imputation of a love affair.[20]

One of Porter's most intense love affairs was with Army sergeant and painter Charles Shannon, in 1944. She sometimes spoke as if she considered Shannon the great love of her life, somewhat as Miranda, in "Pale Horse, Pale Rider," regards her soldier lover Adam as her one true love. Givner calls Shannon Porter's World War II lover as the original of Adam had been her World War I lover. This is somewhat misleading, because there is good reason to doubt that there *was* an original of Adam, in such an emotional sense; but Shannon was real enough.[21] His status as the forbidden (married) man who was continually having to say tortured goodbyes in order to return to his duty surely enhanced the extremity of Porter's romantic attachment to him. Her friends were aware of this romance and puzzled or troubled by it. Wescott noted in his journal as late as 1949 that she had given him "another heart-breaking hair-raising account of the damage Charles Shannon has done to her—I well believe it, but of course at this point her constancy of love is almost as evil as his treachery. (What a fantastic wonderful letter she would write me if I told her this!) Her wits more addled than ever—no integrity (as I use that word, to mean the opposite of sincerity)."[22]

Unlike Wescott, Allen Tate did tell her his opinion, that the reason love had not "worked" for her was her "ambivalence of feeling," a certain "reservation which in the midst of being greatly in love prevents the final commitment."[23] The issue was not sincerity, though, so much as her complex response to the pattern of womanhood that had been inculcated in her throughout her upbringing and her experience as a woman, combined with the damage left by her troubled childhood, especially the absence of her mother and the emotional absence of her father. The roots of such neuroses are, of course, ultimately mysterious, but it appears that she developed a powerful need to prove herself in terms of the old standards of femininity, even as she recognized their speciousness and her need to assert her full autonomy by developing her intellectual and creative powers. At the same time, she needed to control, and perhaps even to punish, men.

The conflict surfaces in her exchanges with scholar Jane Flanders, whose feminist reading of her work Porter had emphatically rejected. Responding in carefully moderated terms, Flanders assured Porter that she recognized her distrust of the word *feminism* and her dislike of being labeled. No one who had read her work at all carefully, she assured Porter, could call her a feminist in any reductive sense. Even so, Flanders remained convinced that there was a strong feminist quality in "Old Mortality." She sent a working paper on Porter's early book reviews to demonstrate her reasoning. That draft remains among Porter's papers. It is marked up throughout in Porter's hand, with the word *feminist* changed, in every instance, to *feminine*. At one point she wrote a protest in the margins: "It has taken me all this time to find what is wrong all the way through with this really good study of the question. I am a woman, that is, a female, which is to say, a human female with strong feminine character. I am not anything ending in -ist. Say female, feminine, even womanly—I am *not* a member of a political or social party, but *very* feminine." She was forgetting, probably, an exchange she had had some years earlier with the well-known Hemingway scholar Carlos Baker. Commenting on that exchange to her friend Jordan Pecile, she said, "*Feminine* is a word I am long accustomed to hearing when I am being described. There is no real disgrace in the word or the state of being—it just gets damned tiresome now and then."[24] When she found herself referred to in the typescript of an interview as an "authoress," she marked out the term. She knew well enough, at that moment at any rate, that she was an author, a writer, and needed no gendered label.

Raised in a time and place in which standards of womanly behavior and appearance were highly schematic and restrictive, she gave one version of those standards in "Old Mortality": "a beauty must be tall; whatever color the eyes, the hair must be dark, the darker the better; the skin must be pale and smooth. Lightness and swiftness of movement were important points. A beauty must be a good dancer, superb on horseback, with a serene manner, an amiable gaiety tempered with dignity at all hours. Beautiful teeth and hands, of course, and over and above all this, some mysterious crown of enchantment that attracted and held the heart." The emphasis given to such standards of physical beauty and charm could only be shattering, of course, to those who did not meet them. Cousin Eva, for example, "wasn't a belle" and consequently lost out in the dreadful contest for husbands. Beyond these qualities, a woman was expected to be pure and to be outwardly dependent on a man, keeping her real strength a secret. It was assumed that she would gain her economic security from that dependent relationship, which would also give her a sense of personal meaning and fulfillment, through marriage and motherhood. Porter, however, advised her niece Ann, "Remember *always* to be on your own about money and get along on what you have gracefully and keep your independence in that and in every other matter."[25]

As Jones points out, the ideal of the southern woman had "much in common with the ideas of the British Victorian lady and of American true womanhood." In Nina Baym's words, it was "a constellation of ideas about women that were not peculiar to the antebellum South [but] took exceptional root there on account of Southern fiction," a great mythmaking force. But it was doubly potent because it was compounded with powerful emotions of regional loyalty. It lay "at the core of a region's self-definition." The image of the lady "meshes profoundly held assumptions about sex with strongly felt class aspirations, beliefs about race, and patriotism for one's homeland."[26] As we have seen, these related values were also powerful ones for Porter. A romantic myth of womanhood was not, however, confined to the South. At the time Porter was growing into adulthood the popular media—stage shows and popular songs and, later, movies—were full of a myth of loving, domestic womanhood, uneasily coexisting with a myth of the femme fatale. Soon that myth was flouted by the contrary but equally demanding image of the 1920s flapper, whose liberation was chiefly sexual, only to be restored in the 1930s. The myth of domestic womanhood was displaced again by the wartime demands of the 1940s, which brought a short-lived ideal of the selfless home-front plugger, but was again reinforced, with a vengeance, in the petticoated 1950s.[27]

A strong woman might reject the myth, of course, and rebel against it, and Porter did rebel. In one of her newspaper columns in Denver, in 1919, she criticized the "nauseating" "ideal of prettiness" the theatergoing public valued in actresses, and in other columns she praised women's boldness in taking up wartime service and in abandoning "frivolity" to pursue their real interests.[28] She would more often manifest an acceptance than a criticism of the ideal of physical beauty, but her comment on "prettiness" demonstrates that she did recognize the problem. She would have a powerful lesson in the destructiveness of the emphasis on physical beauty a decade later when her friend Liza Dallett was admitted to a hospital for psychological treatment. According to Andrew Lytle, Porter helped "persuade" Dallett to "go peacefully." Observing to Herbst that Dallett was "definitely not sane," Porter numbered among her friend's symptoms a conviction of "horrible physical ugliness" and a "horror" of her own body for any real or imagined defect.[29] Dallett's case seems to have been an extreme example of the fixation on the perfect body that manifests itself in anorexia and bulimia, disease syndromes that are now well recognized and studied.

Porter's habitual promiscuousness was also a forceful gesture of rebellion against societal expectations of propriety. But it was a gesture that merely redefined, rather than rejected, the masculine center of the myth of proper womanhood. At the same time, it was a gesture of self-punishment for her failure to gain and to hold the lasting love of a worthy husband. Her work was itself, of course, a demonstration that she did not need a man in her life in order to achieve worth and dignity and meaning. But she was too insecure ever to accept that demonstration. She had to prove to herself again and again that she could also fulfill the myth of romantic womanhood, a myth she could never reconcile with her conception of herself as an artist and superior achiever. The result was a lifelong conflict. In experiencing this conflict within herself, Porter replicated one of the great conflicts of her time as women struggled to achieve political and social equality even as they continued to carry forward a self-defeating pattern of sexual charm and domesticity.

❧ Although her affair with Charles Shannon in 1944 may have been the pinnacle of Porter's tormented romantic history, it was by no means her last love affair. Even well into her seventies she continued to become caught up in torrid romances, generally with younger men. Her turbulent affair with writer William Goyen in 1951 and 1952 especially brings into sharp relief the poignancy and the appalling waste of her subjection to this self-defeating pattern. The story of this affair merits telling because it demonstrates how troubled Porter was by her own destructively romantic mentality.

Porter's attraction to men much younger than herself was established long before she met William Goyen. The age discrepancies in her marriages to Pressly and to Erskine had been a topic of discussion among her friends, and Caroline Gordon had made the sad observation that when young men came to call on her daughter Nancy in the early 1940s, Katherine Anne was "apt to hang around and flirt with them."[30] She first met the handsome and appealingly troubled Goyen—who was also, perhaps not incidentally, a fellow Texan—in 1947, when she was fifty-seven and he was thirty-five. He became, as Givner writes, her protégé, displaying an "unabashed and total admiration of her and [a] tendency to hang on her every word" that "completely disarmed her." He endorsed a copy of his first novel, *The House of Breath:* "For Katherine Anne, this first book and beginning—written and lived in always with you and your great work as a guiding principle, a light shed over it." On the strength of *House of Breath,* which she reviewed in the *New York Times,* she supported Goyen for a Guggenheim Fellowship and an invitation to Yaddo.[31] When she visited Yaddo during his time there, in the winter of 1951, she conceived a violent passion for him.

Porter's friends were acutely distressed by the evidence that she was once again engrossed in the turbulence of a love affair that promised no likelihood of lasting satisfaction. Wescott, for example, noted in his journal that she was "romancing with W. Goyen" and commented that "no one takes a very bright view" either of that fact or of her situation in general.[32] How could they? They had seen on multiple occasions the intensity of her infatuations and the equal intensity of her misery when hopeless involvements proved to be, indeed, hopeless. They knew that the extremes of her infatuation with a man portended extremes of recrimination against that same man later. Moreover, Goyen's diffuse eroticism was at least sporadically homosexual in nature, and it could scarcely be supposed that this element of their relationship would remain irrelevant. Porter had long made clear her aversion to homosexuals, even though she maintained numerous friendships with homosexual men.

She must have been aware of the rampant homosexuality in Greenwich Village from the time she went there; New York seems to have "rivaled Berlin in its tolerance" of "drag balls" during the 1920s. But her prejudice against it is first clearly evident in letters written around 1930, while she was in Mexico. She wrote Herbst in September of that year, for example, that she was "fed to the teeth of fairies and lesbians" and hated "*the slimy feel* they give to writing and music and painting, the kind of lisp they give to everything" (emphasis added). Returning to the subject in connection with disparaging remarks on her sometime friend Liza Dallett, who had been visiting with her for several weeks, she added a note of humor rare in her comments on this issue: "Its all doo butch for bee, said the elephant's child."[33]

Homosexuality was widespread on the Mexican scene—witness the frequency with which it was targeted in newspaper cartoons—and Porter was deep in one of her most insecure periods. She may have felt threatened, too, by one or more lesbian overtures. Peggy Cowley refers jocosely to her having "an ardent desire for no passionate females." At any rate, she was unsettled, then and later, by persons of ambiguous gender—"not-men, not-women, answerable to no function of either sex," as she wrote in her essay on Gertrude Stein. To be sure, she was not alone in her aversion. Caroline Gordon's daughter recalls her mother's similar intolerance of homosexuals, even though she, like Porter, befriended them as individuals.[34]

A pervasive but complex homophobia was characteristic of the cultural scene generally. Like members of distinct ethnic groups, homosexuals were commonly and openly made the targets of demeaning jokes and overt disparagement. A letter from Malcolm Cowley to Porter in January 1931, for instance, relays a "fairy cafe" joke he had heard. The flamboyantly open male homosexuality of Berlin and of Paris in the 1920s and 1930s, which Porter encountered when she went to Europe, was not merely an expression of newfound liberty but frequently an expression through parody of hostility to women. As such, it naturally made her uncomfortable and increased her intolerance. If such open expression of what had been decorously hidden was characteristic of the time, however, so was a reactionary impulse that reinforced the groping for secure masculinity after World War I. Literary modernism, in which Porter was closely though not centrally involved, may have meant in many ways "resistance to the norm," whatever the norm was, but it also "reinforced the normative" (for instance, in T. S. Eliot's essay "Tradition and the Individual Talent"), and it was, as Shari Benstock observes, "indelibly" marked by misogyny, homophobia, and anti-Semitism. Moreover, the powerful influence of Freud among intellectuals of the time and the activity of the scientific community in general in defining homosexuality as an illness contributed to a prevailing homophobia.[35]

When Porter's troubles with Hart Crane erupted into an already troubled scene before she left Mexico, she fixed on his scandalous sexual behavior, denouncing the "*slimy* cattiness of sexually perverted men" (emphasis added) and saying that they made her sick. "I'm all over the juvenile idea that one must be broadminded in these things. Let any one who wishes to be broadminded hop to it. I'm not."[36]

Indeed she was not. Her antipathy toward homosexuals was evident in her correspondence for the rest of her life, even in comments on two of her dearest friends, Wheeler and Wescott, whose relationship was long and mutually supportive. She was vicious in her assessment of known homosexual writers Truman Capote, Tennessee Williams, and Somerset Maugham. Even E. M. Forster, whom she generally venerated, did not escape castigation on this score. Her copy of Forster's *The Longest Journey* is marked in one place "Oh, the dainty homosexual touch!" and in another, "And what about sex, which you have helped to defile?"[37] Why Porter had such an antipathy toward homosexuals is, of course, difficult to say, but one component may well have been her sense that homosexual men were beyond her manipulation and control, and hence a frustration of her need to punish men for her father's neglect.

The same antipathy evident in her comments on Capote, Williams, et al. colored her relationship with Goyen. The letters of the two make harrowing reading, but provide an important resource for understanding Porter's struggles with romantic love and sexuality. From the first, their shared identity as serious writers was a component of their romance, both as an enhancement of its intensity and as a potential disruption. Goyen confessed in January 1951, soon after the visit to Yaddo that initiated their affair, a sense of its being "wrong that our love-letters should be in type; yet with one's fingers most of the day on the keys, it is quite natural." Three months later, as he continued to press forward with his second novel while she complained of his absence, he reminded her, "We are *great lovers* because we love *in work, too,* and out of work our love comes, and because of it. In this way 'staying away' from each other is joining each other—and honey when we really, finally join, we *join.* You know this." She agreed, replying that he "must be absolutely free" and so must she. Exchanging reassurances of the preciousness of their brief times together, they adopted, as would perhaps be inevitable for two linguistic virtuosos, a language of elaborate, even ingenious passion, borrowing figures of speech from one another and elaborating on them. He claimed to wait for their next meeting "quietly, purely, like the star of chastity I found in East House" at Yaddo. Replying, she took up the star image in expressing her confidence that they would "sometimes, somewhere, somehow . . . be together again, and under I hope a happier star than this."[38]

An ominous quality, however, quickly entered their letters. Porter relayed a story she had heard from Donald Elder concerning a friend of Elder's who had picked up a young man, who proceeded to steal the friend's car. She labeled the incident "Notes on Life as it is led by those under the thumb of the Male Eros." "Really," she commented, "it sounds as sordid as an episode, almost any episode, in the life of Auden. I'm sure its no worse than what happens if one goes around picking up women, it just seems worse to me." To have made such a comment knowing, as she said she did, that Goyen had lived as a homosexual was both unfeeling and a clear indication of her hope, perhaps unrecognized at the time, that she might redeem him to normalcy. He was perhaps equally unrealistic, however, in wishing that the two of them could "somehow, maybe, take a little house together on some shore, live primitively, I in shorts and shirtless, barefoot, hours on the beach, hours at work in our rooms, sun and sleep and good exercise." Implicit in this hope is a wish for her to take care of him domestically—not a role she was ever willing to undertake for long. His imagining that the glamorous and intense Katherine Anne Porter would ever live in such a primitive and isolated beachcombing way proves that he did not understand her very well or that he wished to make of her someone she was not.[39]

By April she was caught in the familiar throes of alternation between separation/blame and return/reconciliation. In a letter marked "not sent" she complained of "a strangeness in the air of the distance between us" and begged him not to "punish" her for saying so; then, in only slightly less loaded terms, she complained that missing him had caused her "an inordinate amount of suffering, mysterious and shapeless." The problem was his effort to maintain distance; he had not come to New York from Yaddo as often as she had asked, even when she planned a birthday celebration for him. She claimed to recognize that he was "very naturally absorbed" in his own interests, but she was affronted by it nevertheless. Indeed, she seems to have been affronted all the more because he *was* writing. Goyen, at any rate, believed that her inability to write "at all" during this period, while he was working productively, generated hostility. He would read his stories to her, he said, and she "listened *murderously*"; "really she could have murdered me."[40]

After he came to New York for a brief, intense visit in early May, she claimed to feel "quietened" in her heart. But only two weeks later he departed for Texas, ostensibly for a short visit. Once again she cast her displeasure as loverly impatience: The hawthorn, which her birth date made "her tree," was a "dark fated tree, and one of the fates it visits upon its children is 'enforced chastity.' God help me—will you not save me from that? And hurry!" But the two weeks in Texas stretched into months, and she suspected that he was pursuing a former male lover who had married and moved to Taos, New Mexico. (Goyen did go to Taos in 1952; he had received a Guggenheim Fellowship and spent it there working on a stage version of *House of Breath*.) "There are seeds of wrong in this situation," she scolded, "and they are in you." She accused him of continuing to have homosexual urges. Only a few days later, she begged, "Simply out of your love forgive me for whatever I have written to you that offends you. I wish I knew what it was, and why you took it so bitterly"—a statement requiring almost incredible degrees of willful imperception.[41]

By mid-June she was making telltale use of the slime image she characteristically used for any issue toward which she felt intense moral repugnance, especially homosexuality: Stephen Spender's "sexual perversions," she told Goyen, left "their snail's trail over the arts." From this point on, although there were occasional apologies and expressions of love, their letters became increasingly bitter. She made accusations and told him not to write to her any more, then asked forgiveness. By September, when he had been gone from New York for four months, she was writing distraught fragmentary notes, one after another, most of them unsent. In one of these she said that he had "hurt" her in "so many ways" that she could "no longer count them, and almost to the death."[42]

The last letters in the file are wrenching. After Porter wrote that she realized "the bridges are all down, and the last river has been crossed" and urged that they be "easy in our hearts now, we can't harm or disappoint each other any more," Goyen adopted her bridge metaphor (as she had earlier adopted his star metaphor) in an apparent effort to reach a humane end: "Forgive my weaknesses and my failures, all my errors; and, darling Katherine Anne, if the bridges are down and the rivers crossed, we knew the building and the crossing, we set about it all like good and trusty beavers and I think we done the best we could." But she would not let him off so easily. "Honey, don't you get *too* confused and cloudy out there on that there limb. We didn't build on single thaing, not even enough to make a good ruin." The word *honey* and the exaggerated rural idiom were characteristic when she wished to convey bitter scorn. Over the next several months she accused him of telling intimate details of their affair to others and of holding her up to ridicule, and turned on him the full blast of her abomination of homosexuality. "Bill in the beginning, I knew you had perverted yourself with men for so long, and really had followed your true inclinations, that you could not understand what happens in the natural love between a man and a woman. And yet, I did not think it hopeless." She continued, "You remarked once that sodomy was very subtle . . . I wouldn't know." In the next to last letter in the file, as if to inflict all the damage she could, she added an attack on his writing: "Just keep out of my way, and forget my name and where I live. And write your horrid little lies about what happened as you please; scumble everything up in that mean, ungenerous mind of yours; masturbate with words as you do in other ways; do you not know why I cannot write anything about your work? I do not feel up to a treatise on the subject of self-abuse."[43]

Incredible as it seems, after this spiteful outburst, Porter's last letter to Goyen, so far as the McKeldin collection gives evidence, is a tranquil message of ongoing love implying a recognition that she was sometimes in the grip of a disturbed emotional nature: "Bless you, my darling, and we'll see each other soon away from all scenes and memories of disasters and disappointments and tears." Her forgiveness was not permanent, however. In 1961, in a marginal annotation in her copy of Goyen's *In a Farther Coun-*

try, she called him "the most utter liar and traitor in every relation I have ever known."[44]

It is little wonder that the sketch of Porter left among Goyen's works in progress at the time of his death, part of a work dealing with the influence of six women on his life, is cloaked in a gesture of anonymity. The short sketch "At Lady A's" is developed largely as a monologue, a flood of verbiage spilling from her mouth. Depicting Porter through his impression of her own style, he shows her, in rapid succession, expressing her adoration, reminiscing about her years in Paris, expressing her love of "goddamned" good wine, lamenting the debasement of women, lamenting the debasement of the English language, deploring Jews and homosexuals, expressing a wish to die, and exhorting him to take himself in hand and be the man he ought to be. To quote just that part: "If you'd just *listen* to me, I don't know why you don't listen to me—now I'm talking like your mother, honey, but I don't feel about you like a mother, you understand?—and get this idea out of your head and grow into the man you were meant to be, what did your mother and father do to you when you were young that you haven't grown into the man you were meant to be? What did somebody do to you? Honneeee! There's not a thing I can do for you, you won't listen to me, you won't let me tell you something, I can't do a thing in this world for you, hon-neee! You won't let a thing alone until you have killed it . . . oh honneee! hon-neee! Drink this good wine."[45] The passage reads like a pastiche of their letters. One can only guess what their talk was like.

Porter's turbulent love affair with Goyen was perhaps the most intense of her life in its extremes of ecstatic outpourings and poisonous accusation. But it was a difference in degree, not in kind. A later romance with a young naval officer followed much the same pattern. Porter was sixty-nine years old at the time and he twenty-eight—probably the most extreme difference in age of any of her romantic involvements. The record begins with expressions of breathless excitement and joy and, just as one would by now expect, quickly proceeds to accusations. The tone of succeeding letters fluctuates between infatuation, tenderness, flirtatiousness, and bitter anger. At times she demands that he stop writing to her, after which she pleasantly continues their correspondence. Over the years, as their relationship rather surprisingly settled into an ongoing friendship, Porter enlivened her letters with comments on literature and art and often addressed him by a favorite pet name, Giordano. Then again she could turn vicious and accuse him of inability to love and of having "an atrocious attitude towards women, and towards sex itself." As she typically did with her husbands and lovers, she accused him of disrupting her work. Men always, she complained, did whatever they could to disturb the quietness of her life, so necessary for writing. Interestingly, in one of the later letters, in which she playfully asks whether he will still remember her in, say, the year 2020 and help others celebrate her birthday, she shaves five years off her age—again displaying her intermittent adoption of stereotypical femininity.[46]

❧ As this survey of only a small portion of Porter's amorous history indicates, she was caught, to her own harm and that of others, in the toils of conventional conceptions of women as beings whose lives are defined by romantic love. The causes of both her extreme involvement in her love affairs and her extreme revulsion against them once the inevitable disillusionment came could be adequately explored, perhaps, only by a capable psychologist. It seems clear, however, that her behavior is to be explained in part in Freudian terms, by the insecurity springing from a sense of abandonment by her father, leading to an urge to punish men, a need for romantic affirmation, and a resultant measure of self-disgust. One result of her bondage to this emotional and behavioral pattern was that she was able to achieve very little personal stability or tranquillity. Her life was buffeted and her work disrupted by the turbulent feelings and impulsive actions that resulted from falling violently into and out of love. Glenway Wescott, whose insight into Porter's character was often very keen, observed in his journal that her "relations with young men" made a "tragic story" and led "to the devil and to silence."[47]

Wescott was particularly well qualified to comprehend the torments of literary unproductivity; after *Apartment in Athens*, 1945, although he began several novels, he was unable to complete them and suffered agonies of self-accusation. He pondered in his journal the puzzle of Katherine Anne's inconsistent character, commenting at various times on her vanity, her impulsive changeableness (a quality Pressly had complained of), and her general "daffiness"—all traits we might regard as stereotypically feminine. He noted, too, her "self-pity" and "(deadly) lonesomeness" and the continual need for reassurance.[48]

Porter was notably subject to depression and even black despair. In 1948, with her work in films ended and her serious writing stalled, she wrote to her nephew Paul, "I know now that I have nothing to look forward to at all, and until now I had hope." She once confessed to Goyen that she felt there was "a great cureless suffering at the very root of my life." She would have been keenly incensed at the suggestion that this suffering might have been a primal Freudian wound, but it was clear from her own remarks, let alone the observable pattern of her life, that she never got over brooding over her childhood. Though she reproved Goyen for his "dark and bitter" vision of life, she spoke of "a place in my mind I have to guard, to shut off all thought, a dark place I dare not look into, and that is the long prospect of my loneliness which has been closing down over me for a long time." That dark place, she said, "seems like a punishment that I have brought on myself, but what did I do?" This cry from the depths implies a deep-seated sense of inadequacy or guilt. Wescott at one point cannily attributed Porter's "anger and sorrowfulness" to the fact that men had "ceased to love her" but nevertheless wanted her "to continue loving them, thus depriving her of the sense of their ever having loved her."[49] He may well have been right, but the intensity of her reaction to the loss of romantic love was rooted in an even deeper sense of loss.

During her earlier years, Porter's periods of depression were sometimes linked with her wish to gain feminine fulfillment through having a child. Although one of her early lovers, Sumner Williams, could write jokingly about the nuisance of children—that they tended to be around for such a long time and that she should not by any means have any until she saw him again—the subject was a serious one for her. In 1924 she either suffered a stillbirth or pretended that she did. The father, if indeed there was a pregnancy, may have been Francisco Aguilera, who wrote love letters to her in March and April of 1924 in which he called her Miranda. She told Genevieve Taggard that her baby was due in January 1925 and would be named, if a girl, Miranda. Whatever the truth of this purported pregnancy, it either caused or manifested deep emotional trauma. As late as the mid-1930s, although she had apparently had a hysterectomy in 1925 after a bout of gonorrhea, she continued to pretend that she had menstrual periods, even purchasing hygienic supplies. Givner writes that the loss of her uterus, "so central to her sense of feminine identity," was "traumatic" and that she "handled the situation as she did many other painful experiences—with pretense and pose."[50]

She was oppressed by recurrent feelings of betrayal, lamenting very late in her life, "I have loved so many people and they have loved me and what has killed me now is that when I have needed them they have not responded to my requests for their understanding and assistance." Some fourteen years earlier she had told her nephew, "You know how perpetually hopeful I am." There is a curious incongruity between the two statements. One might be inclined simply to accept the judgment of many who knew her that in her later years she was no longer herself. She did fall into suspicion and gloom, even paranoia, in her last few years. She believed people were plotting against her and urged old friends such as Robert Penn Warren to come let her tell them the truth of what was happening. But these elements had been present in incipient form all along. Bleak statements are scattered throughout her letters, not just in the last years.[51]

Porter's depressions and gloom did not spring from inner tensions alone, of course; sometimes they were a reasonable response to external events. She did live through turbulent times, and her family did fail to give her the emotional sustenance she needed. Often she had drinking problems.[52] Moreover, she was tormented for much of her life by financial strains. Although she received help from literary friends at various times, she was for the most part on her own, trying to make a living by her pen—a notoriously insecure livelihood. For many years her only income was from journalism and marginally literary activities such as book reviewing and piecework editing. It could scarcely *not* have been depressing. But she made her own situation worse by splurging whenever a fairly nice bit of money came in—for instance, buying clothes in 1932 when she received $400 from Scribner's for "The Cracked Mirror." While working in California in the movie industry in the mid-1940s, earning $1,500 a week at first, and later $2,000, she squandered money on expensive clothes ($1,000 for two outfits from a dressmaker who called himself Alain), a car she could scarcely drive, and a piece of land on top of a mountain.[53] At the end of that period she confessed to Warren that she had "nothing whatever to show" for her movie work, "not even a picture." When she returned to the East in 1949, she wrote to her nephew that she was "in absolute bankruptcy," without even enough money to pay her own way back, and had put herself "in the hands of a receiver." He had already instructed her on how to apply for unemployment compensation. She lamented, "Oh God but I am sick and tired of my life."[54] Like her love affairs, her finances kept her on an emotional roller coaster.

❧ Wescott once wrote in his journal that what Porter thought was "wonderfully combined with what she is." On the subject of women's roles and identity, however, what she thought was often at variance with what she was. Despite the multiplicity of ways in which she seemed to reflect stereotypes of the emotional and changeable female, she was deeply sensitive to the devalued position of women in American society and to the revisionary thinking about women that was going on in successive waves throughout her life. She claimed to have no patience with women who complained of gender inequity. When asked once about the "Women's Liberation Movement," she "laughed uproariously" and said, "I don't agree with them. I told them, 'I will not sit down with you and hear you tell me men have abused you.' " She had never, she said, felt that it was "difficult being a woman in a 'man's world.' " Yet her letters show how clearly she perceived that women were abused and repressed by men, especially in professional life.[55]

One of the most noted scholars among Porter's friends, Cleanth Brooks, wrote in his essay "The Southern Temper" that she had "in her own nature a wide streak of the feminist." He might have been surprised to know how strong a reaction his comment evoked. She wrote in the margin of the copy he had inscribed for her "in admiration and with deep affection," "I resent this tag, and I am again astonished at Cleanth's strange lack of understanding of any irony or indeed sensibility or real intelligence in women." At another point in his book she jotted the feminist-sounding marginal notation, "How reluctantly Cleanth admits a woman to any serious discussion"—confirming, perhaps, his point. Tillie Olsen has also testified that she "found in [Porter] what we now call by the name of feminism."[56] That streak of feminism is most clearly evident, perhaps, in "Old Mortality." But it is manifest in much of her other published (and unpublished) work as well and can be traced through her letters and other biographical records from the days of her first marriage, and even before.[57]

Despite her proclivity for marriage, Porter's ideas about marriage and family responsibility reflected, at least intermittently, her sense that work must come first. In 1929, responding to a letter from Kathleen Millay, she said that she had "done a little pondering about this thing of being female AND artist too." She enjoyed being able to control her own time during her retreat in Bermuda. "And I maintain that an artist, I don't give a damn if she is a woman, has the right to use all her resources, in her own time and on her own terms, precisely as all first rate male artists do." For this reason, she said—although as we have seen there were other reasons as well—she had "no family and no husband and no lover." She found that men inevitably tended to act as obstructionists "in any affairs of a woman that removes for one instant her admiring gaze from his own person." A month after writing to Millay, she took up the subject in a letter to Herbst, herself a confirmed feminist who sometimes complained about her husband's readiness to relegate her to housework, debating whether she wanted to live alone for the rest of her life, settle into marriage again, or take lovers. Her answer to all these options, she said, was no. So what did she want? "Answer: I'd like to write two novels and go to Europe: or the other way about."[58]

Probably Porter's most emphatic expression of feminism is to be found in a letter in which she took Matthew Josephson to task for comments he had published in *transition.* She objected to his having labeled Waverley Lewis Root's "mental flabbiness" "'feminine hysteria.'" By invoking a term associated with women in order to "insult him in the profoundest possible manner," she said, Josephson had betrayed a "morbid bias against women." The phrase *morbid bias* echoes her charge, in a 1926 review of *The Plumed Serpent,* that D. H. Lawrence had a "grudge against women." She was clear and emphatic in dissociating intellect from gender, warning Josephson, "If you say, I am being 'feminist' I must warn you not to make a sexual issue of differences founded strictly on a mental conception. I wish to hear what you have to say without once being told I am a woman. I am perfectly aware of it, and it has nothing to do with the case." Some years later, in a similar vein, she scolded Goyen for having called Henry James a spinster, saying, "I don't like the various titles of women used as insults." She must have enjoyed telling Josephson off. She wrote to Herbst four days later that she had "rebuked him severely" for "throwing stink bombs." The substance of the issue she was addressing would have been satisfying enough in any case but was enhanced by the fact that she was then working through the turbulent aftereffects of her love affair with Josephson.[59]

Porter and Herbst were fully in agreement that men did not sincerely support women in their professional endeavors and that housework was a handicapping burden for a literary woman (although both sometimes gloried in cooking, and Porter was extremely conscious of her domestic arrangements). Porter admitted that she "simply hate[d] the thought of cooking and house work," which "takes your time and your forces." When she had trouble getting the *New Republic* to send her one of Herbst's novels to review, she raised the specter of male exclusivity: "I really don't know, Josie, whether its a matter of the gempmun trying to hold us gals down, or what." (About the same time, in a letter to Malcolm Cowley, she praised the *New Republic* for being a place where "a man—or woman, I hope—can speak his mind.") Herbst lamented that, as "an ardent talk-it-over," she had "longed to partake" of a political "talk fest" at a neighborhood tavern where Herrmann was meeting Edmund Wilson, Cowley, Mike Gold, and others, but had received a "gentle stay-in-your place, which may or may not be the home." Herrmann had gone away "full of a masculine importance you and I will never know, alas."[60]

Herbst's account of the uncomfortable position of women in the Greenwich Village literary circle of the late twenties and early thirties was later confirmed by Malcolm Cowley, who admitted in an interview with Caroline Gordon's biographer Veronica Makowsky that "the boys" typically did shut the women out of their talk fests. Makowsky judges, reasonably enough, that it was hard for a woman artist in that society to develop the self-confidence needed for productive work. Her book on Gordon, indeed, centrally interrogates "the place of the woman writer in a literary world dominated by masculine imaginations."[61]

Porter was very much a part of that world and shared the plight Makowsky perceives with respect to Gordon. The two of them, along with Josephine Herbst and Delafield Day, for a time formed a mutually supportive group and held their own "talk fests." But these friendships were transient and subject to explosions—perhaps inevitably so, considering the inherent pressure on such women to regard each other as competitors for the little space allotted them to gain toeholds in the masculine world of letters. Gordon may not have questioned "the way men ran the literary establishment," but it is clear that Porter did, at least sporadically. She shared Gordon's perception of herself as being the rival of other women writers for professional "masculine attention," but she went further. Unlike her sometime friend, she did try to "measure herself against male writers," and she was frustrated when they so often insisted on regarding her only as an attractive woman who happened to write well, not as a serious competitor or peer.[62]

Housework was a symbol of that relegation to a role not taken seriously. Porter's resentment of men's willingness to let domesticity thwart women in their careers was evident as well in her long years of concern for her niece Ann, a talented and well-trained dancer who more than once quit her career for the sake of a marriage. She fretted that her niece was wasting herself in household drudgery and urged her to get back to creative work—

just as she had earlier written screeds on this subject to Herbst and to Janet Winters.[63]

For the most part, the feminist quality one sees in Porter is linked to her commitment to literature and her sense that women as well as men had a right to be treated as intellectual beings. She wrote acidly of "a certain kind of man" who felt that women had "no right to exercise their intellectual powers" and chafed against fellow writers such as William Carlos Williams and Sherwood Anderson, both of whom, she said, had admitted that for years they looked on her as only "a pretty girl making a career in literature."[64] In early reviews she praised Lady Mary Wortley Montagu, Mary Wollstonecraft (author of *A Vindication of the Rights of Woman*), and biologist Amy Catherine Robbins Wells, an "indefatigable" woman who demanded to use at least "one fragment of her mind" as she liked. Anticipating the work of discourse analysts, she once observed to her sister Gay that the men with whom she appeared on the Invitation to Learning radio programs (which featured such notables as Mark Van Doren, John Peale Bishop, Jacques Barzun, and Allen Tate) had interrupted her ten times in the course of just twenty short speeches. "The truth is," she said, "men are really afraid of a woman who can think and express her thoughts." Later, she told Gay that she felt like shooting a reviewer who had called her "an authoress."[65] She wanted her work to stand on its own, without special reference to her sex.

Porter often stated that her sex was irrelevant to her role as an artist and urged a critic to "criticize my work as severely as you like; but please don't expose yourself by putting it on the grounds that I am a woman." But it is clear that she knew gender affected her recognition as a writer. In 1932, when the Scribner's prize she had hoped to win was divided between John Herrmann and Thomas Wolfe, she told Herrmann that it was no surprise. "In these parlous times," she said, "they were certainly not going to give any such sum of coin to any female." The note of resentment evident in this remark is clear, as well, in her 1959 review of *Lady Chatterley's Lover,* in which she derides Lawrence's evident wish that a woman would "stop having any will or mind or indeed any existence of her own." Her recognition and resentment of a common slur on women and their creative works—that they do not involve rational thought but only emotion or instinct—is evident in her rebuttal of John Middleton Murry's comment that Katherine Mansfield's art was "of a peculiarly instinctive kind." Instead, Porter insists, it was "to a great degree a matter of intelligent use of her faculties, a conscious practice of a hard-won craftsmanship."[66] That is, it was fully as deserving of respect as a man's work.

Obviously, she was inconsistent. She insisted on her femininity but defied men to think she was any less tough than they. She spoke of the "womb-shaped female mind" and referred to her own whimsicality as "wombsical," yet demanded that sex be disregarded when ideas were at issue. She promoted women artists but stated flatly that "there aren't and never have been any first-rate women composers," though she would not find musical composition "unbecoming" to women if they had the ability; then conceded that generalization on the basis of sex was unwise. (One wishes she could have known about the work of musicologists Edith Boroff and Marcia Citron, who have demonstrated that there have indeed been many women composers.) She was quick to resent Donald Sutherland's statement that "a woman speaking her mind critically makes herself less interesting." "Believe me," she urged, "it works both ways." Yet she herself, after rejecting Sutherland's idea of a "peculiarly female mind," hazarded her own generalization: "the real difference between the sexes, emotionally and intellectually considered, is that women feel less need for asserting themselves by analyzing and judging everything; they do not, in a word, feel a need to be God." One hears in that comment the voice of a woman who had chafed under the godlike male mind.[67]

❧ It is in "Old Mortality" and the brief stories or sketches grouped under the collective title "The Old Order" that we find Porter's fullest imaginative development of feminist themes. Even in these works, the theme is elusive, embedded in a domestic world that overtly, at least, celebrates the traditional roles of women as centers of family life. Within that milieu she shows the Grandmother, modeled on her own Grandmother Porter, as a powerful matriarch of independent mind, confident of her authority. (Porter's wish to identify with her powerful grandmother, known as Aunt Cat, is indicated by her referring to herself, in letters to her niece, as Aunt Kat.) Nannie, the "faithful old servant," is also apotheosized as a figure of singularity and authority, asserting her right to live as she chooses.

The decisive moment in the "Old Order" stories is given to neither of these older women, however, but to an even more singular figure who can by no means be conformed to traditional femininity, Great-Aunt Eliza. With her scientific interests and her indifference to constraining notions of feminine behavior, Eliza releases Miranda from her imagined guilt over having buried a chick alive. Her power derives, not from beauty or social bearing, but from knowledge, and she possesses that knowledge only because she has pursued her studies in disregard of prevailing notions as to what women should or should not take an interest in. She has climbed onto the henhouse to look through her telescope in defiance of propriety, and she has sat at the dinner table studying bits of this and that through her microscope without regard to conventional manners or charm. It is therefore Eliza whose voice can convey to the child, in nobly simple terms, a vision of "other worlds, a million other worlds" and who can correctly identify the supposed cry of the buried chick as the chirping of tree frogs.[68] Porter's presentation of this character can scarcely be called a feminist argument. But she created in Eliza an image of woman defined by her independence and her mind, not by biological function or social stereotype.

"Old Mortality," first published in 1937 in the *Southern Review*, has often been considered Porter's finest work. It was recognized by Cleanth Brooks and Robert Penn Warren with inclusion in their enormously influential 1943 anthology, *Understanding Fiction*, a watershed of the New Criticism, and it has been included in numerous other anthologies for college students. Warren believed the story had "few peers in any language."[69] In many ways, it stands as the summing up of Porter's creative impulse. Its theme, the struggle toward self-definition, is the central theme of her own life. Thus it can properly be read as a pervasively autobiographical work, though not directly autobiographical in the way that it has sometimes been seen. Details of setting and family circumstance, with their trappings of prosperity and social prominence, convey more of wish than of actual remembrance. Indeed, as George Core has commented in reference to the "Old Order" stories, the surface of the story "often parallels her invented life" more than her actual one.[70] But the deeply embedded thematic action of "Old Mortality," a struggle toward self-definition through acts of separation from family and home, is profoundly self-revelatory. Journeys and displacements were primal symbolic actions in Porter's own developing awareness of self, as they are in Miranda's.

The story follows Miranda's development of a mental independence that will allow her to launch her adult life. She does this largely through studying the important women of her family, past and present, and observing the unreasonable, contradictory responses that these women evoke on the part of fathers, brothers, lovers, and husbands, as well as on the part of the powerful grandmother figure. In particular, she is tormented by the family's idealizing of her deceased Aunt Amy, now "only a ghost in a frame" but still held up to Miranda and her sister as a seemingly impossible ideal of feminine beauty and charm, the "quintessential belle." Besides their family's Amy-olatry, the two girls also puzzle over their father's stubborn denial of the truth about other women in the family.[71] He insists, for example, that "there were never any fat women in the family" despite the plain fact that at least two of their great-aunts are quite obese. Clearly, everyone in the family values slenderness, gracefulness, charm. Their father, who values these qualities to the point of refusing to recognize any departure from them, not only sets the girls an impossible standard of female perfection but makes his love contingent on their approximating these standards. Like Porter's own father, he doles out affection on the basis of their being "prettily dressed and well behaved, and pushed them away if they had not freshly combed hair and nicely scrubbed fingernails."[72]

Porter makes it clear that such demanding models of feminine perfection exert a destructive pressure on those female children and young women who cannot attain them. Not only does Miranda live in continual torment because of her fear that she cannot be another Amy, she learns, late in the story, how cruelly the judging of young women by their beauty alone has blighted the life of her cousin Eva, who lost out to other girls in the vicious contest for husbands simply because she had no chin and therefore could not present herself as a belle. Eva has found her own satisfactions in a career as teacher and crusader for woman suffrage. Even so, she bears emotional scars that are all too evident, and she is depicted in a "stereotypical way" that has been seen as reflecting Porter's ambivalence toward feminists.[73]

In the final section of the story, as Miranda takes a train home for a family funeral along with Cousin Eva, she hears Eva's assault on the family legend of the beautiful Amy. Readers sometimes interpret this assault as a correction of fantasy by fact, but Eva simply replaces the legend of the belle with her own legend, equally overdramatized, of the "impure woman."[74] Listening to her diatribe, Miranda realizes that Cousin Eva hates Amy, dead though she is, but she is not yet sufficiently free of the myth of beautiful womanhood to understand why. What Eva hates is actually the image of the belle which, held up as an impossible yardstick against which she had to measure herself, has left her frustrated and emotionally twisted.

The real Amy, hidden behind the family's idealization, is revealed by Porter in a few deft strokes. The Amy that the family refuses to recognize and Eva cannot recognize because she is blinded by resentment is herself a frustrated model of self-definition through disaffection. Self-willed, defiant of convention, she plays out the expected role of belle and bride in her own style. When she marries she refuses to wear the white dress symbolizing values of propriety and stability, but instead chooses a gray dress accessorized with red, the color of blood, telling her mother " 'I shall wear mourning if I like . . . it is *my* funeral, you know.' " She is remembered in family lore in her moment of departure after the wedding as she "ran into the gray cold and stepped into the carriage and turned and smiled with her face as pale as death." Even without the comment that "none of us saw her alive again," it is quite clear that hers is an ultimate departure. But in the family legend her bold gestures are remembered as evidence of her flamboyant nature, not as a substantive protest. Only the attentive reader sees that she has enacted a parody of the feminine ideal.[75]

The three sections of "Old Mortality" recount the growth of Miranda's and, to some extent, her sister Maria's rejection of the ideal of womanhood their family would fasten on them. In Part I they begin to question its veracity. In Part II, physically separated from their family home by their "immurement" in a convent school, they begin to realize that their father's gestures of affection are unreliable and they pass tacit judgment on his refusal to answer their questions frankly. From this intermediate stage of separation, Miranda launches herself into independence by running away from the convent to get married, thus signaling her rejection of her father's dominance and, by implication, his models for her life. Rejecting his ideal of Amy, she aligns herself with the subversive Amy, the exemplar of the despairing, self-destructive woman and the antithesis of the domestic angel. In Part III, Miranda rejects both her marriage, which seems to her to have "nothing at all to do with the future," and her family of origin. Cousin Eva provides her an alternative model, not one she will adopt but one that helps her think through her position within the family. Eva urges her to "use your mind a little" and not "let yourself rust away." It is a message that, at the end of the story, she is attempting to put to use.[76]

Miranda alights from the train only to realize that she cannot, after all, come home again. Getting into a car for the drive to the house, she is once again caught in transit. At the end, poised for another departure, she recognizes that she "can't live in their world any longer." She "consciously reject[s] her past-intoxicated family" in favor of "homelessness" and the freedom to construct her own life and her own self. Yet even this recognition is blurred as Porter's final words convey the elusiveness of that accurate self-knowledge Miranda seeks. She tells herself that she can at least "know the truth about what happens to me."[77] But the voice of the older and wiser, surely more deeply disillusioned, narrator labels Miranda's silent promise to herself a wish made "in her hopefulness, her ignorance."[78] The older narrator understands just how limited a young woman's freedom to live her own life and develop her own ideas really is. It is on this note of mingled triumph and poignancy that the story ends.

In "Old Mortality," as well as in other works, both fiction and nonfiction, Porter demonstrated that she perceived, even if she could not safely negotiate for herself, the pitfalls prepared for women by a patriarchal society. Her resentment of such pitfalls is occasionally made clear in her letters. She once commented on Thoreau's line "Most men lead lives of quiet desperation" that "at the risk of being called a feminist" she would say "that goes for women, too doubled in spades." In her fiction and her published nonfiction, however, she launched a criticism of gender inequity in more understated and indirect ways. She was never able to achieve in her own life the poise and autonomy she described in the Miranda of "Pale Horse, Pale Rider," facing her future without the props of artificial consolations, or the Hattie Weston of "St. Augustine and the Bullfight," sitting her horse "graceful and composed," so perfectly in control that by comparison the violent games of men seem shabbily cruel.[79] Porter participated in her generation's revaluation of women's roles, but for the most part she made her testimony indirectly, through a spare symbolism, rather than through the resounding exhortations of some of her contemporaries.

CHAPTER NINE

Ship of Fools and the Problem of Genre

Miss Katherine Anne and her 27 years have been giving me nightmares.

—Flannery O'Connor, April 16, 1960, on learning that Porter had been twenty-seven years on her novel

It is appalling to see how these reviewers, you cannot call them critics, apparently can read every word, or at least every line of a work and not understand one idea or emotion it contains. . . . It is so strange they cannot see the difference between flight and a going *towards;* between adventure and a pilgrimage.

—Porter to Caroline Gordon, November 5, 1964

In 1962 Porter published what she hoped would be her crowning achievement, her one novel, *Ship of Fools.* A book of conspicuous weightiness, reflecting ponderous political and moral ambitions, it explores at considerable length the atmosphere of arrogance, suspicion, and fear that pervaded the Western world on the eve of World War II. That is to say, the book essentially reached back thirty years to Porter's own sense of disillusionment and foreboding during her early months in Europe, the consciousness and the historical moment she had already explored in "The Leaning Tower." In part, then, the fact that *Ship of Fools* did not prove to be the artistic triumph she had hoped to achieve—though it was far and away her greatest commercial triumph—can be attributed both to the fact that her material for the book was stale and to the fact that her creative impulse to develop that material was attenuated or simply worn out.

In large part, however, the failure of the book to crown her career artistically can be seen as a problem of genre. Porter had tried to make her mark in a form that seemed in some ways compulsory, the entrée both to the respect of the (predominantly male) literary establishment and to the adulation of a numerous reading public, both of which she keenly desired. Like Eudora Welty, she had felt compelled to shift from the short story to the novel to demonstrate that she belonged in the company of the acknowledged "heavy hitters" of the book world. But the genre was uncongenial.[1]

More characteristic are her novellas (she called them long stories) and her short stories, many of which have puzzled readers by their avoidance of expected patterns of action. Especially the short narratives titled collectively "The Old Order," whose subjects are centered on the everyday lives of girls and women, have seemed to belong to a genre lying somewhere between the story and the sketch.[2] Her achievement here in the development of a revisionary genre has not been adequately noted. It is an achievement she would defend, though without acknowledging either the pertinence of specific works or a link to gendered literary expectations, in her witty essay "No Plot, My Dear, No Story" (1942), in which she neatly captures the male editor's condescension and assaults his authoritative power with one of the primary weapons used by the powerless, laughter. She asserts in the essay that the gender of the author of such seemingly unplotted stories "doesn't matter." But gender was more pertinent than she recognized.

The linkage of gender and genre is a major concern of feminist literary theory. Shari Benstock has argued persuasively that the masculine dominance of the modernist literary world not only marginalized women like Sylvia Beach, who were facilitators of writing rather than producers of it but have not been highly valued in that role in the way that Ezra Pound (to cite a noted example) has been, but also "locked" the woman writer out of the circles of influence and "locked" her into "literary forms conceived by and written for men."[3] It is not, of course, that the novel is intrinsically unsuited to women writers. Still, many women have found shorter, more concentrated forms to be more congenial than large forms, and in general they have suffered reputational penalties when they have followed that inclination. In music, the symphony or the opera is customarily regarded as the test of greatness. In literature it is the book. Aside from the issue of length or scope, however, women have often found the accepted subjects and plot structures of fiction and of autobiography to be based on masculine models of public endeavors and signal achievements, whereas women's lives have traditionally been more often lived in privacy, in the pursuits of dailiness. The dilemma of having to negotiate between expectations based on masculine assumptions and their own aesthetic motivation and experiential material has often led either to the breaking of generic models or to silence.[4] The effects of the dilemma are apparent in Porter's career in both ways, in her periods of troubled silence, linked to her struggles with the novel, and in the forms of much of her short fiction.

❧ A commonplace of criticism has it that painters want to write and writers want to compose music and musicians want to paint. A few, perhaps, have done so successfully, but for the most part not. If the old saw were put in terms of genre, rather than of medium, Katherine Anne Porter would be a prime illustration. Brilliant in the short story and the essay, she yearned to write novels and poetry. Most critics agree that she did not really succeed in either form and that in fact neither the poetic idiom nor the extended structure of the novel was suited to her genius.

Porter's efforts in poetry are little known, certainly not nearly so well known as the fact that she produced a novel that was, in a commercial sense at any rate, a success. She always wished to write poetry, however, just as she always wanted to write a novel, though it was only in the 1920s that she actually gave much effort to the genre. She produced a few poems, none of them really memorable. The almost magical facility with language that created such a distinctive style in prose never, for whatever reason, lent itself to verse. Moreover, unlike her sureness in judging when a story met her high standards, she had little critical sense with regard to her poetic efforts. An appeal to her editor friend Genevieve Taggard in 1924 is indicative. She asked, "Just how good—or bad!—a poem is 'Requiescat,' anyhow?" When Taggard gently (it seems) rejected some offered poems, Porter hastened to reply, defensively, "You aren't to trouble about the poems. I don't. My amazement was not when you decided they weren't good enough, but when you thought they were. I am not a poet, and shall write no more verse." She did not hold to this resolve but continued to try, without notable success, to write poems. In 1926 she offered four more poems for publication, inviting Taggard to take her choice and promising not to be "unreasonable" if she did not choose any. "I realise more and more that I am a prose writer: verse is a strange, always experimental form with me . . . but I love it, and shall probably keep on experimenting from time to time."[5] But her *Collected Essays and Occasional Writings,* published in 1970, offers just eight poems written and published over a wide span of years.

The desire to succeed as a novelist was longer-lived and more compelling, and it had a much more far-reaching effect on her career. It was an entirely understandable ambition. As a stand-alone product lending itself to promotion, sales, and review, the novel was, and is, a far likelier medium in which to achieve literary reputation than the short story. Porter spoke of writing a novel for some thirty years before the publication of *Ship of Fools* and assured publishers that the finished product was just around the corner. But despite several ideas or beginnings, a work of long fiction continued to elude her. She had contracts for both a novel of Mexico and a biography of Cotton Mather, but was unable to complete either. Her old friend Kenneth Durant joked in 1934 that he understood why she didn't return to the United States—too many publishers had made her advances on manuscripts she hadn't completed, and she couldn't face them. But it was hard for her to take a humorous view of the problem. She told Robert McAlmon that she was so "covered down with shame because I don't get any stories done, its been impossible to carry off conversation with any kind of ease."[6] Increasingly, as years passed, that sense of shame became attached to the phantom lure of the novel.

In the mid-1930s, with the Mather book still hanging about her neck but the novel of Mexico discarded, Porter's intentions shifted from a novel about her family history, the material for which went into "Old Mortality" and several shorter stories, to a group of long stories or short novels, some based on the family history material and one based on her voyage from Mexico to Germany in 1931.[7] It was that story, "Promised Land," that finally, in 1962, became *Ship of Fools.*

At first she conceived of it as one of five short novels or long stories to be published along with "Old Mortality," "Noon Wine," "Pale Horse, Pale Rider," and the never-completed "The Man in the Tree" in a single volume. In December 1937, after finishing "Pale Horse, Pale Rider," she reported to Josephine Herbst that "Promised Land" was "half finished" and after all the book would include four rather than five stories, "for they will make a full length book and that is enough." Instead, it appeared in 1939 as a volume of three works. She was still, she reported to Herbst in March of that year, "half way through" but now the "Promised Land" material was making a "full length—or nearly—novel" because it had "kept growing and spreading." By fall she could tell Glenway Wescott that "Promised Land" was "so good in places I can't believe I wrote it." (George Gershwin is said to have made a similar comment about *Porgy and Bess.*) For years she continued to whet readers' appetites for the full feast that she was not able to supply, commenting on it in letters and milking the growing manuscript for magazine publications. During all these years of promise and delay her friends, admirers, and well-wishers agonized for and with her. In 1941, Harcourt Brace announced the book and Eudora Welty wrote to say that she hoped Katherine Anne had put onto paper the last 20,000 words to finish it.[8] Far more than twenty thousand words were in fact lacking. Those who knew her well knew the torment she experienced as she tried to bring the project to some kind of completion. But her delays were also a torment to editors and publishers, some of whom complained that she had driven them, too, to the brink of despair.

The pattern of promises and delays had emerged early in her career. In 1921 she was writing to her sometime lover and fellow political schemer Joseph Retinger that she hoped to have her "mexican book" completed in about a month. She never got past the notes for such a book. In 1924 the editors of the *Survey* wrote that they "could have wrung your lady-like neck on various occasions when we had difficulty in getting contact with you."[9] Two years later she admitted to her friend Taggard that "even the poor Herald Tribune is reduced to nagging me by telegram for reviews." When Horace Liveright demanded that she repay $850 in advances for the Mather book plus $190 spent in preparation for publication, she seems to have ignored the letter. In 1934 Harcourt Brace bought the contract from Liveright for five hundred dollars, despite having been disappointed in the expectation of a novel in 1931.[10] For the most part, she let such nagging roll off her back. At times, however, she felt the expectations of publishers as a dreadful and debilitating pressure. It was a pressure she brought on herself by accepting, perhaps from necessity, advances on work that she had little hope of supplying. Her typical mode of dealing with the resulting problems was evasion.

Publishers' deadlines were almost a guarantee that the writing would not come. In 1951, for example, when she had promised to produce an article on the twenties for *Harper's,* she wrote William Goyen that she was experiencing an "obstinate resistance" of her "entire being" against writing it. "Would you believe that when I thought it done, I let it lie about a while and decided it wouldn't, COULDN'T do, and tore it up and began again. I am now thirteen agonized days over the date set to give it up." According to Wescott's journal, her editor, Russell Lynes, finally assembled the article from scattered notes: "When she bogged down, he came and spread her manuscript out on the floor and selected some fifteen of the disjoined pages and will do the joining himself." Wescott ended his account of the episode with a comic touch, quoting a telephone conversation in which she had laughed and told him, "Honey, you should have an editor like that, ha ha!" But the record is clear that such episodes gave her, as she said to Goyen, "agonized days."[11]

Porter's struggles to produce the writing of which she was capable and the dreadful gaps that occurred in her success in doing so were deeply embedded in her sense of herself and her proper roles as a woman. Throughout her career she experienced conflicts between the demands of her profession and both her romantic involvements and her urge toward domesticity. Caroline Gordon's belief that she "had a natural passion for domestic activity but indulged it to get out of writing" was accurate enough.[12] Just as she engaged in unnecessary bouts of the cooking and canning Gordon observed at Benfolly, she engaged in binges of slipcovering, sewing of clothes, letter writing, and general socializing, all traditionally female activities, when she had writing she wanted and needed to complete.

It was not, of course, a pattern peculiar to herself. Her friend Herbst had similarly, but with less personal connivance, found her writing interfered with by housekeeping, cooking, and the maintenance of a marital relationship. And Gordon's disapproval of Porter's use of retrogressive domestic work as a means of escaping her artistic discipline may well have been fueled by her own uncomfortable self-perception. In 1929 Gordon wrote to Herbst, "I believe that aversion to work is so deep-seated in most of us that we will clutch at anything that distracts." What she sometimes clutched at were duties associated with gender. Although she might, as Makowsky observes, "confront this problem with increasing professional dedication and achievement," she would never "completely conquer it," and her dread of the rigors of writing sometimes "meshed too neatly with the demands placed on her as a woman: wife, mother, and hostess."[13] The poet Louise Bogan, another of Gordon's guests at Benfolly, once wrote that the "delights of the cook and the housewife" were sometimes "substitutes" for writing. When Porter read this statement in Bogan's published letters, she wrote in the margin, "never substitutes for me—delights in themselves adding to the life of my work, KA 24 November 1973."[14] But they were sometimes deviously constructed distractions.

Another plausible explanation of Porter's recurrent and severe writer's block, as it affected the completion of *Ship of Fools,* is Givner's surmise that she had a short attention span. This would no doubt help to explain why the novel was not a congenial form for her. Her work habits, consisting of short periods of total immersion, indicate as much. She was not accustomed to the sustained labor of constructing a long, multidimensional work. Moreover, she was notoriously changeable. This was true in all aspects of her life—in her politics, her affections, her social plans, her choices of where to live. One day she was wanting to buy a mountain in California and live there forever, another day she was deciding that Pennsylvania felt more like home than any place she had ever been, and almost the next, it seems, she was declaring Virginia the most perfect place in the world for her. The complaint of one of her husbands, that she was "inexplicably sudden" in her "whims and fancies," was well founded.[15] Rapid changes in interest and intention are not conducive to the development of a large project requiring some degree of planning and the development of an organic relation of parts to whole.

That Porter recognized, at bottom, the unsuitability of the genre is indicated by a comment she made to Wescott: "Truth is, I am a writer of short stories, and when this novel got simply too much for me, I lightly jumped the track and did something I can do, and a good thing."[16] It was a rare moment of self-knowledge, and the "good thing" about it was good indeed: "The Leaning Tower." For the most part, however, she insisted that she was producing and was going to produce novels, although for years she did not succeed in doing so.

❧ The making of *Ship of Fools* would provide the material for a book in itself. In all literary history there are few such sagas of prolonged promise and frustrated delivery. The book was more than twenty-five years in the making and would probably not have been finished at all if Little, Brown had not bought the contract from Harcourt Brace—and then, even more important, if Porter's editor there, Seymour Lawrence, had not simply taken charge and dragged or cajoled the book out of her. Lawrence wrote to Porter proposing the shift to Atlantic-Little, Brown on October 19, 1955. She eagerly agreed, telling him that it would cost $5,000 for the release from Harcourt Brace and asking for an added $2,500 advance plus $400 a month to free her from having to spend her time in speaking engagements. Her estimate was far off. The advances from Harcourt Brace had totaled $10,435. One can only be amazed that Lawrence's faith in her work was so strong as to induce him to pay that much, when her record of completion was so poor. In March 1956, with contract negotiations for the change of publisher still going on, she wrote to him that she had a complete draft and was starting to make a fair copy. The novel would not be finished and published, however, for six more years.

In the interim, Lawrence found places for her to work, he secluded her, he catered to her. Finally, of course, he was rewarded with a best-seller. But there must have been numerous occasions when he felt doubtful of the outcome. Porter had claimed to Caroline Gordon years before that it had "never in my most disheartened moments occurred to me that the novel was not, in some way, at some time, going to get finished."[17] Her claim was pure bravado; inwardly she was not so confident. At times she despaired of being able to rid herself of the succubus that was draining her strength and tranquillity. She was fortunate to have had the encouragement and assistance not only of Lawrence but of other supportive friends, most of all Glenway Wescott and his sister-in-law, Porter's longtime patron and friend Barbara Harrison Wescott.

Glenway tried for years to encourage and assist her to complete her novel. After she confessed, in 1940, that she had "jumped the track" from working on it, he assured her that she had "nothing to worry about" because her "artistry" was now "mature" and she could "do no wrong"—a wonderful statement of one artist's confidence in another. Even warmer, perhaps, was a tribute he sent in 1944, when *Ship* was again in trouble. After reporting that he had completed a novel called "The Change of Heart" (changed, before publication, to *Apartment in Athens*), he said, "Certainly I admire you more than I admire anyone else, I admire you more than I like anyone, I admire you even more than I like you—is that a riddle? It is a pretty tremendous thing anyway: to be borne in mind by you, please, if the fact that *No Safe Harbor* [another working title] has struck a reef worries you."[18] It did indeed worry her—and well he knew it.

In August of 1943, as she still labored over the book Wescott had thought she could bring off in 1941, and as she found the longed-for house that she had finally bought and remodeled, South Hill, a greater and greater burden, he wrote to express his concern. George Platt Lynes, Monroe Wheeler, and Barbara, he said, shared his worry about her "discouragement" and her "economic status." They all recognized "the necessity of finding some sort of solution" for her and would have suggestions to make shortly. By the end of the month he was asking her to let him see the manuscript in the hope that he could find some way to help. In September he relayed an offer from Barbara to put Porter up in a country inn for three months during the winter so that she could be free of the distractions of operating an inconvenient house in an isolated location and could write. "As soon as you decide where you choose to go," he followed up, "she will pay the place whatever is wanted in the way of an advance, and ask them to send your weekly bill to her here." He thought George Platt Lynes would want to provide her "some spending money" and promised to see him about it. Lynes, he added, had "the camera of Midas just now"—a tactful bit of assurance to her that she need not worry about being a burden to him. (She would later live in Lynes's house in California for several months, during another difficult period.) Wescott called himself a "back seat muse" and offered to monitor her progress; if he detected anything going wrong, he would immediately set himself to try to assist. Apparently she did not accept that offer. If she ever let him go over the manuscript, the record does not indicate as much, and it would have been utterly uncharacteristic of her to have done so. But she accepted the stay at the inn.[19]

Wescott hoped, of course, to bring about a repetition of what he called the "Doylestown travail and miracle," the stay at the Water Wheel Tavern when she had completed both "Noon Wine" and "Old Mortality." Unfortunately, the 1943 retreat at Cold Spring, New York, seems to have yielded only another of her nervous collapses, during which she was unable to work. In a letter dated December 22, Wescott spoke of the fall's having been "a bramble-bush" for her. Her short note to him dated Christmas Day sent greetings "in spite of hell" in a handwriting so notably awry that she must indeed have been ill when she wrote it. On December 27 she wrote at greater length, mentioning a respiratory illness but giving hints of emotional or "nervous" collapse: She was taking a great array of medications, "each with its own mission of soothing, or elevating the spirits, calming the heart or stimulating it, loosening the phlegm and tightening the nerves, stopping the cough and lowering the fever." "My mind is a good sound lasting instrument," she asserted bravely. "There are some fears in me, but not in that place where I truly live. But that it has stood a long siege I will admit." Recovering from whatever combination of physical and emotional illness she had suffered, she wrote apologetically, "I am sure that my reasons for not finishing are entirely human, no doubt natural, perhaps acceptable as excuses, but I don't like them just the same and I don't like excuses. It is also quite horrible to me to find myself in a situation where I must be regarded with various kinds of dismay by my dearest friends." She was indeed so regarded not only then but at various other times. Before the end of her stay at Cold Spring she tried to assure Barbara that her investment had paid off: "The novel is finished EXCEPT for a nasty tough spot in the exact middle of the captain's party." That was not, of course, true.[20]

One can only guess what Wescott et al. must have felt when that very year, 1944, after having accepted both their solicitude and their resources toward the completion of her novel, Porter expended emotional strength she could ill afford to squander on her affair with Charles Shannon and then signed with Metro-Goldwyn-Mayer as a scriptwriter. We do not have to guess what her publisher, Donald Brace, thought; his attempt to discourage her from responding to the lures of Hollywood is on record. Wescott, whatever his disappointment, faithfully reviewed *The Leaning Tower and Other Stories* in the *New York Times Book Review* in September and predicted that if she turned to "larger fiction" she might "give American literature a better novel than it has ever known."[21] He seems to have believed, in fact, that she did almost that. When the novel finally appeared, he reviewed it glowingly and never flagged in his favorable judgment.

Barbara, supportive as ever, wrote in July 1945 to say that she had heard Porter was "working again on That Novel, and you can imagine how I feel about it! But still better news is that you are in a blissful state of good health, after all these weeks, months, years (?) of battling with your own particulare [*sic*] demons." Barbara must have understood about demons. Less than two years later, when she was hospitalized, Wescott wrote to say that "Baba" did not have bronchitis, as they had given out to friends and neighbors, but instead had suffered "the wish to commit suicide." By the end of 1948, still in California, Porter herself seems to have been in an almost equally desperate state, writing to her niece Ann that she had found "rock bottom" and to her nephew Paul, "It is a heavy undertaking to write even a little." She complained, "It is just merely, simply, in a few words, that I know now that I have nothing to look forward to at all, and until now I had hope. I have, with the enthusiastic help of almost everybody who comes near me, managed to destroy my life."[22]

Porter's long correspondence with Wescott was of value to her not only with respect to *Ship of Fools,* which he steadfastly encouraged until its publication and praised afterward, but with respect to her need for personal affection and encouragement. Wescott challenged and amused her and stimulated her thinking. Their correspondence was of great value to him as well. He once confessed that his "rivalry" with her was "one of the too few factors in my life just now which sways me directly toward literature" and that she was one of the few people who held him to his "determination to be no more or less than a literary artist." "Not only are you world-wise," he wrote, "but you know the professional secret, the perilous gestation, the self-reproach. Therefore you do me a (or is it 'an'?) unique good."[23] Among the many writers to whom Porter was a valuable resource Wescott was perhaps unique in being at least as great and perhaps a greater benefit to her than she was to him. On her birthday in 1944 he wrote that he believed "in matters of art" they understood each other "better than any other two in this country (who else is there?)"[24]

In the 1950s, after her reputation was firmly established as a popular as well as an artistic writer, Porter became increasingly distracted by demands for interviews and occasional pieces, appeals for favors, and fan mail. She made little progress on *Ship of Fools* but continued to speak of it as if it were imminent. In 1956, declining J. Frank Dobie's invitation to come speak at a meeting of the Institute of Texas Letters, she cited time pressure to finish the novel, "which will appear early next year"—a familiar refrain and as little based on fact as her earlier references to the Mather book's imminent appearance had been. In 1958 she told a startled Flannery O'Connor that she had been working on the novel for twenty-seven years.[25] It is surprising, then, to find her stating, in 1962, in her acceptance speech for the Emerson and Thoreau Gold Medal of the American Academy of Arts and Sciences, that she did not actually work on *Ship of Fools* for twenty years, but only for about three. The rest of the time, she said, she was working on other things, though she did occasionally "mention" that she thought she might be "writing a novel." The record shows that she was far more definite about it than that.

In 1957, however, she began the series of retreats organized by Seymour Lawrence that would at last lead to publication. By March of that year she was at a country inn near Boston where she could write without distractions. In June she reported that her "third deadline" had passed and the novel was not finished. She was trying to "refresh" herself by "writing a 30th anniversary piece about the Sacco-Vanzetti scandal." That "piece" would be published as *The Never-Ending Wrong*, not for the thirtieth but for the fiftieth anniversary. In July, declining to grant a favor asked by Kay Boyle, she said that she had about 20,000 words to go—the same number she had apparently given Welty in 1941, sixteen years earlier.[26] But she did not reach the end in this stretch either.

❧ Lawrence's role in the completion of Porter's most famous, if not her greatest, book is a remarkable instance of literary midwifery. He assumed the task of coaxing and pressuring her into completing what was at least the fourth book she had undertaken, in some way publicized, and then stalled out on. Moreover, he was not the first capable editor, trusted by her for varying periods, who had tried to play such a role. Why was he successful when others had failed?

One answer is persistence. He was willing to go on and on bolstering her confidence, making arrangements, running interference, doing whatever he had to do to get her going again when she stalled. In August 1956, when she had missed her deadline after telling him months before that she was starting to make a fair copy (when in fact great tracts of the massive novel did not yet exist), he assured her that she must not think he was disappointed by her failure to meet the deadline. The "quality and scope" of the sections of manuscript that had come in "more than compensat[ed] for any technical delay."[27] The comment demonstrates how well he understood his quarry. Knowing her insistence on artistic perfection above all else, knowing that if she became convinced the work was unworthy of her she would never finish it just to fulfill a contract, he assured her that she was indeed meeting that high standard of craft and redefined the process of publication itself as a mere technicality. It was a rhetorical strategy well calculated to power her work.

Some six weeks after Lawrence's encouraging message, Porter sent him the "sad" news that she not only had not finished the book but was breaking off work on it to go on a speaking tour.[28] Again Lawrence showed his astuteness. After the investment of buying out her contract with Harcourt Brace and adding a new advance to what she had already received, he would have had every right to fulminate. He might well have pointed out that he was providing funds which ought to keep her from wasting time on other income-generating ventures. But as we have seen, and as Lawrence must have seen, Porter was as ill-equipped for prolonged effort as she was for prolonged quiet. She had often expressed her need for "a little quiet," but a little was all she could tolerate before she felt an equally compelling need for social diversion and attention. The rhythm of her entire life was one of alternation between the two. Lawrence had to accept this fact, hope that a period of the usual accolades would reenergize her, and make himself ready to utilize the next period when she would want withdrawal.

In March 1957 he seems to have believed that she was, as he said, in the "homestretch." In fact, she was only beginning to give him lessons in frustration. When her energies again flagged and she began to complain of financial worries, he arranged an additional $1,000 advance as a sign of the press's confidence. In August, unable or unwilling to go again to the Atlantic-Little, Brown board, he arranged for her to receive a grant from the Bollingen Foundation, again trying to allay financial worries so that she could or would go on writing.[29] Here, too, Lawrence showed his understanding of this writer whom he had studied as carefully as he had read her books. He knew quite well how financially irresponsible she was and how debilitated she became when she felt money problems closing in on her. In such a frame of mind she would certainly not be able to work.

Until the book was finished, Lawrence would go on providing modest sums of money—$1,600, for example, in January 1958—to keep Porter afloat and fairly tranquil so that she could continue on the magnum opus for which the reading public was so well primed. With every advance, of course, he tied her more tightly, not merely in a legal sense but also through her gratitude and sense of obligation, to his goal of getting the Atlantic-Little, Brown imprint onto the long-awaited novel. Previous publishers had made advances, but far less generously. Lawrence understood that to make money one has to spend money. Not that the financial prize was his only motivation. Clearly, Seymour Lawrence was as literate and discriminating an editor as he was a successful businessman. His discernment of artistic merit and his veneration of Porter's work were unassailable. But he was, as well, a shrewd investor in marketable creativity, and he was a remarkable practical psychologist.

In the summer of 1958 Lawrence arranged for more money from Little, Brown, this time in the form of a loan. By now Porter seems to have realized that she had mortgaged her artistry to the hilt and reduced herself to a kind of bondage of the imagination. In August she reached the section of the captain's party she had told Barbara Harrison Wescott she had reached in January 1944. But she was again in a severe state of discouragement. "It must be my last book under the past conditions," she wrote. "But you do encourage me with your plans to make some money for us, for all of us, and to set me free. I am sure then I shall write again then [*sic*] as I did once, for love and joy, which is the only way worth doing. Or not at all, which will be just as good for me at this point."[30] The novel had become the key to her future identity as a writer, and Lawrence was the one person who could help her turn that key. Small wonder, then, that she would later turn against him when she looked back at the pressure she had endured and, even worse, when she perceived him as still holding power over her.

By the end of 1958 Porter was again flagging in her efforts and apparently again resorting to lying about the status of her work. This time, however, her lie reached so many ears that it threatened to humiliate her. In panic she appealed to Lawrence for complicity: "I have done a desprate [*sic*] thing to get rid of people asking me about this God damned novel. I simply said one evening in New York in a company of friends that it was finished, and please never mention its name to me again. The occasion to my horror turned into a party of celebration, and the news got abroad like a fox with its tail on fire, and so, I am stuck. It is NOT a lie, because the book is finished. But I have NOT finished copying it, and of course it cannot be called finished until the final copy is in your hands. But I beg of you, if any one writes you or says anything to you, DO say, Yes, the bloody thing is finished, or just use your own language, and I still think you are going to get it in a few weeks. But I am so deathly tired I can't see to hit the keys, really."[31]

Lawrence's role was played out with consummate skill and timing. Alternately cajoling and pressuring (it was "really imperative" that the book get out soon), he managed to keep her sense of her own welfare aligned with the welfare of the publishing company and himself, and he managed to keep her believing that the manuscript was up to her own high standards—an essential belief if she was to persevere to the end.

During 1958 and 1959, while she was supposedly making the final copy, she went off on the speaking and teaching circuit and became involved in another distracting love affair. What she needed, she wrote to her old friend Erna Johns, was "solitude and silence." In 1961, she got just that. Lawrence again arranged a retreat for her at a quiet inn, this time in Rockport, Massachusetts, on the Cape Ann peninsula. From there she wrote to Erna exulting that it was "not surprising that I get a lot done—I always did if only I could be left alone long enough to work a little." She described her retreat as having "no telephone, no television, no radio, no gramophone, no telegrams, no doorbells, no callers at all."[32] The litany of absences recalls Miranda's request for things "without," plain things having no extraneous ornaments, at the end of "Pale Horse, Pale Rider"—a passage taken by William Nance as evidence of Porter's pattern of "rejection," in his book that Porter so disliked.[33] Nance's insight was accurate, though, with respect to Porter's career-long but periodic need for working conditions "without." She yearned for company and conversation and pretty clothes and furnishings, but in order to pursue her creative work she needed a place of withdrawal without such distractions.[34]

This time Lawrence's arrangements produced the desired result.

❧ By spring of 1962, with the novel out and reviews appearing, Porter was once again trying to buy a house, this time in New Jersey, about a fifteen-minute drive from the Wescotts, but complaining that her lawyer and publisher had her money locked away and were telling her she couldn't afford it. To the real estate agent as well she complained of interference, in terms that reveal her awareness of the chafing pressure of patriarchy: "Oh, how much better I manage my own affairs than any man has ever been able to do for me. Yet I must be grateful for the friendly interest and concern Mr. Lawrence shows." Her old friend Mary Doherty wrote from Mexico City to congratulate her on the artistic success, which she said was "expected," and on the "money success," which was "indeed a real triumph." She added, without malice but with real foresight, that "it will be none too much. Katherine Anne is quite the person who will know how to pitch it around and spend it gayly."[35]

She did just that, going to Europe and sending back to her nephew parcels of statues, vases, silk blankets, and other beautiful things to be stored for her until she returned. While in Italy, she promised to go to Germany to visit Erna Johns's family, backed out, and thought for a while of flying to Pakistan to visit Barbara Thompson, a "brilliant" and "aristocratic English looking" young woman whom she regarded with great fondness, whose interview with her, now well known, would be published in the *Paris Review* in 1963. Thompson, she reported, once again revealing her prejudices, had "married a Pakistaner in the gummint there" and produced a "dark skinned, thatch-polled, snubby faced fat baby with eyes black as jet and slightly tilted" whose picture gave her a "shock."[36] But she did not make that trip either; she was never really eager to go anywhere outside Europe and Mexico. Instead, she lingered in Italy, moved on to Paris, gathering booty as she went, and then returned home.

Once again lapsing into her persona of "the homeless one," she began looking for a house, but again was frustrated in the effort. The incident seems, in fact, to have become one of the seeds of her later break with Seymour Lawrence. Firmly in control of her funds from *Ship of Fools,* Lawrence first encouraged her to buy the house, then had a staff member look it over to see whether she could afford it. As a result he advised her that the property was too expensive and she should proceed slowly. "Nothing works, nor can be made to work," she lamented to him in what sounds like one of her characteristic fits of depression. "I don't in the least care where I live if only I *could* live, and it is very certain I am not living now. It is just existence and a getting from one day to the next. No way to live. Just a waste. I have managed badly because everything I have done for the past several years has been done in desperation. My life is nearly unbearable; I blame no one, I have done it myself, and I must get out of it myself." She still wanted a house, she said, and was going to have one. "But not yet. Maybe next year." Her tone echoes an earlier lament to her French translator, Marcelle Sibon, "I do understand now what it means to win the war and lose the peace! Is it possible that I am never going to find a quiet place to work again?"[37] The war was, of course, the writing of the novel, but in a larger sense, as it continued into the postnovel "peace," it was her lifelong war: for independence.

Porter's later relations with Lawrence followed the established pattern of dependence, complication, and resentment. In 1964, when he moved to Alfred A. Knopf as editorial vice president, he assumed she would follow. When she wrote saying that she had decided to stay with Little, Brown there were expressions of dismay, a change of mind, and difficulties with the contract for an anthology she had long promised to edit and embellish with prefatory comments. By September she was again, despite having received almost $600,000 for *Ship of Fools* since its publication, "in a terrible jam financially," with only, she said, a few hundred dollars in the bank and "preposterous bills coming." There was also a matter of overdue income taxes. She borrowed some money from Cyrilly Abels. Lawrence, urging her to fulfill her contract with Little, Brown, sent her an advance to tide her over. Such interactions took their toll on her goodwill and her fund of gratitude. Several years later, in 1970, when *Collected Essays and Occasional Writings* was published by Lawrence in conjunction with Houghton

Mifflin, she resented what she took to be his condescending tone in thanking Robert A. Beach, Jr., George Core, William Humphrey, Rhea Johnson, and Glenway Wescott for their assistance. Whenever she signed a copy of the book, she customarily marked out the acknowledgment of their "help and guidance" and wrote in comments such as, "The mystery remains—What gave the publisher and the committee the notion they could help and guide me, even if I had needed it?"[38]

By 1976 Porter was planning a lawsuit against Lawrence, whom she now referred to as her "worst enemy" and a "disastrous . . . plague," and took umbrage when her attorney and friend E. Barrett Prettyman did not seem to take her grievance seriously. It is hard to know how much credence to give these complaints, however, since she was by then coming to suspect enmity on every hand. Not long after reprimanding Prettyman for his lack of sympathy, in fact, she fired him as well. Her affairs had to be taken over by her nephew Paul. The local newspaper noted on October 5, 1977, that she had been "ruled incapable of handling her own affairs" owing to her "deteriorated mental state."[39]

❧ *Ship of Fools* was a major event in the literary world. Yet it was soon spoken of as a disappointment, and most critics have regarded it as a far lesser achievement than Porter's shorter works. In part the problem was simply that the book was dated. It could not possibly have the impact in 1962 that it would have had in the late 1930s, when the tensions between Germany and the rest of the world that appear in the novel were actually building, or in the 1940s, when the events leading up to the war were still relatively fresh in the minds of the public. If she had been able to follow up *then* her 1931 journal letter to Caroline Gordon recounting shipboard observations that ultimately went into the novel, she might, with virtually the same book, have had something that would have swept reviewers off their feet and remained highly esteemed by subsequent critics. By 1962, however, those events and that atmosphere had already been examined and reexamined in countless books, articles, and films. Thus one of the major themes of the novel was simply old hat.

A more important problem is the book's tone, an unremitting sardonic distaste that simply piles up for 497 pages. Porter's own tension and anxiety during the war and her unavoidable (but generally unmentioned) postwar awareness of Nazi atrocities (an awareness that would reshape the philosophical assumptions of a generation) seem to have been read back into the prewar setting of the book. Cut loose from its real cause, however, the overwhelming distaste for German characters seems gratuitous. The structural problem is related. To the extent that the book does succeed it does so as a collection of separate episodes, not as a whole. As a sequence of short episodes stitched onto an overly predictable linear form, the allegorical journey, the book tediously reiterates the same sour theme. With virtually no growth by the characters and little surprise, after the first few episodes, either of incident or of emotion, the whole becomes less than the sum of its parts.

Porter had in fact begun receiving negative reactions to portions of the book long before it was published in full. In 1956 a reader of an excerpt published in the *Atlantic Monthly* wrote to object that the phrase *women peddling tail* showed Porter was a "thoroughly vile woman." That in itself was a trivial irritant. But complaints of distortion in her tone and her view of humankind had apparently begun as well. In a letter to Lawrence she pointed out that she had "some very good people" on her boat as well as some "utterly wicked ones," but for the most part her characters were "a mixture of frailty and virtues."[40] Her defensiveness on this point, then, was established early on.

Although the book was greeted with great fanfare, elicited in part by a major publicity effort, the reviews did not please her. Most reviewers insisted that it was well worth the wait, but many added qualifiers to their praise. Such reservations were most often related to the book's episodic but static form or to its emphasis on the grotesque, the disheartening, the malevolent. In May, a month after its April 1 release, when she might have seen as many as twenty-five reviews—certainly enough to detect a pattern—she puzzled to Barbara Harrison Wescott, "I wonder why some of the reviewers think I take a gloomy view of the state of this world." A few months later, writing to her nephew from Rome, she was more emphatic: Her "constant preoccupation" and "unanswered question" were "WHY the reviewers and some readers think I have been unjust to my characters and made them too outrageously and over-lifesized wicked or hateful or both." Her "poor Ric and Rac," she said, were "not monsters at all," but were based on "children I have known of nice families trying to bring them up well, and Ric and Rac are nearly angelic compared to some of those children. Why dear little Donald and David alone—but we won't go into

THAT."[41] Donald and David were her great-nephews, Ann's children. One almost wonders, seeing her describe Ric and Rac as "nearly angelic," if she was thinking of a different book.[42]

Another complaint about the novel that appeared early and has remained a staple concern relates to the fairly blatant anti-Semitism of its portrait of the Jewish character Herr Löwenthal. Summarizing this aspect of the early critical response in her biography, Givner has added significant evidence of a "virulent anti-Semitism" pervading Porter's attitudes and appearing in such forms as marginal comments written in her personal library. Indeed a study of the library supports that judgment. Theodore Solotaroff, in a review in *Commentary* in October 1962, targeted the portrayal of Löwenthal as a "caricature of Jewish vulgarity," and Josephine Herbst numbered the stereotyped characterization as one of the "nasty things in this book."[43] To a reader who had sent fan mail, Porter claimed that Löwenthal was not a caricature at all but "an all too common sort of low-caste Jew." She had seen his type "in every part of the world," but had also seen "witty cultured good looking people such as Freytag's wife and her mother." "Why," she asked, "can't all of us simply acknowledge that every nation and color and religion has its high and its low, its criminals and its saints, its stupid and gross and its delicate minded, intelligent ones?"[44] The question sounds sensible enough, but the portrayal of the Jew in *Ship of Fools* does not convey so balanced a view.

Response to the novel on the part of certain critics and friends whose views Porter particularly valued was positive. Tate wrote to say that it was very distinguished and had great driving power. Warren found it "unforgettable," a book that "creates its own genre as well as its own world of feeling." He added, "I don't know many books that can do this." Brainard Cheney congratulated her on having produced "a work of genius." Wescott admired the work extravagantly. Cyrilly Abels wrote charmingly, "Well, who else but you would attempt so difficult a structure—and bring it off! The dense, rich texture—but, of course, life." Despite the mustering of her friends, however, Porter was only too aware of the many negative judgments.[45]

Critical estimation of *Ship of Fools* has remained mixed at best. Chief among its defenders are Robert Heilman and Darlene Harbour Unrue, who regards it as the culmination of Porter's long career, bringing to fullness the unifying theme or themes of her work.[46] The contrary view is incisively summarized by Thomas F. Walsh, who calls the novel "the mediocre work of a writer of short fiction." Walsh rejects the idea that *Ship of Fools* continues Porter's earlier use of caricature; deft caricature, he argues, relies on "economy of presentation," while *Ship* belabors its caricatured portrayals in "predictable . . . repeat performances." More inclusively, Walsh views the novel as a tedious presentation of its author's overwhelming dislike of humanity in the aggregate. Except for a very few "complex and sympathetic characters," the book "encourages us to care no more about the fate of others than they do about that of Ric and Rac." The novel is finally, in Walsh's view, Porter's "last revenge against the world that denied her the love and happiness for which she yearned all her life."[47] His estimate seems to me both intelligent and well-stated.

❧ *Ship of Fools* is in many ways, not alone its length, uncharacteristic of Porter's work. She attempted to do something that was not congenial, and the strain shows. The novel is indeed, as various critics have said, episodic, but it is also surprisingly static given that it is cast in the form of a journey, a form relying on movement. Dangerous as it is to hazard a statement of what a novel should be or do, one can surely say that in general a novel should develop ideas or characters in such a way that the reader experiences them as evolving or growing. There should be a sense of discovery, both for the reader and within the experience of the characters as it is presented. But the structure of Porter's novel is more nearly one of assertion, amplification, and reassertion than one of discovery. The unfolding of characters is for the most part the demonstration of how fully they are what we thought they were from their introduction. The unfolding of theme is likewise not so much one of discovery, despite the inherent possibilities of the voyage conceit, but of confirmation. Meanness is asserted in the opening section; the extended middle section displays more and more ways in which people and events are shown to be mean; and the ending confirms that, yes, these people and perhaps all people are indeed mean.

Part of the problem is the way in which Porter handles the basic conceit itself, the voyage. One of the oldest of narrative forms, the fictional voyage exists in a number of recognizable types, defined by clusters of conventions. Familiar as it is, it is generally a form of openness and exploration, endlessly capable of correspondences between real and imaginary, outward and inner.[48] But Porter does not exploit these possibilities of the form. Beginning with the all-too-obvious title, she sets up her fictional voyage as the thinnest of allegories. The ocean crossing is only minimally suspenseful or interesting in its own right as a "real" journey. To be sure, the characters do not know what awaits them at the end of the voyage, but their uncertainty creates little suspense for the reader because the voyage is so patently allegorical. Porter herself characterized it as a "voyage to eternity" taken by "the ship of this world."[49] It is only a device for isolating her microcosm. And the only reason she has for isolating the microcosm is to say how distasteful a microcosm it is after all. Formally, *Ship of Fools* is a *calculated* work—that is, one conceived mentally and even arbitrarily, rather than one that sprang from Porter's deeper consciousness or her response to experience. As Walsh comments trenchantly, "Whereas Porter discovered evildoers and the political context in which they operated at the Hacienda Tetlapayac, she had to create them in *Ship of Fools* to illustrate her sense of evil, later reinforced by her views of German fascism."[50] This is what makes it so unlike her more characteristic and more perfectly achieved works. It is more an intellectualized than an intellectual—that is, thoughtful and thought-provoking—work.

Moreover, it is not an autobiographically resonant work in the way that most of Porter's works are. The autobiographical element in her stories was in general relatively displaced, but it was there in a deep, structuring way. She drew effectively on her own life and her sense of self in, for example, the Miranda stories. *Ship of Fools* does not lack biographical parallels and references—there are a great many; but they lie at a relatively superficial level.[51] They do not convey the ambivalent and often tortured emotions of the biographical elements in such deeply expressive works as "Noon Wine" and "Old Mortality."

The Miranda and Amy characters in "Old Morality" both love and reject their homes. They are caught in a profound inner conflict, impelled to leave yet wanting to return. Here and in other Miranda stories family traditions are shown as being all-important, yet it is only by rejecting family traditions that one can gain autonomy. The fathers in these works, in particular, are centers of powerful emotions that hold the young women in grips of ambiguous love and rejection. Leaving home means leaving the father, and they can never be adult women until they do so, but neither can they be happy after losing their role of favored child. This rich turmoil of conflicted primal emotions projects and defines Porter's own turbulent feelings about her father. By realizing so powerful a theme, she touches on inner conflicts in her readers. Through the limpidness of her style, she is able to define these conflicts with a clarity that reveals them as if for the first time.

In *Ship of Fools,* though she treats many issues that were important to her as an adult, Porter incorporates none of this primary determinant of her own emotional life—no affection for home, little of the turmoil of departing from home, none of the childhood emotions that were so enormously real for her throughout her life because she was never able to resolve them. The novel does not draw on the core of her personality—a troubled core, indeed, but a powerful one to which many readers can relate. The issues of *Ship of Fools* are thus, in a sense, superficial ones *for Porter.* The book remains on balance detached, arbitrary, even contrived. This is largely owing to the absoluteness with which she conceived the novel as an allegorical journey.

For it to represent that idea, the book had to proceed to arrival; it had to be a completed journey. Yet it is the act of departure, not arrival, that has most powerfully gripped the imaginations not only of Porter but of many women writers of the nineteenth and twentieth centuries. Leaving the house, setting one's face toward unfamiliar and even undetermined territories, has been the crucial act as women writers have rejected their known social roles and set out to find or to create new "places" that have not traditionally existed for them. Thus the journey narratives of women writers have often ended precisely at the point traditional literary journeys have begun, the point of departure. The course of the voyage itself, not to speak of the moment of arrival, is often, in Porter's work and in the fiction and poetry of many other women writers, simply uncreated, unprojected.

Not so *Ship of Fools.* For individual characters, the journey may be one of uncertainty in that they can only wonder, when they embark, what their lives will be like after they get to Germany. Jenny and David, for example, do not know whether they will be able to persevere in their stormy relationship. But the destination itself, geographically and figuratively speaking, is charted in advance, and the act of departure is not so much the launching of an exploration as simply the beginning of a transit traced through to its foregone end. The departure of the *Vera* from Vera Cruz is unambiguously unidirectional. There is no love lost for that grimy yet self-satisfied city on the part of any of the characters, and few of them expect to return. The novel is so extended a middle passage that the drama of the departure is dissipated. Perhaps because its action does not (thankfully) continue into the various characters' arrival in Europe and what that might mean to them, the self-definitional aspect of the voyage remains curiously suspended. The reader is told, probably more times than she or he wants to be, how the characters define themselves during the passage, but a change resulting from the act of separation is not evident.

In tracing the allegorical journey with a fullness not found in any other of her works, Porter scants the act of separation, which was in fact the aspect of the symbolic journey most deeply rooted in her own being. She scants, as well, the essential nature of the twentieth-century mind, its dislocation from certainty. *Ship of Fools* is absolutely, dogmatically certain in its scheme and in its thematic burden, the allegorical statement that we are all fools on a voyage signifying nothing. When she had reached this seeming point of no return, Porter's career was, in essence, ended. After 1962 she published only two works of real significance in the canon, "The Fig Tree" and "Holiday," and both had been written long before.

CHAPTER TEN

Porter as Reader and as Critic

At any rate, the arts are real, they survive, I stand by them.
—Porter to Josephine Herbst, November 23, 1938

It seems to me that St. Augustine knew the real truth of the matter: "It doth make a difference whence cometh a man's joy."
—Porter, "The Art of Katherine Mansfield"

Porter's sense of the times was intensely personal and unmediated, based on an acquaintance with many of the people who made her historic moment, or series of moments, what it was. At the same time, much of her awareness of the political and artistic kaleidoscope of the twentieth century as well as scattered portions of its heritage was gained from her reading. Throughout her long life, she was an omnivorous and indefatigable reader. Even in great age, when she had to take up residence in a nursing home, she took a selection of her books with her. She was probably one of the most widely, though not the most systematically, read of all twentieth-century authors outside the academy, and perhaps within it as well.

Her personal library was huge. As preserved at the University of Maryland, it includes some four thousand items. Of course, it is impossible to know how many of the books she owned at one time or another are missing from this collection. In her last two years, living in two joined apartments in College Park under the care of varying teams of nurses before going into the nursing home, her mental faculties in ruins, she tended to press gifts upon visitors of all sorts, strangers as well as good friends, and many of these inappropriately bestowed gifts were undoubtedly carried off. They must have included books from her library. Moreover, her guardian, Paul Porter, who assumed his court-appointed duties on September 28, 1977,[1] may have sold books of particular value as he struggled to meet the rising costs of her care out of shrinking resources. If so, he can surely not be faulted; the immediate need was more pressing than any future importance of the collection. As a result, though, we cannot regard the present library of Porter's own books as definitive. Even in its current form, however, which is being continually enhanced as books bearing her name and often her marginal comments come on the market, it is stunningly extensive and varied.

Porter acquired her library over a great many years during many of which she was strapped for funds, and it bears the stamp of momentary personal interests and impulses as well as the recurrent need to get herself up for particular pieces of writing. These impulses went in all sorts of directions. Marcella Comès Winslow, the Washington artist in whose home Porter rented lodgings for several months in 1944, forming an acquaintance that was maintained for some years, reported to her mother-in-law, the writer Anne Goodwin Winslow, that Porter had "a tremendous interest in *everything*. I have hardly hit upon a subject that she does not know something about (usually a great deal) from old colonial silver to astrology."[2] Astrology is indeed represented in the library, as are old silver and old houses and old roses.

The collection is particularly strong in mythology and anthropology, French literature, medieval and Renaissance English literature, and literary criticism. It includes less extensive but still substantial holdings in German and Spanish literature, philosophy, psychology, and political affairs, with more titles than one might expect covering religious and spiritual subjects, demonology, and arcana. There are two copies of Montaigne's *Essays,* both moderately heavily marked; one, which she acquired in 1937, is noted as having been her "3rd copy." Probably the largest number of volumes are in twentieth-century literature (novels, short stories, poetry, a few plays), criticism, and literary history. Many of these, however, were sent to her by the authors or publishers and appear to have remained virtually untouched except for her customary signing or initialing and dating on the flyleaf. As a result, the mere presence of a book in this category is much less significant than the presence of a book of another kind. One needs to look for evidence of reading and reaction.

Such evidence is abundant. Porter read interactively, pen or, more often, pencil in hand. Her characteristic markings are lines in the margin on both sides of a particular passage, underscoring, sometimes a combination of both, and occasionally double lines in the margins. These markings, absent marginal comments, appear to indicate simply emphasis, whether constituting agreement, interest, or recognition of importance. Comments indicating approval are comparatively rare; she seems to have relied on lines and underscoring to indicate that. Her copy of *The Art of the Novel,* for example, by her adored Henry James, is heavily marked but bears virtually no annotation.[3] When she disagreed she was likely to scribble emphatic protests: "no," "like hell honey—," "absurd," "fool!" In addition, she often recorded reminiscences evoked by the text at hand or new ideas sparked or her own observations on the topic, so that her reading sometimes became a virtual conversation with the author. At times, apparently when her response was particularly emphatic, she recorded the dates and times at which these conversations occurred. They tended to be between midnight and 4:00 A.M.

Porter's library itself together with her annotations gives evidence of a remarkable process of self-education and of intellectual involvement with the great (and lesser) minds among her contemporaries as well as those of the past. She did not generally mark poetry collections or anthologies—indeed, probably did not even read in anthologies except to check the indexes for her own name. Her books of this sort generally appear pristine. Nor did she usually engage in interactive reading of scholarly criticism. Even her friend Cleanth Brooks's *Modern Poetry and the Tradition* remains pretty much as it was when he gave it to her in 1939, and R. P. Blackmur's *Language as Gesture,* 1952, appears unread. It is dangerous to generalize, however. One can flip through a volume and think that she made no annotations, only to spot near the end an exclamation attached to a footnote. In contrast to criticism, literary memoirs attracted her close reading and vigorous response, partly because she knew so many of the cast of characters, whose names in the index she often marked with little plus signs. Biographies of all sorts also engaged her, and she was quick and absolute in her pronouncements on their soundness.

Porter's personal library, then, and especially the marginal annotations in her books provide a rich resource for understanding her and for adequately estimating the keenness of her intellect.

❧ A particularly significant example of the insights to be gained from examining Porter's marginalia is their indication of her reactions to one of the most interesting and important of modern intellectual dynamos,

Sigmund Freud. In general, she was hostile to Freud and his theories and often said so. The evidence is scattered throughout her library as well as her letters. This hostility is somewhat surprising, considering the psychological depth evident in her handling of characters and symbols in her fiction. Nevertheless, she generally preferred moral, theological, and economic explanations of human behavior to those of Freudian theory. The record of her reading of and about Freud, however, demonstrates a more complex process of thought.

In 1956 Porter received from her nephew Paul a two-volume biography, *The Life and Work of Sigmund Freud,* by Ernest Jones, published in 1953 and 1955. She spent many hours reading the two volumes, marking them heavily and making numerous negative, even hostile, annotations. Typical is her pronouncement on page 125 of the first volume: "*What* an idiot he was about human nature. No wonder he had to invent all that rigmarole." That "rigmarole," she said on page 458 of the second volume—betraying one of her fixed prejudices—could only have been developed by a "godless Jew." (In fairness, one should note that she took up the word *godless* from the text.) Various annotations make it plain that she regarded Freud as presumptuous and offensively imperious, dishonest, unreasonable, and egotistical and selfish in his private dealings. She was keenly aware of his rather anomalous personal puritanism. The attitudes she expressed in these volumes and elsewhere are well summarized in her comment on page 4 of the second volume: "He remained the most disgusting person of his century and *that,* considering his century, is quite an achievement. He was a pseudo-scientist and a natural Fraud."

After reading these annotations, it is surprising to take up Porter's copy of Freud's own *General Introduction to Psycho-Analysis.* She initialed and dated the volume October 21, 1947, marking it "Second Copy," which means that she had owned one previously and lost or damaged it. (She customarily indicated replacement copies in such a way, noting, for example, that the copy of *The Confessions of St. Augustine* now found in her library was not merely her second but her "7th copy.") Despite having owned and presumably read the work before, she seems to have read this copy of the *General Introduction* carefully and to have returned to it at various times. It is heavily marked, mostly with the lines or underscoring that she typically used to indicate interest or a positive response. At times she double-marked passages, for example, both underscoring and double-lining Freud's belief that the "terrible evil" evident in dreams is "simply what is original, primitive and infantile in mental life" and his conclusion that "we are not so evil as the interpretation of our dreams would lead us to suppose" (p. 187). At several points she made approving comments or extended his discussion by reference to her own observations. For example, to his commentary on the losing or breaking of objects, page 50, she added: "One loses objects when one is in the company of a person who wearies and bores or annoys one, also whom one *wants to lose*[.] This is mysterious but I know it is true!" When Freud comments, page 318, on "cases in which the childish nervousness is carried on into lifelong illness," she responds, "Yes indeed!"

One of the most interesting (in more ways than one) of Porter's marginal extensions of the doctor's text is her comment on page 130 on the transference of bad impulses to dreams: "I said in the last war that the reason the world loves the Germans so, and forgives them everything, and helps them [illegible], is because they actually *do* all the monstrous things the other 'civilized' people dream of doing. *I hadn't read Freud then*. Even the sentimental refusal of certain individuals to believe that the Germans actually did such things is only a refusal to face their own evil impulses." [Emphasis added.] Here, as in the passage on the lost objects, she uses Freudian interpretation to corroborate Freud's text. The indication that she had not read him yet during World War I (1914 to 1918) is notable in view of several assertions elsewhere that she began to read Freud in *1908* and knew immediately that he was "one of the trinity of evil."[4]

In her annotations in Freud's *Introduction,* contrary to those made after 1956 in the biography, even the instances in which Porter expresses disagreement or qualification are couched in tones of rational or even respectful discourse. She agrees with Freud's belief that every mistake has a meaning, but cautions, "not necessarily *always* a sinister one" (p. 54). Regarding penis envy, a notion she often violently rejected, she demurs mildly, "This is not an inviolable rule," and cites her memories of her own childhood feelings of "curiosity" combined with a sense that "they looked closed up and I thought they must be very uncomfortable!" She added, on page 278, "I never had and have not now any sense of inferiority as a woman. My sexual pride is very natural and very easy. I belong to the sex that has the babies." When Freud refers to the clitoris as "a region of especial excitability," she comments, "This has always been very slight for me." But she does not call Freud a fool or a trickster. Her demurrals are made within a context of rational attention.

What had happened to change her views so dramatically between the time she read and marked Freud's *Introduction to Psycho-Analysis,* some time after October 1947, and the time she read and marked Jones's biography, some time after June 1956? My theory is that in the intervening period, probably while she was still in California, she had had either a direct or a vicarious experience with the psychiatric establishment that startled or offended her. Paul Porter finds it "totally unimaginable that she would have gone to a psychiatrist." He recalls her agreeing with Christopher Isherwood that psychotherapy might take away one's creativity along with one's neuroses and that in any event it was an intrusion on one's personhood. He concedes, however, that she might have done so and "never told anyone." Considering the amount of disposable income she had during this period (which she certainly disposed of) and the fact that in the Hollywood scene in which she was moving recourse to psychiatrists was fashionable, it seems possible. As Marcella Winslow observed, she was "very open to suggestion." Paul recalls that in those years she experimented with various "quack doctors" who "treated her with calcium shots and other bizarre California 'cures' that had nothing to do with what ailed her."[5] One of them may have launched a quasi-Freudian line of inquiry. Or someone close to her may have undertaken analysis and shared a powerfully negative set of reactions. Whatever the cause, a marked change in the tone of her response to Freud and Freudian theory occurred around the late 1940s.

❧ It is easy to see in Porter's habit of immediate, emphatic response to her reading, reflected in the marginal annotations in her books, the genesis of her customary mode as a reviewer and critic. She was, in a word, opinionated, never doubting that her responses were correct and well worth recording. These multitudinous responses issued in a moderate-sized corpus of published commentary providing thoughtful, often thought-provoking personal criticism. Her *Collected Essays and Occasional Writings* includes a number of critical essays varying in length, seriousness, and stylistic polish. In addition, many of her reviews (or, more accurately, her *other* reviews; many of the essays appeared first as reviews) and her letters to literary friends, in which she carried on a lively engagement with the creative minds of her time, offer remarkable insights into Porter's critical and imaginative sensibility. Her critical writings are an open window through which we can share her views of the texts and writers she was encountering, and also a window through which we can examine the quality of her mind.

Porter's correspondence with Glenway Wescott in particular is a rich mine of interactive engagement with the contemporary literary scene. Her letters to her nephew Paul, guiding his reading and commenting on her own, are witty and illuminating; her correspondence with Josephine Herbst is perhaps unmatched for its directness and verve in addressing public affairs as well as literature and both women's work in progress; and her long exchange with Robert Penn Warren presents the record of a deep mutuality of concern with craft and with ideas. Such exchanges were so numerous and so richly diverse that it is impossible to represent them with any fullness here. A few samples, however, from the many comments on writers and books found in her letters may indicate the quality of her engagement with literary issues and the extent to which such issues were embedded in her daily personal interactions.

Her acerbic wit could be a knife thrust. She asked Herbst, for instance, in a long paragraph mostly of gossip, "But Kay [Boyle], what is happening to that girl? She gets slicker and more superficial in her writing every day. Its a crime because she had talent . . . Has it yet, but I am beginning to fear that is all. . . . Sweet, shallow, always in the fourth cocktail height of emotion." To her nephew she confessed, "Jean Stafford is a disappointment to me, because I believed she had a good talent. But she lacks vital marrow. Her first book was a wonderful mixture of all the most fashionable influences: first a layer of imitation Proust, then a layer of James, then a filling of Joyce and a frosting of Yeats." Forgetting, perhaps, that she had written these comments, she remarked to Paul again, just three weeks later, "Well, Stafford: she lacks vital marrow, and will go, is already going, in the trail of Kay Boyle . . . with overtones of Mary McCarthy: there's a crowd of them, Carson McCullers, Anais Nin, and of course, Truman Capote." Capote was her bête noire. She once referred to him as "Mr. Gruesome Caputt."[6]

She was not moderate in her reactions. Günter Grass's *The Tin Drum* struck her as the most "sickening" book she had ever read, "a study in pure loathing, sexual nausea food nausea—all a rotting flesh." Robinson Jeffers wrote "abominable, noisy vulgar, empty poems. How I do abominate that pretentious, Carmel-by-the-Sea Mystic!" (The fact that Jeffers had criticized one of her poems may have contributed to her dislike.) Hemingway, she said after his death, "did great harm in the sense that he confirmed mean little minds and limited intelligences in a kind of Hollywood notion of the deadpan hero." Of Thomas Wolfe she exclaimed, "Oh, that messy, affected, tricky style, that false fat 'gusto' the critics have been wallowing in!" Critics might call Wolfe Rabelaisian, she said, but she "like[d] Rabelais too well to have him diluted with such feeble pee-pee." Norman Mailer she dismissed with a flashing thrust: "I do not think we should encourage middle aged juvenile delinquents even if he has had the courage to write one of the foulest books ever printed in English."[7]

She could be equally glad to pay tribute. Robert Penn Warren was "the best and most distinguished poet in this country." (But fourteen years later John Crowe Ransom was the "greatest living poet in English.") Henry James's "whole life and works is (singular because the life and works is one) a standing rebuke to [his detractors'] frivolity and emptiness." E. M. Forster was "the best man of his time in England." Yeats's poems put her into "a daze of endless enchantment." Robert Frost and William Carlos Williams were "good poets, honorable men." Chekhov and Synge were "two of the best playwrights—THE best—of the world before or since for a hundred years or more."[8] In her letters, such tributes were not so frequent—or so amusing—as were the barbs. Celebrations were generally saved for essays. Letters were more often a venue for wit and for the cutting remarks she usually, though not always, refrained from making publicly.

An instance of her *not* refraining from making blistering comments in public was her speech accepting the Gold Medal of the American Academy of Arts and Sciences. She took swipes at writers who use "a kind of low, base language in which they take a very low, base view of human nature" and tore into J. D. Salinger as an example. She thought *Catcher in the Rye* a "very immoral book" and called *Franny and Zooey* "Frenzy and Phooey." Salinger, she said, "has added blasphemy to his bad English, and his terrible ideas of religion, and his terrible ideas of human relationships" and has presumed to represent as "a typical sort of an American" a set of people who "are not even human." This was perhaps an extreme performance, even for Porter.

The gauntlets she flung down were not usually taken up, but some unguarded comments she once made about her status as a Texas writer led to a lively exchange. In an interview by Winston Bode published in the *Texas Observer* as "A Portrait of Pancho," she either said or was misquoted as having said that she was the only serious writer Texas had ever produced, while the much-noted (in Texas at any rate) and respected J. Frank Dobie was "only a chronicler." She exchanged numerous letters with Bode and with Dallas newspaperman Lon Tinkle attempting to explain that she had intended to distinguish between the nature of Dobie's work, nonfiction, and the nature of her own, fiction. She agreed that she had said, as Bode claimed, that Dobie was "a chronicler, a teller or rather re-teller of tales, legends, myths of the region, and an historian," but denied that she had said he was *only* that. The tiff caused her, she complained, "hellish trouble." Finally, when Bode asked her to write him a favorable comment that might be used in advertising his work, she replied with fire: "I forbid you to mention my name in connection with anything you may publish now or later; nor to publish one line from any letter I may have written you at any time; nor to use my name in any of your schemes of promotion now or in the future. Have I made this clear. You may not quote this telegram. . . . Samuel Butler said, 'I don't mind lying, but I detest inaccuracy.' I detest both. Don't annoy me further."[9] Apparently he didn't.

In addition to the literary comments in her letters, which often served as way stations on the road to critical essays, Porter wrote, especially during the earlier years of her career, a large number of book reviews, most of them for the *New York Herald Tribune*. She published some forty-one known reviews from 1920 through 1929 and thirty more from that time until 1970.[10] As might be expected, many of these were written fairly hastily, as a means of gaining a livelihood, and they are of uneven significance. Some were plainly ephemeral. Thirteen, however, reappear in the *Collected Essays,* and several others, though left uncollected until recently, are well worth reading. She once told Herbst that she disliked contracting for reviews and there was "no excuse" for doing such "low work" unless the "poor hack gives at least an honest opinion."[11] It would appear from the reviews themselves, however, that she often enjoyed such work very much and did indeed give honest opinions. Relying on the quick thrust rather than sustained argument, her reviews provide flashes of wit and of insight. Often they provide flashes of self-revelation as well.

One of the themes apparent in her earlier reviews is a "distaste for contemporary popular fiction"[12] and other light reading. Like her response to the light entertainment she had been assigned to review for the *Rocky Mountain News* in 1919, her comments on such books as *The Chinese Coat* by Jeanette Lee and *A Gringo in Mañanaland* by Harry L. Foster make it clear that she has little patience with a writer who "sees every surface and misses every core." Her dislike of pretentious style and obfuscation and her demand for intelligent form emerge early on, for instance in her title for a 1925 review of John Cowper Powys's *Ducdame,* "Over Adornment." Her reviews of travel books consistently express disapproval of superficial judgments based on hasty impressions and of "imperialistic" condescension on the part of tourists toward Mexican Indians and other people who appear different or have unfamiliar customs. Her dislike of such superciliousness extends also to males who presume to make patronizing comments on the "cause of woman." She pointedly rejects such "good offices," asserting, "We are not a problem." A similar note would be heard in "A Most Lively Genius," her 1951 review of *Short Novels of Colette,* in which she mocked "that tone of particular indulgence, reserved for gifted women who make no pretentions and know how to keep their place in the arts: a modest second-best, no matter how good, to the next ranking male."[13]

One of the most interesting of Porter's reviews is one that was never published. In July 1930 Malcolm Cowley solicited a review of Stuart Chase's *Mexico: A Study of Two Americas* for the *New Republic.* She sent in the review shortly before leaving for Europe. In September, however, it was rejected by Cowley because of its extreme negative tone. Although Porter later conceded that she had used the review as an occasion to vent repressed anger, she resented what she regarded as Cowley's high-handedness, and their friendship suffered an irreparable blow. The review exists in typescript among Porter's papers and has recently appeared in the volume *Uncollected Early Prose,* the editors of which find that it "neatly captures the tone of 'Hacienda' " and Porter's attitude toward Mexico at the time.[14] But the two are actually quite different. Whereas "Hacienda" expresses her disillusionment with the lapsed revolution, the harsh review of Chase's book expresses anger at American tourists and journalists who undermine Mexico's culture by commercializing it and pass off their shallow impressions as informed analysis. The reason Mexico is no longer a good place to live or even to visit is that it has been spoiled and falsified by outsiders. Chase's book not only violated her feelings for Mexico by its condescending idealization;[15] it also violated her strongest literary principles by what she saw as its slipshod workmanship and its fundamental dishonesty.

❧ The most serious, or at any rate the most sustained, of Porter's critical writings are found among the *Collected Essays and Occasional Writings.* Five of the essays that seem to me most interesting and most significant are those on Thomas Hardy, D. H. Lawrence, Willa Cather, Virginia Woolf, and Gertrude Stein. These five are among the most substantively and artistically developed of the essays in their assessment of the essences of their subjects, and they offer, as well, significant insights into Porter's own career and cast of mind. All five exemplify what is perhaps the primary quality of her critical writing and thinking, the combination of an interest in artistic distinctiveness and a concern for general principles. The former might be called a romantic impulse, the latter a classical or, more accurately, an ethical one. She once declared that she had no interest in conceiving of human beings in terms of groups, but was "interested in the thumbprint."[16] In these essays she is interested in the literary thumbprint, but she also appraises the individual subject by reference to a small set of consistently held criteria.

Porter expected literature to display a sense of form, a deliberate structuring that lifts it to a different order of reality from the welter of raw experience. She demanded, as well, that writers exhibit something like Matthew Arnold's high seriousness; that they be willing to address significant material with their fullest and most committed attention. This did not mean that only subjects of ponderous magnitude or social elevation could be formed into great literature (though she did at times betray discomfort with what struck her as unworthy human subjects) but rather that the result of the writer's effort must seem somehow to matter. The writer must be able to convince her that both the subject and the treatment were worth an attentive reading. The style must have a quality of authenticity; that is, it must not be contrived of tricks or imitation, must not be florid, but must show discipline and a measure of restraint. Why these were the essential principles of judgment she did not ask herself; she took them to be self-evident.

Her judgment of current fiction, she once said, was based on a small number of works that she particularly admired: E. M. Forster's *A Passage to India,* Richard Hughes's *High Wind in Jamaica,* Ford Madox Ford's *The Good Soldier,* Virginia Woolf's *To the Lighthouse,* James Joyce's *Portrait of the Artist as a Young Man* and *Dubliners,* and Ernest Hemingway's "Big Two-Hearted River." Her choice of these was in turn, she believed, "formed" by her reading of classic eighteenth- and nineteenth-century novelists, among whom she singled out Jane Austen. It is an important list in demonstrating her commitment to the standards of literary modernism and in providing a context for her critical commentary on specific authors.[17]

D. H. Lawrence

Porter's engagement in print with the work of D. H. Lawrence began early, with a 1926 review of *The Plumed Serpent,* and was resumed thirty-four years later when she published, in the literary quarterly *Shenandoah,* an extended comment on *Lady Chatterley's Lover* and the controversy surrounding it. Both the review and the essay appear in the *Collected Essays and Occasional Writings.*

The publication of *The Plumed Serpent* provided an occasion for Porter to capitalize on her modest reputation as an expert on Mexico. At the time, she had already published four reviews and fourteen essays or other short magazine and newspaper pieces on Mexico, in addition to the catalog of the 1922 folk art exhibit. She was a natural choice to review Lawrence's book for the *New York Herald Tribune,* where most of her reviews were then being published. In responding to the turbid work, she indicated an admiration for Lawrence's musical and richly imaged style, but judged it to be in decay. His prose still had at times a "muscular power," but it lapsed into "booming, hollow phrases" of "artificial raptures." Even at this early stage in her career, then, she had the self-assurance to apply to an accepted master her own yardstick of stylistic discipline and to find him wanting. The book was also, she thought, marred by "pretentiousness" in its quasi-mystical apperception of Mexico. It provided a "summing up" of Lawrence's "mystical philosophy," but that philosophy remained a mishmash of confusion, misunderstanding, personal wish fulfillment, and prejudice.

Mysticism was not a quality of mind Porter found congenial, and her tone in handling ideas of sacred mystery and the occult is uneasy. She regarded herself, during those years, as a thoroughgoing rationalist, believing that one should "take the visible world, and [one's] little lamp of reason, as guides." When her sister Gay took refuge in spiritualism after the death of her child, Porter called it "a superstition for darkened minds" and an "ugly and unworthy means resorted to by mediums to touch the dead again." On the other hand, she described to Gay what one might take to be a mystical experience of her own, one that also involved contact with the dead.[18]

Thus she seems to have encountered Lawrence with mixed preconceptions, which are evident in the review. Lawrence's idea of blood knowledge she dismisses as "artificial Western mysticism" colliding with the "truly occult mind of the Indian." But she describes Indian religious mysteries, at any rate as he depicted them, in condescending terms that call into question her attitudes toward Indian beliefs and ceremonies in their own right. The implication is that reality has no truck with any of this and the honestly realistic writer will choose a fictional milieu true to modern technological society.

Her review of *The Plumed Serpent* was mild, however, compared with her 1960 essay on *Lady Chatterley's Lover* and what she saw as its shabby obscenity. Lawrence's novel of the lady and the gamekeeper, long suppressed in the United States, had just been made generally available by a 1959 court order. A similar decision would be reached in 1960 in England. These events naturally focused Porter's attention on the morality or immorality of the book.

Moral rectitude was not one of her usual avowed standards for judging serious literature except insofar as it was a function of the honesty or the giving of an honest testimony that she demanded of an author. In fact, however, she had little tolerance for scatological or sexually explicit material. In her essay, she applauds the court decision overturning censorship of the novel, deploring in the most emphatic terms the "rise to power of a demagoguery of political and social censorship by unparalleled ignoramuses" who know nothing about art but take a "morbid purblind interest" simply in order to advance their notions of propriety.[19] At the same time, she has come to believe, she says, that she is not obligated to defend a dull or ill-crafted book—as she considers *Lady Chatterley's Lover* to be—simply because she opposes censorship. She had in fact done just that some thirteen years earlier, in 1947, when she supported an effort to get the ban on James Farrell's *Bernard Clare* lifted despite finding it "oh so dull and incoherent."[20] Since then (though she claims she began to change her mind when she first read *Lady Chatterley's Lover* in 1928) she has had a "change of view." She is glad Lawrence's book is no longer censored, but that does not mean she has to praise it.

Listing a number of famous and respected critics who *have* praised the book as being "pure" or "deeply moving"—Archibald MacLeish, Harvey Breit, Edmund Wilson, Jacques Barzun, Mark Schorer—she sets herself directly in opposition, in a way that Flannery O'Connor found "refreshing." The book, she says, is dull, overwrought, and at times unintentionally funny. In essence, she accuses Lawrence of violating one of the chief principles of good writing, honesty and plain statement, by attempting to pass his obscenity off for something it is not. "Instead of writing straight, healthy obscenity, he makes it sickly sentimental, embarrassingly so." She objects to "this pious attempt to purify and canonize obscenity, to castrate the Roaring Boy, to take the low comedy out of sex." "The attempt to make pure, tender, sensitive washed-in-the-blood-of-the-lamb words out of words whose whole intention, function, place in our language is meant to be exactly the opposite is sentimentality, and of a very low order." (In a marginal comment written in F. R. Leavis's *D. H. Lawrence: Novelist,* which she apparently read only a year or two before writing her essay, she also accused him of "vile sentimentality and falseness.") Still, it seems, some degree of discretion should prevail. Whatever a man and a woman want to do in their sexual relations, they should "keep it to themselves," and apparently so should the author. Lawrence's display of artificially stimulated "obscene acrobatics" is a "never-ending wrong" (the phrase she later used as the title of her memoir on the Sacco-Vanzetti case) against "the human imagination." Human sexuality is "one of the more private enterprises," and the book makes her feel that she has "overheard talk and witnessed acts never meant for me to hear or witness."[21] She convicts Lawrence, finally, of a failure of reserve and artistic tact.

Porter's position on the issue does not resolve but merely holds in suspension the conflict between her commitment to free expression and her judgment that in this instance the nature of the expression was artistically and humanly distasteful. Thus in wrestling with one of the most persistent and troublesome civil liberties issues of her time she reached no fuller a resolution than have many other outstanding minds. Her essay, "A Wreath for the Gamekeeper," became more of a cause célèbre than she could ever have anticipated when it was taken up as part of the evidence in the censorship hearing on the book in England. Stephen Spender, editor of *Encounter,* in which a revised version of the essay was reprinted in February 1960, wrote to her that the journal was receiving a great many reactions to the piece, few of which were either neutral or moderate. She replied that the episode reminded her of the uproar following her comically severe comment on Gertrude Stein.[22]

Gertrude Stein

Porter's amusing but controversial attack on another of the reigning personages of modernism, Gertrude Stein, resembles her attack on Lawrence in that it accuses her of pretentiousness and obfuscation. In this case the material that appears in the *Collected Essays* is made up of three earlier pieces: a review of *The Making of Americans,* published in 1927 in the *New York Herald Tribune* with the title "Everybody Is a Real One"; a review of *Useful Knowledge,* published in the *Herald Tribune* in 1928; and an essay published in *Harper's* in 1947 as "Gertrude Stein: A Self Portrait" but here given the title "The Wooden Umbrella." This odd title refers to a ludicrous but distinctive object described by Stein in *Everybody's Autobiography.* The three pieces together are collectively given the descriptive title "Gertrude Stein: Three Views"—an apt designation in that the three parts of the whole are indeed three separate views that not only do not cohere but in fact do not agree. Between the writing of the first and the writing of the third, Porter's view of Stein had undergone a decided change, partly determined by personal experiences.

The 1927 review expressed direct, unembellished praise. *The Making of Americans,* she said, is a "very necessary book" that gives readers the most honest, most directly sensed account of themselves, their friends, and their friends' friends—though only if they are of the American middle class. But that is no problem, she said, because America has hardly anything else—a common but inaccurate view of American society and one based on sweepingly racist assumptions about who Americans, real Americans, are. She implies that she considers it a remarkably wise book and one that meets her standard of authorial honesty. "There are only a few bits of absolute knowledge in the world, people can learn only one or two fundamental facts about each other, the rest is decoration and prejudice. [Stein] is very free from decoration and prejudice."[23]

At the time she wrote this review, Porter's high regard for Stein was well established. Her discovery of *Tender Buttons* in a Corpus Christi bookshop cum shoeshine parlor in or about 1913 is described in the essay "Reflections on Willa Cather," published in 1952, as a momentous but not entirely positive event in that her initial reactions to Stein were "the beginning of my quarrel with a certain school of 'modern' writing in which poverty of feeling and idea were disguised, but not well enough, in tricky techniques and disordered syntax." She wondered, she says, "why she did not say" what she meant.[24] This account, however, is disingenuous. At the time, she had thought Stein brilliant and had read her subsequent books eagerly.

In 1926, a year before the publication of her review of *The Making of Americans,* she said in a letter to Genevieve Taggard that her husband, Ernest Stock, had given her a copy of the book for her birthday and had also carved her "a little elephant paper cutter of soft pine." She seems to have been pleased by both. One assumes that Stock would not have chosen to give her the book if she had not asked for it or if he did not have some other reason to believe she would like it; they had little money to risk on uncertain treats. By June 3, less than three weeks after her birthday, she had read enough to make some summarizing comments: "I find that admirable woman writes in a continual spiral, which is, as you know, the very form of the germ of life; it is not hard to read once you recognise that it is the spiral, and let your mind follow loosely relaxed."[25] She would utilize the spiral image in her review. In the same letter she lists Stein's *Three Lives* among a half dozen titles that she wanted to order. When she was engaged in the controversy that resulted from her publication of "The Wooden Umbrella," in 1953, she again, as in the Cather essay, represented this early reading of Stein very differently. Before meeting Stein in 1933, she said, she had read *Tender Buttons, Three Lives, The Making of Americans,* and *Useful Knowledge,* and "it seemed plain" that "Miss Stein was not for me."[26] In 1926 she had obviously thought Stein *was* for her, and the 1927 review indicates as much.

Only a year later, in 1928, she published a review of *Useful Knowledge,* "Second Wind," which was couched as a parody. She seems in the interim to have become somewhat more bothered by Stein's non sequiturs, flat statements, and odd coordinations than when she wrote the first review. Still, her tone is more one of amusement or good-natured fun than of censure. Some years later, Porter said that *Useful Knowledge* had caused her to "reconsider" Stein's work five years before meeting her and to decide that Stein was "on the whole a bore, and a little of a fraud."[27] Again, however, although the possibility of such a judgment is raised by the parodic style of the review, there is no indication of so fundamental a change in her estimate. Indeed, in a 1931 review of two books by Kay Boyle, Porter labeled Stein and James Joyce, equally, "the glories of their time"—high praise indeed.[28] A letter from Donald Sutherland to Donald Gallup of the Yale University Library, a copy of which Sutherland addressed to Porter, indicates that when he met Porter in 1942 he "had the impression, from our conversations, that she liked Gertrude Stein and her writing as I did, since she said that all anyone had to know about character was already contained in *The Making of Americans*. Or something very like that, and more than I would have said of the book myself."[29]

After settling in Paris in 1932, Porter met Stein at her famous salon apartment at the invitation of Allen Tate and Caroline Gordon. Givner summarizes known information about the visit and subsequent events and conjectures that the "atmosphere may have displeased her." If Stein, "as was her custom," directed her attention to "the male visitor" and consigned the women to a table in the corner with Alice B. Toklas, implying their lesser status, Porter "would have been offended." Porter's June 2, 1953, letter to Sutherland confirms that the "atmosphere itself" had displeased her, evoking a "deep feeling of boredom and futility and sense of suffocation," as if she were "in the wrong place with the wrong people." But she insists that Stein and Toklas were both "perfectly friendly and courteous." It is difficult to know, then, whether Givner's conjecture about something like a snubbing by the great Stein actually occurred, but the guess is plausible, based as it is on Stein's customary behavior. Sutherland's letter to Gallup also alludes to the 1933 visit in terms that indicate it was not a comfortable one, saying simply that he understood Porter "had the traditional difficulty with the small tables and chairs in Gertrude Stein's studio at 27 rue de Fleurus."[30]

Givner provides another possible explanation for Porter's growing distaste, and one that would also have arisen from the 1933 visit with Tate and Gordon, namely, that since Porter was always "suspicious of Lesbians and often spoke harshly of them, she was discomfited by the direct encounter with Stein and Toklas."[31] It is an appropriate reminder. Porter's uneasiness with indeterminacy of gender has already been noted, and Stein, if anyone, would have aroused that uneasiness. But Stein's cross-dressing was, as literary historians Sandra M. Gilbert and Susan Gubar have argued with great thoroughness, a manifestation of one of the central engagements of female modernism, a challenge to male privilege through the redefinition of gender. She was not alone in "defying the conflation of sex roles and sex organs that many of their male contemporaries sought to reinforce" or in doing so in part by "transgressively appropriat[ing] male costumes."[32] Porter's discomfort with blurred sexual identities and her emphatic assertion of her own feminine, not merely female and not feminist, identity through her choice of glamorous costume indicate both her troubled sense of her own sexuality and her ambivalence about one of the major social and intellectual currents of her time, its challenge of inequalities based on sex. Her fundamental and complex anxiety about gender may well have colored her changing response to Stein. Indeed, her jibe in "The Wooden Umbrella" about "Amazons which nineteenth-century America produced among its many prodigies: not-men, not-women" would seem to support this surmise.[33]

Even allowing for the distaste evoked by direct encounter with Stein's lesbianism, it is not clear that, as Givner judges, Porter's "admiration . . . changed abruptly" on the occasion of her visit to 27, rue de Fleurus, though it was surely shaken. By the time she published the essay that appears in *Collected Essays* as "The Wooden Umbrella," however, she had definitely become hostile, having decided that Stein was "a blight on everything she touched." The final determinant of that change was quite personal, contributing to her being "accused" of "ignoble motives" in writing the essay. The incident was a second Porter visit to Stein's Paris establishment, not by Katherine Anne herself this time but by her nephew Paul. It is recorded in a (possibly disingenuous) letter from Stein to Donald Sutherland, quoted in the letter that Sutherland copied for Porter when he made their correspondence available to public view by sending it to Yale.[34]

Stein's account goes: "One day a young gentleman called and he sent in a note saying that he was the nephew of Katherine Anne Porter. Then he came in and I said gently and politely, do I know your aunt, I am afraid said he you have never met, and said I politely who is she, and he went quite white and said you know and I said no, and then he decided to take it as a joke, but it was a blow, he had evidently traveled far on his nephewship." Porter's version is, as one would expect, somewhat different. She calls the entire report "mean little gossip" about a "paltry little episode" occasioned by Sylvia Beach's having sent Paul to Stein with instructions that he should mention his aunt, and says that according to his recollection Stein was neither gentle nor polite. Paul is so far from traveling on his nephewship, she insists, that he is indeed "somewhat overscrupulous" and "will not let me help him."[35] That, of course, was not true. Porter often berated her nephew for being only too eager to let her help him (though she was at other times only too eager to do so).

Clearly, the incident of Paul's visit and Sutherland's exposure of Stein's account of it to public view stung Porter in two ways. It discomfited a relative of whom she was very solicitous, and it affronted her by calling into question her stature among those she wanted to consider her peers. But the fact was, and is, that she never achieved the eminence of a Stein or a Joyce, however much she wanted to believe she did. Her work was of a quality—a beauty, one might as well say—that may ultimately make it loved when theirs is no longer read. Indeed, that is already true except among academic specialists. But she did not have, and would never have, the impact on the sensibility of her age that Stein or Joyce had. And she cannot have enjoyed facing that fact.

She took her vengeance by responding to Russell Lynes's invitation to send him something for publication in *Harper's*. "Gertrude Stein: A Self-

Portrait" appeared in late 1947 and evoked a storm of protest. And rightly so. It is a brilliantly written assassination not merely of Stein's writing, which she had parodied earlier, but of her very self. As Givner observes, Porter portrays Stein as "a compendium of the seven deadly sins," among which greed, acedia, avarice, envy, and sloth are prominent and were named by Porter in correspondence with Herbst.[36] Not that it is not witty, of its kind. Her image for Stein's "tepid, sluggish nature"—something "eating its way through a leaf"—is memorable. The accusation of interminable talking in a "slow swarm of words" constituting the "long drone and mutter and stammer of her lifetime monologue" fits all accounts of Stein's manner as she held court in Paris. If at the end Porter accords her a single redemptive virtue, the fact that she fell so "in love with the whole American army below the rank of lieutenant" during World War II that she wished to extend a blessing to all GIs, that fact is not enough to counteract an entire lifetime of torpor and a mind numbed by "willful ignorance." She is left immobile and useless, like a wooden umbrella that "feeling the rain" was "struggling slowly, slowly, much too late, to unfold."[37]

Several of Porter's friends rallied to praise the essay. Eleanor Clark called it "really extraordinary," especially "the phrase about zombie-ism." Elizabeth Ames said it was a "prize piece." Ernestine Evans wrote asking, "Are you ill, or well? You *must* be well, as the Gertrude Stein piece was written by a strong sabre arm." John Malcolm Brinnin said many years later that he only wished his book on Stein had captured her as cleanly as Porter's essay had.[38] But others were offended by her evident maliciousness. Sutherland could think of no response but to place Stein's letter where it could be consulted in future years, since his affection for Porter, he said, prevented him from attacking her in print. Instead, he made an implicit attack in a personal letter, and when he attempted to patch it up after her furious response he made matters worse by casting slights on "the feminine mind," which, he said, "lives and breathes in the personal and the sensory" so that when women "go on the attack" there is inevitably "the substance and texture of gossip." Porter reproved him again, even more severely. He was welcome to disagree with her and to criticize her work, she said, but shouldn't "expose" himself by "putting it on the grounds that I am a woman."[39]

But it was Herbst who responded most quickly and most directly, incisively distinguishing between matter and manner. "I have to dissent on your Stein piece. It reads so persuasively but it isn't Stein. She was all that your piece divulges but that isn't the whole story. Not by a long shot." In the following year, 1948, Herbst made essentially the same comment publicly in the *Partisan Review.* The essay had "a witty ring," she conceded, "but is it true?" Her argument was not only that Porter had presented a distorted view of Stein, but that her article was part of a general attack on modern art in the name of the reactionary values of safety and conformity.[40] The exchange effectively put an end to their long friendship, which had, in fact, been waning for many years. Porter reported the episode to Tate some years later, taking a swipe at Herbst along the way. Some of her former friends, she said, didn't like her any more. "Josie Herbst for one, quit me cold—or rather, red-hot, over my Gertrude Stein piece, a pity, for she was ever so much better a letter writer than she ever was novelist. . . . I miss her, but it can't be helped."[41]

Thomas Hardy and T. S. Eliot

Porter's 1940 essay "On a Criticism of Thomas Hardy" is unusual among her critical writings in that it was not preceded by frequent references in letters. Although it is clear from the essay itself that she regarded Hardy as an important presence in the history of the novel, we can conjecture that she would not have written on him had she not been provoked by Eliot's attack, which was based not on purely literary but on theological grounds. Freedom of expression and the valuation of literature for its own sake, not for instrumental or ideological purposes, were cardinal principles of Porter's. Not that she was always consistent in applying them; she was greatly displeased, for example, by Warren's *All the King's Men* because she saw it as defending a person whose values were reprehensible—an instrumental rather than artistic judgment. But she was able to see clearly when the same thing was being done by another person, especially if it was in the service of a cause she deplored. She rose to the defense and turned the issue into one of principle. In so doing, she produced an essay of great interest for its critical response to Eliot as well as to Hardy and for the thoughtful way in which it addresses issues of freethinking, orthodoxy, and aesthetic evaluation.

In part, Porter had reservations about Eliot's humanity. She told Wescott in a letter written some years after her essay that he was "a dry damned soul." That view is confirmed in her recollections of a reading she heard at Sylvia Beach's bookshop in 1932. Eliot read in a "dry" voice, "turning the pages now and again with a look very near to distaste, as if he did not like the sound of what he was reading." His expression was "fiercely defensive" and "bitter," and he established no rapport with his listeners. In contrast, James Joyce, who was among those listening, was passionately intense, an artist who "had courage for all of us, and patience beyond belief, and the total intensity of absorption in his gift, and the will to live in it and for it in spite of hell."[42] More seriously, however, she disliked the dogmatism that entered Eliot's work after his conversion to Anglicanism and distrusted what she saw as his dictatorial tendencies.[43] It was the quality of dogmatism in his comments on Hardy that spurred her response.

Her rhetorical strategy is an interesting and powerful one. Beginning with an instance of what she calls "theological hatred," the Bishop of Wakefield's alleged burning of *Jude the Obscure,* she contrasts the bishop's intolerance with Hardy's own charity of mind and the "amiable" advice of another clergyman that potential village rectors learn the "essential dignity of country people" by reading Hardy. She then points to the "calamitous history of institutional religion" and implies, by turning directly to Eliot, that he is a living example of that calamitous history. Quoting at length Eliot's own words, she demonstrates that he judged Hardy according to a prescriptive doctrinaire criterion, the doctrine of Original Sin. By contrast, her own characterization of Hardy emphasizes his breadth of humanity and his honest doubts of orthodox answers to difficult questions. The effect of such a strategy is necessarily positive. Having invoked the unfortunate term *edifying,* Eliot's criticism provided her sharp wit the perfect opportunity to be thankful that indeed the "complacency of edification is absent" from Hardy's work. That Eliot himself is guilty of an immense complacency then goes without saying.[44]

In Porter's view, Hardy becomes a saint of heterodoxy who "knew the master he was serving" (a phrase lifted from Eliot himself): his conscience. Eliot found Hardy to have an untrained mind; Porter replied that "untrained minds have always"—one recalls Sacco and Vanzetti—"been a nuisance to the military police of orthodoxy." Moreover, she saw in Hardy a "Franciscan tenderness in regard to children, animals, laborers, the poor, the mad, the insulted and injured." He was a defender of "the helpless" against the injustices of "entrenched authority and power." Eliot, as a spokesman for orthodoxy, is tacitly arrayed with the oppressors. Hardy was, as well, opposed to war and to capital punishment. He was devoted to the "individual dignity and importance of the country people"—a phrase that may reflect Porter's sometime interest in Southern Agrarianism and her continuing loyalty to the idea, though not the fact, of her rural Texas origins. By contrast, Eliot "speaks as a man of the town," opening himself to easy charges of snobbery by referring to Hardy's rural characters as "period peasants." One can hardly imagine a more inviting rhetorical opening for someone who, like Porter, was adept at turning words into weapons.[45]

After crushing Eliot's argument on the grounds of Hardy's virtue and his sense of moral tragedy, Porter turns to his famous comment on Hardy's style, that it "touch[ed] sublimity without ever having passed through the stage of being good." It is a witty phrase, to be sure, but again she takes the high rhetorical ground. She concedes that Hardy's prose may lumber and creak along, but insists that he achieved scenes and even whole books that live in the memory with "somber clearness." In the end he "arrived at his particular true testimony"—a phrase Porter characteristically used to mean authenticity or integrity of work.[46]

The essay is both a ringing and affectionate tribute to Hardy and a severe criticism of Eliot, whom she sees as having declined into the unimportance of servitude to dogma. The critical vision it conveys is one that might be described as humane. Beyond its effectiveness as a statement of specifically literary principles, it is interesting as an expression of Porter's intellectual and political principles generally. We recall not only her insistence on giving her true testimony but also her pride in maintaining a "free, intransigent, dissenting" mind.[47] It was her insistence on free thought and free expression and her abhorrence of the "never-ending wrong" of repression of those freedoms that fueled her concern with the Sacco and Vanzetti affair. The essay incorporates, as well, her long-standing concern for the politically and economically oppressed and her avowed pacifism. At the time it was written, 1940, she was particularly vocal in maintaining that avowal. "On a Criticism of Thomas Hardy," then, is an important document in Porter's canon both as a literary statement and as a statement of the essential principles of her political liberalism, at a time when she was pulling back from her earlier radical stance.

Virginia Woolf

In 1931 Porter advised her family to try Virginia Woolf's *The Waves* if they wanted "a very beautiful book to read." She continued, "She is ill, I hear, and not young any more, and if she writes another book I shall be surprised.

But may I have as good and solid and honest a body of work behind me when I say Good-bye to All That" (an allusion to Robert Graves's noted 1929 memoir of the Great War).[48]

Woolf was one of the few writers Porter never hesitated to place among the very greatest of her time. Her 1950 review of Woolf's posthumous *The Captain's Death Bed,* originally published with the title "Virginia Woolf's Essays—A Great Art, a Sober Craft," is unique among her critical essays in being an unqualified celebration. A comparable piece from about the same time, her 1951 review of E. M. Forster's *Two Cheers for Democracy,* is perhaps as uniformly positive as the one on Woolf, but its tone is not so celebratory, perhaps because Forster was still living at the time while Woolf was deceased, and thus memorializing was appropriate. Porter always admired Forster, and associated him with that conjunction of technical mastery and wholeness of vision that was her standard for literature of the highest level. She called him "my adoration and my despair for a great number of years—ever since *Passage to India,*" which she said she had first read in 1924. On the flyleaf of a copy she acquired in 1947 (apparently the fifth she had owned) she called it her "favorite 'modern' novel except 'To the Lighthouse' and others by Virginia Woolf."[49] But she did not mention Forster in the company of Yeats, Joyce, and James as she did Woolf.

Woolf, she said, was "a great artist, one of the glories of our time," who "never published a line that was not worth reading." *The Voyage Out,* about a young woman's self-discovery, gave her a "sense of some mysterious revelation of truth." In her independence of taste, sureness of what she meant to say, and commitment to craft, Woolf clearly measured up to Porter's standard of the artist's vocation. What is more, she, like Hardy, "lived outside of dogmatic belief."[50]

Porter's tribute to Woolf is very short; it does not touch on the subtleties of individual works. Indeed, her essays on literature were characteristically expressions either of praise or of blame, meted out according to very personal standards, not close analyses in the manner of her New Critical friends. She once told her nephew that she supposed "if a critic were neutral, he wouldn't trouble to write anything."[51] We can infer that she admired Woolf's technical innovation and subtlety, her emphasis on form, and her tonal control, but she does not discuss these matters specifically. The importance of the review lies in its clear indication of how greatly she esteemed Woolf's achievement.

At various times Porter commented on a number of women writers, including (besides Stein and Woolf) Austen, whom she revered, Caroline Gordon, whom she admired, Eudora Welty and Flannery O'Connor, on whom she doted, and Josephine Herbst, toward whom she had serious reservations. None of her comments on women writers stresses gender. In her treatment of Woolf she mentions a number of essays, but not the two great documents of feminism, *A Room of One's Own* and *Two Guineas*. Perhaps if her review had been written at an earlier time, before her avowed pacifism turned to support of World War II, she would have praised the feminist pacifism of *Two Guineas*. Or perhaps even then its feminism would have proved too strong for her. We can only wonder whether she read Woolf's joyous parable of androgyny, *Orlando*, and if so, what she thought of it.

Willa Cather

The most complex as well as one of the longest of Porter's critical essays is her "Reflections on Willa Cather," published in 1952. The essay is the culmination of a number of scattered critical comments, including a *New York Times* review of a posthumously published book of Cather's essays, *Willa Cather on Writing*. Annotations in Porter's copy of the book indicate a close and admiring reading. Of one essay, "Escapism," she exclaimed, "How fine it is!" Her essay on Cather, however, conveys a response colored by a sense of rivalry.

Porter once remarked in a letter to Eugene Pressly that Cather "should be president of the Girl Scouts" and that she resembled Ellen Glasgow and Pearl Buck in that none of them had any "wilderness" in them.[52] The idea of a lack of excitement or wildness reappears as a major theme in her essay. Despite avowing her admiration of this literary elder sister, she conveys an image of Cather that implies a certain dullness and lack of modernity. The essay is in fact an extraordinarily competent exercise in duplicity through which Porter manages to enhance her own stature while appearing to praise Cather's. Its rhetorical strategy does not so much reflect literary sisterhood as it does the supposedly masculine "anxiety of influence" propounded by Harold Bloom, which describes the relationship of major writers as a rivalry or, in Nina Baym's words, a "quasi-Freudian father and son conflict."[53] Thus it is as interesting for what it tells us of Porter herself as for what it tells us of her view of Cather.

Once again, the tone of the piece is personal rather than analytic. Its method is indeed surprisingly autobiographical. She works narratively, summarizing her acquaintance with Cather's writing and expressing her responses both to the work and, more pervasively, to the quality of Cather's mind and personhood. Her points of emphasis, somewhat surprisingly, are Cather's physical appearance, her home education, and what finally comes to seem her old-fashionedness.

The matter of personal appearance is launched in the opening paragraph: "There are three or four great ones, gone now, that I feel, too late, I should not have missed" because it would have been nice "just to remember how they looked." She knows something of how Cather looked, however, because of the famous Edward Steichen photograph showing "a plain smiling woman, her arms crossed easily over a girl scout sort of white blouse, with a ragged part in her hair. She seemed, as the French say, 'well seated' and not very outgoing. Even the earnestly amiable, finely shaped eyes, the left one faintly askew, were in some mysterious way not expressive, lacking as they did altogether that look of strangeness." Although the tone of the description sounds rather affectionate, it stresses a certain plainness in the visual image. Some might find the ambiguous half-smile caught in Steichen's picture intriguing, the expression in the eyes not so much earnest as guarded or ambivalent. Indeed, when the essay came out in 1952 in *Mademoiselle*—which probably strikes today's reader as an improbable venue for so literary an essay—a former pupil of Cather's wrote to protest, "Please, she was not big and she was not plain."[54]

Porter herself was, of course, extraordinarily beautiful as well as vain. Her photograph had appeared in *Vogue* and other magazines. She could count on many of her readers to know that unlike the Cather she describes she herself was neither "well-seated" nor "plain." By stressing Cather's lack of glamour, she was implicitly striking a contrast that would enhance her own image. The lack of a "look of strangeness" in Cather's eye, or what she goes on to call the "afterlight" of a "wild vision," recalls her earlier assertion that Cather lacked "wilderness." Instead, she looked "awfully like somebody's big sister, or maiden aunt."[55]

Cather came from a family reduced in circumstances but well able to inculcate an "aspiration" toward true "nobility"—very much the kind of family Porter liked to claim for herself. She had "literate parents and grandparents, soundly educated and deeply read, educated, if not always at schools, always at their own firesides," and she read Greek and Latin with a nearby storekeeper—"not the first nor the last American writer to be formed in this system of home education." She was "the true child of her plainliving, provincial farming people, with their aristocratic ways of feeling and thinking; poor, but not poverty-stricken for a moment."[56] That Porter intends this praise of Cather's family and her home education to reflect well on herself is made clear in a letter she wrote to her sister Gay some six years later. Launching into a discussion of the merits of home education and the fact that she herself "never set foot in a college or university until I went there to teach literature, or to take D. Litt degrees," she boasted, "I still think I am a good example of what home education can do." She recalled Gay's studying of Latin and ancient history in "that little public school in Kyle, Texas" (she may actually have been remembering the Thomas School in San Antonio) and linked their experience with Cather's: "I always remember Willa Cather in Red Cloud Nebraska, reading Greek with the little man who kept the grocery store down the road!"[57] Missing from both the letter and the essay is any acknowledgment that, unlike herself, Cather had a university education.

Turning to Cather's writing, Porter makes several rhetorical moves that effectively position her own work nearer the center of modernism and move Cather's toward the periphery. First, after enumerating the books by Cather that she has read, she singles out the short stories, praising them in a language as generous as it is judicious: "They live with morning freshness in my memory, their clearness, warmth of feeling, calmness of intelligence, an ample human view of things; in short the sense of an artist at work in whom one could have complete confidence."[58] But by locating her primary critical esteem in Cather's short stories, she has moved the locus of discourse onto her own terrain. Porter was recognized as a consummate artist of the short story and could well afford to be generous in her praise of a writer who was rarely perceived as an innovator in the form. Not yet having managed to produce a novel, despite her widely publicized efforts to do so, she could scarcely have spoken from such a position of strength if she had directed her attention to Cather's novels, which were *her* strongest ground and the chief source of her reputation.

Having strategically positioned the discourse, Porter then praises Cather for a quality that is equally characteristic of her own work, reticence or reserve. Last, she praises Cather's independence of mind, but does so in a way that implies a certain stodginess. "Freud had happened"; "Stravinsky had happened"; "The Nude had Descended the Staircase"; "Joyce had happened." But, point by point, Cather preferred the old ways. Overtly, Porter praises her for resisting what we might call trendiness. But in their cumulative effect the sequence of ignored innovators leads to the conclusion that she was not abreast of her time. Even Joyce, whose greatness Porter always acknowledged, "caused not even the barest tremor in Miss Cather's firm, lucid sentences."[59]

In its emphasis on Cather's family, early life, and appearance, "Reflections" is more a biographical than a critical essay, but it is finally in effect more *auto*biographical than biographical. The primary rhetorical strategy is to make of it a story in which Porter herself is the protagonist. The first word of the essay is "I," and the first person pronoun retains its primacy throughout. The main actions giving the essay its dynamic movement are not Cather's but Porter's own. She discovers books in a little Texas town (not only Cather's books, but Stein's, James's, Conrad's, and Joyce's as well), reads, moves restlessly among plays and concerts, goes to Europe, makes up her mind about Cather, changes her mind. Clearly, she has been as adventurous as Cather was, in her depiction, dull. Seeming to praise Cather, she takes over center stage herself. Reflecting on Cather, she makes of her a mirror reflecting her own image.

Several years after writing her essay, Porter commented in a letter to a friend that Cather had "only vast emotional friendships with women, and lived forty years with a devoted faceless, selfless female creature" who wrote a memoir that was the best we have but gave Porter "a slight shudder because it is the sort of thing infatuated wives write about their husbands." Even so, it was "impossible" for her "to believe that those two housemates were ever anything but two old maids—one of them a genius, that's true—who shared a kind of nunnery against their loneliness." After rejecting the unspeakable, however, she comments, "But the mere notion of that kind of existence gives me the horrors." Was her horror a response to their perceived loneliness or to the hint of lesbianism in the picture she had drawn? Either would have been entirely fitting to Porter's sensibility. She had said in her essay that "nobody, not even one of the Freudian school of critics, ever sat up nights with a textbook in one hand and her works in the other, reading between the lines to discover how much sexual autobiography could be mined out of her stories."[60] She proved to be a poor prophet on this point. More interesting, though, is the fact that she herself manifested an interest in the line of thought that led to the Freudian criticism she deplored.

❧ Porter's aesthetic principles are not stated systematically in any one document but are scattered throughout her letters, reviews, and essays. Still, they are fairly coherent and consistent. In what she called her first speech, she stated "maybe too simply" that the writer's business is "first to have something of his own to say; second, to say it in his own language and style." But if the style was "forced" or "exclamatory"—that is, if it was florid or did not have the genuine ring of a "true testimony"—woe to the artist. It should be a "good measured spare style."[61] Formally, art should not replicate life but reshape it. In working on her book on Cotton Mather she complained that there was "too much material, the subject is too well documented, and I can't turn my imagination loose." The balance between craft and material was threatened. An art "not rooted in human experience" would not be "worth a damn," but craft, not raw experience, should predominate.[62]

She also placed strong emphasis on the writer's independence of mind and sensibility—a quality that was, indeed, the key to her own nature. "Artists are not political candidates," she believed, "and art is not an arena for gladiatorial contests." If a writer begins to ask what some external group, whether family or friends or political party, will think of something, he or she has taken "the road by which the artist perishes." Pressures that threaten art may come from the political right (for instance, from publishers' advertising departments) or from the left. Either way, the effect is much the same. "I surmise the same kind of threat to freedom in a recently organized group of revolutionary artists who are out to fight and suppress if they can, all 'reactionary' artists—that is, all artists who do not subscribe to their particular political faith." It took a bit of nerve to mention this threat as she did: She was responding at the time to a series of questions posed by the editors of the *Partisan Review*. Her statement was in effect a declaration of independence.

Porter never moderated her belief in the necessity for art to pursue its own aims and not become a tool of other aims. It was this belief that turned her away from communism. She debated the question inwardly and in her letters to Herbst, especially, over a period of years. Regarding the Communist party in Germany, she declared, "I know which side I'm on, all right, without having to inquire. But how far will they let me go with them, since I cannot possibly agree with them about writing: about all the arts." The reason writers and painters had left the party, she thought, was their "feeling of futility about art. The social question comes first, and dwarfs everything else." But for the real artist art must come first. In a capitalistic society the artist risks becoming "either Pet or Prostitute," but in a "revolutionary" society the risk is of becoming "Pariah or Pander." The true and honorable artist will avoid these traps, going on "in spite of hell, making his gloss, his notes, on the world as he found it; if we give up this freedom then we are enslaved more terribly than any other people."[63]

It was on art, finally, that she pinned her faith: "I feel more and more that the workers in the arts must simply do their work, leave their testimony, make their statements, too. I do not believe we are going to be destroyed. What the artists do now will be alive when the political questions of this time are as out dated as the long war between predestination and free will."[64] She made this statement at a time when the arts were under pressure from the left, but she would hold to the same faith when the arts were under pressure from the right. Whatever the pressures, she demanded that the artist maintain autonomy and state as honestly as possible his or her vision of reality. That insistence gave her nowhere to position herself but the narrow center, even though it was so very hard to "stand in the middle."

CHAPTER ELEVEN

Artistry and Achievement

Abundance is a great gift, but . . . no orchard is any good without the pruning hook freely used.

—Porter to Allen Tate, January 27, 1931

She never sold out . . . the art was the main thing all along.

—Joan Givner to Paul Porter, May 17, 1977

Porter's stature as a political observer and activist and her role in public discourse respecting issues of region and gender are at times problematic. As a literary artist, however, her stature is indisputable. Especially in the short story and in that form usually called the novella, she holds a place of eminence among American modernists. From the time she published her first few stories, in the 1920s, she was regarded, initially within a relatively small circle but later by great numbers of readers, as a perfecter of craft, a writer's writer.[1]

Porter's work, a fiction of memory and of style, was firmly based in reality, specifically in the reality of her own experience and observations. She did not have strong powers of invention and was not interested in writing heavily plotted or romanticized fiction. On the other hand, she had no inclination toward unshaped reportage and never regarded highly a naturalistic art that was content to reproduce raw actuality, unmediated and unshaped. Fiction, she believed, should not imitate the formlessness and messiness of life; it must achieve significant form. As she turned increasingly, after the 1920s, to memories of her own earlier life for the material of her fiction, she did not simply recount her remembered experiences or touch them up so as to make stories. Her artistic standards demanded a higher degree of conscious shaping than mere recapitulation. How she got from the one to the other, from the confusions, frustrations, and emotional muddles of her life to the formal perfection of her work, is an elusive but richly rewarding study.[2]

Porter once told Eugene Pressly that the "two best things" she had done were "Hacienda" and "the sections of the novel to which The Grave belongs." That projected novel, which she sometimes called "Many Redeemers" and sometimes "Midway of This Mortal Life," or some variant thereof, was to be based on family history and reminiscence. It was from a section of the intended book to be called "Legend and Memory" that much of her most important work was developed.[3]

Legend and memory were indeed the deep roots of her fiction. Her own experiences and her family stories are deeply implicated and generally recognizable in most of her work. The fictional theories, the habits of work, and the emotional pressures that shaped this process are complex and elusive. Yet despite their ultimate mystery we may be able to sort them out sufficiently to gain some inkling of the process of her creation and her craft. In addition, by examining three factors—the import of her compressed style as symbol and ethical standard, the rigor of her artistic discipline and her devotion to art, and her place in the larger phenomenon of modernism—we may be able to arrive at a clearer understanding of the nature and significance of her achievement.

❧ The essence of Porter's reputation has been her recognition as a stylist. She wrote prose of a disciplined elegance and luminousness that have seemed to many readers to achieve a kind of perfection. This very quality, however, has been problematic for her reputation, and was so in her own view. She once said that she had been called a stylist so often she could tear her hair out.[4] But it was perhaps inevitable that a writer of limited output, devoted to short forms and so restrained a tone that it has sometimes seemed to elude identifying description, and in whose work great social and philosophical issues are not conspicuous, would be more highly regarded for manner than for matter. Except in *Ship of Fools,* she did not write "big" fiction. Instead, it is the distinctive limpidness of her compressed style, together with her subtle symbolism, that is her hallmark.

The stylist is at risk, of course, of being trivialized by that label. Few critics and probably fewer general readers are willing to accord the highest importance to a writer who seems to expend enormous effort on the minutiae of technique. Especially if the artist is female, there has traditionally been a reluctance on the part of academic critics, at any rate, to treat such work with seriousness. Such undervaluation is particularly severe when combined with the reluctance to accord brief forms and works addressing private or quotidian experience a respect equal to that accorded the "large forms" and works that treat subjects perceived as being of major importance. These have not traditionally included the elements of daily domestic life, sometimes rendered in fictions following what Ann Romines has designated "the home plot."[5] Jane Austen and Virginia Woolf are two notable examples of artists who were once and are perhaps still regarded with a degree of condescension because of supposed limitations of content and excessive devotion to manner. They—and Porter—have been tarred with the brush of preciousness, while writers characterized by thematic grandeur and prolific production have generally been accorded greater respect.

Critical focus on Porter's style began early, with reviews of *Flowering Judas* (1930), *Katherine Anne Porter's French Song-Book* (1933), and *Flowering Judas and Other Stories* (1935). The prevailing note in these reviews is praise of her "careful, disciplined craftsmanship." In 1930 poet Louise Bogan found her style to be "straightforward" and without "exclamatory tricks." In the same year Allen Tate called it brilliant. In 1934 a reviewer of the *French Song-Book* called Porter's fiction "exquisite," a term that clearly implies emphasis on style, and reviewers in *Booklist*, the *Christian Century*, the *New York Times*, the *Saturday Review of Literature*, the *Nation*, and elsewhere praised her stylistic "economy and distinction." The emphasis on style was so well established that Herbst titled her 1936 review "More than Style," and Samuel French Morse, the following year, called his review of *Noon Wine* "Style—Plus."[6]

When Herbst read "Noon Wine," published in part in 1936 and in full in 1937, the "something more" that appealed to her was social consciousness. She praised the title for its "softness in comparison to this terrible grim reality of the insane man with his touching tune, the touch of the harmonicas dropping from his blouse—that whole picture of his being trapped is so fine," and continued, "As for social significance, you can't ask for anything more deeply terribly significant. The very ingredients that make for bedeviling the poor and the harmless are here, the horrible elements that trap the harmless and humble."[7] It is an eloquent commentary on the story, but one that has not often been followed in subsequent criticism, much of which has continued the early reviewers' emphasis on style, with an added effort to analyze what all agree in admiring. In a pacesetting essay first published in 1942, Robert Penn Warren, noting the "exceptional precision of her language," found irony (that touchstone of the New Criticism) the key to her elusive tone. James William Johnson in 1960 explained the character of her work by its combination of a "limpid" style with "an adroit use of symbols" and a "consistent and complete" point of view. George Hendrick's biographical study in 1965 also invoked the ideas of discipline, understatement, and appositeness of symbolic detail by calling her art "as subtle and perceptive as the best works of Joyce or James." M. M. Liberman, in another of the earlier general studies, described her as a "classical writer" and viewed the "verbal and rhetorical" properties of her work as the revelation of a "first-rate and peculiarly feminine intelligence"—a generalization that does not greatly clarify his insight.[8] Just what a feminine intelligence might be is hard to say. At any rate, feminist critics in the decades since Liberman's book have made great strides in raising theoretical issues that call such a conception into question and demand an examination of the process by which a gendered intelligence, however it be defined, might have come into existence.

Among the most illuminating of those critics who have focused on Porter's style is Robert Heilman, who frankly acknowledges a "certain elusiveness" that makes the effects it achieves "not quite easy to account for." Heilman proposes that her style is hard to describe because it is "without mannerisms, crotchets, or even characteristic brilliances or unique excellence." His meaning is not that her style is flat but rather, I believe, that it has a quality of full achievement unmarked by distortion or peculiarity.[9] Heilman's view, then, converges with the line of thought earlier invoked by Liberman in the designation "classical writer." Both imply that the elusive defining qualities of Porter's style are poise, restraint, and brevity. We will return later to the appropriateness of the label *classical,* as well as to the more useful label *modernist.*

Eudora Welty, perhaps the greatest of the writers whose careers Porter helped to foster, called Porter's style "distilled."[10] It is a wonderfully apt term, one that does not deny the elusiveness Heilman discerned but captures a quality of refinement to essence that characterizes Porter's work at its best. Any number of examples of moments in her stories that achieve such a quality of distillation and take us very near the center of her art might be cited. The blowing out of the candle at the end of "The Jilting of

Granny Weatherall" melds ideas of life, death, God, and the assertion of identity. The ending of "He," with the mentally defective son, who might have been supposed unable to comprehend what was happening to him, crying wretchedly and the neighbor "driving very fast, not daring to look behind him," conveys in the most painful terms a whole complex of human difficulties, economic as well as emotional. That brief scene, especially its concluding sentence, captures in a few words not only the terrible plight of the Whipple family but the plight of all who face situations in which there is no good, or even tolerable, answer. It *distills* the fact of human inadequacy in a dreadfully imperfect world and the impossibility of comprehending such mysteries as why deficiencies and miseries like those of the Whipples' son are visited on some lives and not on others—a searching question, to be sure. A lesser story but a very good one, "Rope," presents what might well be called a distillation of the swirling tangles of false emotions and hidden hostilities constituting a marital quarrel. This story manages to make its readers distinctly uncomfortable with very little narrated action and little elaboration of its succinct ironies. "The Fig Tree," one of the early stories though it was not published until 1960, distills a child's dawning comprehension of the interrelation of life and death—an enormous theme indeed—into a mere drop of simple understatement: "'Thank you, ma'am,' Miranda remembered finally to say" to the well-informed aunt who had relieved her of needless guilt for having buried a chick alive (or so she believed) by identifying the "weep weep" sound she hears as the song of tree frogs.[11]

Given Porter's devotion to artistic perfection and given the compressed nature of her style, it is tempting to think of her as a Baudelairean searcher for the right word, the *bon mot*. That would not, however, be an accurate or an adequate conception of her art. Her words *qua* words do not often call attention to themselves. She is more accurately described as a searcher for the right sentence, the "succinct, summarizing sentence" that achieves effects of "pithy" observation or pronouncement.[12] It is at this level that her writing achieves its distinction. Glenway Wescott, one of her finest readers, pondered her style with great care and more than once, in his journal, expressed both his delight and his judgment that its distinction lay at the level of the sentence. Contemplating her statement, "Even when I was a small child, I knew that youth was not for me," he remarked on both its meaning—"her lifelong mild foreboding and great patience from start to finish"—and its rhythm. This sentence "as such," he found, was "characteristic" in its "vague speedy first phrase, and little or no middle, and the coming to the point or the end with a kind of little swoop and bump."[13] Wescott, himself a recognized master of prose style, is responding here to what is often called voice, a quality of distinctive verbal presence. It is worth noting, too, that he responds to the substance of her statement even as he responds to its stylistic flourish. This dual attention, to theme as well as form, is what is required if one is to read Porter well.

Style was, to be sure, a value in itself for Porter. She shared in the modernist logocentrism. There is ample evidence that she labored hard, and only after a long apprenticeship, to produce the distinctively evocative prose style that has so often been recognized and praised. "I do not know why I go on writing," she once lamented to Robert Penn Warren, "when it is so hard to do." Or again, "I must have simply so much time in solitude and silence to work, literally and physically will my brain and my two hands to get the words down on paper. It takes everything I've got while it goes on." The intensity of her commitment to style as value is evident in her praise of John Herrmann's story "The Big Short Trip": "The style is clean and firm as if you'd whittled it out in good sound wood." The word *clean* is richly connotative. An honest or "clean" style was for Porter an indication of integrity. Truth and truth telling were not only represented by but enacted in a verbal style of unevasive, uncomplicating restraint, even of "clean" minimalism.[14]

Style was important to her also for its expression of mind, of personality, and of purpose. As she said herself in a well-known interview, "The style is you."[15] But by itself it was not enough. "When virtuosity gets the upper hand of your theme," she said, "or is better than your idea, it is time to quit." Her own style becomes part and parcel of her total response to her time and her human experience. As Susan Stanford Friedman has said of another traditionally marginalized modernist, H.D., she had "a reason to write beyond the pleasure of the play of empty signifiers." Her "pure" style is, in Darlene Unrue's words, at once "the medium of the honest vision and also a symbol of it," or in Robert H. Brinkmeyer's, "the foundation of her ethics."[16]

Porter's aspiration, she said, was to give an honest testimony about her experience and her understanding of the world about her. Her notes for a speech given before the American Women's Club in Paris in 1934 include statements of this intention: "I shall try to tell the truth, but the result will be fiction," and "the writer must have honesty, he should not wilfully distort and obscure."[17] But to give an honest testimony it is necessary to have an honest medium. The two are inseparable. In developing a style at once direct, compressed, and evocative, Porter created an emblematic representation of what honest testimony means—despite her proclivity for personal dishonesty. In her fictional structures, the style becomes the person and represents or even constitutes the theme. Style, then, is both a medium for conveying values and a symbolic enactment of those values. We are well cautioned, as one critic has put it, "not [to] miss the moral achievement for which the art is testimony."[18]

The values that most occupied Porter and that, at her best, she managed to convey in her work are integrity, restraint, and alertness to the continuing presence of what has been valuable in the past. Frequently her characters define themselves in relation to these values by their speech. Those whose speech is excessive, either unrestrained or forced, are thereby revealed as unreliable, devious, or simply undisciplined. Those who have something to hide throw up a smokescreen of words. Those characterized by personal authenticity and directness are generally spare of speech.

Nowhere, perhaps, is verbal style used as a manifestation of values more fully than in what is perhaps her finest single work, "Noon Wine." In its outlines, it is a simple, direct story. Mr. Thompson, a somewhat shiftless farmer in Texas, hires a handyman, Mr. Helton, who proves to be capable and hardworking but oddly taciturn, perhaps because his English is limited. After nine years, during which Helton brings the farm from slovenly subsistence to well-ordered prosperity, a stranger calling himself Homer T. Hatch comes looking for Helton, saying that he is an escaped mental patient who once killed his own brother. When Hatch tells Mr. Thompson that he intends to take Helton back to North Dakota and collect a reward, Thompson kills Hatch with an ax. After this, although he is acquitted of murder, because he seems to have believed that Hatch had attacked Helton with a knife, Thompson spends his time driving around the countryside explaining his innocence to his neighbors. At last, despairing of ever fully exonerating himself, he commits suicide.

Much of the subtlety of this beautifully achieved story is conveyed through the differing speech styles of the three men. Speech serves as a powerful index to character. In contrast to the taciturn Helton, Mr. Thompson is given to empty talk, filling conversational space just for the sake of filling it. Moreover, he sometimes becomes jovially talkative in pursuit of profitable business deals, warming to a forced geniality when he senses a bargain at hand. This volubility of Thompson's is more an amusing fault than a vicious one, but it indicates his willingness to use a friendly manner and a stream of talk for purposes of minor dissembling. In its parallel contrasts of Thompson's manner and Helton's and of the work habits of the two, the story firmly associates Thompson's kind of talkativeness with shiftlessness or shallowness, and reserve (though perhaps not to the degree exhibited by Mr. Helton) with conscientiousness and competence. Still waters, Porter seems to suggest, do run deep.

When Hatch appears, he is at once marked as a shabby character by the simple fact that he talks too much. The contrast of Thompson and Helton has prepared the reader to recognize the signs. Hatch is like a demonic double of Thompson, his roar of false laughter an exaggerated parody of Mr. Thompson's joviality. He has a "free manner" which in its excess reveals the "forced amiability" of Mr. Thompson's "public self."[19] Moreover, Hatch's seemingly loose talk is actually sly, calculated, and thus doubly reprehensible. If Helton is taciturn and Thompson is garrulous, Hatch is voluble. The reader quickly distrusts him. Indeed, Mr. Thompson himself notices that Hatch's jokes and laughter do not ring true; he seems to be "laughing for reasons of his own."[20] Hatch's talk is shot through with simple untruth, and his manner is an attempted disguise. To assist the reader in navigating these fairly subtle implications, the narrative voice serves as a model of reserve and a standard against which looseness and fakery are measured, underscoring the moral significance of the contrasts among the characters' speech styles.

Near the end of the story, as Mr. Thompson drives about the countryside trying to convince his neighbors that he is not a murderer, he is embarrassingly voluble in the attempt. His wife sits by "with her hands knotted together," knowing, as he too comes to realize, that no one believes him. In contrast to his wordy groveling before unsympathetic neighbors, his suicide note is honest, direct, and terse. After attempting to explain once more that the reason he killed Mr. Hatch was that he had believed Hatch was about to knife Helton, he pauses to think and decides against invoking his wife's witness, which had been false all along. Instead, he makes a new start on the whole story, stating it directly and without the slightest evasion: "It was Mr. Homer T. Hatch who came to do wrong to a harmless man. He caused all this trouble and he deserved to die but I am sorry it was me who had to kill him." This unembellished statement of the facts is Thompson's "true testimony." The act of giving it accords him an enhanced moral stature, and its conciseness and evident honesty measure his distance from the speciously talkative Hatch. Porter's narration of the suicide, in its simplicity, spareness, and concreteness, underscores the verbal ethic of reserve, implying but not stating a quality of terrified determination in the face of the ultimate: "Taking off his right shoe and sock, he set the butt of the shotgun along the ground with the twin barrels pointed towards his head. It was very awkward. He thought about this a little, leaning his head against the gun mouth. He was trembling and his head was drumming until he was deaf and blind, but he lay down flat on the earth on his side, drew thc barrcl under his chin and fumbled for the trigger with his great toe. That way he could work it."

In "Noon Wine," reticence becomes an ethical standard against which slackness and inauthenticity are measured. It is posed in the story line, in the characterization, and in the narrative voice. Porter's restrained, incisive style defines and delineates, but at the same time poses ambiguities and ironies. The one communicative act that it does not perform is to belabor. As one reader has commented, "There is a depth of dignity and reticence to the story, and all the garrulity of explanation should finally rest on this."[21]

Critics have not, however, refrained from explaining or commenting. Indeed, "Noon Wine" has been a favorite object of analysis. Its combination of strangeness with ordinariness has been examined by M. Wynn Thomas, Roy R. Male, and Louis Leiter.[22] It has been read as tragedy by Thomas F. Walsh, J. Oates Smith, and Edward Groff.[23] Its concern with the common people of the South has been praised by Elmo Howell and Winfred Emmons.[24] Almost universally, the story has been placed as one of her greatest works. Robert Penn Warren said once in an interview, "Of the world's best twenty novelettes, she might probably have two of them." He then named not two but three that he considered to be "at the world level, you know": "Old Mortality," "Pale Horse, Pale Rider," and "Noon Wine." "She has this power," he added, "of getting these ranges of meaning into the short form."[25] Much the same might be said of her triumphs in the short story—"The Grave," "Flowering Judas," "He," "The Jilting of Granny Weatherall," "The Downward Path to Wisdom," and probably some half dozen others.

❧ Porter's struggle to put the shapelessness of life into significant form was waged against enormous obstacles, including obstacles of temperament. She worked in intense bursts of creativity, broken by long periods in which she gave herself up to love affairs, hard living, talking, and the writing of great bales of letters. During these fallow periods she might make scattered notes that would later be gathered up into completed works, but for the most part she procrastinated, telling her friends that whatever project was on her mind was actually almost finished. *Ship of Fools* is the obvious example, but another is her book on Cotton Mather. For years she claimed that it was coming along or was only a few days from going to the publisher. It was listed in the announcement of the Harcourt Brace fall 1934 line; Donald Brace wrote to Porter in May of that year reminding her that he would need the completed manuscript by July in order to fulfill that announcement. She never completed it. In 1936, almost a decade after beginning, she wrote to her husband, "This book will be the death of me if I let it be. . . . I have not been able to get it done, and it has stood in the foreground of my mind as a terrible worry."[26]

Another obstacle to productivity was money. Wescott once said he believed "all that had hindered" her was "livelihood, little or no livelihood"—that and her "great lapses into weariness and sadness."[27] Although much of her financial problem can be blamed on her own inability to control her expenditures when she had money in hand, there were periods when she lived on resources so inadequate that she was driven to short rations and the acceptance of any kind of hackwork that might bring in a few dollars. Needing stability and concentration in order to produce the kind of polished, perfectly faceted work that was her mode and her standard, she lived in continual insecurity and upheaval.

She struggled, as well, against the disruptions of history, living through a period of enormous and distressing political, social, and economic instability. When that struggle seemed not to avail, she fell into deep depressions, sometimes taking refuge in hospitals to evade her own inability to produce the work of which she knew she was capable. And she refused to accept less. During a period of unproductivity and deep gloom she once exclaimed, "Oh, God, let me die in a ditch before I do half-things and mistake them for good." When she was engaged in the phenomenal effort that produced the final drafts of both "Noon Wine" and "Old Mortality" in a period of about a month, a temporary setback cast her nearly into despair: "I have had some sort of severe derailment, absolutely unable to think or work, sick in my mind and spirit." Wisely, she consoled herself, "But it will pass."[28]

At times, writing was Porter's refuge and mainstay against other problems, personal or public. When she was leaving California in 1949 during one of her recurrent financial emergencies, her spirits were so low that she lamented, "Oh God but I am sick and tired of my life," adding, however, that it was "still true that if I can be let alone and allowed to live I can do my work." Being able to work at the pitch she demanded would relieve her of having to feel sick and tired of life. At other times, however, she spoke of her writing in terms of a "horrible grim burden" or a prison sentence: "I wouldn't do it if I were not morally engaged to do it; yet, I wonder sometimes if the mere moral engagement hasn't clamped down this smothering lid on me, as if I had to serve a term and then would be free."[29]

❧ Porter's method of transforming personal experience into fiction was not a simple matter of setting out to write the story and drawing on what she could remember. Rather, she drew her observations and memories together into a structured whole through a long process of gradually cohering notes and drafts. The making of "Pale Horse, Pale Rider," based on her experiences in Denver during the late days of World War I and the great flu epidemic, is a particularly interesting example of that prolonged gestation. In January 1935 she told Robert McAlmon that she might have "one more story to add" to *Flowering Judas and Other Stories,* called, so far, "Pale Horse and Pale Rider." She added, "I work on it when I can." A month later she told Robert Penn Warren that she had "on hand, trying hard to finish it, a fairly long story which I call 'Pale Horse and Pale Rider.'" In July, five months later, she reported to Warren that she had been "trying unsuccessfully to finish Pale Horse and Pale Rider" but it wasn't "done yet." According to a later note to Genevieve Taggard, she had begun it, as well as "Noon Wine," "Old Mortality," "The Man in the Tree," and "Promised Land" (which ultimately became *Ship of Fools*), "in Mexico City, Basel, Paris, Berlin, and on board ship between Vera Cruz and Bremerhaven." She had gone to work "in Deadly Earnest" (a joking reference to her former husband Ernest Stock) on October 30, 1936, and by January 5, she said, had the "first three finished. Two to go." In fact "The Man in the Tree" not only was not finished then, it never would be; but she did finish "Noon Wine" and "Old Mortality" during her stay at the Water Wheel Tavern in Doylestown, Pennsylvania, the period she refers to here.[30]

She was not able to finish "Pale Horse, Pale Rider" at that time. About midway into her stay at Doylestown, on November 29, 1936, she reported to Pressly that she did not know when it would be finished. The next day she was "stuck again" on it. She remained stuck for quite some time but resumed work on the story after settling in New Orleans in 1937. On December 3 of that year she wrote to Wescott that she had just finished "Pale Horse, Pale Rider," though most of it had been written "years ago," having been begun in Mexico and continued in Berlin, Basel, Paris, New York, and Doylestown. She would now, she said, begin "Promised Land." Four days later she reported to Albert Erskine that she had done so that very morning—although she had spoken of working on it at Doylestown over a year earlier.[31] These statements exemplify the kind of smokescreen she typically blew about her work, which was actually carried out in a privacy amounting almost to secrecy.

Porter's claims that she produced her works in short, intense bursts of speedy writing were misleading, then, but not entirely inaccurate. She did write in short bursts. But at best, such claims belied the long period when a story was working itself out in her mind; at worst, they misrepresented the process of development through scattered notes into drafts that she corrected and retyped mercilessly. She claimed, for example, to have done the "actual writing" of "Noon Wine" in "exactly 14 days" at Doylestown. But she had written to Pressly seven months earlier, in April 1936, that she had "added five pages to the Noon Wine story," which she proceeded to describe by reference to a memory of a man who "murdered another, was out on bail, and driving around the country with his poor red-eyed crushed wife, a noisy man trying to bluster and shout his way through his trouble, trying to work up the sympathy of the country side in his defense." It is a close description of the final section of the completed work, and she knew that it would be: "I am going to use that in this story."[32] Moreover, not only did the structure of the work as well as something over five pages of text, at minimum, exist months before the phenomenal fourteen days, but she had actually published a portion of the story, with the title "Noon Wine," in the spring (in *Signatures: Work in Progress,* Volume 1). Although the completion of her stories did come in bursts of intense work, those bursts occurred after long preparation, jotting of notes, and experimenting with fragmentary drafts. She herself said that "Noon Wine" had been begun years before, in Mexico, and scattered notes are indeed found among her papers from that time. Although the notes that became the germs of her stories seem to have erupted almost spontaneously from her memory, often from troubled memories, the effort that turned them into art was prolonged, difficult, and keenly conscious.

Porter herself pondered the mysterious connection between memory and creativity in a letter to Herbst. "I believe that we exist on half a dozen planes and in at least six dimensions and inhabit all periods of time at once, by way of memory, racial experience, dreams that are another channel of memory, fantasy that is also reality, and I believe that a first rate work of art somehow succeeds in pulling all these things together and reconciling them." The meditation on memory and art that she refers to here would reappear in one of the fragments collected as "Notes on Writing" and included in the *Collected Essays*. "I must very often refer far back in time to seek the meaning or explanation of today's smallest event, and I have long since lost the power to be astonished at what I find there. This constant exercise of memory seems to be the chief occupation of my mind, and all my experience seems to be simply memory, with continuity, marginal notes, constant revision and comparison of one thing with another. Now and again thousands of memories converge, harmonize, arrange themselves around a central idea in a coherent form, and I write a story."[33] Her emphasis is on the act of recombining the memories in which fiction begins so that they are reconstituted into a new whole with a newly revealed meaning. This is the difference between Porter's art and a simple recounting of remembered events.

Such an act of reconstitution is traced in " 'Noon Wine': The Sources." A beautifully finished essay in its own right, the piece ponders the creative process that went into the making of "Noon Wine," presenting that process narratively in a kind of story that may have a factual basis but is essentially a fiction itself. The essay opens with a statement of the synthesizing quality of the imagination: "By the time a writer has reached the end of a story, he has lived it at least three times over—first in the series of actual events that, directly or indirectly, have combined to set up that commotion in his mind and senses that causes him to write the story; second, in memory; and third, in recreation of this chaotic stuff." "Endless remembering," Porter says, "surely must be the main occupation of the writer." But when the act of writing takes place it is as a "meditation" rather than an "exposition" of the thing remembered. Accordingly, the meditation that went into "Noon Wine" included a great omnium gatherum of things remembered: the Texas countryside itself, with its rivers and colors and smells and plants; a Negro family dependent who does not in fact appear in the story; the hereditary background of the people in Porter's section of Texas; her years abroad, which "gave me back my past and my own house and my own people—the native land of my heart"; the tobacco-chewing men she remembered seeing in conversation with her father; the men's knives and farming tools and guns; vague memories of hearing a gunshot, of seeing a funeral procession, and of witnessing a visit to her grandmother's house by a man and his wife intent on explaining a killing; a memory of a Swedish hired man playing a harmonica. Most of these elements have the ring of authenticity; some we might doubt. Certainly we doubt her emphatic assertion that Mr. and Mrs. Thompson were based on types, not individuals, for she "never knew them" and "never knew her name." This is another smokescreen. The Thompsons were in fact poor cousins with whom she spent a period of time after her grandmother died. They are perhaps the most totally real source of the story. Yet they are denied while other elements are reported as fact. All come together, whatever their origin, in the power of Porter's imagination and her prose style.[34]

Her faith in the importance of her calling was high. "What the artists do now," she said in the dark days preceding World War II, "will be alive when the political questions of this time are as out dated as the long war between predestination and free will." The arts, she insisted, were "real" and would "survive." The price she was willing to pay to achieve art of the first rank was equally high. It involved, as she said of Katherine Mansfield, "a triumph of discipline over the unruly circumstances and confusions of her personal life and over certain destructive elements in her own nature." She drew on agonies of "deep dissatisfaction" with draft after draft, but that "painful aspect of self-criticism," she believed, was essential because without it she would be "lost from the beginning." She had, she wrote to her nephew, "a life engagement, something that will last me until I die."[35]

She could be extremely upset by negative criticism. Indeed, she was never able simply to ignore reviews and critical comment. When her agents "objected" that her work was "too 'literary' for easy sale," she exclaimed, "So much for agents. I'm finished." When a reviewer said she had learned a lot from Somerset Maugham, she called it "the cruellest blow I ever received" and felt tempted to "sit down and tell that fellow that he is a gourd headed imbecile." However upsetting she found such remarks, she held to her own judgment of when a work was right and when it was not. When the first editor to whom she sent "The Leaning Tower" asked her to revise it slightly to make it not quite so hard on the Germans, she refused and demanded the return of the manuscript.[36] The integrity of her work was not to be compromised.

❧ In her devotion to her work and to an ideal of art as a counterpoise to the aimlessness and meaninglessness of ordinary life and a redemption of it, Porter evidenced her participation in the central project of modernism. Indeed, to describe her style by reference to classicism obscures the degree to which her stylistic qualities themselves can be seen as a manifestation of the artistic paradigm shift that occurred late in World War I. Her emphasis on language as a means of constructing a system of values is of a piece with her affinity for that vast literary and intellectual movement that elevated style to supreme heights but connected style with a great set of issues and responses. For Porter, as for the modernists whose goals and techniques she shared, a disciplined style and artistic form were responses to a disordered world, both a defense against it and a means of establishing a more valid system of meaning and value, a "world elsewhere." The modernist project was essentially the creation of an alternative and superior reality.

For a generation shattered by the Great War, the ironic gesture became a means of retaining a sense of empowerment and of separating oneself from the cant that had contributed to launching and prolonging the carnage. The restrained, ironic style of the modernist was a mode of self-preservation and self-validation in a violently unstable world in which the old pieties had become untenable. Perhaps that mode is seen most clearly, in its most definitive expression, in the clipped style of Ernest Hemingway's *The Sun Also Rises,* a novel explicitly of response to the war and its destruction of social and moral foundations. The earlier poetry of T. S. Eliot is best interpreted within this same framework, with its images of social disorder and the bankruptcy of the easy verities, against which the poet poses a language of irony, ambiguity, and self-created order. The "obsessive need for order and discipline," as Shari Benstock terms it, was, however, linked to an impulse not of conservatism but of reaction, a retrogressive invocation of ideas and systems of order so long dead that they were in fact new. It is this impulse that is the germ of modernism's "Janus-faced" conflict between innovation and repression, as it "peer[s] both backward and forward." In its backward look, defiant modernism "reasserts hierarchies of sexual and racial difference, and reconstructs traditional authority in restrictive ways."[37]

Sandra M. Gilbert and Susan Gubar agree with such interpreters of modernism as Benstock and Langdon Hammer that it was a reactive and repressive cultural phenomenon. Their account of the rise of literary modernism differs from that of many critics, however, in that they reject the notion that modernism was primarily a response to the war. Viewing it in equally reactive terms, they see it, instead, as a response to the upsurge of feminism at the end of the nineteenth century, which reached its peak during the war years. Eliot, for example, in their view of the period, "constructs an implicitly masculine aesthetic of hard, abstract, learned verse that is opposed to the aesthetic of soft, effusive, personal verse supposedly written by women and Romantics. Thus, in Eliot's critical writing, women are implicitly devalued and the Romantics are in some sense feminized."[38] Gilbert and Gubar's massive work in *No Man's Land* shares in an even larger critical undertaking, termed by Susan Stanford Friedman the "(en)gendering of modernism" and carried forward over the past decade or so by a number of scholars. It is now fully evident that the modernist movement in which Porter participated, in however marginalized a way, was "a far more eclectic and richly diverse literary movement than has previously been assumed."[39] It is evident, too, that many of her personal inconsistencies and conflicts reenact those writ even larger in modernism itself.

If for male writers such as Eliot the response to women's insurgence, only too evident during the war, was one of anxiety and resistance, for numerous women writers it was one of zestful release.[40] Porter was not one of these. Her sense of gender was too conflicted for so unidimensional an enthusiasm. But by this definition as well, much of her artistic development can be understood with reference to her participation in modernism. She, too, responded to aggressive feminism with anxiety, because she was uncertain of her own self-definition as a woman. Like an Eliot or a Joyce, she retreated from the undermining of secure structures of gender relationships by creating a fictional world in which language itself—a tautly disciplined language, restrained much in the way of Hemingway's—constituted meaning.

Porter lived at a time and in personal circumstances in which the external world did not provide a structure of meaning that she could find acceptable. Like Hemingway, then, and like Eliot and others, she wrote, as she said, in order to "try to wangle the sprawling mess of our existence in this bloody world into some kind of shape." Through this effort to achieve clarity of form she was able to come to terms with the great unnerving flux of the first half of the twentieth century as well as with her own vagaries of temperament and allegiance. Like others of the great modernists, she characteristically worked by reaching into the past and at the same time formulating an autonomous order responsive only to its own self-validation. Unlike an Eliot or a Tate, however, she rejected "corporate authority" in favor of solitary acts of memory and self-scrutiny.[41]

Compared to a really prolific writer, a William Faulkner, say, or a Henry James, an Iris Murdoch, or a Willa Cather (who also got off to a slow start and whose career included gaps of unproductivity), Katherine Anne Porter would seem to have expended enormous effort on little result. Almost her entire corpus is contained in three volumes, one of stories, one of essays with a few poems, and one a novel. If importance as a writer were proportional to volume of output, she would have to be considered a minor figure indeed. If sheer intellectual or philosophical depth were the sole criterion, she could by no means be compared to a Herman Melville, a T. S. Eliot, a Toni Morrison, a Thomas Pynchon. Though her stories are richly suggestive, evocative of a place and situation securely possessed by the creative imagination and conveying a quality of enormous thought and caring, her place in American letters can scarcely be attributed to profundity of ideas or to plenitude, either of topics or of pages. What gives Porter's stories their literary significance is that they represent a convergence of two great forces: consummate artistry and significant response to deeply human concerns.

CHAPTER TWELVE

"a free, intransigent, dissenting mind"

> My life, after its enormous fret and fever and confusion and all the burden and waste and disappointment, has come to this quiet cool clear place, where I am free to remember without rancor or bitterness.
>
> —Porter's notes concerning Charles Shannon, July 9, 1945

> I met you in the summer of 1927. And that event did much to change my life.
>
> —Robert Penn Warren to Porter, August 24, 1977

To arrive at an understanding of Katherine Anne Porter's stature as an intellectual presence on the twentieth-century scene, we need to address both her involvement in prevailing currents of thought and her independence from them. She liked to believe that she had an independent mind, but at times she was more of an intellectual chameleon, taking on the coloration of people around her. The question of whether she was, as she claimed, intellectually independent, a dissenting freethinker not only in religion, as the term is commonly applied, but in other respects as well, is one of the two key issues to be addressed in arriving at that understanding. The other is the problem of consistency or inconsistency.

Porter was not a systematic or profoundly influential thinker. Through her wide acquaintance and through her interest in both public and literary matters and in serious human concerns, she was, however, involved in the social and intellectual currents of her time. She reacted to those currents in her own distinctive ways, and she evoked the reactions of others. She lived foolishly at times and passionately always. She valued truth and claimed to seek it, but what she meant by truth is not easy to say. Sometimes she spoke as if truth were a determinate, unitary thing one could grasp and hold, and sometimes she seems to have used the word to mean an attitude or a code of integrity, being truthful. In personal dealings, however, she was often devious, and in her emotional composition and inner conflicts she was so complex that she was unable to be truthful even to herself. Hubert Humphrey said, when he wrote to congratulate her on winning the National Book Award, that she was, for many people, "a source of inspiration and insight." It was true. But she achieved such a role more in spite of her personal character than because of it.[1]

This troubled complexity makes her, at times, a difficult or even disturbing object of study. It also makes her a deeply human one—not one of the Olympians, but a flawed, irritating, and often appealing human being much like oneself, only more troubled (perhaps), more adventurous, and surely more artful—artful in all meanings of the word. Responding to the culture and the historical period in which she lived, she exhibited an intelligence at once deeply individuated and reflective of widespread intellectual trends. She was notoriously changeable, even self-contradictory in her views. But if this is true of Porter, it was true of many others as well. It was a time of rapid technological, social, and political change, and as conditions changed, so, necessarily, did responses. The inconsistencies in Porter's stated positions are clear evidence of her deep involvement in the ideological upheavals of her day, as well as in the multilayered intellectual and aesthetic movement we call modernism.

She was, for instance, as we have noted, by no means alone in her shift from leftist politics in the 1920s and early 1930s to a variably centrist position in the 1940s and after—indeed, a centrist position so variable that it sometimes included denunciation of those on the left who had formerly been her comrades. American society in general experienced dramatic turnabouts during her lifetime. The labor movement and populism of the 1890s carried over into the first decade and a half of the century, contributing to a powerful socialist agitation. This leftist movement yielded to the Red Scare, racial oppression, and general chauvinism of the late teens, which in turn yielded to the slow growth of Marxism culminating in the Red Decade of the 1930s. Porter did not participate in the outburst of superpatriotism that came with U.S. entry into the war. The leftward-leaning political ideas she had already begun developing by the time she went to New York in 1919 carried through without interruption into her Marxist enthusiasm of the 1920s and, with questioning, into the 1930s. The arc of her rising and falling attraction to the politics of the left was much like that traced by numbers of American writers in 1929 and the following decades, except that hers preceded the general pattern. The disillusionment that then drove American intellectuals into accommodation with conservatism after, say, 1939 had begun influencing her earlier in the decade, in the disillusionment that produced "Hacienda." In Europe in the early to mid-1930s her disillusionment was reinforced as she observed the rise of Nazism, the threat of another war, and the Communist demand for a party line in the arts. This demand for writers and artists to subordinate their individual visions to a leftist orthodoxy joined with revelations of Stalinist atrocities as the impetus to her rapid disaffection from leftist-communist sympathies.

In the late 1930s, however, Porter was still vacillating. Despite representing herself as only "another liberal" to Monroe Wheeler and the Wescotts, she marched in the May Day parade in New York in 1937, a statement of alliance with the left. At some time after March 1936 (when Kenneth Durant wrote urging that she affiliate with "the only organization" that kept its position "clearly on the record" as being "against war and fascism"), she joined the League of American Writers, a group with Communist party affiliations. In 1939 she resigned, apparently signaling a change of heart. The meaning of this sequence of events is ambiguous. Retrospective notes she made in the margins of Durant's 1936 letter assert that although she "knew" the League was Communist she "did not get actual proof" until she "joined for a few months." Perhaps this is true; she was, after all, still in Europe until 1936 and therefore not so directly in touch with leaders of the group as she might have been. Even so, she usually stayed abreast of American journals, and it is hard to believe that she would not have understood the League's position. Daniel Aaron points out that the party's "domination of the League" was quite open. At any rate, when a League representative visited her in 1939 to discuss her reasons for dropping her membership, she explained angrily that she had "not felt at home" with them. "Also I said something about moral blackmail. Also about the gang spirit; also about the low standards of criticism imposed when writing was judged purely by its political point of view."[2] The gang spirit, as well as any devaluation of art, was anathema to her.

Porter's disaffection from the politics of the left was based largely on the high ground of her conviction that the arts must remain independent of political orthodoxy, but also on personalities. As her friendship with liberals Wescott and Wheeler warmed, she began to vilify her longtime radical friend Josephine Herbst. The impetus of that disaffection would apparently carry her to the point of contributing to an FBI investigation of Herbst. Certainly it carried her far enough to the right for her to make patriotic America-first statements during World War II, to characterize communists as troublemakers in various letters during the 1940s, and later to write aggressively anti-communist comments in the margins of earlier letters.

Porter's alliance with the Southern Agrarians provides another measure of her ideological wavering, but a very complex one. It was an alliance cemented by at least three factors, separate though related. One was simply friendship. She had become acquainted with Tate, Gordon, and Lytle in the late 1920s in New York and had carried on an intermittent but amiable correspondence with them since that time. It was to Gordon that she addressed the journal letter about her voyage from Mexico to Germany on the *Werra* in 1931 that became the germ of *Ship of Fools*. Her association with the group was reinforced when Warren wrote to her from Baton Rouge in 1934 praising her work and urging her to send a manuscript for publication in the *Southern Review*[3] and again when Tate and Gordon arranged for her to join them in teaching at the Olivet College Writers' Conference in 1937 and then invited her to return with them to their home in Tennessee. A second factor was her deep-seated feelings for the South. However stridently she might declare her independence of her Texas origins, she retained a nostalgia for the South. Indeed, her sometime hostility toward Texas seems to have fed a compensating idealization of the Old South and southern manners—precisely the kind of attitude espoused by the Agrarian "Brethren." Thus Porter's participation in a conservative discourse about the South and traditional values was powered by deep emotions of compensatory regional loyalty and family affection.

A third factor cementing her alliance with the Agrarians provides a more intellectual basis for the apparent incongruity between that alliance and her leftist sympathies. Both the leftists Porter was drawing away from and the Agrarian rightists with whom she more and more identified offered critiques of capitalism and capitalist society. As the American economy foundered helplessly in the 1930s, intellectuals of both the left and the right vented their frustration in disaffection from the capitalist industrialism that had brought society to such a pass. Their programs were, of course, quite different. The radicals of the left touted the new society emerging in the Soviet Union and a global vision based on collectivism. The radicals of the right, as represented by the Agrarians, envisioned a regional cure that entailed, not a march into a collective future, but a return to a past perceived as being at once individualistic and communitarian. But their dissatisfaction with the existing capitalist system of industry was a shared link. There is another link as well. Porter's early radicalism had centered on the Mexican Revolution, with its vision of land distribution to the deprived. Land ownership, especially by sturdy yeomen farmers, was also at the heart of the Agrarians' vision. Thus, although the shift in her political views was real enough, we can perceive some elements in common that enabled her to make the turn she made without being overcome by intellectual vertigo.

An equally profound disparity is evident between Porter's avowed support for labor and the laboring poor, a concern that seems to have arisen primarily from her early acquaintance with populist and socialist ideas, and her yearning to claim an aristocratic heritage. For many years she spoke, more or less vaguely, in terms of class conflict, cheering on in her letters the struggles of those oppressed by capitalism in Mexico and elsewhere and sometimes (for example, in "Theft" and in "Magic") couching her fictional conflicts in terms that imply class struggle. In letters to members of her family she made clear her support of organized labor. Yet at the same time she boasted of her (specious) roots in the landed aristocracy. Moreover, as we have seen, despite her radical principles she held profoundly conservative beliefs about race. Again, however, the disparity is reconcilable, at least in part, by reference to the not entirely consistent visions of lower-class empowerment in the populism of her regional roots and her more recent socialist involvements.

There was a great disparity, as well, between, on the one hand, the feminist tone of some of her early reviews and the feminist implications of much of her fiction and, on the other, her aggressive hostility to the emergent feminism of the 1960s. Urging women to give up the complaints and demands of the women's liberation movement and make themselves charming for their men, she avowed her own femininity and reacted angrily when called a feminist. Yet her awareness of the inequalities that Betty Friedan and other voices of the sixties were bringing to wide attention and her insistence that women writers be judged by their achievements alone are clear and undeniable. Unwilling to be subsumed in any mass movement yet determined to resist the masculinist dictates that had cramped her life, she asserted her intransigent dissent from traditional patriarchy and from mass feminism alike.

Porter's response to Simone de Beauvoir's *The Second Sex* demonstrates not only her thinking about gender but the stubborn independence of her mental life generally. On the flyleaf of her personal copy of de Beauvoir's massive work, she sketched out a thesis for a projected, but never completed, review. Her position, she thought, would be that de Beauvoir was "the victim of man's idea of woman," which she had fought against but not adequately resisted. Only a victimization by male ideas, Porter thought, would account for the traces of self-hate she saw in the book. Rough notes folded into the volume call it a "great study, honest and impassioned" but also "informed, instructed." Yet her unusually heavy annotations indicate resistance to de Beauvoir's thinking. She concedes that the French feminist is a brilliant mind and indicates her agreement with particular statements here and there, generally those asserting the mistreatment or failure of understanding of women by men. More often, however, she rejects de Beauvoir's excessive theorizing on grounds of common sense and independent experience. She tests de Beauvoir's argument on her own pulses and finds it wanting. The pattern is much like that of Porter's response to Freud. What de Beauvoir asserts as universals of childhood experience Porter doesn't "believe a word of" because her memories of her own childhood don't tally with it. Moreover, she sometimes finds that de Beauvoir is not feminist *enough*. Marking an assertion that Catherine of Siena was of a "rather masculine type," she protests, "You mean because she could think?"[4] Porter *could* think for herself, she insisted on doing so, and she regarded herself as feminine, not "rather masculine."

To anyone looking for logical coherence, Porter's political and social principles must appear a riddle of inconsistency. But it is the expectation itself that is the error; coherence is not the appropriate model for Porter's political and social views. Efforts to interpret her writings and her ideas as parts of a unified whole, from Nance's embracing view of a fiction of "rejection" to Unrue's argument that she strove to communicate a positive "truth" or "large design," are incommensurate with the nature of her thought and her sensibility, which were structured not by a single meta-belief or truth-statement but by variance and tension. She thought as an empiricist, and the variability that this entailed was accentuated by her emotional volatility and her lack of systematic education at anything but a basic level.

❧ A particular locus of tension and movement in Porter's mind and sensibility was her religious sense. In this respect, as in others, her ideas did not so much evolve as vary. Adopting a posture of devoutness, she manifested, at any rate, a delight in the trappings of religion. In the early 1940s, for instance, while living at Marcella Comès Winslow's house in Washington, she "sent for her rosary and heavy crucifix" and "spoke so feelingly of her Catholic childhood and convent education" that she convinced her hostess she was a "cradle Catholic."[5] With equal facility, however, she could mock religious belief and deplore the authoritarianism of traditional hierarchical religion. Frequently she displayed a rationalist skepticism akin to her father's insistence that he didn't "know" and didn't believe anyone else did either.[6] She could be aggressively anticlerical, telling Herbert Klein in 1931, in Berlin, "We are groping around in the dark, like in a cellar, with only the feeble flame of our reason to aid us. And along comes the theologian and blows out the light."[7] Yet in the last years of her life she turned again to the Church and was greatly comforted by the visits of Sister Kathleen Feely, president of the College of Notre Dame in Baltimore, and a priest, Father Gallagher, who came at Sister Kathleen's instigation to hear her confession and give her the Eucharist. After Father Gallagher's first visit, her nephew Paul reported that she was "happier and more at peace with her situation, at least for now."[8] The tension between her rationalist skepticism and her wish for religious underpinnings to life is, perhaps, more paradigmatic of the nineteenth century than of the twentieth, but it reflects the uncertain secularism of her own time as well.

One constant of Porter's spiritual thought, however much her statements of belief and her attitudes toward religious institutions might vary, was her devotion to *The Confessions of St. Augustine.* A copy that remained in her personal library at the time of her death, inscribed February 1936, is marked "7th copy." Also on the flyleaf is the inscription, in Porter's hand, "God is, and He is the rewarder of them that seek Him." On the following page she wrote a favorite quotation from Book VI, par. 10, "It doth make a difference whence cometh a man's joy." The book is fairly heavily marked up, indicating continuing reading. In Book VII, par. 4, she marked a passage on free will and sin, "But again I said, Who made me?

Did not my God, who is not only good, but goodness itself? Whence then came I to will evil and nill good, so that I am thus justly punished?" In the margin she wrote, "This is the great question." It is typical of the kind of elusive questions she continually turned over in her mind, resisting easy or institutionalized answers.

Her religious roots were actually not in Roman Catholicism at all but in conservative Protestantism. The chief religious presence in her early childhood was her stern grandmother, who had come from a Cumberland Presbyterian background but attended the Methodist church in Kyle and took her son's orphaned children with her. Erna Johns, Porter's childhood friend there, recalled that the two of them had stood up before the congregation at the Methodist church and sung a duet.[9] After his mother's death in 1902, Harrison Porter was apparently at pains to espouse an agnosticism that knocked the last underpinnings of security from his children's lives. One of Porter's earliest fictional depictions of him, in a draft fragment, shows him attempting to shake Miranda's belief in the Virgin Birth. If we can credit a story she told Isabel Bayley long afterward, she was reaching back in memory, in this fragment, to an actual incident that occurred when she was ten years old. Her father, she recalled, had asked her why she was dressed up, and she had replied that it was the Feast of the Immaculate Conception, whereupon he "sent her into the library to 'drive all the nonsense' out of her head by reading Voltaire and the Encyclopedists." The story does not entirely ring true, either in the detail of his sending her "into the library," as if they had such a room in their house, or in the idea of a Methodist child knowing about the Feast of the Immaculate Conception, but it may catch accurately enough the quality of his influence.[10] Her later religious doubts and conflicts may well have sprung from her father's assault on her childhood faith.

After marrying John Henry Koontz in 1906 she converted to Catholicism and remained Catholic in a nominal sense throughout her life, though for much of the time until her last few years she seems to have been either indifferent or hostile to religion and the religious establishment. During her years in Mexico she was consistently anticlerical. Several of her essays and an uncompleted work of fiction from 1922, "The Dove of Chapacalco," pursue themes of the degeneracy of the Church, its disruption of native Indian beliefs, and its exploitation of the poor in Mexico. She indicts the Church for forming an unholy alliance with the landowners and foreign oil companies. The linkage between Porter's expressions of religious skepticism and her laments over the world's griefs was typical of her thinking. An example is her outburst to her father in 1934 about widespread starvation caused by a teaming of natural disaster, "drouth and flood and pest," with "thugs" in the government manipulating the economy to the detriment of the poor. "Old-fashioned religious folk," she went on, "would undoubtedly see the hand of an avenging God in it. I sometimes wish there were a God, and that he really would avenge some of the wrongs and putrid nonsense of such criminal morons as are ruining the world now. But nature is a kind of god, I suppose, blind and indiscriminate. Always destroying the innocent with the guilty." With the outbreak of World War II, her despairing view deepened. Although a new baby in her husband's family seemed to represent "all the beauty and charm and promise and good temper that continually renews [*sic*] hope for the human race," she knew that "these things pass" and "corruption sets in early." Religion seemed to provide no recourse from such a spectacle of doom. "God. How the name keeps recurring. What did they mean by it I wonder and what do we mean?"[11]

A mere nine months after pondering this mystery, however, Porter claimed to have received a divine visitation: "I had to take a tablet every four hours for two nights and two days, and never once did my mind fail to wake me at the right hour, on the hour like a little radio station. Once I slept stubbornly, had to be waked by the sharp rapping at my door. It was four in the morning the whole house asleep and quiet. I sat up knowing instantly Who had done it."[12] Had she experienced a conversion? Hardly. She found such modes of speech reassuring at times, for instance, when recalling that Gay and her little daughter had had a mass said for her when she lay near death with the flu. On the whole, however, she enjoyed even more vaunting her heterodoxy: "There is no time in our western world at least until very lately that I would not have been liable to the rack and stake for heresy of one kind or another. And indeed, if I stay around much longer, with the Catholic Church on the one hand and the Communists on the other, they may get me yet." The paralleling of Church and Party seems to indicate that after membership in both she had drawn away into a freethinking that would be condemned by the orthodox. She told Robert Penn Warren that she was "a born heathen" and that no religion she had ever heard of had given her the "consolation and pleasure" she derived from intervals of good health. The tone of that perhaps momentary feeling would be reflected in the new spirit Wescott thought he saw in her in 1948, five years after her announcement of the mysterious knocking—not a new religious spirit but a "new inspirational paganism" enlivening her "old Roman Catholic intellect."[13]

In 1951 Porter took the time to respond at length to a routine inquiry from a publisher wishing, apparently, to assemble a marketable set of comments by the famous on the subject of prayer. Jealous as she was of her time, and resentful as she was of the floods of unsolicited mail that poured down on her, it is odd that she would have bothered. Perhaps it was a momentary impulse. But the exchange is worth quoting at length because it provides an interesting expression of the intransigent dissent that constituted one dimension of her complex religious sensibility. The question was, "Is there any reward—inward, if not outward—from *prayer* in your own experience?" She answered:

> The whole notion of prayer, theologically considered, has always seemed to me very blasphemous; the notion that an All-wise, All-seeing Creator should grant us our small mundane wishes—rather often at the expense of some other human being possibly as dear to him—on the grounds that we know what is best for us; what could be more unsound from every point of view? If we ask him to save our souls, on our promise to practise the beliefs and virtues we think are pleasing to him, we are presuming on his mercy, and on our knowledge of his will. If we ask for his mercy in spite of our failings, we are assuming that he has no sense of justice, for we are taught to believe he has damned many a one for his own mysterious reasons; if we escape, what are we to think of such criminal partiality on the part of Divine Perfection?
>
> When we are in danger, as in war and other disasters, we pray for him to help us destroy our enemies, souls which he created also. No doubt millions pray earnestly for their daily bread—as well as working for it—but only a chosen few really get enough bread. Are we to suppose that there is not enough bread to go round, and that God distributes only to his favorites?
>
> Shall we pray then strictly for spiritual favors, peace of mind, peace of soul? What self-love, what insensibility it must require to cultivate either in this bloody shambles of a world to which religion has added the touch of supernatural horror, on the one hand, and material assistance to its evils on the other.[14]

She seems to have enjoyed such toying with theological puzzles.

In the same year, 1951, her review of Christopher Sykes's *Character and Situation* takes much the same tone, mocking Evelyn Waugh for making "a great point" of Sykes's Catholicism, as if this gave him "a superior moral and philosophical outlook." In a witticism conveying the pagan sense Wescott thought he had seen in her three years earlier, she found it "a pity" that both Waugh and Sykes could "manage to make religious doctrine and feeling so repellent to one's better nature." She thought they must have "driven hundreds of promising souls away from the very gates of the fold." Of another prominent figure she regarded as both a spiritual watchman and a disagreeable would-be gatherer-in of souls, evangelist Billy Graham, she later commented, "I took another look at Grahams face today in the Paris paper, and he really has the meanest gimlet eye and nastiest self-righteous smirk I ever saw." Again toying with theological puzzles, she wrote jokingly to her French translator, "Marcelle, what a scandalous situation in Heaven: The Virgin was seduced by the first god in his second shape, the dove, and bore this same god in his third shape, Jesus, and now this ambiguous family group is re-united; and I ask myself, Are there really four Gods there, or only two? Certain there is not only One, I know that." [15] Her tone in these witty barbs is one of detachment from religious tradition, neither believing nor yearning after belief.

In 1953, only two years after her diatribe on the theological and ethical folly of prayer, Porter wrote to Eleanor Clark Warren that she was "shocked as only one can be who hears of a new, totally undreamed-of wickedness" when she heard someone remark "horridly about the conceit of those who fancied other people needed their prayers." She preferred to separate "morals, and ethics and a sense of personal responsibility for one's acts" from their traditional theological bases, but found it personally very hard to maintain a rebellion against doctrine. Although she was at times a "very bad Catholic," as she told Erna Johns, she felt "quite unable to be anything else, its that or nothing." Only a few years before, however, she had insisted to a Reverend Fahey, who had written to her about her work, that she was "not a Catholic" and could not "be judged as one." [16]

In the late 1950s, Flannery O'Connor thought she saw a "terrible need" in Porter's religious skepticism. She was right. Porter was sincere in her longing to believe, and Catholicism spoke to her through her aesthetic sense and her need for a sense of community through identification with a stable whole. When she was in Italy following the publication of *Ship of Fools,* she found herself "very serenely and happily" saying her prayers, lighting candles, and going to High Mass at San Marco's, and thought it "wonderful to feel a *part* of a world so strong and sure and so nobly beautiful with all the arts." Her added comment that it was hard for her to "feel a part of anything" may offer a partial explanation for her recurrent attraction to the Catholic church, however much she might revile it at other times: She longed to feel a part of something.[17] When Allen Tate said that he detected in her a deeply, though perhaps unintentionally, Catholic perspective, she assured him that "of course" she had "a Catholic view." This was in 1962. But in her copy of Tate's book *On the Limits of Poetry: Selected Essays: 1928–1948,* on page 305, she marked a sentence he had written in 1930: "One must think for oneself—a responsibility intolerable to the religious mind," and noted in the margin, referring to his conversion, "How did these words taste when you eat [*sic*] them, dear Allen?" We are wise not to take any one statement as Porter's final position on so complex and emotional a matter as religious belief. She wrestled with the issue and asserted her intellectual freedom by dissent. Very near the end of her life, however, she marked several favorites in a book of prayers, including, "Help me to overcome my failings, my fear of suffering, my dread of the unknown."[18]

In her last two decades Porter engaged in a curious correspondence with a priest and poet, Father Raymond Roseliep, whose letters regularly assured her that he was remembering her by name in his daily Mass and recommending her "to the Eucharistic God" while carrying the Sacrament to hospital patients. If she disliked the fervency of his devotion or the way in which it was mixed with a diffuse eroticism ("I think of you, read your books over and over, pray for you, and yes, I still dream about you in color"), she left no record of remonstrance with him. Apparently she did write to a friend, David Locher, that Roseliep had been "a source of uneasiness" because of the ambiguity of his tone. Joan Givner, who was also "drawn into a false friendship" with Roseliep, found the experience "troubling indeed." However, Givner concluded that Father Roseliep's telephone calls "never failed to make [Porter] happy," and reported to Paul Porter that Roseliep was quite certain she had an "indestructible" faith at this time in her life.[19]

In her 1940 essay "On a Criticism of Thomas Hardy" Porter pronounced the history of institutional religion "calamitous" and "theological hatred," of all "evil emotions generated in the snake-pit of human nature," "perhaps the most savage." The voices of orthodoxy struck her as a kind of spiritual "military police" in contrast to those good souls like Hardy who were "sound in heterodoxy" and free to serve only conscience.[20] The Porter who speaks here is the dissenting rationalist, her father's daughter and better. It is perhaps her most eloquent published statement on religion, and ringingly conveys her own heterodoxy.

Porter lived in an age of scientific secularism. She had a keen awareness of the debates going on around her, having heard them indeed since her childhood. It would be easy to say that she had recourse to religion in her weaker moments but in her stronger moments stood firmly against it—for instance, when she pronounced Christianity a "Jewish heresy" that had brought upon the Western world a "terrible tide of Oriental custom and superstition," or when she labeled the doctrine of bodily resurrection "absurd" and demanded, "How do they *know?*"[21] But to take such a view would be to adopt simple value judgments about a very complex matter. Givner's restraint from making such a judgment, one way or the other, is appropriate when she writes simply, "Her deep need to believe and her equally deep skepticism formed another area of ambivalence in her character."[22]

One can perhaps go slightly further than Givner does in searching out the reasons for her religious wavering. The ambivalence of Porter's attitude toward religion demonstrates her sensitivity to a wide range of intellectual, as well as emotional and aesthetic, experience and also demonstrates, once again, her inability to resolve an intellectual issue with any firmness except the firmness of the moment. In part this was because she so keenly sensed the complexity, the radical ambiguity, within which human life is lived. Whatever else the world might seem to offer, she said, "never once did it promise to be simple." She spent all her life, she once claimed, "trying to reconcile forces that are in opposition from the very germ. Mutually destructive, possibly by necessity." Although editors and reviewers sometimes found her fiction thin, it is hard to imagine an alert reader ever supposing that it was shallow. Beneath it yawned the depths. Indeed, Robert Penn Warren once commented that the true modernism of Porter's stories consisted in their pondering and "scrupulously" reporting those depths, "the dark pit where motives twine and twist."[23]

❧ As Warren perceived, Porter's vision was profoundly pessimistic, despite her gregariousness and her occasional insistence that she had really a hopeful and cheerful disposition. Even aside from her periodic lapses into depression, she tended to see the world in terms of misery and trouble, as a vale of sorrows. She had, after all, seen wars, depression, famine, the Holocaust (to which she does not seem to have reacted very strongly), the disappointment of political and artistic hopes, and the repeated souring of love. Her world had proved to be a place that frustrated her attempts, sporadic as they may have been, to establish a stable basis for her personal life. She might, in moments of exaltation, claim that even "in the midst of the most appalling apparent confusion" she could see the "firm core of order" in her life. "I could see the plot very clearly," she once told Wescott, "perhaps for the first time."[24] But these moments did not stay with her.

At times she became so focused on the world's sufferings that the natural joys of life seemed only to lend irony to the fact that "human trouble" was so "pervasive and incurable." At other times it was what she saw as the pervasiveness of moral evil that troubled her most. The world seemed to be made up largely of those who were actively evil and those who were innocent in themselves but so passive that they "assist[ed] all evil."[25] Justice did not seem to be a part of the scheme of things. Noting that with people starving all over the world, food was being dumped as waste in order to drive up prices, she asked rhetorically what people would do when they got to the moon. "We will only take our miseries and failures and ordures there." She sometimes felt a "great cureless suffering" at the "very root" of her life and felt "sick of living." All she heard on the news, she said, was the "cureless, endless, monotonous horrors of this world."[26]

She was a complex and troubled person, though abundantly charming and the most delightful of companions when she felt like being so. Confirmation of both sides of her character is scattered throughout her papers. Cleanth Brooks's wife, Tinkum, for example, once assured her that she had "made" their Thanksgiving with her "happy visit." She had an enormous number of friends, many of them evidently more loyal to her than she was to them, yet she suffered a persistent sense of betrayal. Her nephew Paul remembers her as a person of fun and inventiveness who loved jokes and the funny papers—forgetting, apparently, or at any rate forgiving the many difficult times she caused him. Isabel Bayley, a friend of many years, recalled her with an affection that seems to have closed her eyes to all faults. A "goodness of heart," she said, "runs through her letters."[27] It is surely true. But that is not all that runs through them.

Most of her friends recognized how difficult she could be. After a visit to Tate and Gordon, "Red" Warren told Robert Lowell that "never until the other night had he heard anyone speak ill of Katherine Anne." Gordon, ever sharp-tongued, commented, "As if people hadn't been sitting around for twenty years talking about Katherine Anne." It was mutual, to say the least. Porter confessed to feeling at times not only a "serious . . . detachment from life" but a "loath[ing]" of human nature. It is that loathing that is so overwhelmingly evident in *Ship of Fools*. "I wish I liked people better," she said. "It would make things so much more bearable." Fortunately, such feelings were not continuous, and her friends, despite their occasional dismay, seldom deserted her. Wescott, recognizing as he did her occasional evasions of truth and her crankiness, celebrated their long friendship: "How I have loved you! What honor you have done me, at all times! How consonant our thoughts have always been, with so great an amount of non-agreement!" Sharing her enjoyment of gardening, he often filled his letters with talk of roses and varieties of iris. They enjoyed sharing their interest in flowers much as she and her sister Gay enjoyed sharing the simple pleasures of backyard birds and squirrels, flowers, and Gay's fig tree.[28]

Toward the end of her life Porter became increasingly irascible, even paranoid. She accused Malcolm Cowley of planning to publish her letters to him without permission, going so far as to have an attorney contact him to forestall the action he assured her he had no intention of taking. When asked, years after *Ship of Fools* had brought in thousands in royalties, to make a donation to Yaddo, the artists' colony that had aided her so much in earlier years, she replied that she could not afford to help.[29] After she suffered strokes in early 1977 she became convinced that people were plotting against her in bizarre ways. She turned on those who had been close to her, including her nephew Paul, her assistant Bill Wilkins (Lieutenant Commander William R. Wilkins, retired, who had helped her complete *The Never-Ending Wrong*), her kind and attentive visitor Jane DeMouy, and many others. This clearly pathological hostility was only an intensification of the irritability and rages she had manifested for some years—indeed, sporadically all her life—but it led to her being assigned a guardian on September 28, 1977, at the request of Paul Porter and E. Barrett Prettyman, with the endorsement of several members of the family.

More and more, after the publication of *Ship of Fools*, she had resented the intrusions of people who wrote and asked her to read their books or endorse their work or simply answer questions about herself. When Winston Bode lost a letter she had sent him and asked if she could replace the gist of it, she replied crossly, "You can't possibly exaggerate in your mind the kind of hellish trouble this sort of thing causes me, multiplied as it is daily by regiments of people who can't remember what they said, or did, or engaged to do or wanted me to do, and would I please straighten it all out for them?" When Virginia Spencer Carr, the biographer of Carson McCullers, approached her about the possibility of writing her biography as well, apparently having received or thinking she had received encouragement during an earlier visit in College Park, Porter replied viciously that the study of McCullers which Spencer Carr had "perpetrated" was "appalling." Referring to the visit or to the book or both as an "invasion and slander," she said that she had no intention of "giving" her life story to people who would "undoubtedly misuse it." "As my final word to you," she told the professor (who now remembers her with amusement and affection), "kindly leave my name and stories about me out of your writings from now on. I will not even take the trouble to answer any questions you might ask me about any incident in my past life."[30] Such encounters must have been startling indeed to the victims of her snappishness.

Even in these distorted last years, however, Porter was sometimes able to regain the sense of hopefulness and the delight in worldly beauty that had been her counterpoise to gloom in the past. She had once told William Goyen, whose vision of life she thought excessively "dark and bitter," that his gloomy account was not the "whole view." "There is also, always has been, a whole world of love and faith and vital energy." She continued to try to hang onto that world. Even in the depths she sometimes enjoyed the flowers and potted plants that crowded her apartment. She had once written her sister that life might be so "beastly" and "tiresome" that it seemed like a prolonged punishment for early misdeeds, but she could still occasionally sing "a song of hope" for whatever there was to sing about "in *this* world, too, before we go to that other world to sing."[31] Intermittently, she retained that urge to sing a song of hope. At times she expressed a wish that the end would come. She had once written of death as a friend, in correspondence with Glenway Wescott about his mother's death: "We have I suppose no choice but to be whatever we are, and die the death appropriate to us. With Saint Francis let us praise our sweet sister Death, who sometimes comes late but never fails us."[32] Her inclination toward death was, to be sure, intermittent. She enjoyed her reading, the receiving of honorary degrees and other recognitions, and even, as late as 1977, the completion (with help) of her long-delayed memoir of the execution of Sacco and Vanzetti.

During her last working days, when with the help of Bill Wilkins she was putting together her memories of this event that had reverberated down half a century, she wrote Robert Penn Warren one of her typical sparkling letters, one that perhaps more than most sends illumination in many directions. The letter touches on her joy in Warren's own new poetry and its language, "as if the bone marrow had found a voice"; on her memories of her stay in Italy after the publication of *Ship of Fools;* and on her zest in being able to work again. It opens with the liveliness and pace in phrasing that make so many of her letters such good reading, and expresses the joy in living that has returned to her under the magic of Warren's friendship and, even more, under the magic of being once again involved in the making of a book. "Your letter was a bracer, like a spring breeze in October, and we had some sunshine to make it seem like a pretty good world after all. I am working again. I, too, am getting out a book." A note of doubt as to her ability to finish the book enters, but then the magic of friendship returns to remind her of her human resources: "I will wait until you come back, maybe to see me, to tell you about it. It is something I have had in my mind for years." And at this point comes one of her concise phrases that could put its finger on the subject at hand and light it up with a compressed glow: "You do know my habit of rather not exactly thinking things over but feeling them over."[33] It is a very precise definition of the quality of her intellect—not systematic, not abstract, but deeply fused with physical life and the life of the emotions. She did indeed *feel* things over.

Despite the impediments posed by her deeply neurotic, often depressive temperament, Porter lived the life of the mind in a vital, responsive, and richly creative way until very nearly the age of ninety. The pathos of her last years, which were so great a trial to her nephew Paul and to a number of loyal friends, was rendered the more pronounced by its contrast with her many years of lively and imaginative responsiveness to the spectacle of her time. She sensed, to an unusual and distinctive degree, the interactions of personal identity and memory with the shaping ideas that emerged from the world's uncertainties.

❧ Although Porter had had a sizable following for some years and had regularly appeared in the pages of large-circulation magazines, she became recognized and celebrated by the general public, in great numbers, only after the publication of *Ship of Fools*. Long before that, however, she had been warmly admired by a coterie of serious artists, most of whom knew each other. Glenway Wescott, Ford Madox Ford, Allen

Tate, Andrew Lytle, Caroline Gordon, Yvor Winters, Robert McAlmon, Malcolm Cowley, Ernestine Evans, Genevieve Taggard, perhaps Gertrude Stein knew the excellence of her work. She was a writer's writer long before she became a popular one, and she remained a writer's writer, in the eyes of most of her early devotees, to the end. Eudora Welty, fretting over Givner's unvarnished biographical approach, celebrated her as such an artist: "She cared about her *work* above all, and in it she practiced the greatest truth an artist is capable of. . . . The truth of art is what mattered to her and what will endure of her. For which she should be honored."[34]

Early recognition was, as we have seen, centered on her style, but she quickly became established, among the discerning few, as an exemplary symbolist as well. Robert McAlmon claims to have thought in 1929 that both she and Kay Boyle were "better writers" than Katherine Mansfield, and Porter was "the sounder of the two, for she wrote with greater authenticity." A letter from Dorothy Day probably written in 1930 or 1931 tells Porter that Kenneth Burke, already recognized by then as a serious critic, was "unreservedly enthusiastic" about her work, a rare tribute since he was "extremely rare in his praise and . . . seldom even rea[d] any of his contemporaries." After the enlarged edition of *Flowering Judas and Other Stories* was published by Harcourt, Brace in 1935, Fort Madox Ford wrote to pay homage: "I guess you get your niche, though I never had any doubts of it." His favorites, he said, were "Hacienda," "The Cracked Looking Glass," "Theft," "María Concepción," and "He," "rather in that order."[35]

Her own favorite, she told Glenway Wescott, was "The Grave," though it was "hardly ever" remembered or mentioned.[36] That was in 1942. She would be gratified by the attention the story receives today. It is sometimes read as the key to her works, especially as to the important role of memory and the centrality of childhood (a centrality she recognized in the works of Henry James, whose "remarkable memory of his experiences and feelings and states of mind as a child is naturally the source").[37] Wescott, having praised her letters, hastened to mend any fences that might by implication have been broken by assuring her that his "ardor" respecting their letters did not "reflect upon your lifework of fiction. Have I not praised your masterpieces as such, as best I knew how?"[38] He sounds rather plaintive, knowing, as he must have, how easily she could take umbrage at unintended slights.

Among friends who were also peers the critical regard of Robert Penn Warren and Eudora Welty probably meant the most to her. Both had published landmark essays on her work, Warren his "Irony with a Center" in 1942 and Welty "The Eye of the Story" in 1965. When *Collected Essays and Occasional Writings* appeared in 1970, although she was angered by what she regarded as the insulting acknowledgment Seymour Lawrence had added to the back of the title page, she could enjoy the praise of these same faithful friends. Welty extended her congratulations on "that big weight of treasure, 496 pages of it," with its essays "better, sharper, clearer and more valuable with their bloom of time." Warren sent a tribute in which he called the essays "fresh and enslaving" with a "wonderful life-sense."[39] Those whose judgment she valued most highly still valued her work.

Praise came from unexpected quarters as well. Folksinger Pete Seeger, upon learning that one of the songs he frequently performed was from *Katherine Anne Porter's French Song-Book,* wrote to say that he had been "singing the song at various concerts for over half a year" and was "very grateful" to her for having written "such a good set of lyrics." Barbara Harrison Wescott assured her that whether the copyright technicalities were handled correctly or not, Seeger "*does* mention you."[40]

Scholarship on Porter and academic criticism of her works began to appear in the 1960s. An influential article by James William Johnson was published in the *Virginia Quarterly Review* in 1960, William Nance's *Katherine Anne Porter and the Art of Rejection* in 1964, and George Hendrick's volume in the Twayne series in 1965. (Harry John Mooney's *The Fiction and Criticism of Katherine Anne Porter* had anticipated the growth of scholarly interest in 1957, with a revised edition in 1962.) With these works, critical assessment of her short fiction, in particular, moved beyond the appreciations and commentaries published earlier by literary essayists. Hendrick's work raised questions about biographical fictions or misconceptions that had been accepted as facts, such as her Louisiana birth and her education in a New Orleans convent. She herself disliked the book, marking in her own copy many errors or points on which she disagreed, and rejected what she saw as an excessive ingenuity or overinterpretation on points that she regarded simply as accurate reports of reality.[41] In the 1970s, however, after the appearance of M. M. Liberman's *Katherine Anne Porter's Fiction* in 1971 and John Edward Hardy's *Katherine Anne Porter* in 1973, scholarly attention to Porter subsided, although several fine articles that are still consulted appeared during the decade, including the first of Thomas F. Walsh's works on Porter's Mexican interests.

Professor Hardy's book on Porter contained many inaccuracies then generally regarded as fact—the result of accepting Porter's own stories of herself. He accepted the New Orleans education and elopement without question, reported that she was divorced from her first husband after three years, rather than the actual nine, and said that she had met Hitler as well as Goering in Berlin. He seems not to have known about the marriage to Ernest Stock. On the other hand, he was astute enough to question Porter's claims to a Catholic rearing, and one of his comments, in particular, has proved to be both perceptive and prophetic: "Katherine Anne Porter's evasiveness about her personal history may be a more rewarding subject of study than any number of particular, verified facts."[42]

The pace of scholarship quickened again in the early 1980s, with Hank Lopez's *Conversations with Katherine Anne Porter: Refugee from Indian Creek* in 1981 and Joan Givner's *Katherine Anne Porter: A Life* in 1982. Givner's biography remains the standard source of information despite a scattering of minor errors and disputed interpretations. In addition, Jane Krause DeMouy's *Katherine Anne Porter's Women: The Eye of Her Fiction*, 1983, began the long overdue consideration of Porter's attention to the lives of women and what may be called, despite her rejection of the term, her feminism. DeMouy's book was the first, as well, of a series of intensive studies from special interpretive perspectives, including, notably, Darlene Unrue's *Truth and Vision in Katherine Anne Porter's Fiction*, 1985, and Walsh's *Katherine Anne Porter and Mexico*, 1992. Most recently, scholarship on Porter has centered on the unearthing, in some cases, and the preparation for print of interviews and uncollected work, mostly nonfiction. These materials are of great value to specialists.

❧ Porter studies in the past decade have been in a state of discovery and lively discussion. The controversy generated by Givner's biography, the first study based on extensive use of Porter's papers as well as on searches of public records and interviews with long-ago acquaintances, provides an interesting case study in the methods, uses, and reception of biographical scholarship. Scholarly detachment came into collision with personal devotion, and the result was—and is—considerable acrimony on both sides.

The roots of the controversy are Porter's own fictionalized accounts of her early life and the sense of betrayal felt by many who had loved her in life when Givner's researches made it clear that those accounts deviated from fact. Givner explained her intentions early on as "neither to sanctify nor to villify [*sic*]" and praised Paul for his "enlightened attitude" in having said that he too "would have no part in any effort to sanctify."[43] But some friends of Porter, as well as some scholars, believe that Givner did indeed vilify her.

Even people who knew Porter well had accepted her fictionalized accounts of her early life. Robert Penn Warren, for example, when preparing a volume of critical essays, had occasion to look into biographical questions and was dismayed. He wrote to Bill Wilkins, her amanuensis and aide, "The biographers, in their various researches, come up with the fact that the family was Methodist, not Catholic. They find no record of any particular Catholic school where KAP went, and no record of the one in New Orleans. They also raise the question of where and when she became Catholic. Or if she formally did. It suits me just as well to leave it all unsettled, but I have to show myself aware of the questions. The three marriages are mentioned, but with no detail."[44] There were, of course, more marriages than the three Warren seems to have been so sure of, and Givner would unearth the solution to the puzzle of her conversion to Catholicism. Warren's unsettlement would be felt by many others, friends and scholars alike, as questions were raised and then in renewed form when Givner's revelations appeared.

Porter herself had anticipated the possibility that biographical investigation would make her out to be a different personality from the gracious self she liked to portray. She told her Texas journalist friend Lon Tinkle, in 1965, that there were "a great many things" about her life that would "reward richly the most hostile and malicious research." "If you liked, you could make a monster out of me by putting in one set of things and leaving out all the rest."[45]

In the view of some—notably Seymour Lawrence, Isabel Bayley (Porter's literary executor until her death in 1993), and Paul Porter—Givner's work precisely fits that description. Regarding the book as a massive character assassination, they have taken the lead in launching a counterattack on several fronts. But the discrepancies and character flaws Givner speaks of are scarcely of her own making. Granting some degree of negative interpretive slant manifest both in her selections from her great wealth of material and in her comments, it is nevertheless clear that Porter's letters and other records provide abundant evidence of the misrepresentations, vanity, and instability Givner asserts. A different biographer may present a different interpretive slant; that is the nature of biography. But only a willful degree of excision of the record will make it possible to eliminate those traits from the portrait. The intentionality of Porter's works is a more complex matter, to be sure, but not an unrelated one.

Givner began to publish scholarly commentary on Porter in 1969. She first met her in May 1976 when both attended a symposium held at Howard Payne University in Brownwood, Texas, the first academic celebration solely of Porter's work. While there, Porter was feted by Howard Payne faculty and again visited her mother's grave at Indian Creek. Persons near Dr. Roger L. Brooks, the president of the institution at the time, have recalled that Porter did not want Givner to be invited to any of the more intimate occasions and have inferred from this a degree of hostility toward her on the part of the octogenarian author. Givner, however, points out that since they had never met until that time there was no reason for her to be included in private parties.[46] In June 1976, a month after the Howard Payne celebration, Porter told Lon Tinkle, the book editor of the *Dallas Morning News,* that Givner was "a miraculous apparition" in her life and praised her astuteness in reading *Ship of Fools* through the "spyglass" of "Theft." Givner had "hit two birds with one shot," she said, and the study gave her "a strange very deep inner delight." "There is delicacy and unbelievable strength in that critic. I would like so much to know her personally but then I don't at all believe in arranging such things. It is happiness enough to know she lives, and knows my work." In reply, Tinkle suggested that she consider allowing Givner to visit her.[47]

In August of 1976 Porter again mentioned her pleasure in Givner's work, and in September Tinkle reported having shown Givner around Dallas and having pointed out especially the Woodlawn Hospital, where Porter had been a tuberculosis patient. On September 29, 1976, Porter invited Givner to be her biographer. "I know what I am asking for," she wrote, "and I am not taking it lightly." Givner accepted immediately.[48] Through Tinkle's initiative, Givner visited her in November 1976 and would make five more visits, some extended, during the next two years.

It appears from the record that insinuations of an early disharmony between the two are examples of retrospective reading. At first, at least, Porter not only cooperated with Givner's work but expressed esteem and affection for her. In mid-1978, after Givner had begun her research interviews, Porter's old friend Erna Johns wrote Porter, after a lapse in their correspondence, to say that Givner had informed her of her illness. She characterized Givner as a person "who is so devoted to you and whom I have grown to love too." One can guess how much Givner's friendly service in instigating the resumption of their correspondence must have meant to Porter by noting the tenderness in Johns's letter and her reference to shared childhood experiences. "I am deeply touched that you do want me to write you and wish I could come and hold your hand. Dont [*sic*] be afraid of dieing [*sic*], darling.—it is only going on to a new experience and you dont [*sic*] know how I long for my day to come. I remember well the big old barn we played in, the patient mules we tried to do circus stunts on—once I even rode an indignant white hog who scraped me off his back by running under the barn." If Givner had by then fallen from favor (perhaps by resisting Porter's demands to review her notes), it is scarcely surprising. During that period everyone was falling from favor.[49]

When the biography came out in 1982, it quickly attracted hostility, especially among those who had known Porter. Even before its publication William Goyen was writing to Givner demanding to see what she was saying about him. In reporting Goyen's testiness to Paul Porter, still prior to release, Givner attempted to head off his own possible (or even likely) hostility with thanks for his assistance and reassurances that she had tried to maintain a fair, balanced stance.[50] Almost at once upon publication Porter's erstwhile attorney Barrett Prettyman wrote Givner to complain of her treatment of him in the book and to list errors in her account.[51] Jordan Pecile, who had enlisted both Paul's and Joan Givner's assistance in developing a film on Porter's work, "The Eye of Memory," confided to Paul that he had found the book a "depressing" reading experience because of "too much emphasis on debunking the legend, resulting in a lifeless book." He added, expressing a view that other friends would seem tacitly to share, "Our job is to keep the legend alive, Paul, not to debunk it."[52]

Some readers who were well acquainted with Porter have explained the disparity between the friend or benefactor they knew and the troubled and sometimes malignant figure they encounter in Givner's pages by the fact that Givner knew Porter only in her later years. Paul Porter believes she missed his aunt's joie de vivre. On the back of a photograph of his aunt being hoisted onto an army tank, he wrote: "*So* typical! The kind of thing about her that Givner missed—the reckless joy & exuberance of letting herself be tossed up on top of a tank—'letting' indeed! she probably suggested it!"[53] A story in one of his letters to Givner illustrates the quality he feels is missing from the biography. He once took his aunt, along with a friend named John, to a tugboat race on the Hudson River sponsored by an organization for which he was doing publicity work.

> The river was churned by all kinds of boats going in every direction; the races were going on, really an exciting uproar, the kind of thing Aunt Katherine loved to be smack in the center of. . . . Suddenly a helicopter began to descend just a few dozen yards away from our tugboat, ruffling the water below into waves. Aunt Katherine was absolutely enraptured, exclaiming, clapping her hands with joy; but as the machine descended to just above the surface of the water behind us, she tilted too far back in her chair, lost her balance completely, and crashed against the rail. As she fell, the entire crowd around us turned to gape, and then, in her words, "I reached and caught at the first thing at hand . . . and it was John's manhood I caught!" The incredible thing was, John and I rather lost our composure, our faces red as furnaces; but Aunt Katherine, who on occasion could . . . go spectacularly to pieces, simply let go her grip, and, helped to her feet, went right on applauding and calling everyone's attention to the wonderful helicopter. Quelle femme![54]

It is indeed easy to believe that direct experience of Porter's late irascibility might have skewed the biographer's version of the whole human being, although Givner's letters in 1976, 1977, and 1978 express great affection and speak of Porter's graciousness. She told Paul in 1977 that she had never believed in "fraternization between critic and subject" because it tended to "destroy objectivity," but "wouldn't now have missed knowing her this past year for anything."[55] Another explanation altogether has been provided by Tillie Olsen, whom Porter generously fostered early in her career. Olsen believes that Givner failed to take into account the social and economic pressures Porter faced and thus did not temper her judgments with an appropriate degree of charity.

The Givner biography became an even greater bone of contention when the revised edition appeared in 1991 with comments on the Herbst controversy added. Elinor Langer's biography of Herbst had by then appeared, making the case that Porter had discussed her friend's politics with the FBI. To those who saw themselves as Porter's rightful defenders, Givner's acceptance of this calumny came as a last straw, even though Givner offered a more understanding account of the possible causative factors than Langer had. No rebuttal of the evidence has yet been offered by the defenders, whose position can be summarized by Olsen's statement, made at one of several recent conferences devoted to Porter's work, "I don't think anyone should say she was a betrayer. I am convinced she was not." Isabel Bayley, also rejecting the charge, pointed out that Porter mentioned in a letter to her agent, Cyrilly Abels, an instance of having been called on by an FBI agent asking about "a friend of mine suspected of communism" and that she said in this letter she had told him truthfully that "so far as I had ever known she had no politics at all, Right Left or Center." Bayley believed that Porter's 1942 comment to Donald Elder, "it is surprising to find how little one does know about the actual life of one's friends," corroborates her statement that she did not know her friend (clearly Herbst) was a Communist "and had been all along."[56] But the letters between Porter and Herbst demonstrate beyond doubt that they did discuss politics. Thus her statement to Abels can only be regarded as disingenuous.

The intransigently freethinking Katherine Anne Porter has remained a figure of conflict and contradiction even after her death. In part, that is only to say, once again, that she responded to and reflected her time, in all its countercurrents and bewilderments, with extraordinary sensitivity. But in part the continuing controversy over her character and her achievement arises from her own distinctive conflicts. It has been said that Porter's "actual life" was a great deal more "memorable and admirable" than the life she "invented for herself."[57] That, I believe, is true. The heights she attained, starting from those actual beginnings and by way of such struggles, were astonishing. However "difficult" she might be at times, she was also, as Givner said at one point during her research, "heroic" in her ability to transcend impediments such as her contemporary culture's implicit and sometimes explicit discouragement of intellectual and professional achievement by women. She was heroic, as well, in her commitment to the discipline of her art,[58] and she was irrepressible in her engagement with the currents of public life. Not only did she have a sense of her time remarkable for its fullness and astuteness, she drew on that sense in creating symbolic structures that resonate with the tone of genuine intellect.

NOTES

BIBLIOGRAPHY

INDEX

NOTES

PREFACE

1. An interview by Hank Lopez, "A Country and Some People I Love," *Harper's*, September 1965, pp. 58–68; rpt. *Katherine Anne Porter: Conversations*, ed. Joan Givner, pp. 120–34.

2. Ruth M. Vande Kieft refers to Porter's "uncanny timing in being in the right place at the right time to involve herself with important historical persons and events": "The Love Ethos of Porter, Welty, and McCullers," in *The Female Tradition in Southern Literature*, p. 236. Nancy Tate Wood, the daughter of Caroline Gordon and Allen Tate, recalls that Porter "made a big to-do" about the dinner date with Goering. Telephone interview with the author, Dec. 12, 1993.

3. Hubert H. Humphrey to KAP, March 21, 1966, Porter Collection, McKeldin Library, University of Maryland.

4. KAP to Allen Tate, Jan. 12, 1962, McKeldin.

5. Glenway Wescott, *Continual Lessons: The Journals of Glenway Wescott, 1937–1955*, ed. Robert Phelps, with Jerry Rosco, p. 355.

6. KAP to Josephine Herbst, "Saturday 1928," from Salem, Mass., Beinecke; KAP to Becky Crawford, June 18, 1934, McKeldin.

7. Glenway Wescott reported to Porter in a letter dated July 25, 1948, that Monroe Wheeler had called her that at a cocktail party. Wescott added, "Which is true enough."

CHAPTER ONE: A Career as Big as Texas

1. Barbara Thompson, "Katherine Anne Porter: An Interview," *Paris Review*, 1963; rpt. *Katherine Anne Porter: Conversations*, ed. Givner, pp. 78–98.

2. Daniel Joseph Singal, *The War Within: From Victorian to Modernist Thought in the South, 1919–1945*, p. 138, quoting Howard W. Odum's description in *An American Epoch: Southern Portraiture in the National Picture*. Odum did not leave that description unchallenged, however.

3. KAP to Eugene Pressly, April 20, 1936, McKeldin.

4. KAP to Josephine Herbst, April 16, 1930, Beinecke. KAP to Malcolm Cowley,

Oct. 13, 1942, McKeldin. George Hendrick, in *Katherine Anne Porter,* rev. ed., with Willene Hendrick, p. 1, comments that the "biographical information" Porter relayed about herself was "often romanticized or patently false." In a paper delivered at Baylor University in May 1992, Hendrick conjectured that the Porter family itself, not just Katherine Anne, may have fictionalized its status. George Core observes that Porter's "actual life . . . is much more memorable and admirable than the life that she had invented for herself." See "Lives Fugitive and Unwritten," in *Located Lives: Place and Idea in Southern Autobiography,* ed. J. Bill Berry, p. 59.

5. Harrison Boone Porter to Mary Alice Jones, Jan. 15, 1882, McKeldin. The identity of Castillo remains a mystery; he may have been a businessman or perhaps a regional insurrectionist.

6. Joan Givner, *Katherine Anne Porter: A Life,* rev. ed., pp. 34–36.

7. KAP to Cora Posey, Oct. 21, 1952; KAP to Albert Erskine, March 8, 1938; KAP to Gay Porter Holloway, Nov. 5, 1955; McKeldin. The number of Porter's marriages is usually given as four. Between the first and the second, however, there was an additional brief and apparently unconsummated marriage. See Givner, *The Self-Portrait of a Literary Biographer,* p. 104.

8. Givner, *A Life,* p. 51.

9. Givner, *A Life,* p. 46. Also Hendrick, *Katherine Anne Porter,* rev. ed., p. 3.

10. Annotation in Morton Dauwen Zabel, *Craft and Character: Texts, Method, and Vocation in Modern Fiction* (1957), p. 273; McKeldin.

11. Veronica A. Makowsky, *Caroline A. Gordon: A Biography,* p. 45.

12. Thomas F. Walsh, in "From Texas to Mexico to Texas," *Katherine Anne Porter and Texas: An Uneasy Relationship,* ed. Clinton Machann and William Bedford Clark, p. 84, corrects the accepted dating of 1923.

13. KAP to Gay Porter Holloway and Anna Gay Holloway, Dec. 15, 1943; KAP to Harrison Boone Porter, March 30, 1935; KAP to Gay Porter Holloway, July 3, 1936; McKeldin. In Givner's words, she "wavered in her class identification, now agitating on behalf of downtrodden, exploited people, now speaking proudly of belonging to a slave-owning, aristocratic class." Givner, *A Life,* pp. 61–62.

14. The formal letter of appointment from H. A. Moe, July 14, 1931, began, "I HEREBY CERTIFY, That Miss Katherine Anne Porter of San Antonio, Texas, has been appointed . . ."; McKeldin.

15. Givner, *A Life,* p. 88.

16. Paul Porter to Joan Givner, May 7, 1980, personal collection of Paul Porter. KAP to "Cousin Leo" (Leo Porter), Nov. 11, 1964; KAP to Corporal Adams (a person who had written to her seeking biographical information), Jan. 10, 1952; KAP to Rita Johns, Jan. 21, 1963; McKeldin.

17. Givner, *A Life,* pp. 89–98.

18. KAP to Harrison Boone Porter, March 22, 1933, McKeldin.

19. Dr. Frank C. Wilson of the Medical School of the University of North Caro-

lina summarized this standard information on the disease at the American Literature Association meeting in May 1993 in a paper entitled "In Search of the Tubercle Bacillus: The Death of Thomas Wolfe."

20. Givner, *A Life,* pp. 112–17.

21. Givner points out the coincidence of Porter's career initiatives with her departures from her home state in arguing that her "ambivalences as a woman" played a part in her ambivalent attitude toward Texas ("Problems of Personal Identity in Texas' 'First Writer,'" in *Katherine Anne Porter and Texas,* pp. 48–49). KAP to Harrison Boone Porter, Jan. 21, 1933, McKeldin.

22. Harrison Boone Porter to Gay Porter Holloway, Oct. 23, 1918; KAP to "Baby," n.d. except 1919; McKeldin.

23. Andrew Lytle, foreword in *The Southern Mandarins: Letters of Caroline Gordon to Sally Wood, 1924–1937,* ed. Sally Wood, p. 3. KAP "To my Bunch," Jan. 3, 1920, McKeldin. The three stories have been reprinted in *Uncollected Early Prose of Katherine Anne Porter,* ed. Ruth M. Alvarez and Thomas F. Walsh. Porter would again have a contract for a children's book in the 1950s and would again default on it; Paul Porter to Joan Givner, April 7, 1978, personal collection of Paul Porter.

24. Janice R. MacKinnon and Stephen R. MacKinnon, *Agnes Smedley: The Life and Times of an American Radical,* p. 275.

25. Porter complained that Shapiro had not bothered to get accurate information before writing his poem, but conceded that Thomas, while "entirely drunk," had "at one point" held her "above his head." KAP to Jordon Pecile, April 18, 1961, McKeldin. In pencil comments written on the page proofs of John Malcolm Brinnin's *Dylan Thomas in America,* at McKeldin Library, she characterized Thomas as being "intimate as a hot water bottle *with hands*" and claimed, "I never was so swarmed over at first sight in my life."

26. Besides the *Collected Essays and Occasional Writings,* Porter's book reviews have been collected in *"This Strange, Old World" and Other Book Reviews by Katherine Anne Porter,* ed. Darlene Harbour Unrue, and other pieces have recently been published in *Uncollected Early Prose,* ed. Alvarez and Walsh. She complained to Caroline Gordon on Dec. 14, 1931 (*Letters,* p. 70), "I could have throttled my good friend Malcolm. . . . Even if it is true, (God forbid!) somehow there was an echo of cheerful masculine voices down the centuries saying, 'On his mother's side also our hero inherited some gleam of literary talent, for she was a writer of delightful letters.'" Her father had once suggested that she satisfy her literary aspirations by writing letters.

27. KAP to Delafield Day, July 17, 1928; KAP to Becky Crawford, March 11, 1929 and March 22, 1929; John Crawford to KAP, Sept. 25, 1930; KAP to Henry Allen Moe, Oct. 19, 1933; John Crawford to KAP, Dec. 3, 1933; Monroe Wheeler to KAP, Oct. 1, 1934; KAP to Henry Allen Moe, Dec. 21, 1935; McKeldin.

28. KAP to Harrison Boone Porter, from New York, n.d. but subsequently dated, uncertainly, 1927; McKeldin.

29. Givner, *A Life,* p. 387. KAP to Gay Porter Holloway, April 30, 1958; Gay Porter Holloway to KAP, Feb. 9, 1965; McKeldin.

30. *CE,* p. 101.

31. Although she can well be described, as Will Brantley characterizes her, as "unmistakably liberal" throughout her life, the term allows for such wide variability, from well to the left to broadly centrist, that it does little to resolve the puzzle of her political inconsistency. See Brantley, *Feminine Sense in Southern Memoir: Smith, Glasgow, Welty, Heilman, Porter, and Hurston,* p. 136.

32. Ruth Moore Alvarez, in her dissertation "Katherine Anne Porter and Mexican Art," attributes the change from rebelling aesthete to smartly dressed socialite to Porter's settling into a middle-class domestic life with Eugene Pressly in the 1930s and to her new friendships with such persons of wealth as Barbara Harrison Wescott.

CHAPTER TWO: Establishing an Identity

1. KAP to Caroline Gordon, First Day of Spring, 1935, McKeldin.

2. KAP to Josephine Herbst, July 27, 1932, Beinecke.

3. "*Rapsodia chilena* a Katherine Anne Porter," bearing the pencil date April 23, 1923; telegrams from Aguilera to KAP dated March 25, 1924 and April 10, 1924; Erna Johns to KAP, May 3, 1939; McKeldin.

4. KAP to Porter family, Jan. 3, 1920, and n.d. but subsequently identified as 1920; KAP to Gay Porter Holloway, Dec. 17, 1949; McKeldin.

5. KAP to Harrison Boone Porter, Feb. 24, 1931, McKeldin.

6. KAP to "Darling Baby Child" (Mary Alice Porter Hillendahl), Sept. 14, 1920, McKeldin.

7. KAP, "Notes on Mexico"; KAP to Gay Porter Holloway, n.d. but "1928?" penciled in; McKeldin. KAP to Gay Porter Holloway, April 1, 1930, *Letters,* p. 17.

8. KAP to Kenneth Durant, March 30, 1936; KAP to Harrison Boone Porter, July 15, 1929; Gay Porter Holloway to KAP, April 22, 1930; McKeldin.

9. KAP to William Goyen, May 28, 1951, McKeldin.

10. KAP to Gay Porter Holloway, June 12, 1928, McKeldin.

11. KAP to Gay Porter Holloway, Jan. 18, 1959, McKeldin.

12. KAP to Gay Porter Holloway, Oct. 10, 1930; KAP to Tinkum Brooks, Feb. 19, 1963; McKeldin.

13. KAP to Paul Porter, May 2, 1958, McKeldin.

14. KAP to Mary Alice Porter Hillendahl, May 21, 1969, McKeldin. She wrote at the top of her letter, instead of a return address, "I do not send you my new address because I do not want to hear or read any more of your evil nonsense."

15. Gay Porter Holloway to KAP, April 14, 1963; KAP to Gay Porter Holloway, April 18, 1963; McKeldin.

16. KAP to Gay Porter Holloway, July 4, 1931 and January 11, 1945; KAP to Paul Porter, June 5, 1948; McKeldin.

17. Givner, *A Life,* p. 88.

18. Don Graham, "A Southern Writer in Texas: Porter and the Texas Literary Tradition," in *Katherine Anne Porter and Texas,* pp. 59–60.

19. Flannery O'Connor, *Mystery and Manners: Original Prose,* ed. Sally and Robert Fitzgerald, p. 29.

20. KAP to George Sessions Perry, Feb. 5, 1943, HRC.

21. Graham, "A Southern Writer in Texas," pp. 59–60, 65. Graham also comments that "the period of her use of Texas Southern materials—the mid 1930s through the 1940s—corresponded to a flowering of Texas writing in the Southern tradition" (p. 60). I have argued in "Estranging Texas: Porter and the Distance from Home," *Katherine Anne Porter and Texas,* pp. 90–91, that "Old Mortality" is "surprisingly centered on New Orleans," but that, at the same time, it "would need to be farther south and west in Texas than Kyle, to make it possible for a person to ride horseback to the Mexican border and back in three days, as the story has it."

22. Jane Anderson to KAP, n.d. except 1918, McKeldin. In 1968, Porter recalled that "summer 1918 on the side of Cheyenne Mountain" and labeled Seldes "impudent, climbing, uninvited, except by Jane, Kitty's guest and old schoolmate." Marginal annotations in Robert McAlmon, *Being Geniuses Together,* p. 13; McKeldin.

23. KAP to Paul Porter, Aug. 16, 1963, McKeldin. The United States did not actually enter the war until 1917.

24. Tate to Bishop, Jan. 12, 1941, in *The Republic of Letters in America: The Correspondence of John Peale Bishop and Allen Tate,* ed. Thomas Daniel Young and John J. Hindle, pp. 172–73.

25. KAP to Becky and John Crawford, July 25, 1935, McKeldin. In this letter she says she had begun "Pale Horse, Pale Rider" "years ago." Brantley, in *Feminine Sense* (p. 181), finds that at the end Miranda "sinks into a listless depression" but attributes this lassitude, which he seems to find rather unattractive, to the ravages of the "world of men." Alfred W. Crosby, Jr., in *Epidemic and Peace, 1918,* p. 319, points out that her state of mind at the end is in part "an evocation of the crushing depression that so often followed Spanish influenza."

26. KAP to Harrison Boone Porter, Jan. 21, 1933, *Letters,* p. 90.

27. Crosby, *Epidemic and Peace,* p. 322. The Spanish influenza of 1918 spread "explosively" as flu typically does but differed from other outbreaks of influenza in that it had an unusual "propensity for pneumonic complications" and "characteristically killed young adults," whereas either influenza or pneumonia alone

was generally a killer of young children and the elderly. Some patients died within forty-eight hours of the onset of cough and ache. Crosby, pp. 5, 322, and 8.

28. KAP to Mary Alice Porter Hillendahl, n.d., McKeldin.

29. Crosby, *Epidemic and Peace*, p. 322.

30. *CS*, p. 294.

31. David M. Kennedy, *Over Here: The First World War and American Society*, p. 103.

32. Kennedy, *Over Here*, pp. 80–82.

33. Kennedy, *Over Here*, pp. 99–106.

34. *Over Here*, pp. 26–27, 70. William Z. Foster, longtime secretary of the American Communist party, writes that the Socialist party convention in St. Louis in 1917 was "heavily anti-war." See Foster, *History of the Communist Party of the United States*, p. 134. The Socialist party in the Southwest was suppressed after 1917 because of its pacifist stand. See James Robert Green, *Grass-Roots Socialism: Radical Movements in the Southwest, 1895–1943*, pp. 345–95, and Garin Burbank, *When Farmers Voted Red: The Gospel of Socialism in the Oklahoma Countryside, 1910–1924*, p. 123.

35. Porter would later, however, call her rejection of propaganda depicting the Germans as monsters "my sentimental error and a fashionable attitude of the time," adding, "It was all true and worse than we had been told." Marginal annotations in George Hendrick, *Katherine Anne Porter* (1965), p. 79.

36. *CS*, p. 293.

37. KAP to Malcolm Cowley, March 16, 1965, McKeldin.

38. March 31, 1951, KAP to a Mr. Stallings, and Oct. 24, 1945, to a Miss Campbell, filed in "Miscellaneous Correspondence"; Imogene Clayton, Walnut Springs, Texas, to KAP, Jan. 18, 1951; McKeldin.

39. KAP to Harrison Boone Porter, Dec. 21, 1916; M. E. Foster to KAP, Oct. 7, 1918; KAP to "Dear Angel," presumably Gay, on March 5, 1928; McKeldin.

40. Givner, *A Life*, pp. 132–37.

41. Marginal annotation in Donald McDonald, *Catholics in Conversation* (1960), p. 211; McKeldin.

42. KAP to Gay Porter Holloway, May 22, 1947, McKeldin. Givner, *A Life*, p. 139.

43. KAP to Gay Porter Holloway, July 21, 1924, McKeldin.

44. See Givner, *A Life*, pp. 138–39. The style of the poem is reminiscent of "Janet Waking" by John Crowe Ransom, whose work Porter certainly knew, but since her poem is undated it is impossible to say whether she may have been influenced by Ransom. KAP to Eugene Pressly, Dec. 7, 1931, McKeldin.

45. KAP to Gay Porter Holloway, "partial copy of a letter written in Pencil from Denver in 1919," April 1, 1920, McKeldin. It should be noted that despite her stance of rationalism Porter sometimes consulted astrologists.

46. KAP to Gay Porter Holloway, n.d. but penciled in, in Porter's hand, "1928";

Gay Porter Holloway to KAP, Dec. 2, 1959, and Jan. 10, 1959; McKeldin.

47. KAP to Paul Porter, Aug. 14, 1948, McKeldin. Harry Ransom attempted to soothe her hurt feelings, explaining that the plan to establish a Katherine Anne Porter Library "still stands at Texas," though "changing assignments here may have caused confusion," partly because Porter never responded to his written proposal. Harry Ransom to KAP, Feb. 1, 1967, McKeldin. Marginal note in Louis D. Rubin, Jr. and C. Hugh Holman, eds., *Southern Literary Study: Problems and Possibilities* (1975), p. 234.

48. *CE*, p. 470.

49. John Graves, "The Old Guard: Dobie, Webb, and Bedichek," in *The Texas Literary Tradition: Fiction, Folklore, History,* ed. Don Graham, James W. Lee, and William T. Pilkingham, p. 17. Graves comments elsewhere that the "Texas atmosphere has probably been more of a hindrance to the development of artists' careers than it's been a help" because of the "major emphasis" on action rather than "thought and feeling." Graves, "The Southwest as the Cradle of the Writer," in *The American Southwest: Cradle of Literary Art,* ed. Robert W. Walts, p. 18.

50. KAP to Josephine Herbst, Dec. 29, 1930, Beinecke.

51. KAP to Paul Porter, Sr., March 8, 1932, *Letters,* p. 79; KAP to "Mr. Champion" (John Herrmann), Aug. 3, 1932, HRC.

52. KAP to William Humphrey, Oct. 8, 1950, McKeldin.

53. KAP to Albert Erskine, from Yaddo, July 30, 1940, McKeldin; Robert McBride and Company was offering, she said, $2,500 to writers to do the history of a state. KAP to Josephine Herbst, July 27, 1932, Beinecke.

CHAPTER THREE: Politics and Art in the Radical Twenties

1. Darlene Harbour Unrue aptly characterizes the pattern of Porter's political life as one of idealism followed by disillusionment. See Unrue, "Katherine Anne Porter, Politics, and Another Reading of 'Theft,' " 119–26.

2. Elinor Langer, *Josephine Herbst,* p. 91.

3. *CE*, p. 15.

4. Cleanth Brooks, letter to the author, May 27, 1992. Brooks added, "We believed her and had no reason to do otherwise. If she ever had a card to show membership, we never saw it." He conceded that he had learned Porter "sometimes embroidered her stories." Cheney, interview with the author, April 24, 1993. Daniel Aaron, in the Preface to *Writers on the Left: Episodes in American Literary Communism,* emphasizes that only a "very small fraction of the Left Wing writers" in the United States were party members. The same could be said of supporters of the political left in Mexico. Socialists, however, might also be enthusiastic supporters of Bolshevism and the Russian Revolution; John W. F. Dulles, *Yesterday in Mexico:*

A Chronicle of the Revolution, 1919–1936, p. 129. Similarly, Richard L. Harris, in *Marxism, Socialism, and Democracy in Latin America,* p. 107, cites the theories of Marx and Engels to the effect that a period of socialism is "the early stage of the transition to communism." All three—Aaron, Dulles, and Harris—argue that the leftist socialists and the communists of the period cannot clearly be distinguished.

5. KAP to Andrew Lytle, July 5, 1947, McKeldin. Porter's phrase appears later as the title of chapter 12.

6. Mary Doherty to KAP, Dec. 13, 1963, McKeldin. Barry Carr, *Marxism and Communism in Twentieth-Century Mexico,* pp. 1–2. Membership in the Partido Comunista de México, founded 1919, is estimated to have reached only 1,500 by the end of 1922, from which it dropped precipitously to 191 in April 1925 (p. 10).

7. Carr, pp. 1–2. Richard H. Pells, *Radical Visions and American Dreams: Culture and Social Thought in the Depression Years,* p. 14.

8. Porter, "Mr George on the Woman Problem," in *"This Strange, Old World,"* ed. Unrue, p. 35.

9. Porter, "A Singing Woman," in *"This Strange, Old World,"* p. 43.

10. Porter, "Sex and Civilization," in *"This Strange, Old World,"* p. 25.

11. KAP to Herbst, July 27, 1932, Beinecke. KAP to Caroline Gordon, First Day of Spring, 1935; KAP to Harrison Boone Porter, June 26, 1931; McKeldin.

12. Givner proposes no explanation of her development of radical political views, but mentions the presence of radical friends. Unrue, "Katherine Anne Porter, Politics, and Another Reading of 'Theft,'" pp. 119–20, believes that preexistent socialist and feminist views "found encouragement and nourishment in the bohemianism of Greenwich Village," where she became acquainted with "left-wing writers and intellectuals." Alvarez, "Katherine Anne Porter and Mexican Art," especially pp. 6–16, discusses more specifically Porter's acquaintance with Greenwich Village "intellectuals who held leftist political sympathies." Andrew Lytle remarks of the 1920s in Greenwich Village that "Communism, socialism, and sympathizers with both differed widely from the southern attitude" (foreword to *The Southern Mandarins,* p. 3). He does not point out that Porter was an exception.

13. Thomas F. Walsh agrees, in *Katherine Anne Porter and Mexico: The Illusion of Eden,* that political dynamics in Texas influenced Porter's early political development. Henry C. Schmidt points out that during the years 1912 to 1920 the nation as a whole "had seen a rousing version of socialism and an exuberant bohemianism, which fused revolutionary politics and experimental art." See "The American Intellectual Discovery of Mexico in the 1920's," p. 336.

14. Green, *Grass-Roots Socialism,* p. xi: "In the turbulent years before World War I the American Socialist party won its strongest grass-roots support in the area then known as the Southwest—Oklahoma, Texas, Louisiana, and Arkansas." According to Green, the Populist party was "strong in the Southwest, especially in Texas, and when it declined in the years after 1896, some of its leading activists

became Socialists." Moreover, the Socialist party was strong in Houston and had strength as well, though somewhat less, in Dallas and in San Antonio about 1900 (pp. 34–52).

15. Voting records for these decades indicate not only the Populist and Socialist strength by county, but by precinct, enabling us to see how strong this radical ferment was in the very precincts where the family lived, to the extent that we know what those were. During the 1890s, for example, the Populist party garnered 43 percent of all votes cast in the Indian Creek precinct in Brown County. I am grateful to Professor Worth Robert Miller, of Southwest Missouri State University, for sharing the data he has so painstakingly collected.

16. Green, *Grass-Roots Socialism,* pp. 144, 149. KAP to Porter family, Dec. 31, 1920, McKeldin. Green comments, in summary, that radical leaders in Texas generally "supported insurrectionary activity in Mexico" (*Grass-Roots Socialism,* p. 316).

17. Gay Porter Holloway to "Dear Ones," meaning KAP and Eugene Pressly, April 16, 1933, McKeldin. It is interesting to find Porter's father, in 1931, after lamenting the widespread unemployment in the United States, predicting that "the country may go bolshevic yet," but it is impossible to determine his tone in making this prediction. Harrison Boone Porter to KAP, Oct. 25, 1931, McKeldin.

18. Harrison Boone Porter to Breckenridge Porter, Sept. 29, 1934, McKeldin. Regarding the gubernatorial campaign of 1934 and the political characterization of the candidates, Dr. Robert A. Calvert, private correspondence with the author.

19. Harrison Boone Porter to KAP, April 18, 1938, and undated "Early Reminiscences" in HBP's hand, McKeldin.

20. Green, *Grass-Roots Socialism,* p. 248.

21. KAP to Kenneth Durant, March 30, 1936, McKeldin.

22. Green, *Grass-Roots Socialism,* p. xiii. David DeLeon, *The American as Anarchist: Reflections on Indigenous Radicalism,* p. 105. Socialist platform quoted by Green. Professor Worth Robert Miller, in private communication with the author, has called the Socialists in Texas "neo-Populists."

23. Green, pp. 355–68; also, Burbank, *When Farmers Voted Red,* p. 123.

24. Quoted by Burbank, *When Farmers Voted Red,* p. 70.

25. Lewis L. Gould, *Progressives and Prohibitionists: Texas Democrats in the Wilson Era,* p. 29, quoting Harry Y. Benedict and John A. Lomax, *The Book of Texas* (Garden City, N.J.: Doubleday, Page and Company, 1916), p. 58.

26. Alvarez presents evidence that Porter was at least aware of Best-Maugard by December 1919. See "Katherine Anne Porter and Mexican Art," pp. 6–8. Also, Walsh, *Katherine Anne Porter and Mexico,* p. 5.

27. Pells, *Radical Visions,* p. 101.

28. Helen Delpar, *The Enormous Vogue of Things Mexican: Cultural Relations between the United States and Mexico, 1920–1935,* pp. 193, 25. Delpar points out

(p. 8) that enrollments in Spanish-language courses in U.S. secondary schools increased from about 5,000 in 1910 to over 260,000 in 1922. Schmidt, "The American Intellectual Discovery of Mexico in the 1920's," p. 338.

29. Walsh, *Katherine Anne Porter and Mexico,* p. 14, and Givner, *A Life,* p. 151; Delpar, *The Enormous Vogue,* p. 23. Samuel Gompers had "flirted with socialism" in his youth but had given up most of his socialist views by 1886, when he helped found the American Federation of Labor. Socialists in the organization were an opposition faction. Harvey A. Levenstein, *Labor Organizations in the United States and Mexico,* pp. 13–14.

30. Dulles, *Yesterday in Mexico,* pp. 122, 136–40.

31. KAP to Josephine Herbst, May 14, 1927, Beinecke. Notes on Mexico dated June 12, 1922, McKeldin. Retinger was by his own avowal an adventurer during these years. See *Joseph Retinger: Memoirs of an Eminence Grise,* ed. John Pomian, p. 50. Pomian comments (p. 66), "It is hard to keep track of all Retinger's movements in the twenties and the early thirties."

32. Givner (*A Life,* p. 147) believes that Porter went to Mexico in order to gather material for the *Magazine of Mexico.* Alvarez argues convincingly, however, that she had probably gone for the purpose of working on a ballet-pantomime with Best-Maugard for the celebration of the centenary of Mexican independence in September 1921 and did not obtain the contract for work on the *Magazine of Mexico* until December. Alvarez, "Katherine Anne Porter and Mexican Art," pp. 9, 28–29. Porter's first reference to the magazine is in a letter to her family dated December 31, where she says that she is managing editor and that the first issue will "go to press next week." This would be very fast work if she did not get the job until December. In fact, however, the first issue did not appear until March. *Uncollected Early Prose,* ed. Alvarez and Walsh, pp. 28–31, 32–37, 38–42, and 43–44.

33. Delpar, *The Enormous Vogue,* pp. 20–22. On Alvarado, see G. M. Joseph, *Revolution from Without: Yucatán, Mexico, and the United States, 1880–1924,* pp. 122–49 and 185–88. It may have been Porter's connection with Alvarado, via *El Heraldo,* that led to her relationship with Felipe Carillo Puerto, the fervent socialist who had been Alvarado's propaganda minister in the Yucatan and served as governor of the state from January 1922 until his assassination in 1924. During that time Carillo Puerto pushed Alvarado's reforms steadily leftward. See Carr, *Marxism and Communism in Twentieth-Century Mexico,* p. 27.

34. KAP to Porter family, Dec. 31, 1920, McKeldin. Porter, "The New Man and the New Order," *Magazine of Mexico,* March 1921: 5–15; rpt. *Uncollected Early Prose,* ed. Alvarez and Walsh, pp. 46–50. "A Country and Some People I Love," rpt. *Katherine Anne Porter: Conversations,* ed. Joan Givner, p. 123. However, see Walsh, *Katherine Anne Porter and Mexico,* p. 132, where both the visiting of prisoners and the carrying of letters are indeed traced to actual experiences, but to very different ones than Porter claimed.

35. Dulles, *Yesterday in Mexico,* p. 273. McKeldin, "Notes on Mexico," n.d. but probably written in 1922 or very early 1923. The passage can be dated with near certainty by a reference to diplomatic relations between the United States and Guatemala. Porter seems to confirm here Morones's ambition: "For oil—The government will give a certain concession to the labour party, who will get a company—a corporation, preferably French or Swiss, to work it, for them. This should bring in about three hundred thousand pesos a year for the Labour party. If this goes through, Morones, in spite of his youth, will be next president."

36. KAP to Paul Hanna, April 19, 1921, McKeldin. Thomas M. Leonard, *Central America and the United States: The Search for Stability,* p. 88. Joe C. Ashby notes, in his respected *Organized Labor and the Mexican Revolution under Lázaro Cárdenas,* pp. 12–13, that "Communists, the I.W.W., revolutionary Socialists, and radical agrarian elements" were "in considerable force" at the meeting of labor groups in May 1918 that led to the formation of CROM, which was under Morones's leadership from the beginning.

37. Morones and Samuel Yúdico both took losing stands against affiliation with the newly organizing Communist Party of the United States in 1919; see Dulles, *Yesterday in Mexico,* pp. 274–75. Walsh, *Katherine Anne Porter and Mexico,* p. 11, quoting Robert Haberman, "Mexican Workers Celebrate Labor Day with Great Parades and Demonstrations," *New York Call,* Oct. 18, 1920, p. 4. Regarding the Casa's aims, see Levenstein, *Labor Organizations,* pp. 18–21 and 50–65. Doherty told Walsh in an interview in 1982 that Morones was a moderate and both Haberman and Retinger were anti-Communists. Walsh concludes that Morones was not a Bolshevik at all and in fact "had no relationship with the tiny Communist Party in Mexico" (p. 11). One needs to remember that Doherty was well into her eighties at the time and was looking back on events of sixty years before; however, a part of the difficulty of fixing the political affiliations of such persons as Morones or even Doherty herself is that leftist politics of various stripes shaded into each other. Also, the government was at the time attempting to maintain a fluid identity in order to appeal to a wide spectrum of supporters. Morones was, at any rate, a moderate in comparison to those of the far left who were avowed Communists.

38. Linda B. Hall, *Alvaro Obregón: Power and Revolution in Mexico, 1911–1920,* p. 94. Delpar, *The Enormous Vogue,* pp. 11–12.

39. Walsh, *Katherine Anne Porter and Mexico,* pp. 9, 13, 26. Delpar, *The Enormous Vogue,* p. 33, notes that Bertram D. Wolfe, who had joined the Communist party in Mexico in 1923, accused Morones of being "an instrument of Samuel Gompers" in *El Machete,* November 1924. Wolfe became a biographer of Diego Rivera. KAP to Harrison Boone Porter, July 28, 1928, McKeldin. Dulles confirms that the "more Communist labor elements" were "critical" of Morones's and CROM's "association" with Gompers and the AFL; *Yesterday in Mexico,* p. 274. David M. Kennedy points out that Gompers and the AFL were "notoriously hos-

tile to anything that smacked of socialism" and that, although Gompers had once been a pacifist (like the Socialists), by 1916 he supported national preparedness. *Over Here,* pp. 27, 256. Debs attacked Gompers directly in a speech in Coalgate, Okla., on July 4, 1908, for "cooperating with big capitalists in the National Civic Federation"; Green, *Grass-Roots Socialism,* p. 195. Walsh, *Katherine Anne Porter and Mexico,* pp. 13–28.

40. Walsh, *Katherine Anne Porter and Mexico,* pp. 10, 38–39. Paul Hanna to KAP, April 2, 1921; KAP drafts to Paul Hanna, April 19, 1921 and May 29, 1921; McKeldin. John Pomian, the editor of Retinger's memoirs, refers to Seldes only as a friend of Retinger.

41. J. H. Retinger to KAP, March 3, 1921, McKeldin.

42. KAP to Porter family, Dec. 31, 1920, McKeldin.

43. J. H. Retinger, *The Rise of the Mexican Labor Movement,* pp. 15–35, 86–93. *New York Times,* June 24, 1960. Walsh, *Katherine Anne Porter and Mexico,* p. 25, quoting intelligence reports. Pomian says that Retinger was "never a card-carrying member" of the Socialist party (he does not so much as mention the possibility of the Communist party) or of the British Labour party, though he was thought to be, but acknowledges that during the 1920s he was "in close touch with socialist politicians, particularly in England" and his friends in Mexico were "radical and Labour" (*Joseph Retinger,* pp. 68, 75).

44. KAP to J. H. Retinger, a fragment, possibly never mailed, bearing in pencil the date 1921 and the comment, "Retinger in jail in Laredo"; McKeldin, "Notes on Mexico." Retinger's memoirs incorrectly place his imprisonment as 1926 (pp. 60–64). Walsh, *Katherine Anne Porter and Mexico,* pp. 23–44. Paul Hanna wrote to Porter on April 2, 1921, two and one-half months before Mendez's execution, "Of course I should like to know what you have learned since you gave us that glimpse of portentious [*sic*] private correspondence. The interventionist plot thickens fast here." McKeldin. In fragmentary notes that seem to date from about this time, since they contain references to Retinger, she mentions "my getting of the letters." "Notes on Mexico," McKeldin.

45. Givner, *A Life,* pp. 157–58; Walsh, *Katherine Anne Porter and Mexico,* pp. 47–49. The incidents that led to Porter's fleeing the country were not, however, the first time her political beliefs had led her to court danger. By 1919, at about the time she was becoming identified with socialist/communist circles, the United States was swept by what has been called a "national hysteria" of anticommunism. Even earlier, in 1917 and 1918, the years depicted in "Pale Horse, Pale Rider," where Porter's surrogate is unwaveringly opposed to the war, hostility to socialist pacifism and a wave of antiradicalism in general erupted in instances of vigilantism and lynching in Wyoming, Montana, Ohio, Missouri, and elsewhere. See Robert K. Murray, *Red Scare: A Study in National Hysteria, 1919–1920,* and Kennedy, *Over Here,* pp. 67–69, 73–75.

46. KAP to Mary Alice Porter Hillendahl, n.d., but subsequently identified in Porter's hand as 1921; Mary Doherty to KAP, April 22, 1922; McKeldin.

47. José Clemente Orozco credits Dr. Atl with having awakened Mexican art students to a sense of national competence and independence and with animating them to a "spirit of rebellion." See Orozco, *An Autobiography,* trans. Robert C. Stephenson, p. 21. KAP to Harrison Boone Porter, July 27, 1922, McKeldin.

48. Cynthia Newman Helms, ed., *Diego Rivera: A Retrospective,* p. 53. Orozco, *An Autobiography,* pp. 30, 40–41. Orozco states (pp. 91–93) that Siqueiros, Rivera, and Guerrero were the "most conversant" in the "socialistic theories" on which the Syndicate and its "extraordinarily important" manifesto were based. Siqueiros, he says, had attended Communist meetings of workers in France and brought back the ideas that went into the manifesto when he was recalled to Mexico by Vasconcelos in 1921. Quoting David Siqueiros, Jean Charlot reports that Orozco "refused to attend" the organizational meeting of the Syndicate (held at the home of Rivera and Marín) because of "personal enmity with Rivera," but "agreed to take up active membership." Charlot, *The Mexican Mural Renaissance, 1920–1925,* p. 242.

49. Adolfo Best-Maugard, *A Method for Creative Design,* p. 110. Best-Maugard's emphasis throughout is on the development of individual creativity through the use of motifs common in the art of primitive peoples.

50. Henry C. Schmidt, *The Roots of Lo Mexicano: Self and Society in Mexican Thought, 1900–1934,* pp. 74, 118. Schmidt regards Vasconcelos as "the most political" of the leading intellectuals of the 1920s (p. 118).

51. Unrue, *"This Strange, Old World,"* pp. 83–88. Thomas M. Leonard points out that the "exaltation" of Mexico's Indian heritage "inspired" Augusto C. Sandino, who led resistance to the U.S.-backed conservative government of Nicaragua from mid-1927 to 1933 (*Central America and the United States,* pp. 87–89).

52. In an interview with Hank Lopez, Porter explained the sidetracking of the collection by reference to politics; *Conversations,* ed. Givner, p. 126. Alvarez explains it by simple bungling; "Katherine Anne Porter and Mexican Art," pp. 45–46. Edward Weston, the photographer, is thought to have seen the exhibition. He went to Mexico shortly thereafter. Amy Conger, *Edward Weston in Mexico,* p. 11. Conger terms the collection "monumental" and notes that Porter's catalog was "the first work in English on the subject." A photograph of Xavier Guerrero taken at the folk art exhibition in Los Angeles in late 1922 appears in Margaret Hooks, *Tina Modotti, Photographer and Revolutionary,* p. 59.

53. Xavier Guerrero to KAP, Jan. 1, 1923, McKeldin. Helms, ed., *Diego Rivera,* p. 54. Years after her residence in Mexico, Mary Doherty's sister Peggy wrote to Porter that "Xavier Guerrero always asks for you" (Peggy Doherty to KAP, Aug. 21, 1939, McKeldin). Porter had included Guerrero among a "list of Mexicans" with the label "Indian painter and Communist" in a letter to Josephine Herbst written May 4, 1927 (McKeldin). He was, in fact, an active Communist party organizer

and speaker, and was sent to Moscow to the Lenin School in 1927 (Hooks, *Tina Modotti,* pp. 82, 141, 146). The slogan of *El Machete,* composed by the communist feminist Graciela Amador, was:

The machete is used to reap corn,
To clear a path through an underbrush,
To kill snakes, end strife,
And humble the pride of the impious rich.

Charlot, *The Mexican Mural Renaissance,* pp. 245, 251.

54. Liza Allen Dallett Monk to KAP, undated except for " '22" in Porter's hand, McKeldin. Givner, *A Life,* p. 163.

55. Walsh, *Katherine Anne Porter and Mexico,* pp. 49, 89.

56. Nancy Newhall, ed., *The Daybooks of Edward Weston: Volume I, Mexico,* pp. xviii, 17–19, 25. Helms, *Diego Rivera* (p. 53) places Modotti's meeting of Rivera, Guerrero, and others of that circle in the fall of 1922. Citing Guadalupe Marín's recollection, Hooks, in *Tina Modotti* (p. 53), places their meeting earlier that year.

57. Carr, *Marxism and Communism in 20th-Century Mexico,* p. 35. Doherty visited Modotti in prison and saw her off on the train when she was deported; Hooks, *Tina Modotti,* pp. 197–98.

58. Margaret Gibson, Preface to *Memories of the Future: The Daybooks of Tina Modotti, Poems,* p. xiii.

59. Mary Doherty to KAP, Dec. 13, 1963, McKeldin. In 1982, Doherty told Walsh in an interview that she was upset when Modotti was deported; it seems strange that she would have been upset if she believed then that Modotti had been implicated in Mella's murder.

60. William Spratling, *File on Spratling: An Autobiography,* p. 21. Diego Rivera, *My Art, My Life,* p. 162. Mildred Constantine, *Tina Modotti: A Fragile Life,* p. 104. Margaret Gibson, in the preface to her poems based on Modotti's daybooks, asserts that her bad press was planted in "an attempted political cover-up" of the assassination, which both she and Rivera attribute to Machado, the dictator of Cuba (p. xiv). Rivera also claims that after his own testimony in court at Modotti's trial the Cuban government's involvement was "officially recognized." Modotti had been indicted, he says, strictly for political reasons. Rivera, *My Art, My Life,* p. 162; also, Bertram D. Wolfe, *The Fabulous Life of Diego Rivera,* p. 230. Barry Carr agrees that Mella was killed by agents of the Machado government (*Marxism and Communism,* p. 340).

61. KAP to Pressly, Dec. 21, 1931, McKeldin. Modotti was reported, perhaps apocryphally, to have thrown her camera into a river in a gesture signifying that she would thereafter turn her energies to direct social action. She apparently sold or gave one of her cameras to Eugene Pressly when she left Mexico. Porter had

a camera in Paris that she said had belonged to Modotti. Hooks, *Tina Modotti,* p. 198. KAP to Robert McAlmon, Nov. 12, 1932, McKeldin. *"This Strange, Old World,"* p. 124.

62. A well-preserved copy of the *Survey Graphic,* vol. 2 (May 1924), is in the Porter Collection at the McKeldin Library. John Womack, Jr., *Zapata and the Mexican Revolution,* p. 205. Also, Ramón Eduardo Ruíz, *The Great Rebellion: Mexico, 1905–1924,* p. 211.

63. Schmidt comments that in the 1920s "Communism and art formed the ideological basis of the 'syndicates' of painters and writers who strove for reform." *The Roots of Lo Mexicano,* p. 99. Edward Weston, in an entry in his daybook from his period in Mexico, notes that Rivera was called "the Lenin of Mexico." "The artists here," he wrote, "are closely allied with the Communist Movement; it is no parlor politics with them." Newhall, ed., *The Daybooks of Edward Weston,* p. 35.

64. Roy Newquist, "An Interview with Katherine Anne Porter," *McCall's Magazine,* August 1965; rpt. *Conversations,* ed. Givner, p. 114.

65. Alicia Azuela, "Rivera and the Concept of Proletarian Art," in Helms, ed., *Diego Rivera,* p. 125.

66. Helms, *Diego Rivera,* pp. 59, 71, 79. The article in the *New Masses* was Joseph Freeman's "Painting and Politics: The Case of Diego Rivera." Rivera, *My Art, My Life,* pp. 164–66. Bertram D. Wolfe, Rivera's admiring biographer and himself a hearty Communist, attributes the denunciation to misunderstanding or misrepresentation of Rivera's work at the National Palace, *Mexico of the Future,* which ironically was "the most 'Marxist' work in the history of art." Wolfe, *The Fabulous Life of Diego Rivera,* pp. 266–67.

67. KAP to Peggy Cowley, n.d., from Paris, McKeldin. The year can be established by internal evidence and comparison with other letters. KAP to Josephine Herbst, July 27, 1932, Beinecke.

68. "The Fiesta of Guadalupe" is dated 1923 in the *Collected Essays,* but Thomas F. Walsh has established that it appeared in a newspaper in Mexico shortly after Porter's arrival there. Walsh, "From Texas to Mexico to Texas," p. 73.

69. *CE,* p. 400. KAP to Porter Family, Dec. 31, 1920, McKeldin.

70. *CE,* p. 408. Unrue, *"This Strange, Old World,"* pp. 52–55. Her list of vested interests in "The Mexican Trinity" foreshadows the list she would give in "Pale Horse, Pale Rider" when denouncing the unacknowledged interests behind World War I.

71. Porter, Review of Blasco Ibáñez, *Mexico in Revolution, El Heraldo de México,* Nov. 22, 1920: 7; rpt. *Uncollected Early Prose of Katherine Anne Porter,* ed. Alvarez and Walsh, pp. 28–31. She reviewed the book negatively, saying it "should be devoured and forgotten by the third day."

72. V. Blasco Ibáñez, *Mexico in Revolution,* trans. Arthur Livingston and José Padin, pp. 2–3, 150. Walsh, *Katherine Anne Porter and Mexico,* p. 68. Even before

her completion of "Where Presidents Have No Friends," she expressed in a 1921 letter to J. H. Retinger, then languishing in a Laredo jail, her disillusioned "conviction that, in a pinch, the working of this monstrous machine was not without some balance of discrimination. If I had not friends to set a hand on the lever, I would have been gone [i.e., deported] by now." In notes dated May 1921 she commented, "More deportations . . . such poor, simple people. It's sickening to see nobody with any friends, or a little money, has been touched. Only quite helpless people. Some of them need not have been helpless. They honestly chose to be poor, to work for a true revolution." In 1965, reviewing what she called "these old ragged notes," she commented on that last sentence, "Poor dupes!"—using the word Blasco Ibáñez had applied to the Mexican people in general. McKeldin, "Notes on Mexico."

73. Walsh, *Katherine Anne Porter and Mexico,* p. 17.

74. *CE,* p. 400. But in 1931 she seems to have all but given up hope that revolutionists, at any rate those of the lower classes, would achieve any real change. She wrote to her father while on board the *Werra,* on her way to Europe, that "even the most wretched soul has in his heart a nasty little idea that if he hangs on long enough, he'll get rich too, and then to hell with it . . . So he doesn't do anything that might upset the present system." KAP to Harrison Boone Porter, n.d. except 1931, McKeldin.

75. *CE,* pp. 417–20.

76. *"This Strange, Old World,"* p. 54.

77. MacKinnon and MacKinnon, *Agnes Smedley,* p. 275. Brantley, *Feminine Sense,* pp. 150 and 158.

78. David Felix, *Protest: Sacco-Vanzetti and the Intellectuals,* p. 225. Felix refers to the later notoriety of the case as "a legend of innocence betrayed" (p. 240). Malcolm Cowley wrote in a 1935 article in the *New Republic* (cited by Felix, p. 12) that the protests gave intellectuals a rallying cry in a period when their only "group manifestations" had been "literary teas" and "their only political platform was a cocktail tray."

79. KAP to John Herrmann, Aug. 3, 1932, HRC.

80. Alvarez, "Katherine Anne Porter and Mexican Art," p. 414.

81. KAP to Genevieve Taggard, June 3, 1926, and n.d., McKeldin. Aaron, *Writers on the Left,* pp. 113, 88. James F. Murphy, *The Proletarian Moment: The Controversy over Leftism in Literature,* p. 57. Murphy points out (p. 13) that unlike the *Daily Worker,* the *New Masses* was never an official organ of the Communist party.

82. KAP to Robert McAlmon, Aug. 21, 1934, McKeldin. Walsh, *Katherine Anne Porter and Mexico,* p. 5. Kenneth Durant to KAP, Nov. 7, 1935, McKeldin.

83. Walsh, *Katherine Anne Porter and Mexico,* p. 117.

84. She said later that it was a "cheap little idea by a cheap publisher" who had paid her "several hundred dollars to assemble a kind of anthology." She added, "This kind of thing should have no place in the list of my works." KAP to Edward Schwartz, Nov. 7, 1951, McKeldin.

85. David Shi, *Matthew Josephson: Bourgeois Bohemian,* pp. 124–26. Robert McAlmon, *Being Geniuses Together, 1920–1930,* rev. and with supplementary chapters by Kay Boyle, p. 332. Joan Givner reported to Porter's nephew Paul, during her research for her groundbreaking biography, that the Harcourt Brace file confirmed that Josephson was instrumental in sending Porter's stories there. She also stated that he did "place" the story "Magic" in *transition* for her; Givner to Paul Porter, May 6, 1979, private collection of Paul Porter.

86. KAP to Dorothy Day, July 20, 1930, the Dorothy Day-Catholic Worker Collection, Marquette University: She had been, she said, "curled up in bed for several weeks, utterly miserable" while "curing of T B." She was now feeling that "it was wrong to come back" and "wish[ed she] had not." But she added, "It is a question of how much of it is illness, and whether I should not have felt the same anywhere."

87. KAP to Josephine Herbst, June 1, 1931, Beinecke. KAP to Mary Doherty, Oct. 21, 1932, McKeldin. In excerpting from the letter for her volume *Letters of Katherine Anne Porter,* Isabel Bayley deletes the phrase about Crane's death being "well done," but does not point out the excision. This is one instance of Bayley's supporting her thesis that "goodness of heart runs through her letters" (*Letters,* p. 2). Susan Jenkins Brown, in *Robber Rocks: Letters and Memories of Hart Crane, 1923–1932,* argued that Porter exhibited "kindness, generosity and reasonable tolerance" toward Crane after the "alcoholic explosion" for which he "abjectly apologized," and that she had "tried to limit the spread of this story," though "there were others in Mexico who felt no qualms about repeating it" (pp. 127–40). Porter's correspondence shows that this belief was incorrect.

88. Philip Horton, *Hart Crane: The Life of an American Poet,* p. 285.

89. In her copy of Spratling's autobiography, *File on Spratling,* p. 101, McKeldin, Porter marked an account of Crane and Cowley, whom Spratling refers to as Mrs. X, and called her, in a marginal notation, "a highly non-literary camp follower, 'alley-cat fatàle.'" In response to Spratling's saying that Mrs. X "laid her proposition [to Crane] on the table," she wrote, "Peggy laid her proposition anywhere any time." She also commented on Spratling's interesting phrasing. Elsewhere, however, she referred to Spratling as "the fraud who ran the silver-works racket in Taxco"; KAP to Mary Doherty, May 4, 1960, McKeldin-MLD.

90. KAP to Josephine Herbst, Feb. 11, 1931, Beinecke. Delpar, *The Enormous Vogue of Things Mexican,* p. 195.

91. Ruíz, *The Great Rebellion,* pp. 304–39. According to Ruíz's data (pp. 323–33, 420), land redistribution reached a "gentle" peak in 1921, Obregón's first year as president, then declined, and American businesses were more active in Mexico in 1924, when Obregón's term ended, than before, though the country itself was less prosperous. Frank Tannenbaum earlier took a jaundiced view of the gains of the Revolution in his *Mexico: The Struggle for Peace and Bread.* The trade union movement, for example, he called a "stick" for the government to lean on or to wield (p. 85). Tannenbaum, unlike the more securely researched Ruíz, depicted

Obregón, Calles, and Cárdenas as having wholeheartedly embraced land redistribution and other aspects of the "social revolution," but having been thwarted in their "transcendental" hopes by a stubbornly unyielding backward culture (pp. 63–72, 105). Tannenbaum is to be read with caution. He insists that, with only minor "turns," the United States dealt with Mexico according to "ideals long cherished by the American people," including the principle that "social justice takes precedence over property rights" (pp. 291–92). As to the "visitation of locusts," see Womack, *Zapata and the Mexican Revolution,* p. 375. Womack points out that Zapata's own state of Morelos benefited more from agrarian reform than other parts of Mexico.

92. Harry M. Geduld and Ronald Gottesman, eds., *Sergei Eisenstein and Upton Sinclair: The Making and Unmaking of Qué Viva México!,* p. 130.

CHAPTER FOUR: The Harvest of Mexico

1. KAP to Dorothy Day, July 20, 1930, Marquette University Archives.

2. Unrue, "Katherine Anne Porter, Politics, and Another Reading of 'Theft,'" p. 121. The review of Brenner appears in *"This Strange, Old World,"* p. 124. Unrue's judgment in the preface that a study of the reviews collected in this volume "reveals no substantial change in her social values or artistic standards" (p. xi) may be true in its narrowest sense, but there is ample evidence that Porter's social views changed enormously over the course of her life.

3. Unrue, *"This Strange, Old World,"* p. 83–88.

4. Leonard, *Central America and the United States,* p. 88, refers to the "effervescence of ideas characterizing the Mexican Revolution."

5. This connection has been searchingly studied by Thomas F. Walsh, by Darlene Harbour Unrue, and by Ruth Moore Alvarez in her dissertation "Katherine Anne Porter and Mexican Art."

6. "A Country and Some People I Love," *Conversations,* p. 120. Givner attributes Porter's relatively late emergence as a writer to her sense that she lacked "a body of material that she considered worthy of being used in fiction" (*A Life,* pp. 146–47).

7. Glenway Wescott, *Images of Truth: Remembrances and Criticism,* p. 45.

8. Porter, "Why I Write about Mexico" (a Letter to the Editor of *The Century*), first published in 1923, *CE,* p. 355. In "A Country and Some People I Love," she told Lopez, "My father brought me to Mexico when I was ten years old." Writing to Malcolm Cowley in 1965, she moved the date back somewhat: "My father took me on a trip to Mexico before I was ten years old"; KAP to Malcolm Cowley, March 16, 1965, McKeldin. A press release dated Nov. 18, 1964, publicizing her State Department-sponsored visit to Mexico, elaborated on the report: "Miss Porter is no stranger to Mexico. Born near San Antonio, Texas, she first visited the country at the age of ten, and returned there many times with her family." McKeldin, from the file labeled "Mexico." Walsh does not acknowledge

an early visit. Porter's nephew, Paul Porter, says that he never heard his father or his other aunts speak of such a visit and has never found any evidence that it occurred (private communication to the author). Givner to Thomas Walsh, Feb. 24, 1986, McKeldin-TFW.

9. During the period 1890 to 1910 (the first twenty years of Porter's life) there occurred a 300 percent increase in the Mexican population of the state while the total population increased by only 75 percent. Larry D. Hill, "Texas Progressivism," in *Texas through Time: Evolving Interpretations,* ed. Walter L. Buenger and Robert A. Calvert, p. 247.

10. Harrison Boone Porter to Mary Alice Jones, 1882; Gay Porter Holloway to KAP, Oct. 22, 1931; McKeldin. Givner says that she went with "expectations of high adventure"; *A Life,* p. 147. Lopez interview, in Givner, *Conversations,* p. 121. Walsh, *Katherine Anne Porter and Mexico,* p. 6.

11. Ernestine Evans to KAP, May 23, 1920; Ethel R. Peyser to KAP, May 27, 1920; McKeldin.

12. KAP to Porter family, from Mexico City, Dec. 31, 1920, McKeldin.

13. The phrase "spring fullblown into life" was used by Virginia Spencer Carr in her paper " 'What you write is a sum of your experience and yourself': Katherine Anne Porter's 'Flowering Judas,' " at a conference on Porter's work held at Baylor University, May 16, 1992, in describing the reaction of Porter's first readers to the publication of "María Concepción" and "Flowering Judas."

14. Unrue reads the story as a statement of the "difficulty" of "educating" or "civilizing" the Indian; *Truth and Vision in Katherine Anne Porter's Fiction,* pp. 107, 113. Although I reject that reading, in favor of seeing the story as a tribute to the persistence and even the resurgence of indigenous elements in Mexican culture, it is by no means an unreasonable one. The story is startlingly polished for its place in Porter's canon, but it is not a fully controlled work, and its theme is not clearly worked out.

15. Helen Fiddyment Levy, *Fiction of the Home Place: Jewett, Cather, Glasgow, Porter, Welty, and Naylor,* p. 136.

16. *CS,* p. 21. Helen Levy analyzes "María Concepción" in comparison with the unpublished essay "The Children of Xochitl," written in 1921, through their common development of a theme of small communities centered on a maternal figure who repels invasion by alien powers, here the gendarmes. See "The Children of Xochitl," *Uncollected Early Prose,* ed. Alvarez and Walsh, pp. 78–85.

17. Alvarez, "Katherine Anne Porter and Mexican Art," p. 215.

18. In notes she made on an excursion with the archaeologist Manuel Gamio, Porter commented on the "statues of the Christ, his body a mass of bloody suppurating wounds." "Notes on Teotihuacan," 1921–22, McKeldin; rpt. *Uncollected Early Prose,* pp. 99–106.

19. Both Unrue (*Truth and Vision,* p. 115) and Alvarez (pp. 306–20) comment

on the link between Rivera's "Creation" and "The Martyr." Alvarez gives close attention to Porter's use of genre scenes and portraits throughout her study of Porter and Mexican art.

20. Orozco, *Autobiography,* p. 120. Erika Billeter, in "Mexico's Contribution to 20th Century Art," trans. Maureen Oberli-Turner, states that *pulqueria* painting had been present "since time immemorial." See *Images of Mexico: The Contribution of Mexico to 20th Century Art,* ed. Billeter, p. 25.

21. Porter, *Outline of Mexican Arts and Crafts.* In a later article "translated" by Porter ("From a Mexican Painter's Notebook," *Arts* 7 [January 1925]: 21–23), Rivera would call the Indian the "true Mexican."

22. KAP to Eugene Pressly, Nov. 11, 1931, McKeldin.

23. "A Letter from Mexico and the Gleam of Montezuma's Golden Roofs," *Christian Science Monitor* June 5, 1922: 22; rpt. in *Uncollected Early Prose,* ed. Alvarez and Walsh, pp. 131–35. *Outline,* pp. 40 and 13. Orozco, who took an active role in the Manifesto of the Syndicate and in the early issues of the *Machete* (though he claimed he "played no part in the Revolution"), later viewed the issue of communal artistry as Porter did, declaring that the idea simply does not work. The artist "cannot efface himself from the work as the Manifesto seems to hope." Orozco, *Autobiography,* pp. 40–41, 99.

24. Levy, *Fiction of the Home Place,* pp. 133–35.

25. KAP to Malcolm Cowley, March 16, 1965, McKeldin. Lopez, "A Country and Some People I Love," *Conversations,* pp. 120–34.

26. Walter Frank, an attorney in New York, wrote to Porter on April 16, 1930, confirming that he was sending her a check to cover traveling expenses to Mexico and would send $45 twice a month until the end of the year. In January 1931 he wrote that he would extend the support for a few more months to enable her to resist economic pressures to publish. He hoped that in this way she could avoid "another breakdown." Since he goes on to say that he hopes she will be "entirely 'arrested,' " it appears that the breakdown was a return of tubercular symptoms rather than an emotional breakdown. Walter Frank to KAP, April 16, 1930 and January 17, 1931, McKeldin.

27. Porter variously projected novels to be titled "Thieves Market," "Men and Women," "Historical Present," and "Many Redeemers." The last title was surely drawn from Blasco Ibáñez's use of the word *redeemers* in his book *Mexico in Revolution,* which she reviewed in 1921, referring to the Mexican as "the everlasting dupe whom the redeemers shower with fine phrases, never telling him the truth."

28. Typical of such claims is a comment written in a copy of *Pale Horse, Pale Rider* owned by Sandy M. Campbell, a friend of Donald Windham: "I knew this story all my life, but I wrote it in one draft in seven days—." The volume, from the "Fifth Printing, February 1942," stamped "Ex Libris Sandy Montgomery Campbell," is located in the Donald Windham Collection, Hargrett Rare Book and

Manuscript Library, University of Georgia. Porter's claim appears on the title page of "Old Mortality." This and similar claims, of course, ignore the earlier production of jottings on which she drew when the story finally came together.

29. Harcourt Brace had paid her an advance on a novel to be delivered Sept. 1, 1931. Even after she received her Guggenheim Fellowship in March, she seems to have made a commitment to deliver the novel personally on her way to Europe. Throughout the spring and summer of that year she was receiving letters from Alfred Harcourt asking how she was progressing and why they were not hearing from her. In addition, Horace Liveright was writing to her demanding that she repay the $850 they had advanced to her on the Cotton Mather book, plus $190 expended on dummies and advertising.

30. Becky Crawford to KAP, June 24, 1930; KAP to Delafield Day, February 17, 1931; McKeldin. KAP to Josephine Herbst, Dec. 29, 1930, Beinecke. KAP to Peggy Cowley, Feb. 18, 1931, McKeldin.

31. Walsh points out that Laura's detachment in the story is not a fair representation of Doherty's "honest and genuine devotion to revolutionary reform." He identifies Yúdico as the primary model for Braggioni, to whom Porter added Morones after Yúdico's death in 1928. *Katherine Anne Porter and Mexico*, pp. 125–28. Porter herself made the dual identification of Braggioni in a copy of *Flowering Judas and Other Stories* that she inscribed for Sandy M. Campbell on April 6, 1943. The Table of Contents page bears the instruction, "Look at all Title pages." On the title page for "Flowering Judas" she wrote: "Braggioni is based on two Mexican labor leaders I knew—Luis Morones and Samuel Yúdico. The girl Laura still lives in Mexico and had a fate very different from what she feared for herself—." Donald Windham Collection, University of Georgia. The girl, of course, is Mary Doherty. Notes made for a projected long work Porter called Historical Present, available among her papers in a file marked "Notes on Mexico," demonstrate that she was thinking of including many of her acquaintances as characters under fictional names. The earliest reference to the incident of the serenade, however, seems to be a fragment of typed notes dated in pencil 1921, reading, "Yúdico came in tonight bringing his guitar, and spent the evening singing for Mary. Mary sat in a deep chair at the end of the table, under the light, a little preoccupied, infallibly and kindly attentive. She is a modern secular nun."

32. See, for example, Eduardo del Rio, ed., *Un Siglo de Caricatura en Mexico*, p. 50.

33. Levenstein, *Labor Organizations*, speaks of rumors of "Nero-like debauches" held at Morones's country home (p. 65). We can only wonder whether Porter had direct experience of these. Historian Henry Schmidt indicates that her reputation among persons whom he has interviewed in Mexico is one that would accord with such experience; private communication with the author. Walsh comments on Porter's role in revolutionary activities and her sense of guilt for the harm

that resulted: "A few years before her death, Porter, in tears, told me she herself had given sleeping pills to a prisoner who hoarded them until he had enough with which to kill himself, adding that only the death of the man who caught influenza from her in Denver had affected her as much. . . . Porter's claim of visiting prisoners in their cells is based on her visits to Haberman in hiding [during the arrests and deportations of 1921] and to Retinger in his cell [in Laredo]. Her claim of smuggling letters is based on her copying William Niven's letters about Sidronio Mendez and his co-conspirators." *Katherine Anne Porter and Mexico,* p. 132.

34. Walsh, *Katherine Anne Porter and Mexico,* p. 124, regards her preoccupation with death as the "firm link" between her Mexican stories and her Miranda stories. The pervasive presence of death in Mexican folk festivals and art was captured by Sergei Eisenstein in many sequences in *Qué Viva México!* in which he often depicts skulls. Porter, of course, knew of Eisenstein's work, but she did not need that to alert her to the motif, which she knew directly from observation. Victor Fosado discusses customs relating to the prevalent death-consciousness in Mexico in concise and useful form in his short essay "Death in Mexico," trans. Maurice Harrah, in *Images of Mexico,* ed. Billeter, pp. 431–32. Fosada summarizes, "Since pre-Hispanic times, death has been considered part of daily life, duality, the beginning and the end, the everlasting." In the same volume, the essay "Folk Art in Mexico" by Porfirio Martinez Penaloza, pp. 422–30, includes comments on the objects customarily produced in connection with the commemoration of the dead on November 1 and 2, and includes a color photograph of painted sugar calaveras. A number of reproductions of José Guadalupe Posada's caricature calaveras appear on pages 152 through 155.

35. KAP to Monroe Wheeler, Nov. 13, 1933; KAP to Caroline Gordon, Dec. 14, 1931; McKeldin.

36. Mary Seton, *Sergei M. Eisenstein: A Biography,* p. 160.

37. KAP, "Hacienda," *Virginia Quarterly Review* 8 (1932): 561. For ease of reference, this version of "Hacienda" will be identified in parenthetical notes as H-1. The later version, as it appears among Porter's *Collected Stories,* will be designated H-2.

38. Darlene Harbour Unrue comments ambiguously that because most of the characters are "fictional counterparts of the real people present during Porter's visit" the story "was taken to be almost a documentary." *Understanding Katherine Anne Porter,* p. 39.

39. KAP to Eugene Pressly, n.d. but evidently written in November 1931, McKeldin. Givner, in *A Life,* p. 239, refers to "Hacienda" as a "summation" of Porter's feelings about Mexico.

40. Seton, *Sergei M. Eisenstein,* p. 225.

41. Monroe Wheeler to KAP, Dec. 5, 1934; KAP to Porter family, Jan. 8, 1935; McKeldin.

42. Unrue, *Understanding KAP,* p. 39.

43. Alvarez has pointed out that the details of posture and position (outside on the balcony) may also express her solidarity with the peons, who are seen sitting in the courtyard in Eisenstein's film; private correspondence with the author.

44. Mary Seton seems to believe that Porter caught accurately enough the grotesque atmosphere of the entire undertaking, which she reports would strike "an uninitiated outsider as the escapade of a group of ill-assorted eccentrics" (*Sergei M. Eisenstein,* p. 224).

45. KAP to Harrison Boone Porter, July 28, 1928, McKeldin.

46. KAP to Josephine Herbst, Feb. 11, 1931, Beinecke.

47. Unrue, "*This Strange, Old World,*" pp. 39–41.

48. The caricature of Hidalgo is reproduced in Walsh, *Katherine Anne Porter and Mexico,* p. xix, and in Givner, *A Life,* illustration number 16, where, however, it is misidentified. The sketch of Herrmann is at the HRC. Caricatures of Katharine Anthony (the author of *Catherine the Great*), Genevieve Taggard, and Stein were published in the *New York Herald Tribute* on Jan. 29, 1925, April 18, 1926, and Jan. 16, 1927. She also drew a fine caricature of Elinor Wylie that was not published until some years later.

49. Robert Penn Warren, "Introduction" to Edward Schwartz, *Katherine Anne Porter: A Critical Bibliography.*

50. KAP to Dorothy Day, July 20, 1930, Marquette University Archives.

51. *CE,* p. 423.

52. *CE,* p. 422.

53. *CE,* pp. 423–25; "The Mexican Trinity," *CE,* p. 402.

54. *CE,* pp. 92–93.

55. *CE,* p. 99.

56. *CE,* p. 470.

57. Alvarez discusses at length the relationship of "Holiday" to the work of Porter's Mexican exemplars. See "Katherine Anne Porter and Mexican Art," pp. 355–91.

58. A. Everett Austin, Jr., Director of the Wadsworth Atheneum, Hartford, Connecticut, to KAP, May 6, 1930, McKeldin; KAP to A. Everett Austin, Jr., July 1, 1930, Wadsworth Atheneum (quoted by permission of Mr. Eugene Gaddis, Curator).

CHAPTER FIVE: " 'between two wars in a falling world' "

1. KAP to Josephine Herbst, Feb. 11, 1931, Beinecke. Caroline Gordon reported to Sally Wood on Feb. 21, 1931 that Porter was "getting restless": "I detect signs in our friend of being tired of Mexico"; *The Southern Mandarins,* p. 72. The title of this chapter is from Porter's "The Wooden Umbrella."

2. Unrue, "*This Strange, Old World,*" p. xiv.

3. KAP to Freda Kirchway, Feb. 5, 1942, *Letters,* p. 221.

4. Conan Fischer, *The German Communists and the Rise of Nazism,* p. 115. Susan Sontag, "Fascinating Fascism," in *Women and the Cinema: A Critical Anthology,* ed. Karyn Kay and Gerald Peary, p. 374. See also Susan Gubar, " 'This Is My Rifle, This Is My Gun': World War II and the Blitz on Women," in *Behind the Lines: Gender and the Two World Wars,* ed. Margaret Randolph Higonnet et al., p. 230: "Because European fascism evolved as a reaction against the emasculation associated with the First World War and the Depression, the fascist 'father' regarded his leadership as a sexual mastery over the feminized masses." Gubar offers abundant evidence of women's sense that the war constituted a sexual threat. Porter's linkage of politics and amorous emotion is perceptively elucidated by Thomas Austenfeld in "Katherine Anne Porter Abroad: The Politics of Emotion," pp. 27–33.

5. Studies of the constituencies of the KPD (the Communist Party of Germany) and the NSDAP (the National Socialists) show that there was a "sociological affinity between the two radical extremes." Both drew membership from unemployed workers, as well as from urban industrial workers and some rural workers. Although the NSDAP was also strong among the middle class, the two extremist parties were rivals for members among similar groups. Fischer, *The German Communists and the Rise of Nazism,* pp. 102–17, 138–39.

6. KAP to "Baby" (Mary Alice Porter), 1919, from Denver; J. H. Retinger to KAP, "November or December" 1921; Mary Doherty to KAP, from Victoria, Texas, Aug. 5, n.y., but penciled guesses of 1922 or 1923 written in Porter's hand; J. H. Retinger to KAP from London, April 3, 1924; McKeldin. Despite her avowed distrust of Retinger, it must have contributed to his charm for her to know that he was a close friend of Joseph Conrad. KAP to Mary Doherty, Oct. 24, 1932, McKeldin.

7. KAP to Rita Johns, Jan. 21, 1963, McKeldin. Porter's recollection that her friend had hated Germany is confirmed by a letter Erna wrote to Porter on May 3, 1939, from Steiner Valley Ranch, in Whitney, Texas, her country home. "You remarked on what I said as a child about hating Germany. I realize now that I didn't want to be thought German. I wanted to be like the rest of you and have a Confederate Grandfather!"

8. KAP to Josephine Herbst, July 19, 1929, Beinecke. KAP to "Darling Old Sister and Dad," April 1, 1920, McKeldin.

9. KAP to Josephine Herbst, Aug. 25, 1931, Beinecke. KAP to Caroline Gordon, Aug. 28, 1931, *Letters,* pp. 46–60. KAP to Mary Doherty, Oct. 24, 1932; KAP to Malcolm Cowley, Oct. 3, 1931; McKeldin. When she was going through her papers years later, she wrote in, "What an illusion! How could I have been so blind, so stupified [*sic*]?" KAP to Mary Doherty, Oct. 21, 1932, McKeldin.

10. KAP to Malcolm Cowley, Nov. 5, 1931; KAP to Pressly, n.d., but 1931 penciled in later; McKeldin.

11. KAP to Eugene Pressly, Dec. 1, 1931, McKeldin.

12. KAP to Cyrilly Abels, Sept. 13, 1958, McKeldin.

13. KAP to Eugene Pressly, Dec. 21, 1931; Pablo O'Higgins to KAP, n.d., but identified in Porter's hand as "late fall or winter 1931"; KAP to Yvor Winters, Jan. 1, 1932; McKeldin.

14. KAP to Eugene Pressly, Jan. 3, 1932; KAP to Mary Doherty, Oct. 24, 1932; KAP to Erna Schlemmer Johns, Jan. 21, 1963; McKeldin.

15. KAP to Gay Porter Holloway, July 25, 1932; KAP to Josephine Herbst, July 1, 1932; McKeldin. KAP to Harrison Boone Porter, March 2, 1933, *Letters,* p. 92.

16. KAP to Peggy Cowley, Feb. 20, 1932, McKeldin. At the bottom of the last page of Goldman's *Living My Life* (1934), McKeldin, Porter wrote an account of having "sat at her table" at the Café Select and finding her sad and ignored, with "nearly everyone gone who had once known what she was." She wished she could tell her that she, at least, "really knew," but it would have been "no good at all."

17. KAP to Paul Porter, Sr., March 8, 1932, *Letters,* p. 79.

18. KAP to Caroline Gordon, July 8, 1934; KAP to Eugene Pressly, April 13, 1934, April 20, 1934, and May 9, 1934; McKeldin.

19. In a letter to her niece, Ann Holloway Heintze, dated Jan. 21, 1943 (McKeldin), but apparently written on Jan. 21, 1944, Porter speaks of "trying to finish a heavy piece of work" there after having rested in bed for a week. She says it is expensive but does not mention the fact that her way is being paid by Barbara Wescott. In August 1943 she had written to Glenway that she would have to get a paying job; she could not remain in her house, South Hill, unless she had an income. In the next letter, dated Sept. 19, it seems that Barbara has offered to put her up at an inn for the winter to enable her to write. This is clarified in Glenway's letter of Sept. 21, 1943, indicating that George Platt Lynes may want to contribute "some spending money." A few days later, Porter writes back agreeing to the proposal.

20. KAP to Eugene Pressly, May 21, 1932, McKeldin. Later that year, on Nov. 22, in another letter to Pressly, she took some more swipes at Glenway and others "rolling around Europe" with their "little side partners" and went so far as to hint that the "mumblings of the abnormal and the subnormal" might be "partly responsible for our present messy conditions of mind and material life." It is hard to find a more blatant instance of scapegoating.

21. Wescott, *Continual Lessons,* p. 378.

22. KAP to Josephine Herbst, Aug. 5, 1934, Beinecke.

23. Larry Ceplair and Steven Englund, *The Inquisition in Hollywood: Politics in the Film Community, 1930–1960,* p. 150. Richard J. Golsan, in his Introduction to *Fascism, Aesthetics, and Culture,* pp. x–xi, points out that it is difficult to define fascism clearly. "In the French context, for example, historians disagree as to whether fascism was fundamentally leftist or rightist."

24. KAP to Eugene Pressly, Nov. 18, 1931, Nov. 21, 1931, and Dec. 25, 1931; McKeldin.

25. KAP to Eugene Pressly, Feb. 6, 1936, Feb. 29, 1936, March 16 and 17, 1936; Pressly to KAP, March 19, 1936; McKeldin.

26. KAP to Eugene Pressly, April 2, 1936, McKeldin.

27. *CE,* p. 489.

28. KAP to Eugene Pressly, April 10, 1936, McKeldin.

29. KAP to the Fords, Jan. 25, 1936, McKeldin.

30. KAP to Eugene Pressly, March 11, 1936, Nov. 9, 1936, and Nov. 28, 1936; McKeldin.

31. "'Noon Wine': The Sources," *CE,* p. 470. KAP to Eugene Pressly, Dec. 21, 1936, McKeldin.

32. KAP to Gay Porter Holloway, Aug. 24, 1947, McKeldin. KAP to Cinina Warren, Dec. 12, 1947, Beinecke.

33. KAP to Ann Holloway Heintze, Walter (Ann's husband), and "lil David," May 20, 1952; KAP to Ann Holloway Heintze, Aug. 29, 1952; KAP to Paul Porter, Jr., Aug. 16, 1963; McKeldin.

34. KAP to Gay Porter Holloway from Naples, May 15, 1963; KAP to Cyrilly Abels, June 15, 1963; KAP to Paul Porter, Jr., July 17, 1963; McKeldin.

35. KAP to Mary Doherty, Oct. 13, 1945, McKeldin-MLD. Frances N. Cheney, who is herself familiar with Japan and other parts of Asia, confirms that Porter never, to her knowledge, expressed any interest in visiting the Orient. "Paris was what she liked." Interview with the author, April 24, 1993.

36. "Remarks on the Agenda," *CE,* p. 220.

37. She wrote in her copy of E. M. Forster's *A Passage to India,* "The West has its own civilization and does not need to 'acquire' others"; McKeldin.

38. Brooks, "The Woman and Artist I Knew," in *Katherine Anne Porter and Texas,* ed. Machann and Clark, p. 15.

39. KAP to Ann Holloway Heintze, Jan. 21, 1943, McKeldin.

40. She had boasted to her family about the award of the Guggenheim and had written them scintillating letters from here and there in Europe, while they were enduring the depression at home. It is scarcely surprising that they responded to her plea for money with silence—of which she complained bitterly. "If I let myself think of it, it quite scares me, such an exhibition of total indifference by that family of mine. Otherwise, its probably a good thing: will work a great cure in this sentimental feeling I have about them. Dem um!" KAP to Eugene Pressly, Dec. 12, 1932.

41. *CE,* p. 491.

42. KAP to Yvor Winters from Berlin, Jan. 1, 1932, McKeldin.

43. *CE,* pp. 436, 445, and 456.

44. *CS,* pp. 451 and 486.

45. Porter said, in notes found among her papers, that Eugene Pressly had simi-

larly touched a souvenir of the Leaning Tower of Pisa when they were looking for rooms in Berlin, causing it to crumble. Givner, *A Life,* p. 254.

46. Warren, "Uncorrupted Consciousness: The Stories of Katherine Anne Porter," p. 280. Wescott, *Continual Lessons,* p. 83. One interesting point about Wescott's comment is that Porter actually had no journal except for a few scattered fragments.

CHAPTER SIX: Among the Agrarians

1. It is thus more than a little interesting to note that neither Porter nor Caroline Gordon appears in the index of Gray's book *Writing the South* (from which this chapter's second epigraph is drawn), despite their being, along with Ellen Glasgow, the two most noted women "writing the South" during a time period to which he gives much of his attention.

2. Ann Waldron, *Close Connections: Caroline Gordon and the Southern Renaissance,* p. 56. Makowsky, in *Caroline Gordon: A Biography,* identifies Lytle as Gordon's closest friend among the Agrarians.

3. Richard H. King, *A Southern Renaissance: The Cultural Awakening of the American South, 1930–1955,* p. 27. Southerners have tended to see "Southern society as the family writ large." King's comment regarding the Freudian family romance, that "at the core of the young child's reaction Freud saw resentment at having been abandoned and a fantasized denial of abandonment" (p. 28), describes with an almost uncanny accuracy Porter's tortured sense of her family and, by extension, her home region. Allen Tate also saw the "center of the South" as the family, "for Virginia was a great aggregate of families that through almost infinite ramifications of relationship was almost one family"; "A Southern Mode of the Imagination," *Essays of Four Decades,* p. 588. Andrew Lytle comments that the Southerners who went to New York for literary reasons "generally came home" because of a "conscious entanglement" with the family and its "long cords"; Foreword to *The Southern Mandarins,* p. 3.

4. Elizabeth Fox Genovese, "Between Individualism and Community: Autobiographies of Southern Women," in *Located Lives,* ed. Berry, p. 25.

5. Singal, in *The War Within,* p. 317, refers to this "plantation belt" as "the periphery of the South."

6. Buenger and Calvert, "The Shelf Life of Truth in Texas," in *Texas through Time,* p. xvi, citing Ramsdell's *Reconstruction in Texas* (New York: Columbia Univ. Press, 1910). Harry Y. Benedict and John A. Lomax, *The Book of Texas* (Garden City: Doubleday, Page and Company, 1916), p. 58, quoted by Gould, *Progressives and Prohibitionists,* p. 29.

7. Buenger and Calvert, "The Shelf Life of Truth in Texas," p. xxxi. Norman D.

Brown, "Texas's Southern Roots," in *The Texas Literary Tradition,* ed. Graham, Lee, and Pilkington, p. 40, reports that Southerners of the slaveholding class exercised a disproportionate share of the political power in antebellum Texas, with 68.3 percent of "political leaders" coming from this class although only 27.3 percent of all heads of households in 1860 belonged to the "wealthy slaveholding aristocracy." Obviously, this picture could and would have shifted by the time Porter came to a sense of her regional origins, but the point is that the traditional social authorities of her culture would have been southern.

8. KAP to Josephine Herbst, April 16, 1930 and July 27, 1932, Beinecke.

9. Robert Brinkmeyer points out that the "very title" of Porter's essay about her grandparents, "Portrait: Old South," signals her "choice to rewrite her Texas roots as Deep South tradition." *Katherine Anne Porter's Artistic Development: Primitivism, Traditionalism, and Totalitarianism,* p. 150.

10. C. Vann Woodward, *The Burden of Southern History,* pp. 35–36. Historian Robert A. Calvert, in a private letter to the author, however, asserts that conceiving of Porter as a southern writer is a mistake.

11. Cleanth Brooks, "The Southern Temper" and "Southern Literature: The Wellsprings of Its Vitality," in *A Shaping Joy: Studies in the Writer's Craft,* pp. 198, 217.

12. Robert Penn Warren, ed., *A Southern Harvest: Short Stories by Southern Writers;* Ben Forkner and Patrick Samway, S.J., eds., *A Modern Southern Reader: Major Stories, Drama, Poetry, Essays, Interviews and Reminiscences from the Twentieth-Century South.* Warren stated that Porter's stories about the South had been "very important" to him, as had Caroline Gordon's. Floyd C. Watkins and John T. Hiers, eds., *Robert Penn Warren Talking: Interviews, 1950–1978,* p. 132.

13. Woodward, *The Burden of Southern History,* pp. 15–20. A number of scholars have agreed. For example, C. Hugh Holman, in his Introduction to *Southern Fiction Today: Renascence and Beyond,* ed. George Core, pp. x–xi, reflects on the experience of "tragic defeat" as the defining quality separating the South from the rest of the American nation, with its "high-flying optimism." King, in *A Southern Renaissance,* p. 11, observes that the southern intellectual's sense of being "out of touch with the main action in the centers of cultural ferment" was "accentuated" by the "trauma of defeat and occupation." Sociologist John Shelton Reed demonstrates through the technique of survey data that "a sense of grievance" is a key component of the South's "regional identification and regional consciousness"; *Southerners: The Social Psychology of Sectionalism,* p. 77. *CE,* p. 160.

14. Tate, "A Southern Mode of the Imagination," p. 592. William Howarth, in "Writing Upside Down: Voice and Place in Southern Autobiography," in *Located Lives,* ed. Berry, p. 7, writes, "Usually, success has many authors and failure none; but the South has inverted that wisdom."

15. Nina Baym, "The Myth of the Myth of Southern Womanhood," in *Feminism*

and American Literary History, pp. 183–85. As recently as 1990, however, the year in which Baym's essay first appeared, the vision of the South as a region distinctive for its "sense of tragedy" arising from defeat was endorsed without qualification by Jefferson Humphries in the Introduction to *Southern Literature and Literary Theory*, p. xiii. Humphries finds that the historical experience of "defeat, decline, and loss" gave the South something that "America as a country does not know, or did not begin to know until the war in Vietnam." In 1985, Kathryn Lee Seidel in *The Southern Belle in the American Novel*, p. 30, took the same view: "the Southerner's experience has been unique among Americans until the defeat in Vietnam."

16. "Portrait: Old South," *CE*, p. 161. Gay Porter Holloway to KAP, April 22, 1930, McKeldin. *CE*, p. 470.

17. Josephine Herbst to KAP, "four days out on Norddeutscher Lloyd Bremen," 1930, Beinecke. Herbst and John Herrmann were then on their way to Russia, with Mike Gold's help, to attend the Second World Plenum of the International Bureau of Revolutionary Literature. Allen Tate, "To Whom It May Concern," Nov. 24, 1930, McKeldin. Nancy Tate Wood says that her parents knew Porter had grown up "in terrible circumstances" and felt sorry for her; interview with the author.

18. Dorothy and Delafield Day, the latter of whom also became a longtime friend, lived across the street.

19. Waldron, *Close Connections*, p. 58. Givner is somewhat less specific, saying in *A Life*, p. 179, that the "chief benefit of her association" with the Agrarian group was that "they caused her to change her attitude to her southern background." Thomas Daniel Young and Elizabeth Sarcone, eds., *The Lytle-Tate Letters*, p. 3.

20. Makowsky, *Caroline Gordon*, pp. 69–70.

21. Aaron, *Writers on the Left*, p. 110. Pells, *Radical Visions*, p. 47. Aaron actually places the great turn to the left in 1929. Pells comments that many radicals and "old-stock Progressives" saw the Bolshevik revolution as a "natural continuation of the socialist tradition which was the special hope and dream of Western intellectuals" (p. 62).

22. King, *A Southern Renaissance*, p. 16. King explicitly identifies this sense of estrangement and need for order as one of the stimuli that produced the Agrarians and the Southern Renaissance. It should be acknowledged, nevertheless, that the Southern Agrarians were allied with "anti-modernist critics," an alliance pointed out by Paul K. Conkin is his remarkably cogent essay "The South in Southern Agrarianism," in *The Evolution of Southern Culture*, ed. Numan V. Bartley, p. 133. Pells agrees that the Agrarians were "as alienated from American attitudes as their socialist counterparts" but locates that alienation in the great revulsion from capitalist industrialism that followed the war; *Radical Visions*, p. 103. Lytle viewed the goal of the Twelve Southerners who wrote *I'll Take My Stand* as being "to restore what was lost" of "their inherited European culture," namely, "Christendom"; Foreword to *The Southern Mandarins*, p. 4.

23. Fred Hobson, *Tell About the South: The Southern Rage to Explain,* pp. 184–205, places the Agrarian manifesto within the setting of contemporary events such as the "dramatic" rise in lynchings in 1919 and 1920, textile mill violence, and the Scopes trial in 1925, in all of which the South "called attention to its ignorance, violence, and religious bigotry." The response of most intellectual leaders in the South was a call for reform and enlightened advance. The Twelve Southerners—Hobson refers to the group as Davidson et al. because of his own scholarly focus on Donald Davidson—were severely outnumbered by the southern progressives such as Howard Odum, of the University of North Carolina, but nevertheless "took their stand in 1930 knowing they were going *against* that 'official' enlightened Southern position."

24. The varying interpretations of the Agrarians' central thrust are summarized by Richard Gray in *Writing the South: Ideas of an American Region,* p. 133. Gray points out, however, that the conflicts reflected in these differing readings were *in* the symposium, for example, in the different contributors' use of both populist and "patriarchal" models (p. 134).

25. Yvor Winters to KAP, Nov. 16, 1930, McKeldin. Winters called Davidson's essay "pure hooey" and said that he wished Fletcher had been content to stay with his teaching. Ann Waldron points out that Winters' jibe at Tate was "not quite fair" because Tate and Gordon had indeed realized $200 that year from a crop of hay and had raised turnip greens. Waldron concedes, however, that none of the Agrarians except Lytle "knew anything about farming" and that they wished to defend their region "in order to protect their literature." Waldron, *Close Connections,* p. 101. Tate's gardening interests had not proved durable when he and Gordon lived in rural upstate New York in 1926; Makowsky, *Caroline Gordon,* p. 69.

26. Hugh Ruppersburg, in *Robert Penn Warren and the American Imagination,* p. 30, writes that Warren's essay in *I'll Take My Stand* "expressed surprisingly broad-minded attitudes for the time and place," so much so that, as he points out, Donald Davidson "even refused to believe Warren had written the essay," calling it, pejoratively, " 'progressive.' " See *The Literary Correspondence of Donald Davidson and Allen Tate,* ed. John Tyree Fain and Thomas Daniel Young, pp. 329–32. Warren, Ruppersburg continues, "apologized" for the essay "on several occasions."

27. Aldon Lynn Nielsen, *Reading Race: White American Poets and the Racial Discourse in the Twentieth Century,* p. 103. Warren emerged, Nielsen concludes, in a position of "radical uncertainty." Robert Penn Warren, *Segregation: The Inner Conflict in the South,* pp. 64–65; *Who Speaks for the Negro?,* pp. 425, 431, 440–42. Ruppersburg, *Robert Penn Warren,* p. 34.

28. Twelve Southerners, *I'll Take My Stand: The South and the Agrarian Tradition,* pp. 210; 341, 350, 339; 119; 137–38. Porter, "A Country and Some People I Love," *Conversations,* p. 132. Conkin points out that the twelve writers of *I'll Take*

My Stand "never agreed" on whether the "good society" they envisioned for the South was "feudal, established, hierarchical" or "a society made up of independent yeomen." "The South in Southern Agrarianism," p. 131.

29. *I'll Take My Stand,* pp. 141, 69, 195–200. Langdon Hammer, *Hart Crane and Allen Tate: Janus-Faced Modernism,* p. 66. Although he retained throughout his life a self-identification as an agrarian, Nixon moved steadily leftward. By the mid-1930s he was more identified with the social scientists of the University of North Carolina than with his former colleagues at Vanderbilt. He supported the New Deal and in 1939 became executive secretary of the Southern Conference for Human Welfare, a liberal group "tainted from its beginning by charges of communist infiltration and promotion of racial equality"; Sarah N. Shouse, Introduction to *Lower Piedmont Country: The Uplands of the Deep South,* by H. C. Nixon, p. xvii. See Conkin, "The South in Southern Agrarianism," pp. 132–33, for points of commonality between the Agrarians and Marxists.

30. Andrew Lytle to KAP, Nov. 1, 1930, McKeldin. KAP to Josephine Herbst, Dec. 29, 1930, Beinecke. KAP to Harrison Boone Porter, June 26, 1931, McKeldin. KAP to Gay Porter Holloway, May 30, 1930, *Letters,* p. 22.

31. KAP to Glenway Wescott, April 24, 1966, McKeldin. William Howarth generalizes the Southerner's need for separation from a starting point in the "feverish denial" at the end of *Absalom, Absalom!* Howarth, "Writing Upside Down," *Located Lives,* p. 5. KAP to Caroline Gordon, June 9, 1935, *Letters,* p. 127. Warren, *Segregation,* p. 51.

32. KAP to "Dear Family," March 22, 1934, McKeldin. Interestingly, despite the ambivalence revealed in this and similar comments, Richard H. King explains his omission of Porter from his book *A Southern Renaissance* by reference to his purpose of focusing on "works which take the South and its tradition as problematic" (p. 8). One might think "Old Mortality" problematic enough. Tate to Lytle, July 28, 1937, *The Lytle-Tate Letters,* p. 114.

33. Tate to Lytle, March 19, 1938, *The Lytle-Tate Letters,* p. 118. Sure enough, on Dec. 22, 1940, Tate reported to Lytle that Erskine was "now as if he had never been."

34. Waldron, *Close Connections,* pp. 24–25.

35. *CE,* pp. 4, 10. KAP to Josephine Herbst, Aug. 15, 1937, *Letters,* p. 149. The word "no" is rendered "not" in the published volume.

36. Tate to Lytle, Sept. 10, 1937, *The Lytle-Tate Letters,* p. 115. KAP to Monroe Wheeler, Sept. 24, 1937; KAP to Glenway Wescott, Oct. 11, 1937; McKeldin.

37. KAP to Glenway Wescott, Dec. 3, 1937, *Letters,* p. 154.

38. *CS,* p. 298.

39. "I am stuck again on Pale Horse, Pale Rider, so think I shall do the ship story, 'Promised Land.'" KAP to Eugene Pressly, Nov. 30, 1936, McKeldin.

40. *CE,* pp. 169–72. Porter claimed a love of "leisure and calm" for her grandmother in "Portrait: Old South" (*CE,* p. 162), thereby emphasizing her right to a place in an Agrarian pantheon.

41. Walsh writes, however, that the arguments of her socialist friends and her Southern Agrarian friends "uneasily coexist[ed] in separate compartments of Porter's mind"; *Katherine Anne Porter and Mexico,* p. 108.

42. Frank L. Owsley, "The Irrepressible Conflict," *I'll Take My Stand,* pp. 68, 77.

43. Conkin agrees that Owsley, together with Davidson and Lytle, "not only slighted the black influence" on southern culture but "put blacks down by nasty, racist statements." "The South in Southern Agrarianism," p. 137.

44. The phrase is Hobson's, *Tell About the South,* p. 230. Ruppersburg, in *Robert Penn Warren and the American Imagination,* p. 29, argues that the public image of the Southern Agrarians as "reactionary, racist apologists for the Old South" does not allow for "objective understanding." It is hard, however, to avoid those labels. Nielsen, *Reading Race,* pp. 103–104. Nielsen judges (pp. 106–7) that Tate's expression of racial guilt in "Sonnets at Christmas"—"When I was ten I told a stinking lie/That got a black boy whipped"—was only against "abuse" of "white privilege," not against its existence.

45. Hobson, *Tell About the South,* pp. 25, 47, 141–42, 288–89.

46. KAP to Josephine Herbst, July 12, 1930, Beinecke. KAP to Caroline Gordon, Nov. 5, 1964; Gordon to KAP, March 11, 1928; McKeldin. Gordon to Sally Wood, Oct. 1, 1934, *The Southern Mandarins,* p. 167. Allen Tate to KAP ("To Whom It May Concern") Nov. 24, 1930; McKeldin.

47. KAP to Josephine Herbst, Dec. 29, 1930, Beinecke. Harrison Boone Porter to KAP, March 13, 1935; KAP to Harrison Boone Porter, March 30, 1935; McKeldin.

48. "On Modern Fiction," *CE,* pp. 87–88.

49. KAP to Gay Porter Holloway, May 27, 1964, July 2, 1964, July 10, 1964, and Feb. 16, 1965; McKeldin.

50. KAP to Barbara Harrison Wescott, April 7, 1968, McKeldin.

51. Roy Newquist, "An Interview with Katherine Anne Porter," *McCall's Magazine,* 1965; rpt. *Conversations,* ed. Givner, p. 103. KAP to Allen Tate, Jan. 22, 1965; "Notes and Reviews"; McKeldin. "Jacqueline Kennedy," *CE,* p. 307.

52. *CS,* pp. 330–34.

53. *CS,* p. 349.

54. The manuscript of "The Man in the Tree" is found in the Porter Collection at McKeldin Library, the University of Maryland. My quotations from the manuscript will not give page numbers because the pagination is fragmentary and repetitive. Porter originally intended this as one of five long stories to be published together in the volume that became *Pale Horse, Pale Rider;* KAP to Genevieve Taggard, Jan. 5, 1937, McKeldin.

55. Jan Nordby Gretlund, "'The Man in the Tree': Katherine Anne Porter's Unfinished Lynching Story," p. 13.

56. Josephine Herbst to KAP, May 5, 1945, McKeldin. Two months before Herbst's letter, Porter had published a review of Glenway Wescott's *Apartment in Athens* in which she praised him for exposing "that streak of Germanism in the rest of us which made possible the Germany we know today." Unrue, "*This Strange, Old World*," p. 125.

57. She was convinced that "only the lowest of either [race] will associate sexually." Marginal notations in Warren, *Who Speaks for the Negro?* p. 82; McKeldin.

58. Porter commented at greater length on Indian peoples in a letter to her close friend Donald Elder, an editor at Doubleday: "I have been pleasantly tinkering with the idea of going to live in Puerto Rico, or some other picturesque backward country, but the thought of all those natives gnawing my bones to get at the marrow—I haven't lived among Negroes and Indian servants for nothing, I ought to have learned by now—simply wearies me. Here, you can at least get away from Negroes in your own house; and if I were ever able to have a servant, I should most certainly have a white one; but in Mexico and South America the Indians simply swarm over you like those ants who sweep all clean before them. I do not for a moment mean to say the Indian and the Negro are anywhere near the same level—the Indians are infinitely superior, and they have [a] superb history; but oh, I am so wearied out with being blackmailed by persecuted minorities." KAP to Donald Elder, Sept. 20, 1957, McKeldin.

59. KAP to Glenway Wescott, April 24, 1966; KAP to Gay Porter Holloway, May 15, 1963; McKeldin. She may have been feeling particularly pensive on this day, however, because it was her birthday and she was far from whatever might be called home, in Naples. Like Miranda at the end of "Old Mortality," however, she had chosen her exile from the South, or what Joan Schulz calls her "orphaning," in order to "improv[e] her chances that she [could] manage her life"; Schulz, "Orphaning as Resistance," in *The Female Tradition in Southern Literature,* ed. Carol S. Manning, p. 93.

60. KAP to Albert Erskine, March 14, 1938, McKeldin.

61. Richard Dillard and George Garrett, interviews with the author.

62. Aaron, *Writers on the Left,* p. 205.

63. Hobson, *Tell about the South,* p. 215.

64. Porter's longtime friend Frances (Fanny) Cheney says, however, that the visits of nuns were "a great comfort" to her late in life, after she became ill. Private conversation with the author, February 1993.

CHAPTER SEVEN: From Radical to Moderate

1. Ceplair and Englund, in *The Inquisition in Hollywood,* p. 56, note that the call to found the League of American Writers as a "nationwide Popular Front organization" against war, fascism, racial discrimination, and other illiberal ills was "characteristic of the new, ecumenical, moderated communism."

2. KAP to Mary Alice Porter Hillendahl, May 3, 1937, McKeldin. Aaron, *Writers on the Left,* p. 378.

3. David Seideman, *The New Republic: A Voice of Modern Liberalism,* p. 146. David DeLeon calls the American Communist party "not a native radical party but a local sect of Soviet communism." *The American as Anarchist,* p. 107.

4. Ceplair and Englund, *The Inquisition in Hollywood,* p. 233. Josephine Herbst to KAP, June 15, 1938, McKeldin. In January 1932, Porter expressed her disgust with "Becher the communist poet and several of his group" for their partisan aesthetic judgments. "When I heard them tossing Thomas Mann and Rainer Maria Rilke on the scrap heap, I decided to reserve judgment." KAP to Yvor Winters, Jan. 1, 1932, McKeldin. Given her firmness on freedom of expression, it is startling to see her, under the pressure of multiple countercurrents during the war years, denouncing the American Communists "of either wing" for their "treasonable" acts and saying that the government should really suppress all firms on a "banned list," for example, Bayer's, the German manufacturer of the most successful brand of aspirin. She did not exactly call for repression of speech, but confessed to being "wearied out a little with the noisy minorities who keep up such a continual clamor about their wrongs." KAP to Freda Kirchwey, Feb. 5, 1942, *Letters,* pp. 221–23. The views expressed in this letter are uncharacteristic. In 1947, in a letter to the *Nation* published in the May 24 issue, she would advocate the jailing of both fascist and communist "conspirators."

5. KAP to Harrison Boone Porter, June 26, 1931, McKeldin. She added, "I would stay in Moscow except that there is no room now, and the winters are so frightful I probably couldn't survive there." Walsh points out that she called herself a fellow traveler as late as 1938 (*Katherine Anne Porter and Mexico,* p. 195). KAP to Malcolm Cowley, July 22, 1931, McKeldin.

6. KAP to Josephine Herbst, Dec. 21, 1931, Beinecke.

7. KAP to Josephine Herbst from Berlin, Nov. 30, 1931, apparently unsent, McKeldin. James F. Murphy, *The Proletarian Moment,* pp. 44 and 17. KAP to Malcolm Cowley, Jan. 22, 1932, McKeldin. Thomas Austenfeld has searched the files of *Linkskurve* and found no evidence of Porter's work. If she wrote for the publication she did not sign her work, and if she contributed unsigned work that was translated into German before publication the style is not recognizable. Private communication of Austenfeld to the author.

8. O'Higgins's earnestness was gently mocked by Porter in a letter to Peggy

Cowley dated Dec. 9, 1931. After he arrived in Berlin they had a dinner conversation over beer: "Ah, the Russians. Ah, the USSR! Yes, but, and maybe; the German Communists, when they give a rally, don't put on half so good a show as the Hitlerites. One regrets this because one hates the Hitlerites, and loves the Communists." Tellingly, she adds parenthetical remarks that are characteristic in terms of their ambivalence: "Or does one, really? It is possible to love *A* Communist, but in the mass personal charm is not their long suit, maybe not even their aim? but—and it isn't human to love an embodied principal [*sic*], is it?"

9. Pablo O'Higgins to KAP, Dec. 23, 1931, McKeldin. After returning to Mexico, O'Higgins was involved with a succession of organizations devoted to bringing news and political opinion to the common people through the printing of posters, *corridos,* and other inexpensive publications. In spite of "violent anti-Communist repression" in Mexico in the early 1930s, he and a small group of fellow artists, including David Siqueiros, continued to try to promote an "art of revolutionary propaganda." As late as 1937, O'Higgins was occupied in organizing graphic artists (including Porter's friend Xavier Guerrero) to promote Communist candidates for office and in denouncing fascism. Francisco Reyes Palma, "Workshop of Popular Graphics during the Times of Cardenas," trans. Kenneth W. Johnson, in *Images of Mexico,* ed. Billeter, pp. 111–14.

10. KAP to John Herrmann, Aug. 3, 1932, HRC.

11. Herrmann's and Josephine Herbst's roles in the Ware-Chambers-Hiss affair are summarized in David D. Anderson's "John Herrmann, Midwestern Modern, Part II: The Alger Hiss Case and the Midwestern Literary Connection," *Midwestern Miscellany* 1991: 42–52, and, earlier, in Langer, *Josephine Herbst,* pp. 269–73. KAP to Josephine Herbst, June 1, 1931, *Letters,* p. 42. KAP to John Herrmann, Aug. 3, 1932, HRC. KAP to Josephine Herbst, Jan. 16, 1932, Beinecke.

12. Young and Sarcone, eds., *The Lytle-Tate Letters,* p. 77.

13. KAP to Eugene Pressly, April 1, 1936; Eugene Pressly to KAP, March 21, 1936; Monroe Wheeler to KAP, November 1936; KAP to Monroe Wheeler, Nov. 24, 1936; McKeldin. Fanny Cheney does not recall any discussion of politics when MacLeish came to visit while Porter, Tate, and Gordon were living in the Cheneys' house in Washington in 1944. Private conversation with the author.

14. KAP to Josephine Herbst, April 8, 1938, Beinecke. Josephine Herbst to KAP, April 5, 1938, McKeldin. Porter's old friend Diego Rivera was also "aroused to hatred towards Stalin and Stalinism and all it represented" by the purges of 1936. Wolfe, *The Fabulous Life of Diego Rivera,* p. 237.

15. Josephine Herbst to KAP, Sept. 24, 1937, McKeldin; KAP to Josephine Herbst, April 8, 1938, Beinecke. A founding editor of the *Partisan Review,* Dwight Macdonald, is described by Richard Pells as "a Marxist polemicist with a distinct sympathy for Leon Trotsky"; *The Liberal Mind in a Conservative Age* (1989 ed.), p. 21.

16. Porter, Letter to the Editors, *Partisan Review* 4 (March 1938): 62. Herbst wrote that she had seen the letter and that she believed "the real thing wrong in Russia is not its original aim, that is still the one aim worth striving for, but that it has somehow been unable to work it out." Josephine Herbst to KAP, April 5, 1938, McKeldin.

17. André Gide, "Second Thoughts on the U.S.S.R.," pp. 21–28. Like Gide, historian Richard L. Harris notes that the distribution of "special privileges" to "those in the higher positions of Soviet society," including "differential distribution of material incentives," increased under Stalin, although such a difference in material rewards was not approved by Lenin; *Marxism, Socialism, and Democracy in Latin America,* p. 108.

18. KAP to Josephine Herbst, April 8, 1938, Beinecke.

19. Marginal notations in Henry Morgenthau, Jr., *Germany Is Our Problem* (1945), p. 153; McKeldin.

20. KAP to Mary Doherty, Oct. 21, 1932, McKeldin; KAP to John Herrmann, Aug. 3, 1932, HRC.

21. KAP to Eugene Pressly, Dec. 27, 1931; Eugene Pressly to KAP, Dec. 1, 1932; McKeldin.

22. Glenway Wescott, *Fear and Trembling,* pp. 87–89, 357.

23. KAP to Harrison Boone Porter, May 31, 1934, McKeldin; KAP to Barbara Harrison Wescott, Nov. 18, 1935, *Letters,* p. 132.

24. Selig Adler, *The Isolationist Impulse: Its Twentieth-Century Reaction,* p. 240.

25. See Sebastian D. G. Knowles, *A Purgatorial Flame: Seven British Writers in the Second World War,* on the British literary response to the coming of war and the war years themselves. Knowles seeks to demonstrate that World War II was "no less a literary war than its predecessor" despite the commonplace belief that the kind of serious writing about the war that was done in World War I was not done during the second. William E. Dodd, Jr., and Martha Dodd, eds., *Ambassador Dodd's Diary, 1933–1938,* pp. 134, 307. Porter marked these passages in her copy and commented that he was a good prophet. Shari Benstock, *Women of the Left Bank: Paris, 1900–1940,* p. 127. Sanford J. Smaller, *Adrift among Geniuses: Robert McAlmon, Writer and Publisher of the Twenties,* p. 258.

26. Louis MacNeice, *The Collected Poems,* ed. E. R. Dodds (New York: Oxford Univ. Press, 1967), pp. 101–53. Porter does not seem to have commented on "Autumn Journal," if she knew of it, but she did tell Cyrilly Abels once that MacNeice had "a kind of no-nonsense stance toward a good many human idiocies" and she "did like him!" KAP to Cyrilly Abels, Oct. 3, 1963, McKeldin.

27. Charles Chatfield, *For Peace and Justice: Pacifism in America, 1914–1941,* pp. 167, 236.

28. Chatfield, *For Peace and Justice,* p. 297. Jean-Baptiste Duroselle, *From Wil-*

son to Roosevelt: Foreign Policy of the United States, 1913–1945, trans. Nancy Lyman Roelker, p. 270.

29. KAP to Robert Penn Warren, June 20, 1940, *Letters,* p. 182. Ambassador Dodd also noted, with concern, that various elements were "pressing" in the "Fascist direction"; *Diary,* p. 348; also cf. pp. 195 and 212.

30. KAP to Glenway Wescott, June 28, 1940, McKeldin. The polarization between the left and the extreme right in the mid-thirties is spotlighted by David Seideman: "Liberals, socialists, and communists forged the alliance [the Popular Front] as a bulwark against fascism"—and not only against Hitler, but also against the "forces of reaction in the United States," a "cabal" including "big business, the Ku Klux Klan, the American Legion, professional patriots, and conservative politicians." *The New Republic: A Voice of Modern Liberalism,* p. 149. KAP to Freda Kirchwey, Feb. 5, 1942, *Letters,* p. 221. Sara Alpern, in *Freda Kirchwey: A Woman of The Nation,* p. 177, writes that Kirchwey was "adamant" that the "anticommunist liberals" who saw Soviet communism and German fascism as being virtually equivalent threats were gravely mistaken.

31. KAP to Peggy Cowley, Oct. 1, 1931, McKeldin. *CE,* p. 9.

32. KAP to Harrison Boone Porter, May 31, 1934; McKeldin. KAP to Robert Penn Warren, June 22, 1940, Beinecke. KAP to Caroline Gordon, n.d., McKeldin.

33. KAP to Albert Erskine, March 13, 1938; KAP to Monroe Wheeler, Sept. 5, 1939; McKeldin.

34. Albert Erskine to KAP, June 19, 1940 and Oct. 13, 1940, McKeldin.

35. KAP to Albert Erskine, June 14 (but corrected in the body of the letter to June 16), 1940, June 18, 1940, and June 19, 1940; McKeldin.

36. KAP to Albert Erskine, Oct. 18, 1940, McKeldin. She campaigned for Roosevelt, however, in 1944. KAP to "Red and Cinina," Robert Penn Warren and Cinina Warren, Dec. 11, 1941, Beinecke. KAP to Mary Alice Porter Hillendahl, Jan. 11, 1942, McKeldin.

37. Dodd, *Diary,* p. 307.

38. KAP to Monroe Wheeler, Oct. 24, 1942; KAP to Donald Elder, Jan. 30, 1941 and Dec. 16, 1941; McKeldin.

39. *CE,* pp. 193–94.

40. *CE,* pp. 194–96. KAP to Gay Porter Holloway, July 20, 1945, McKeldin.

41. KAP to Josephine Herbst, April 29, 1945, Beinecke. KAP to Gay Porter Holloway, July 16, 1947 and Oct. 31, 1947, McKeldin. Similarly, she deplored the presence of Italians in the United States, where they had "enjoyed the status of full citizens while the great majority of them were Fascist in belief and act"; draft of a letter responding to a solicitation for "Friendship with Italy Week," March 7, 1947, McKeldin.

42. Sigrid Schultz, *Germany Will Try It Again,* pp. 6–9, 44, 101. Morgenthau, *Germany Is Our Problem,* pp. 113, 127, 194.

43. KAP to Ann Holloway Heintze, Dec. 1, 1942; KAP to Gay Porter Holloway, Dec. 23, 1944; KAP to "Baby," Mary Alice Porter Hillendahl, Jan. 11, 1942; Josephine Herbst to KAP, May 5, 1945; McKeldin. Adler, *The Isolationist Impulse,* p. 292, confirms that "Nazi propaganda . . . for a time seemed very formidable in the United States" and mentions a number of "super-patriot groups along semi-fascist lines" during the early years of World War II.

44. Her comment about keeping the Western world in a state of disorder has a very similar ring to statements attributed to the female informant identified by Langer as Porter: "[Herbst] said that her only interest [in being present at a labor strike in Detroit in 1937] was to cause as much dissention [*sic*], strife and bloodshed as possible in order to prolong the strike. She said that it was the Communist purpose to try to prohibit a fair settlement of strikes and to arouse as much class hatred as possible." Photographic reproduction of FBI report, Langer, *Josephine Herbst,* p. 253.

45. KAP to Mary Doherty, Aug. 30, 1963, McKeldin. Two examples of such marginal comments are: Executive Secretary of the League of American Writers to KAP, July 8, 1938; Book and Magazine Guild, Local 18, United Office and Professional Workers of America, CIO, to KAP, Dec. 11, 1940; McKeldin.

46. Langer, *Josephine Herbst,* pp. 270–73. Givner, *A Life,* pp. 4–10. Walsh, *Katherine Anne Porter and Mexico,* p. 195.

47. Pells, *The Liberal Mind,* p. 285. It was "easy," Pells states, for liberal intellectuals, even as they "strove to moderate its worst abuses," to "internalize" such "assumptions of the right" as the idea that citizens should "accept certain constraints on academic freedom and civil liberties in the interests of national security."

48. KAP to Josephine Herbst, Jan. 28, 1947; *CE,* p. 215.

49. *CE,* p. 206. Two years later, in 1949, she would again publicly denounce American sympathizers with prewar fascism in a letter to the editor of the *Saturday Review* relating to the controversy over Ezra Pound's selection for the Bollingen-Library of Congress Award for Poetry for 1949. See *CE,* pp. 209–15.

50. Givner, *A Life,* p. 4.

51. Two examples, besides Herbst and Herrmann, though by then they were some years in the past: Malcolm Cowley was active in Communist-supported labor activities in the early 1930s and in 1937 was still "Stalinist" despite the purge trials in the USSR; Matthew Josephson supported William Z. Foster for president in 1932. Ceplair and Englund, *The Inquisition in Hollywood,* pp. 53, 240.

52. Eleanor Clark Warren to KAP, March 19, 1949; KAP to Donald Elder, n.d. except 1942; McKeldin. Porter wrote on the statement in behalf of Ames attached to Clark's letter, "I am signing this." Ames had been accused of harboring Communists by Robert Lowell and possibly also Flannery O'Connor. KAP to Leonie Adams, March 30, 1949, McKeldin; Joan Givner to Thomas F. Walsh, May 5, 1979, McKeldin-TFW. Ames thanked Porter for her statement of support, which she said

shone brightly and effectively in her defense like a star. Elizabeth Ames to KAP, April 3, 1949, McKeldin.

53. KAP to Paul Porter, June 5, 1948, McKeldin.

54. KAP to Gay Porter Holloway, Aug. 24, 1947; KAP to Josephine Herbst, July 20, 1947; McKeldin. KAP to Dr. William Ross, March 4, 1951, *Letters,* ed. Bayley, p. 394.

55. Pells, *The Liberal Mind,* p. 286.

56. KAP to Paul Porter, July 13, 1948; KAP to Janet Winters, Aug. 18, 1948; McKeldin.

57. KAP to Gay Porter Holloway, May 22, 1947 and July 1, 1947, McKeldin.

58. Notes on Mexico bearing a pencil date, probably affixed later, of 1931, McKeldin. KAP, Letter to the Editor, *The Nation* 164 (May 24, 1947): 640. KAP to Andrew Lytle, July 14, 1947; KAP to Josephine Herbst, July 20, 1947; KAP to Paul Porter, June 5, 1948 and July 13, 1948; McKeldin. Ceplair and Englund, *The Inquisition in Hollywood,* point out that the Catholic hierarchy in America supported Franco in Spain and the inquisitions in Hollywood.

59. Adler, *The Isolationist Impulse,* p. 292.

60. Givner, *A Life,* p. 178. On Day, see, for example, Robert Coles, *Dorothy Day: A Radical Devotion,* pp. xv–xxi, 2–16. KAP to Glenway Wescott, March 19, 1947, *Letters,* p. 334. The quarrel between Porter and Gordon is explained by Nancy Tate as having originated in their differing versions of an old verse. At a luncheon party, Porter recited "The turkey was so cool and calm/She would not give a single damn." Gordon said the lines came in the reverse order. Interview, Dec. 12, 1993. Makowsky astutely reads this "ludicrously trivial" quarrel as an indication of their literary rivalry: "Porter's version of reality, her fiction, was accepted, indeed acclaimed in a way that Caroline's was not, and Caroline wanted her version to prevail, at least in her own house" (*Caroline Gordon,* p. 167). Tate expained the quarrel between them as having arisen from the "Lon" Cheneys' being "more interested in Katherine Anne than they were in Caroline" (Waldron, *Close Connections,* p. 222)—a not incompatible account. Fanny Cheney's recollection of the event would seem to bear out his view in that she paints Katherine Anne with great sympathy as the wronged party. Porter was quite ill, she recalls, and Caroline decided to bathe her. "She was scrubbing her raw, calling her a lazy, lazy bitch, and saying she had no talent and all that attention was undeserved." (Nancy Tate Wood does not recall such an incident.) Caroline, Mrs. Cheney reports, "thought she improved after she went into the Church, but she didn't." Interview, Feb. 27, 1993.

61. Brantley, *Feminine Sense,* p. 259.

62. Brinkmeyer, *Katherine Anne Porter's Artistic Development,* pp. 202–3. Brinkmeyer views her, not as a vacillating liberal, but as a onetime liberal whose views hardened into "conservatism" and "aristocratic elitism." A similar dilemma

arises in studying the career of Freda Kirchwey, who, like Porter, wished to suppress the fascist press during the early days of World War II despite her longtime commitment to civil liberties. See Alpern, *Freda Kirchwey,* p. 149.

63. KAP to Josephine Herbst, Jan. 16, 1932, Beinecke.

64. KAP to Muriel Rukuyser, July 17, 1949, McKeldin. The Rukuyser file in Porter's papers is curious in that little of Porter's side of the correspondence is there, although she customarily kept carbon copies of her letters, and at least one letter from Rukuyser has been torn off irregularly at both the top and the bottom. One wonders if she destroyed some of this correspondence. Yet that seems unlikely, given the nature of many letters in other files that remained untouched. The title of the essay was adopted for its reprinting in *The Days Before.* It had originally been published as "Yours, Ezra Pound," a review of *The Letters of Ezra Pound, 1907–1941,* in the *New York Herald Tribune,* Oct. 29, 1950. Kathryn Hilt and Ruth M. Alvarez, *Katherine Anne Porter: An Annotated Bibliography,* p. 122.

65. *CE,* pp. 40–44.

66. KAP to Paul Porter, March 23, 1963, published as part of "Letters to a Nephew," *CE,* p. 115. KAP to Fr. Raymond Roseliep, Jan. 29, 1962; KAP to Leonie Adams, March 30, 1949; McKeldin.

67. William Barrett, "Comment: A Prize for Ezra Pound," 344–47; Symposium, 512–22.

68. The terms are Virginius Dabney's in a classic study, *Liberalism in the South,* p. xv.

69. Tate to Davidson, May 1, 1952; Fain and Young, eds., *The Literary Correspondence of Donald Davidson and Allen Tate,* p. 364. The six who attended were Tate, Porter, William Faulkner, "reformed Marxist" (as Tate exclaimed to Davidson) James T. Farrell, Glenway Wescott, and W. H. Auden. Diego Rivera to KAP, June 25, 1957.

70. KAP to Paul Porter, July 19, 1960; Paul Porter to KAP, July 14, 1960; McKeldin.

71. KAP to Paul Porter, Jan. 31, 1963; KAP to Gay Porter Holloway, July 6, 1965; McKeldin.

72. KAP to Gay Porter Holloway, July 6, 1965, McKeldin.

CHAPTER EIGHT: The Issue of Gender

1. Baym, "The Myth of the Myth of Southern Womanhood," p. 193. John Shelton Reed identifies the grande dame as a recurrent southern type and comments that the belle is the "larval form" of the Southern lady. Porter, for all the distinctiveness of her life history and her abilities, confirms this typology. Reed, *Southern Folk, Plain and Fancy: Native White Social Types,* pp. 48–50.

2. KAP to Professor Beverly Whitaker, University of Texas, June 10, 1975; KAP

to Ann Holloway Heintze, March 5, 1954; McKeldin. On the other hand, she sometimes complained that her speaking engagements kept her away from her real work. "Its sadly true—I've been derailed into colleges and universities to make a living until I was hardly writing at all—just talking about it—a most horrible end!" KAP to Kay Boyle, April 1, 1957, McKeldin.

3. *The Habit of Being: Letters of Flannery O'Connor,* ed. Sally Fitzgerald, p. 276.

4. Seidel, *The Southern Belle,* pp. xi–xiv. In these years, Seidel asserts, the figure of the belle changed "from a representation of the virtues of Southern society to an embodiment of its vices." Observing the same duality, Ruth M. Vande Kieft comments that Porter "assumed and played out the dual roles of Southern belle modernized and liberated, and legendary femme fatale"; "The Love Ethos of Porter, Welty, and McCullers," p. 236.

5. Josephine Novak and Elise Chisholm, "Don't Scare the Horses, Miss Porter Tells Liberation Women," *Baltimore Evening Sun,* March 25, 1970; and Maurice Dolbier, "I've Had a Good Run for My Money," *New York Herald Tribune,* April 1, 1962; rpt. Givner, *Conversations,* pp. 156 and 76. Andreas Huyssen, *After the Great Divide: Modernism, Mass Culture, Postmodernism* (Bloomington: Indiana Univ. Press, 1986), pp. vii, 47. Hammer, *Hart Crane and Allen Tate,* pp. 4–7.

6. *Conversations,* ed. Givner, p. 178.

7. "*This Strange, Old World,*" ed. Unrue, p. 35. KAP to Donald Elder, Feb. 6, 1942; Paul Porter, Sr., to Mrs. K. R. Koontz, March 23, 1909; McKeldin.

8. Alvarez, "Katherine Anne Porter and Mexican Art," p. 414. Coles, *Dorothy Day,* p. 2.

9. Joseph, *Revolution from Without,* pp. 216–19. Hilt and Alvarez, *Bibliography,* p. 108. Givner, citing Paul Porter's letter, comments that she was "a vocal feminist" (*A Life,* p. 101).

10. KAP to Lodwick Hartley, May 4, 1940, *Letters,* ed. Bayley, p. 178. KAP to Lon Tinkle, Aug. 19, 1976; KAP to Jane Flanders, Aug. 16, 1976; McKeldin. Suzanne W. Jones, "Reading the Endings in Katherine Anne Porter's 'Old Mortality,'" p. 43.

11. "*This Strange, Old World,*" ed. Unrue, p. 29. KAP to Marcelle Sibon, Lady's Day, 1963, McKeldin. Marginal annotations in Tolstoy, *War and Peace,* pp. 526–27.

12. The importance of the horse race sequence and the connection of the bloodied filly to the various women of the story was pointed out by Jane Flanders in "Katherine Anne Porter and the Ordeal of Southern Womanhood," pp. 47–60. Porter seems to have liked Flanders, or at any rate the fact that she had spent "several years" studying her work, but regarded her feminist interpretation as "entirely wrong." KAP to Jane Flanders, Aug. 16, 1976; KAP to Lon Tinkle, Aug. 19, 1976; McKeldin. For a searching examination of Porter's works from the perspective of feminist concern with the social and biological demands on women, see

Jane Krause DeMouy, *Katherine Anne Porter's Women: The Eye of Her Fiction.* DeMouy's work has proved influential in subsequent scholarly criticism on Porter.

13. Brinkmeyer, *Katherine Anne Porter's Artistic Development,* p. 117. Seidel identifies subservience as one of the pernicious qualities expected of the southern belle.

14. Anne Goodwyn Jones, *Tomorrow Is Another Day: The Woman Writer in the South, 1859–1936,* p. xi. Jones's account of the countervision of the South offered by women writing as early as the Civil War has been pushed back to the antebellum period by Nina Baym in "The Myth of the Myth of Southern Womanhood."

15. Givner, "Problems of Personal Identity," p. 46. "*This Strange, Old World,*" ed. Unrue, p. 43.

16. Paul Porter, "Remembering Aunt Katherine," in *Katherine Anne Porter and Texas,* p. 34.

17. O'Connor, *The Habit of Being,* p. 260. Givner, *Self-Portrait,* p. 104. KAP to Becky Crawford, May 1, 1929, McKeldin. The "phantom" marriage was reported to Joan Givner by Kitty Barry Crawford during Givner's research for her biography; Porter had apparently told Barrett Prettyman about it at some time prior to the publication of Givner's book. Joan Givner to Paul Porter, Dec. 30, 1978, and E. Barrett Prettyman to Joan Givner, Nov. 22, 1982, private collection of Paul Porter.

18. KAP to Robert Penn Warren, Feb. 24, 1935, *Letters,* p. 119. *CE,* p. 186.

19. KAP to Barrett Prettyman, Feb. 5 and Feb. 16, 1968, McKeldin. Walsh, *Katherine Anne Porter and Mexico,* p. 28.

20. E. Barrett Prettyman to Joan Givner, Nov. 22, 1982, personal collection of Paul Porter. Porter's "amorous adventures were the compulsive attempts of a love-starved woman to find what she could not possibly attain"; Vande Kieft, "The Love Ethos of Porter, Welty, and McCullers," p. 237.

21. Marcella Comès Winslow, in whose house Porter was staying, told Givner that she returned home after a weekend when Shannon had stayed with Porter "to find the room he had occupied filled with corked-up bottles of urine. He had not troubled to walk down the one flight of stairs to the bathroom and had left to his hostess the task of disposing of the bottles." Givner, *A Life,* p. 343.

22. Wescott, *Continual Lessons,* p. 232. Fanny Cheney recalls that Porter talked about Shannon "all the time" during the period when they were in close contact in Washington; interview with the author. Nancy Tate Wood remembers that "everyone" thought the affair "very pathetic"; interview with the author, Dec. 12, 1993.

23. Allen Tate to KAP, Nov. 16, 1945, McKeldin.

24. Jane Flanders to KAP, Sept. 4, 1976; KAP to Jordan Pecile, May 1, 1963; McKeldin. The draft Flanders sent to Porter was later published as "Katherine Anne Porter's Feminist Criticism: Book Reviews from the 1920's."

25. KAP to Ann Holloway Heintze, July 8, 1938, McKeldin.

26. Jones, *Tomorrow Is Another Day,* pp. 4–5. Jones points out that almost all the former Confederate states refused to ratify the Nineteenth Amendment, seeing the vote for women as inconsistent with woman's role of being a lady and safeguarding social traditions (p. 15). Baym, "The Myth of the Myth of Southern Womanhood," p. 185.

27. The changes in the image of American women that occurred with home-front mobilization for World War II were "superficial" and "had no permanent impact on women's status in society" because their employment in industry was "meant by the government, and understood by the public, to be temporary." Leila J. Rupp, *Mobilizing Women for War: German and American Propaganda, 1939–1945,* pp. 138, 160, 181.

28. *Rocky Mountain News,* July 13, July 8, and June 12, 1919.

29. Andrew Lytle to Allen Tate, Jan. 31, 1929, *The Lytle-Tate Letters,* ed. Young and Sarcone, p. 17. KAP to Josephine Herbst, n.d. but possibly Jan. 30, 1929, Beinecke.

30. Waldron, *Close Connections,* p. 222. Nancy herself says that Waldron's statement is rather silly because Porter "flirted with anything that walked"; interview, Dec. 12, 1993. One of the most curious of her flirtations is recorded in her correspondence with Fr. Raymond Roseliep, who wrote to her frequently and fervently, assuring her that he prayed for her, especially when carrying the Blessed Sacrament to infirmary patients, that he dreamed about her in color, and that the sight of her picture or even just thinking about her made him "all goosebumps." In one letter Roseliep assured her, "Our Love Affair is sketched in the stars," and in another he instructed her to wrap the rosary he was sending her around her finger "like a love-knot." It seems to have been a meeting of equivalent needs. Raymond Roseliep to KAP, April 29, 1962, June 27, 1972, May 1, 1979, and June 17, 1979; McKeldin.

31. Porter's copy of *House of Breath,* flyleaf. Givner, *A Life,* p. 377. Henry Allen Moe wrote to her on March 29, 1951, to say that Goyen had been awarded the Guggenheim. Also Givner, p. 377.

32. Wescott, *Continual Lessons,* p. 291.

33. George Chauncey, Jr., "The Way We Were," *Village Voice,* July 1, 1986: 29. KAP to Josephine Herbst, Sept. 30, 1930, Beinecke.

34. Peggy Cowley to KAP, n.d. except 1931, McKeldin. *CE,* p. 260. As to Gordon, "They were always sitting around her feet"; interview with the author, Dec. 12, 1993.

35. Malcolm Cowley to KAP, Jan. 14, 1931, McKeldin. Benstock, *Women of the Left Bank,* pp. 6, 33, 51–52, 173. Wyndham Lewis was an example of the combination of the stylistic innovativeness and resistance to moralism and hypocrisy that are components of the now-mainstream modernism with a "polemic hostility to feminism" and an "obsessive phobia against homosexuals." Fredric Jameson, *Fables of Aggression: Wyndham Lewis, the Modernist as Fascist,* p. 4.

36. KAP to Josephine Herbst, Nov. 30, 1931, McKeldin.

37. Marginal annotations in E. M. Forster, *The Longest Journey,* pp. 326 and 302; McKeldin. Tennessee Williams said of her, however, that she was "someone I would love to please." *Tennessee Williams' Letters to Donald Windham, 1940–1965,* ed. Donald Windham, p. 82.

38. William Goyen to KAP, Jan. 14, 1951 and April 3, 1951; KAP to Goyen, April 6, 1951; Goyen to KAP, March 21, 1951; KAP to Goyen, March 25, 1951 and April 6, 1951; McKeldin.

39. KAP to William Goyen, March 27, 1951; Goyen to KAP, March 31, 1951; McKeldin.

40. KAP to William Goyen, April 16, 1951 ("not sent"), April 19, 1951, McKeldin. Reginald Gibbons, *William Goyen: A Study of the Short Fiction,* p. 135.

41. KAP to William Goyen, May 3, 1951 and May 19, 1951, McKeldin.

42. KAP to William Goyen, May 28, June 3, June 19, Aug. 8, Aug. 10, and Sept. 17, 1951, McKeldin.

43. KAP to William Goyen, Sept. 26, 1951; Goyen to KAP, Oct. 3, 1951; KAP to Goyen, Oct. 11, 1951, Dec. 14, 1951, and Feb. 24, 1952; McKeldin.

44. KAP to William Goyen, June 20, 1952, McKeldin. Marginal annotation in Goyen, *In a Farther Country* (1955), dated July 20, 1961; McKeldin.

45. William Goyen, "At Lady A's," unpublished manuscript, HRC, used by permission of Goyen's literary executor, Reginald Gibbons. The other five women are Freda Lawrence, Dorothy Brett, Margot Jones, Millicent Rogers, and Mabel Dodge Luhan.

46. KAP to Jordan Pecile, Feb. 10, 1963, Sept. 2, 1960, and Jan. 4, 1964, McKeldin. Near the end of her marriage to Eugene Pressly, in 1937, she also accused him of continually disrupting her work. Near the end of her warm relationship with attorney Barrett Prettyman, in 1975, she said that he too was interrupting her work by telephoning her and told him to stop.

47. Wescott, *Continual Lessons,* pp. 327–28.

48. *Continual Lessons,* pp. 236 (observing that another person was "so unvain, unlike K.A.P. in this regard"), 275, 302, and 68. Eugene Pressly to KAP, March 1, 1937: "But besides you're, to me, inexplicably sudden in your whims and fancies—not to make use of your own word, wombsical"; McKeldin.

49. KAP to Paul Porter, Dec. 4, 1948; KAP to William Goyen, May 26, 1951, July 3, 1951, and June 28, 1951; McKeldin. Wescott, *Continual Lessons,* p. 317.

50. Sumner Williams to KAP, July 5, 1923, McKeldin. Givner, *A Life,* pp. 175–76.

51. KAP to Paul Porter, Oct. 19, 1977 and July 6, 1963; McKeldin. Richard Dillard of Hollins College, in a telephone conversation with the author, observed that Joan Givner knew Porter "when she was old and cranky" and that therefore her biography does not catch her real character.

52. She wrote to Josephine Herbst, for example, on Feb. 6, 1930, "Well, anyhow, I'm going to try to keep sober." On Feb. 25, 1931, she boasted that "all day long"

she was "sober as a crow," and again on Nov. 23, 1938, reported to Herbst that she had "no need, ever, for a drink to buck me up." On July 30, 1940, she wrote Robert Penn and Cinina Warren, "I am being sober, too, in several ways. No liquor, for one thing." All at the Beinecke Library. In 1945, when she was working for Paramount Pictures in California, she wrote to Monroe Wheeler that after a night out drinking with "a nice Navy Lieutenant who is a kind of Nightclub Beau" she was "hung-over like a cliff." Apparently knowing that Wheeler would be concerned, she added, "But this doesn't happen often darling." McKeldin.

53. A visitor to her office at MGM in March 1945 reported that she was "very nice and fun" but unhappy "even with her $2000 a week," of which she said she was saving $500 a week. "And she rolls her own cigarettes which is funny." Sandy M. Campbell to Donald Windham, March 10, 1945, private collection of Donald Windham.

54. KAP to Ann Holloway Heintze, Jan. 21, 1958, McKeldin. KAP to Robert Penn Warren, Dec. 15, 1946, Beinecke. A year later she told Warren about some movie work she had hoped to pick up but just missed out on when the producer was called to testify before the House Un-American Activities Committee. After that he was suspected "as one who favors you-can-guess-what," a word she had become "wary of." KAP to Robert Penn Warren, Dec. 12, 1947, Beinecke. Clearly, she had not entirely turned against the possibility of work in motion pictures despite her earlier discouragement. Paul Porter to KAP, Aug. 8, 1949; KAP to Paul Porter, Aug. 24, 1949; McKeldin.

55. Wescott, *Continual Lessons,* p. 68. *Conversations,* ed. Givner, pp. 155 and 77.

56. Brooks, "The Southern Temper," in *A Shaping Joy,* p. 208. Marginal notations in *A Shaping Joy,* pp. 208 and 251; McKeldin. Olsen, remarks at the conference "Katherine Anne Porter: Centennial Celebration," Georgia State University, Nov. 10, 1990.

57. She said that she had written a letter to the editor of a Houston newspaper when she was fourteen, protesting against "a stupid, foolish, ignorant man who had published his personal opinion that in effect women should . . . curb their willful resistance to the authority of men, their God-sent masters." KAP to Jane Flanders, Aug. 16, 1976, McKeldin.

58. KAP to Kathleen Millay, April 12, 1929, McKeldin. KAP to Josephine Herbst, May 21, 1929, Beinecke.

59. KAP to Matthew Josephson, July 15, 1929; KAP to William Goyen, July 22, 1951; McKeldin. KAP to Josephine Herbst, July 19, 1929, Beinecke. Shi, *Matthew Josephson,* pp. 124–26.

60. KAP to Josephine Herbst, June 6, 1930, Beinecke, and Oct. 16, 1933, McKeldin. KAP to Malcolm Cowley, June 17, 1930; Herbst to KAP, July 20, n.y.; McKeldin.

61. Makowsky, *Caroline Gordon,* pp. 72 and viii. Benstock comments on the

"patriarchal repression" inherent in the male hegemony over writing in Porter's day, which led to women's being "locked out of the societal power structure" of letters; *Women of the Left Bank,* p. 7.

62. Makowsky, *Caroline Gordon,* p. 167.

63. To Winters, the wife of Yvor Winters, she had written, "DON'T do housework! . . . of all wasteful occupations for women in our vocation, that is the most utterly wasteful." KAP to Winters, Aug. 3, 1934, McKeldin.

64. *CE,* p. 281. KAP to Robert Penn Warren, Dec. 22, 1944, *Letters,* p. 295.

65. "*This Strange, Old World,*" ed. Unrue, pp. 78, 80, 72. Radcliffe Squires calls "Invitation to Learning" "the most intellectually mature program ever produced by an American network"; *Allen Tate: A Literary Biography,* p. 155. KAP to Gay Porter Holloway, March 30, 1943, and July 15, 1947; McKeldin.

66. *CE,* pp. 281, 25, 49–50. KAP to John Herrmann, Aug. 3, 1932, HRC. She herself remarked of Willa Cather, however, that she "did everything by emotional, instinctive choice"; marginal comment in Cather, *The Troll Garden* (1961 ed.), p. 151; McKeldin.

67. Eugene Pressly to KAP, March 1, 1937, McKeldin. *CE,* pp. 261, 283, 280.

68. *CS,* p. 361.

69. Robert Penn Warren to KAP, Jan. 12, 1972, McKeldin.

70. George Core, "Lives Fugitive and Unwritten," in *Located Lives,* p. 59.

71. Peggy Whitman Prenshaw, "Southern Ladies and the Southern Literary Renaissance," in *The Female Tradition in Southern Literature,* p. 83. I see Miranda as being more independent in her ideas, or at any rate more questioning of the ideas of her elders, than does Edward G. Schwartz, who reads "Old Mortality" as the story of Miranda's "fall[ing] under the sway of family legend and social taboo," so that she is "shaped by the values of the old order" before she begins to "struggle to be free in the present by going in search of the determining past." I take the latter phrase to mean becoming conscious of how determining the past can be. Schwartz, "The Fictions of Memory," *Southwest Review* 1960; rpt. *Katherine Anne Porter: A Critical Symposium,* ed. Lodwick Hartley and George Core, pp. 67–82. While acknowledging that Miranda comes to accommodate the old ways, Richard Gray seems on firmer ground in observing that she does not accept "predigested information" but only "knowledge that is experienced directly, felt upon the pulses." Gray, *The Literature of Memory: Modern Writers of the American South,* p. 188. Nancy Tate Wood conjectures that a composite of Amy the ancestress and Miranda the contemporary is the woman Porter wished she had been; telephone interview with the author, Dec. 12, 1993.

72. *CS,* pp. 173, 184.

73. Jones, "Reading the Endings," p. 40.

74. *CS,* p. 211.

75. *CS,* pp. 182, 176. Mary Titus, following Jane DeMouy's argument that Porter is deeply distressed by the biological specters facing women, emphasizes the "trail

of blood" running through "Old Mortality": "Beneath the surface of the smiling Belle, she saw women oppressed and destroyed by an ideology which enforced obedience to men and endorsed repeated childbearing while simultaneously denying women's sexuality." "The Agrarian Myth and Southern Womanhood," in *Redefining Autobiography in Twentieth-Century Women's Fiction,* ed. Janice Morgan and Colette T. Hall, p. 204. Edwin W. Gaston, Jr., had earlier commented that in "Old Mortality" Porter undercuts the myth of the southern belle, in "The Mythic South of Katherine Anne Porter," pp. 81–85.

76. *CS,* pp. 213, 108–10. DeMouy points out that Miranda's marriage was "an impetuous elopement"—that is, rather Amy-like. *Katherine Anne Porter's Women,* p. 157. That Porter considered her own father domineering is clearly indicated by her marking the phrase "massive, dominating figure of Mother" in Germaine Greer's *The Female Eunuch* (1970) and writing in "or Father."

77. Schulz, "Orphaning as Resistance," p. 93. William Nance, in a book that was long accepted as the standard critical commentary on Porter although she herself found it infuriating, comments that at this point Miranda is "more romantic than she realizes with her vision of unobstructed autonomy and self-sufficiency." *Katherine Anne Porter and the Art of Rejection,* p. 130.

78. *CS,* p. 221.

79. KAP to Jordan Pecile, July 3, 1961, *Letters,* p. 588. Christine Hanks discussed Porter's account of Hattie Weston's riding in "Riding in the Bullring: Katherine Anne Porter and the Challenge of Female Artistry," Baylor University, May 1992.

CHAPTER NINE: *Ship of Fools* and the Problem of Genre

1. Carol S. Manning cites a review of Eudora Welty's *Losing Battles* by John W. Aldridge, *Saturday Review* 1970, as an example of the linking of full-length genres and masculine hegemony that produced such pressure to produce novels. The reviewer acknowledged that until the publication of the novel he had regarded Welty as a talented writer pursuing " 'minor and peripheral' " interests. The long novel showed him she was "capable of standing with the boys." "Introduction: On Defining Themes and (Mis)Placing Women Writers," in *The Female Tradition in Southern Literature,* p. 5. In contrast, Caroline Gordon "always regarded herself as a novelist and the short story as a lesser genre." Makowsky, *Caroline Gordon,* p. 84.

2. Baym notes, in "The Myth of the Myth of Southern Womanhood," that these stories present "a view of antebellum women's lives much more in accord with reality than with myth." For the most part, the stories are set in postbellum times, but Baym's comment is accurate to the extent that it applies.

3. Benstock, *Women of the Left Bank,* p. 7.

4. Theoretical work on autobiography has brought into sharp focus the in-

hospitableness of traditional expectations to women. See, for example, Sidonie Smith, *A Poetics of Women's Autobiography: Marginality and the Fictions of Self-Representation,* and Shari Benstock, ed., *The Private Self: Theory and Practice of Women's Autobiographical Writing.* Tillie Olsen's classic *Silences* examines related issues. Also, Ann Romines discusses expectations of narrative structure in *The Home Plot: Women, Writing and Domestic Ritual.*

5. KAP to Genevieve Taggard, Nov. 14, 1924, Dec. 31, 1924, June 3, 1926, and April 3, n.y.; McKeldin.

6. Kenneth Durant to KAP, Dec. 25, 1934; KAP to Robert McAlmon, Sept. 13, 1932; McKeldin.

7. In 1936, however, she was still avowing an interest in the book about her family past, "Many Redeemers," in requesting support from the Guggenheim Foundation. KAP to Henry Allen Moe, Nov. 5, 1936, McKeldin.

8. KAP to Josephine Herbst, Dec. 21, 1937 and March 21, 1939, Beinecke. Donald Brace to KAP, May 19, 1941; KAP to Glenway Wescott, Sept. 5, 1939; Eudora Welty to KAP, Dec. 17, 1941; McKeldin.

9. KAP to Joseph Retinger, Sept. 29, 1921; Paul Kellogg to KAP, April 23, 1924; McKeldin. In 1931, when Porter's Guggenheim Fellowship was awarded, Caroline Gordon mentioned to Sally Wood that Porter "says she is going to stay in Mexico till she finishes her novel"; Gordon to Wood, May 4, 1931, *The Southern Mandarins,* p. 75.

10. KAP to Genevieve Taggard, June 3, 1926; Horace Liveright, Publisher, to KAP, July 8, 1930 and May 8, 1931; Donald Brace to KAP, Jan. 5, 1934; McKeldin.

11. KAP to William Goyen, June 24, 1951, McKeldin. Wescott, *Continual Lessons,* p. 297.

12. Waldron, *Close Connections,* p. 25.

13. Caroline Gordon to Josephine Herbst, March 22, 1929; Makowsky, p. 83.

14. Ruth Limmer, ed., *What the Woman Lived: Selected Letters of Louise Bogan, 1920–1970* (1973), p. 284; McKeldin.

15. Eugene Pressly to KAP, March 1, 1937, McKeldin.

16. KAP to Glenway Wescott, Sept. 13, 1940, from Yaddo; McKeldin. She had earlier admitted to Albert Erskine that the novel was going "with terrible, unreal slowness. Truth is, I don't do as well as I should, or as I hoped, but you know how long it takes me to settle after any change, and I have had the most awful, painful and uprooted feeling of all my life here." KAP to Erskine, June 27, 1940, McKeldin.

17. KAP to Caroline Gordon, July 18, 1948, McKeldin.

18. Glenway Wescott to KAP, April 17, 1941 and May 15, 1944, McKeldin.

19. Glenway Wescott to KAP, Aug. 22, 1943 and Aug. 30, 1943; KAP to Wescott, Sept. 19, 1943; Wescott to KAP, Sept. 21, 1943; McKeldin.

20. Wescott to KAP, Feb. 1, 1966 and Dec. 22, 1943; KAP to Wescott, Christmas 1943; McKeldin. KAP to Wescott, Dec. 27, 1943, *Letters,* pp. 277–79; KAP to Barbara Harrison Wescott, Jan. 19, 1944, *Letters,* p. 282.

21. Donald Brace to KAP, Dec. 15, 1944, McKeldin. Wescott, "Stories by a Writer's Writer," quoted in Hilt and Alvarez, *Bibliography,* p. 169.

22. Barbara Harrison Wescott to KAP, July 23, 1945; Glenway Wescott to KAP, Feb. 12, 1947; KAP to Ann Holloway Heintze, Nov. 1, 1948; KAP to Paul Porter, Dec. 4, 1948; McKeldin.

23. Glenway Wescott to KAP, April 30, 1941, Dec. 26, 1939, and Aug. 15, 1939, McKeldin.

24. Glenway Wescott to KAP, May 15, 1944, McKeldin. Porter seems to have picked up Wescott's little question for the opening paragraph of her essay on Ezra Pound, " 'It Is Hard to Stand in the Middle' ": "In Mexico, many years ago, Hart Crane and I were reading again *Pavannes and Divisions,* and at some dogmatic statement in the text Crane suddenly burst out: 'I'm tired of Ezra Pound!' And I asked him: 'Well, who else is there?' " *CE,* p. 40.

25. KAP to J. Frank Dobie, Oct. 3, 1956, HRC. Fitzgerald, ed., *The Habit of Being,* p. 275.

26. KAP to Wescott, March 6, 1957, McKeldin. KAP to Wescott, June 29, 1957, *Letters,* p. 540. KAP to Kay Boyle, July 21, 1957, McKeldin.

27. Seymour Lawrence to KAP, Aug. 27, 1956, McKeldin.

28. KAP to Seymour Lawrence, Oct. 9, 1956, McKeldin.

29. Seymour Lawrence to KAP, March 5, 1957, May 17, 1957, and Aug. 15, 1957, McKeldin.

30. KAP to Seymour Lawrence, Aug. 21, 1958, McKeldin.

31. KAP to Seymour Lawrence, Nov. 13, 1958, McKeldin.

32. KAP to Erna Schlemmer Johns, Aug. 18, 1959 and Aug. 31, 1961, McKeldin.

33. She called Nance's book a "cup of cambric tea seasoned with arsenic." "He manages in the midst of what sometimes nearly seems to be serious and honest consideration of a literary problem, to slip in the mean hint, the innuendo, sometimes the outright slander, that nullifies all the rest. As for negation! He is its embodiment, if I know any of the signs." KAP to Caroline Gordon, Sept. 30, 1964, McKeldin.

34. Wescott, who understood her so well, commented in his journal that he had learned something Porter had unfortunately not learned, the "grave ill effect of my tremendous talk upon my poor writing, and of my involvements in life and others' lives generally," a "waste of time" and "of energy." He had observed of Porter "how in the city overstimulation would kill her, . . . how in the country she bored herself to death. We need both ways of life in fairly frequent alternation." *Continual Lessons,* p. 225.

35. Barbara Harrison Wescott to KAP, April 21, 1962, McKeldin. KAP to Barbara Harrison Wescott, May 3, 1962 and May 19, 1962, *Letters,* pp. 591–94. KAP to Mrs. Matson, Dec. 19, 1961; Mary Doherty to KAP, Aug. 7, 1962; McKeldin.

36. KAP to Paul Porter, Dec. 17, 1962, McKeldin.

37. KAP to Seymour Lawrence, Dec. 14, 1963; KAP to Marcelle Sibon, Lady Day, March 25, 1963; McKeldin.

38. Givner, *A Life,* pp. 490–91. KAP to Cyrilly Abels, Oct. 20, 1964, McKeldin. Inscription in a copy belonging to George Thomas Parsons, III, of Houston. The same page bears the signature of E. Barrett Prettyman, dated July 10, 1991, with the notation, "Actually, Beach, Core, Humphrey, Johnson and Wescott—all great friends of KAP at one time or another—were of enormous help in getting the book together, and KAP was most appreciative until she reached the stage reflected in her comments above."

39. KAP to E. Barrett Prettyman, June 14, 1976; Prettyman to KAP, June 16, 1976; KAP to Prettyman July 2, 1976 and Sept. 2, 1976; McKeldin. *Prince George's Journal,* Oct. 5, 1977, A8.

40. KAP to Seymour Lawrence, April 5, 1956, *Letters,* p. 500.

41. KAP to Barbara Harrison Wescott, May 3, 1962, *Letters,* p. 592. KAP to Paul Porter, Dec. 17, 1962, McKeldin.

42. See, however, Myron M. Liberman, *Katherine Anne Porter's Fiction,* pp. 18–19, arguing that the children's viciousness is mitigated by the need to sympathize with them for their victimization by their parents. But then, the account of that victimization increases the dreariness of the whole.

43. Givner, *A Life,* pp. 450–51.

44. KAP to Mrs. Eva F. Ronell, July 10, 1962, McKeldin.

45. Allen Tate to KAP, Nov. 11, 1962; Robert Penn Warren to KAP, July 20, 1962; Brainard Cheney to KAP, May 9, 1962; Cyrilly Abels to KAP, March 6, 1962; McKeldin.

46. Heilman, "*Ship of Fools:* Notes on Style," in Hartley and Core, eds., *Katherine Anne Porter: A Critical Symposium,* pp. 197–210. Unrue, *Truth and Vision,* pp. 161–217, 219.

47. Walsh, *Katherine Anne Porter and Mexico,* pp. 205, 215, and 229. Vande Kieft calls *Ship of Fools* a book touched by "cynicism"; "The Love Ethos of Porter, Welty, and McCullers," p. 250.

48. Janis P. Stout, *The Journey Narrative in American Literature: Patterns and Departures,* p. 13: "The journey is a convenient form for fiction because its parameters are so obvious and at the same time so flexible." Robert Scholes and Robert Kellogg point out in *The Nature of Narrative,* pp. 73–77, that the traveler's tale is a "persistent oral form in all cultures." For the history and relationships of various forms of journey narrative, see pp. 228–37. Ihab Hassan, in examining twentieth-century quest narratives, has seen their unifying quality as the act of placing personal safety and identity at risk in confrontations of otherness. Hassan, *Selves at Risk: Patterns of Quest in Contemporary American Letters,* pp. 3–14.

49. Thompson, "Interview," in *Conversations,* ed. Givner, p. 97.

50. Walsh, *Katherine Anne Porter and Mexico,* p. 206.

51. Fanny Cheney has pointed out, for example, that like La Condesa, Porter had a "lazy little belly." "That wasn't made up at all." Telephone conversation with

the author, Feb. 27, 1993. Walsh, *Katherine Anne Porter and Mexico,* pp. 206, 210, and 224, identifies biographical referents.

CHAPTER TEN: Porter as Reader and as Critic

1. *The Prince George's* [Maryland] *Journal,* Oct. 5, 1977, A8.

2. Marcella Comès Winslow, *Brushes with the Literary: Letters of a Washington Artist, 1943–1959,* p. 56 (letter of April 23, 1944).

3. Darlene Harbour Unrue identifies Porter's collection of books by and about James as "a representation greater than that of any other author"; Unrue, "Katherine Anne Porter and Henry James: A Study in Influence," p. 17.

4. Marginal annotation in Louis D. Rubin, Jr., and C. Hugh Holman, eds., *Southern Literary Study* (1975), p. 135; McKeldin.

5. Paul Porter, private conversation with the author, July 21, 1993. Winslow, *Brushes with the Literary,* p. 60.

6. KAP to Josephine Herbst, May 24, 1933, Beinecke. KAP to Paul Porter, Feb. 21, 1949 and March 11, 1949; KAP to William Goyen, July 19, 1951; McKeldin.

7. KAP to Jordan Pecile, Jan. 17, 1963; KAP to Eugene Pressly, Dec. 18, 1931; McKeldin. KAP to Jordan Pecile, July 3, 1961, *Letters,* p. 588. KAP to John Herrmann, Aug. 3, 1932, HRC. KAP to Glenway Wescott, March 20, 1961, McKeldin.

8. KAP to Donald Elder, April 15, 1942; KAP to Ann Holloway Heintze, Nov. 29, 1956; KAP to Glenway Wescott, Sept. 19, 1951, March 27, 1939, and April 3, 1959; KAP to Paul Porter, March 23 and 24, 1963; McKeldin.

9. KAP to Winston Bode, Dec. 18, 1964, Dec. 12, 1965, March 26, 1965; Bode to KAP March 22, 1965; KAP to Lon Tinkle, March 26, 1965; McKeldin.

10. The Hilt and Alvarez *Bibliography* lists thirty-nine of these. Two more, which appeared in *El Heraldo de México* in 1920, are reprinted in *Uncollected Early Prose,* ed. Alvarez and Walsh.

11. KAP to Josephine Herbst, May 5, 1928, Beinecke.

12. Alvarez and Walsh, *Uncollected Early Prose,* p. 38.

13. Porter, "Mexico," in "*This Strange, Old World,*" ed. Unrue, p. 3; "Shooting the Chutes," p. 14; "Mr. George on the Woman Problem," p. 35; "A Most Lively Genius," p. 137.

14. Alvarez and Walsh, *Uncollected Early Prose,* pp. 343–45.

15. Pells, *Radical Visions,* p. 102, comments that Chase thought the "only other nation in the world that promised similar psychological and spiritual satisfactions was the Soviet Union." Porter regarded this as a glib judgment.

16. *CE,* p. 455.

17. *CE,* p. 87.

18. *CE,* pp. 421–25. KAP to Gay Porter Holloway, April 1, 1920 and n.d., bearing Porter's pencil notation "1928?"; McKeldin.

19. *CE*, pp. 14–15.

20. KAP to Josephine Herbst, Jan. 28, 1947, McKeldin.

21. *CE*, pp. 20–23. Fitzgerald, ed., *The Habit of Being*, p. 390. O'Connor commented that Porter "cuts away a lot of the grease around the Lady Chatterley business."

22. Stephen Spender to KAP, Jan. 28, 1960, McKeldin.

23. *CE*, pp. 251–54.

24. *CE*, p. 33.

25. KAP to Genevieve Taggard, June 3, 1926, McKeldin.

26. KAP to Donald Sutherland, June 2, 1953, *CE*, p. 274.

27. *CE*, p. 274.

28. "*This Strange, Old World*," ed. Unrue, p. 101.

29. *CE*, pp. 271–72. Sutherland's correspondence with Porter over the donation of his correspondence with Gallup to the Stein Collection at Yale is printed as "Ole Woman River: A Correspondence with Katherine Anne Porter."

30. Givner, *A Life*, p. 353; *CE*, p. 274; KAP to Donald Sutherland, June 2, 1953, *CE*, p. 272. Porter marked a statement in Edith Sitwell's autobiography, *Taken Care Of* (1965), p. 159 (McKeldin), to the effect that "Gertrude talked to the husbands, it was the job of Alice B. Toklas to entertain the wives and the less interesting of the guests."

31. Givner, *A Life*, p. 353.

32. Gilbert and Gubar, *No Man's Land: The Place of the Woman Writer in the Twentieth Century; Volume II, Sexchanges*, p. 327. Three pictures of Stein reproduced on pages 357–59 of *Sexchanges* illustrate the plurisignificant forcefulness of her expressionism in dress. The entire last chapter of the volume, "Cross-Dressing and Re-Dressing: Transvestism as Metaphor," provides a useful and clearly apposite context for Porter's concern with gender and lesbianism.

33. *CE*, p. 260. Porter's attitude toward male sexuality may similarly have colored her estimate of such contemporaries as Truman Capote and Tennessee Williams. Wescott tacitly judged as much in attributing her "attitude toward homosexual writers" to "her (deadly) lonesomeness." In "one of her tirades" against Capote, she called him "a pimple on the face of the literature." Wescott, *Continual Lessons*, p. 302.

34. *CE*, pp. 275 and 271.

35. *CE*, pp. 272–76.

36. Givner, *A Life*, p. 354.

37. *CE*, pp. 261, 259, 269–70.

38. Eleanor Clark Warren to KAP, Nov. 17, 1948; Elizabeth Ames to KAP, Jan. 18, 1947; Ernestine Evans to KAP, n.d. except KAP's later note, 1948; John Malcolm Brinnin to KAP, Nov. 17, 1959; McKeldin.

39. Donald Sutherland to KAP, June 4, 1953; KAP to Donald Sutherland, June 10, 1953; *CE*, pp. 278–81.

40. Josephine Herbst, "Miss Porter and Miss Stein," pp. 568–72.

41. Josephine Herbst to KAP, Jan. 8, 1947; KAP to Allen Tate, Jan. 12, 1962; McKeldin.

42. KAP to Glenway Wescott, March 19, 1947, *Letters,* p. 335; *CE,* p. 300. In her copy of *James Joyce in Paris: His Final Years,* by Gisèle Freund and V. B. Carleton (1970), McKeldin, she wrote beneath a picture taken at the reading at Shakespeare and Company, "I was present, unseen, seeing and hearing."

43. Marginal annotations, T. S. Eliot, ed., *Literary Essays of Ezra Pound* (1954), signed and dated Jan. 10, 1958, pp. 58–59, 63; McKeldin.

44. *CE,* pp. 3–7.

45. *CE,* pp. 7–10.

46. *CE,* p. 13.

47. KAP to Andrew Lytle, July 14, 1947, McKeldin. Hendrick, in *Katherine Anne Porter* (1965), p. 17, comments that her "intransigence seems to have been inherited from her grandmother."

48. KAP to "the whole family," Nov. 8, 1931, filed with the Mary Alice Hillendahl correspondence; McKeldin.

49. KAP to Glenway Wescott, March 27, 1939, McKeldin.

50. *CE,* pp. 68–71.

51. KAP to Paul Porter, June 5, 1948; *CE,* p. 114.

52. KAP to Eugene Pressly, Nov. 28, 1932, McKeldin.

53. Nina Baym, "The Madwoman and Her Languages: Why I Don't Do Feminist Literary Theory," in *Feminist Issues in Literary Scholarship,* ed. Shari Benstock, p. 47.

54. Margaret Doane Gilson to KAP, Nov. 21, 1952, McKeldin. *Mademoiselle* was, at the time, a magazine designed to interest the educated young woman. It published such writers as James Baldwin, Truman Capote, and Frank Conroy, in addition to fashion pieces. Moreover, the editor, Porter's friend Cyrilly Abels, paid her top dollar. Phyllis Rifield, assistant to Cyrilly Abels, interview with the author, Oct. 13, 1993. Porter had published "Marriage Is Belonging" in *Mademoiselle* the year before and would publish "A Defense of Circe" there in 1953 and her poem "After a Long Journey" in 1957, as well as other pieces.

55. *CE,* pp. 29–30.

56. *CE,* pp. 30–31.

57. KAP to Gay Porter Holloway, April 30, 1958, McKeldin.

58. *CE,* p. 35.

59. *CE,* pp. 37–38.

60. KAP to Jordan Pecile, June 5, 1961, McKeldin. *CE,* p. 29.

61. *CE,* pp. 438–39. KAP to Josephine Herbst, July 1, 1932, Beinecke.

62. KAP to Josephine Herbst, n.d., Beinecke, and Feb. 11, 1931, *Letters,* p. 34.

63. KAP to Josephine Herbst, Jan. 16, 1932, Beinecke.

64. KAP to Josephine Herbst, Nov. 23, 1938, Beinecke.

CHAPTER ELEVEN: Artistry

1. Glenway Wescott used the phrase "writer's writer" in the title of his review of *The Leaning Tower and Other Stories, New York Times Book Review,* 1944.

2. On "the shapelessness of life," *CE,* p. 278. Brinkmeyer, *Katherine Anne Porter's Artistic Development,* p. 21, observes that the writing of "Holiday" in 1924 and the publication of "He" in 1927 "signaled the new direction of Porter's art and vision, drawing upon memory for inspiration and meaning." Eileen Baldeshwiler, in "Structural Patterns in Katherine Anne Porter's Fiction," pp. 45–53, distinguishes among three modes: a mode of conflict leading to a resolution (in which she groups "He," "Noon Wine," and "The Downward Path to Wisdom"), a mode of memory (in which she mentions "The Old Order"), and a new form tracing an emotion or a complex of emotions that develops into wisdom (including "Theft," "Flowering Judas, "Old Mortality," and "The Leaning Tower"). In my reading, the works do not sort themselves out so neatly, and the mode of memory is implicated in virtually all the stories Baldeshwiler mentions.

3. In 1935 Porter wrote to Robert Penn Warren that she had drawn from that section of her novel a "fragment" called "The Grave" (later grouped with several other stories or sketches under the collective title "The Old Order"). "That leaves," she said, "only three other fragments, "The Grandmother,' a short portrait; 'The Circus,' which might not stand by itself, I don't know; and a very long middle section called 'The Old Order.'" KAP to Warren, Feb. 24, 1935, *Letters,* p. 118. At other times she said (and her notes clearly indicate) that "Old Mortality" also came out of her work on this never-to-be-completed novel.

4. Thompson, "An Interview," in *Conversations,* ed. Givner, p. 92. I sometimes wonder if she would have liked the term I once used to describe her work, the "little black dress" of literature.

5. Romines, *The Home Plot,* pp. 3–18.

6. Hilt and Alvarez, *Bibliography,* pp. 259–66.

7. Josephine Herbst to KAP, undated, McKeldin.

8. Robert Penn Warren, "Irony with a Center," in *Selected Essays,* p. 139. James William Johnson, "Another Look at Katherine Anne Porter," pp. 598–613. Hendrick, *Katherine Anne Porter,* p. 96. Liberman, *Katherine Anne Porter's Fiction,* pp. 52, 7.

9. Heilman, "*Ship of Fools:* Notes on Style," in *Katherine Anne Porter: A Critical Symposium,* ed. Hartley and Core, p. 202. Here and elsewhere I am drawing on my own previous work, chiefly in *Strategies of Reticence: Silence and Meaning in the Works of Jane Aústen, Willa Cather, Katherine Anne Porter, and Joan Didion.*

10. Welty, "The Eye of the Story," 265–74. Porter recommended Welty for a Bread Loaf fellowship in 1940 and wrote the introduction to her first book.

11. *CS,* pp. 58, 362.

12. Heilman, "*Ship of Fools:* Notes on Style," pp. 202–3.

13. Wescott, *Continual Lessons,* p. 68 (April 4, 1940).

14. KAP to Robert Penn Warren, July 15, 1943, Beinecke. KAP to Erna Johns, Aug. 18, 1959, McKeldin. KAP to John Herrmann, Aug. 3, 1932, HRC.

15. Thompson, "An Interview," *Conversations,* p. 92.

16. Susan Stanford Friedman, *Penelope's Web: Gender, Modernity, H.D.'s Fiction,* p. xi. *CE,* p. 443. Unrue, *Truth and Vision,* p. 219. Brinkmeyer, *Katherine Anne Porter's Artistic Development,* p. 9.

17. *CE,* pp. 433, 440. Porter once wrote to the *Washington Post* a contrast of art and science that turned the usual cliché on its head: "I am an artist, and I have to keep my feet on the ground and deal with reality, with truth as far as I am able to find it, I have to be practical; and you men of science carrying on your wild games on Cloud Nine, and then telling fibs, make it very hard for me to convince my writing students" to keep things in the proper perspective. *CE,* p. 227.

18. Edward G. Schwartz, "The Fictions of Memory," *Southwest Review* 1960; rpt. *Katherine Anne Porter: A Critical Symposium,* ed. Hartley and Core, p. 82.

19. Thomas F. Walsh, "Deep Similarities in 'Noon Wine,'" pp. 83–91.

20. *CS,* pp. 243–45.

21. M. Wynn Thomas, "Strangers in a Strange Land: A Reading of 'Noon Wine,'" p. 245.

22. Thomas, "Strangers in a Strange Land"; Male, "The Short Story of the Mysterious Stranger in American Fiction," pp. 281–94; Leiter, "The Expense of Spirit in a Waste of Shame: Motif, Montage, and Structure in *Noon Wine,*" in *Seven Contemporary Short Novels,* ed. Charles Clerc and Louis Leiter, pp. 185–219.

23. Walsh, "Deep Similarities," also "The 'Noon Wine' Devils," pp. 90–96; Smith, "Porter's *Noon Wine:* A Stifled Tragedy," pp. 157–62; Groff, "'Noon Wine': A Texas Tragedy," pp. 39–47.

24. Elmo Howell, "Katherine Anne Porter and the Southern Myth: A Note on 'Noon Wine,'" pp. 252–59; Winfred S. Emmons, *Katherine Anne Porter: The Regional Stories,* pp. 2–3 and 28–34.

25. *Robert Penn Warren Talking,* ed. Watkins and Hiers, pp. 133–34.

26. Donald Brace to KAP, May 10, 1934; KAP to Eugene Pressly, March 27, 1936; McKeldin.

27. Glenway Wescott to KAP, Feb. 1, 1966, McKeldin.

28. KAP to Eugene Pressly, Dec. 7, 1931 and Nov. 29, 1936, McKeldin.

29. KAP to Paul Porter, Aug. 24, 1949, McKeldin. KAP to Caroline Gordon, Dec. 14, 1931, *Letters,* pp. 69–70. Her comment on serving a "term" was made in 1931, when she had just gone to Germany on her first Guggenheim Fellowship and was feeling the award as an unnerving pressure to produce.

30. KAP to Robert McAlmon, Jan. 29, 1935, McKeldin. KAP to Robert Penn Warren, Feb. 24, 1935, *Letters,* p. 118. KAP to Robert Penn Warren, July 17, 1935; KAP to Genevieve Taggard, Jan. 5, 1937; McKeldin.

31. KAP to Eugene Pressly, Nov. 29 and 30, 1936, McKeldin. KAP to Glenway

Wescott, Dec. 3, 1937, *Letters,* pp. 153–54. KAP to Albert Erskine, Dec. 7, 1937, McKeldin.

32. KAP to Eugene Pressly, Nov. 28, 1936 and April 2, 1936, McKeldin.

33. KAP to Josephine Herbst, n.d. except 1928, Beinecke. *CE,* p. 449.

34. *CE,* pp. 467–68, 478, 481. Givner, *A Life,* pp. 73–75. An interesting parallel is Porter's account of the origin of her story "The Downward Path to Wisdom." On Nov. 13, 1936, she wrote to Pressly that the story was "based on your childhood." But a letter from Glenway Wescott to Porter on Dec. 26, 1939, implies that she had told him the story was based on something he had related to her about his childhood. The truth may be that she simply picked up bits and pieces, or just the emotional tone, from both.

35. KAP to Josephine Herbst, Dec. 1, 1938; KAP to Robert Penn Warren and Cinina Warren, July 5, 1945; Beinecke. *CE,* pp. 50, 118.

36. KAP to Janice Ford, Nov. 5, 1933; KAP to Janice Biala and Ford Madox Ford, Nov. 20, 1935; KAP to Glenway Wescott, Jan. 23, 1941; McKeldin.

37. The later Eliot, who reached out to established structures of political reaction and religious orthodoxy as means to order, was alien to Porter's way of thinking. In her essay "On a Criticism of Thomas Hardy," she likened Eliot's orthodoxy to "military police" patrolling for heterodox untrained minds like Hardy's. *CE,* p. 7. Benstock, *Women of the Left Bank,* pp. x, 33, and passim. Hammer, *Hart Crane and Allen Tate,* p. 9. Fredric Jameson sees in Wyndham Lewis's "brief flirtation with Nazism" and the "comparable enthusiasms of Pound, Yeats, Shaw, and others" reason to raise the issue of "the affinities between protofascism and Western modernism"; *Fables of Aggression,* p. 5.

38. Gilbert and Gubar, *No Man's Land,* Vol. I, p. 154.

39. Friedman, *Penelope's Web,* p. 2. Benstock, *Women of the Left Bank,* p. 6. Friedman's opening chapter discusses H.D.'s very different theorizing of modernism as an "Eleusinian gynopoetic" reaching outside the twentieth century (pp. 1–32).

40. See Chapter 7, "Soldier's Heart: Literary Men, Literary Women, and the Great War," of Gilbert and Gubar's *Sexchanges,* pp. 258–323. Porter is discussed here as one of those who feared that "if men were sick they must have fallen ill because women were sickening," in reference to Adam's dying at the end of "Pale Horse, Pale Rider" of flu caught from Miranda.

41. *CE,* p. 93.

CHAPTER TWELVE: "a free, intransigent, dissenting mind"

1. Hubert H. Humphrey to KAP, March 21, 1966, McKeldin. Darlene Unrue says in *Truth and Vision,* p. 219, that truth meant, for Porter, "finally life itself."

The phrase has a noble ring and avoids a distorting reductiveness, but is too vague to be very useful. The phrase that is used as the title to this chapter is from KAP to Andrew Lytle, July 5, 1947, McKeldin.

2. Kenneth Durant to KAP, March 9, 1936, McKeldin. Malcolm Cowley had written to her about the League earlier, on June 8, 1935. Aaron, *Writers on the Left,* p. 284. KAP to Albert Erskine, July 23, 1939, McKeldin. Durant's widow comments that he was a "journalist of surpassing integrity" and that of the various persons who have "tried to implicate Kenneth Durant with communist activities" none has "ever succeeded"; personal letter from Mrs. Kenneth Durant to the author, Oct. 31, 1993.

3. Robert Penn Warren to KAP, Dec. 22, 1934, McKeldin.

4. Annotations in Simone de Beauvoir, *The Second Sex,* trans. H. M. Parshley (New York: Alfred A. Knopf, 1953), pp. 379, 396, 279, 674, and passim.

5. Givner, *A Life,* p. 332.

6. Harrison Boone Porter to KAP, n.d., McKeldin. A statement that he had "led a lonely miserable life for forty years or more" would seem to place the letter in the early to mid-1930s in that it had then been forty years or slightly more since the death of his wife.

7. Herbert Klein to Joan Givner, quoted in Givner, *A Life,* p. 258.

8. Givner, *A Life,* pp. 493, 508. Paul Porter to Joan Givner, Feb. 2, 1978, private collection of Paul Porter.

9. Erna Johns to KAP, Feb. 1, 1963, McKeldin.

10. Bayley, Introduction to *Letters,* p. 4.

11. KAP to Harrison Boone Porter, May 31, 1934; KAP to Glenway Wescott, June 28, 1940 and March 10, 1943; McKeldin.

12. KAP to Glenway Wescott, Dec. 27, 1943, *Letters,* p. 279. The story appears in other letters as well.

13. KAP to Gay Porter Holloway, May 22, 1947; KAP to Andrew Lytle, July 14, 1947; McKeldin. KAP to Robert Penn Warren, Feb. 27, 1947, *Letters,* p. 333. Wescott, *Continual Lessons,* p. 209.

14. KAP to Samuel Duff McCoy (of Dial Press), Jan. 12, 1951, McKeldin.

15. *CE,* pp. 64–65. KAP to Gay Porter Holloway, May 15, 1963; KAP to Marcelle Sibon, Lady Day, March 25, 1963; McKeldin.

16. KAP to Eleanor Clark Warren, May 8, 1952, *Letters,* p. 423. KAP to Robert Penn Warren, Oct. 16, 1953, Beinecke. KAP to Erna Johns, Aug. 18, 1959; McKeldin. KAP to Rev. John F. Fahey, Oct. 5, 1948, Bayley, ed., *Letters,* p. 358.

17. KAP to Jordan Pecile, June 4, 1963; McKeldin. Fitzgerald, ed., *The Habit of Being,* p. 275.

18. Allen Tate to KAP, Nov. 11, 1962; KAP to Tate, Nov. 21, 1962; markings in *Lord Hear Our Prayer,* ed. Thomas McNally and William Storey (1978); McKeldin.

19. Raymond Roseliep to KAP, April 29, 1962 and June 27, 1972, McKeldin. Givner, *The Self-Portrait of a Literary Biographer,* p. 151. Joan Givner to Paul Porter, June 25, 1979, personal collection of Paul Porter. Givner, *A Life,* pp. 508–9.

20. *CE,* pp. 3–4, 7, 11.

21. KAP to Edward Schwartz, March 26, 1958, *Letters,* ed. Bayley, p. 549. Marginal notations in Pierre Benoît and Roland Murphy, eds., *Immortality and Resurrection* (1970), pp. 103 and 131.

22. Givner, *A Life,* p. 102.

23. Porter, "St. Augustine and the Bullfight," *CE,* p. 98. KAP to Josephine Herbst, April 16, 1930, Beinecke. Warren, "Uncorrupted Consciousness," p. 280.

24. KAP to Glenway Wescott, April 19, 1942, McKeldin. Similarly, she told Warren that her views were not "hasty" and wouldn't "change much": "my principles are really principles, and they work." KAP to Warren, Dec. 27, 1939, Beinecke.

25. KAP to Robert Penn Warren, May 1, 1940 and Dec. 22, 1946, Beinecke.

26. KAP to Tinkum Brooks, July 15, 1963, McKeldin. KAP to William Goyen, May 26, 1951, McKeldin. KAP to Cinina and Robert Penn Warren, July 5, 1945, *Letters,* p. 305, and Sept. 15, 1975, Beinecke.

27. Tinkum Brooks to Porter, Nov. 29, 1957, McKeldin. Bayley, Introduction to *Letters,* p. 2.

28. Caroline Gordon to Andrew Lytle, May 19, 1942, quoted by Waldron, *Close Connections,* p. 204. KAP to Cleanth Brooks, Oct. 5, 1954 (but actually dated, through an obvious typographical error, 1984; it was written from Liège), McKeldin. Glenway Wescott to KAP, May 24, 1965 and July 12, 1965; Gay Porter Holloway to KAP, June 2, 1966; McKeldin.

29. Malcolm Cowley to KAP, Jan. 9, 1969; KAP to Malcolm Cowley (addressing him, despite their long friendship, as "Mr."), Nov. 11, 1974; McKeldin. Porter had occasionally spoken ill of Cowley ever since he refused her intemperate review of Stuart Chase's *Mexico: A Study of Two Americas.*

30. Winston Bode to KAP, Jan. 6, 1965; KAP to Bode, Dec. 12, 1965; Virginia Spencer Carr to KAP, Oct. 8, 1976; KAP to Spencer Carr, Oct. 25, 1976; McKeldin.

31. KAP to William Goyen, July 3, 1951; KAP to Gay Porter Holloway, Dec. 3, 1966 and July 6, 1966; McKeldin.

32. KAP to Glenway Wescott, Jan. 5, 1960, McKeldin.

33. KAP to Robert Penn Warren, Oct. 31, 1975, Beinecke.

34. Welty to Givner, March 8, 1975, in *The Self-Portrait of a Literary Biographer,* p. 184.

35. McAlmon, *Being Geniuses Together,* p. 332. Dorothy Day to KAP, letter dated only July 5, but penciled at the end, in Porter's hand, "1930? I was still in Mexico"; Ford Madox Ford to KAP, Dec. 21, 1935; McKeldin.

36. KAP to Glenway Wescott, Jan. 12, 1942, McKeldin.

37. KAP to Robert Penn Warren, Oct. 8, 1942, *Letters,* p. 250.

38. Glenway Wescott to KAP, Sept. 9, 1965, McKeldin.

39. Eudora Welty to KAP, Aug. 3, 1970; Robert Penn Warren to KAP, May 29, 1970; McKeldin.

40. Pete Seeger to KAP, Dec. 10, 1965; Barbara Harrison Wescott to KAP, Jan. 24, 1966; McKeldin.

41. Marginal annotations in George Hendrick, *Katherine Anne Porter* (1965); McKeldin.

42. John Edward Hardy, *Katherine Anne Porter,* p. 12.

43. Joan Givner to Paul Porter, May 17, 1977, personal collection of Paul Porter.

44. Robert Penn Warren to Bill Wilkins, April 1, 1977, Beinecke.

45. KAP to Lon Tinkle, March 26, 1965, McKeldin.

46. Charlotte Laughlin, at the conference "Katherine Anne Porter and Twentieth-Century Culture," Baylor University, May 15, 1992. Joan Givner, private interview with the author.

47. KAP to Lon Tinkle, June 10, 1976; Lon Tinkle to KAP, June 24, 1976; McKeldin.

48. KAP to Lon Tinkle, Aug. 19, 1976; Lon Tinkle to KAP, Sept. 17, 1976; McKeldin. KAP to Joan Givner, Sept. 29, 1976; Givner to KAP, Oct. 5, 1976; McKeldin-PP.

49. Erna Johns to KAP, April 13, 1978, McKeldin. Joan Givner to Paul Porter, Feb. 23, 1978; KAP to Joan Givner, April 12, 1978; personal collection of Paul Porter.

50. Joan Givner to Paul Porter, May 28, 1982 and Oct. 12, 1982, personal collection of Paul Porter. A decade later Paul states that his attitude toward his aunt's biographer has "turned around 180 degrees" from his early cordiality. Paul Porter to the author, telephone conversation July 6, 1993.

51. E. Barrett Prettyman to Joan Givner, Nov. 22, 1982, personal collection of Paul Porter.

52. Jordan Pecile to Paul Porter, Dec. 12, 1982, McKeldin-PP.

53. The jaundiced view of Givner that Paul finally came to hold is evident, too, in his comments on the back of a picture of Givner standing in front of the portrait painted by Marcella Comès Winslow: "Joan Givner & that godawful painting by Marcella Winslow. Joan liked it, of course." Both photographs, with inscriptions, are in the McKeldin collection.

54. Paul Porter to Joan Givner, May 10, 1978, personal collection of Paul Porter.

55. Joan Givner to Paul Porter, May 17, 1977, personal collection of Paul Porter.

56. Tillie Olsen at "Katherine Anne Porter: Centennial Celebration," Georgia State University, Nov. 10, 1990. KAP to Cyrilly Abels, Dec. 31, 1960, and to Donald Elder, June 14, 1942, *Letters,* p. 582.

57. Core, "Lives Fugitive and Unwritten," in *Located Lives,* p. 59.

58. Joan Givner to Paul Porter, May 17, 1977, personal collection of Paul Porter.

BIBLIOGRAPHY

WORKS BY PORTER

The Collected Essays and Occasional Writings of Katherine Anne Porter. Boston: Houghton Mifflin/Seymour Lawrence, 1970.

The Collected Stories of Katherine Anne Porter. New York: Harcourt Brace Jovanovich, 1979.

"From a Mexican Painter's Notebook," by Diego Rivera. Translated by Katherine Anne Porter. *Arts* 7 (Jan. 1925): 21–23.

"Hacienda." *Virginia Quarterly Review* 8 (1932): 556–69.

Letter to A. Everett Austin, Jr., located at the Wadsworth Atheneum, Hartford, Connecticut.

Letters and other papers in the Katherine Anne Porter Collection, the Paul Porter Collection, the Mary Louis Doherty Collection, and the Thomas F. Walsh Collection, McKeldin Library, University of Maryland.

Letters of Katherine Anne Porter. Selected and edited by Isabel Bayley. New York: Atlantic Monthly Press, 1990.

Marginal annotations in books in the personal library of Katherine Anne Porter, McKeldin Library, University of Maryland.

Outline of Mexican Arts and Crafts. Los Angeles: Young and McCallister, 1922.

Papers located in the Donald Windham Collection, Hargrett Rare Book and Manuscript Library, University of Georgia, including a copy of *Pale Horse, Pale Rider* owned by Sandy M. Campbell and endorsed by Porter.

Papers located in the Dorothy Day—Catholic Worker Collection, Marquette University.

Papers located in the John Herrmann Collection, Harry Ransom Humanities Research Center, University of Texas.

Papers located in the Josephine Herbst Collection and the Robert Penn Warren Collection, Beinecke Rare Book and Manuscript Library, Yale University.

Rocky Mountain News, items with Porter's byline published Feb. 8, 1919, through August 17, 1919.

Statement in *Writers Take Sides: Letters about the War in Spain.* League of American Authors, 1938.

Survey Graphic, Volume 2 (May 1924).

"This Strange, Old World" and Other Book Reviews by Katherine Anne Porter. Edited by Darlene Harbour Unrue. Athens: Univ. of Georgia Press, 1991.

Uncollected Early Prose of Katherine Anne Porter. Edited by Ruth M. Alvarez and Thomas F. Walsh. Austin: Univ. of Texas Press, 1993.

SECONDARY WORKS CITED

Aaron, Daniel. *Writers on the Left: Episodes in American Literary Communism.* New York: Harcourt, Brace & World, 1961.

Adler, Selig. *The Isolationist Impulse: Its Twentieth-Century Reaction.* London: Abelard-Schuman, 1957.

Alpern, Sara. *Freda Kirchwey: A Woman of The Nation.* Cambridge, Mass.: Harvard Univ. Press, 1987.

Alvarez, Ruth Moore. "Katherine Anne Porter and Mexican Art." Ph.D. dissertation, Univ. of Maryland, 1991.

Anderson, David D. "John Herrmann, Midwestern Modern, Part II: The Alger Hiss Case and the Midwestern Literary Connection." *Midwestern Miscellany* 1991: 42–52.

Ashby, Joe C. *Organized Labor and the Mexican Revolution under Lázaro Cárdenas.* Chapel Hill: Univ. of North Carolina Press, 1963.

Austenfeld, Thomas. "Katherine Anne Porter Abroad: The Politics of Emotion." *Literatur in Wissenschaft und Unterricht* 27 (1994): 27–33.

Azuela, Alicia. "Rivera and the Concept of Proletarian Art." In *Diego Rivera: A Retrospective,* ed. Cynthia Newman Helms. Detroit: Founders Society, Detroit Institute of the Arts, in association with W. W. Norton, 1986.

Baldeshwiler, Eileen. "Structural Patterns in Katherine Anne Porter's Fiction." *South Dakota Review* 11 (1973): 45–53.

Barrett, William. "Comment: A Prize for Ezra Pound." *Partisan Review* 16 (1949): 344–47.

Baym, Nina. "The Madwoman and Her Languages: Why I Don't Do Feminist Literary Theory." In *Feminist Issues in Literary Scholarship,* ed. Shari Benstock, pp. 45–61. Bloomington: Indiana Univ. Press, 1987. Also in *Feminism and American Literary History: Essays,* pp. 199–213. New Brunswick, N.J.: Rutgers Univ. Press, 1992.

———. "The Myth of the Myth of Southern Womanhood." In *Feminism and American Literary History: Essays,* pp. 183–96. New Brunswick, N.J.: Rutgers Univ. Press, 1992.

Benstock, Shari. *Women of the Left Bank: Paris, 1900–1940.* Austin: Univ. of Texas Press, 1986.

———, ed. *The Private Self: Theory and Practice of Women's Autobiographical Writing.* Chapel Hill: Univ. of North Carolina Press, 1988.

Best-Maugard, Adolfo. *A Method for Creative Design*. 1926. Rev. ed. New York: Alfred A. Knopf, 1927.

Billeter, Erika. "Mexico's Contribution to 20th Century Art." Translated by Maureen Oberli-Turner. In *Images of Mexico: The Contribution of Mexico to 20th Century Art*, ed. Erika Billeter, pp. 24–28. Dallas: Dallas Museum of Art, 1987.

Blasco Ibáñez, V. *Mexico in Revolution*. Translated by Arthur Livingston and José Padin. New York: E. P. Dutton, 1920.

Brantley, Will. *Feminine Sense in Southern Memoir: Smith, Glasgow, Welty, Heilman, Porter, and Hurston*. Jackson: Univ. Press of Mississippi, 1993.

Brinkmeyer, Robert H., Jr. *Katherine Anne Porter's Artistic Development: Primitivism, Traditionalism, and Totalitarianism*. Baton Rouge: Louisiana State Univ. Press, 1993.

Brooks, Cleanth. "Southern Literature: The Wellsprings of Its Vitality." In *A Shaping Joy: Studies in the Writer's Craft*. New York: Harcourt Brace Jovanovich, 1971.

——. "The Southern Temper." In *A Shaping Joy: Studies in the Writer's Craft*. New York: Harcourt Brace Jovanovich, 1971.

——. "The Woman and Artist I Knew." In *Katherine Anne Porter and Texas: An Uneasy Relationship*, ed. Clinton Machann and William Bedford Clark, pp. 13–22. College Station: Texas A & M Univ. Press, 1990.

Brown, Norman D. "Texas's Southern Roots." In *The Texas Literary Tradition*, ed. Don Graham, James W. Lee, and William T. Pilkingham, pp. 40–45. Austin: College of Liberal Arts, Univ. of Texas, and the Texas State Historical Association, 1983.

Brown, Susan Jenkins. *Robber Rocks: Letters and Memoirs of Hart Crane, 1923–1932*. Middletown, Conn.: Wesleyan Univ. Press, 1968.

Buenger, Walter L., and Robert A. Calvert. "The Shelf Life of Truth in Texas." In *Texas through Time: Evolving Interpretations*, ed. Walter L. Buenger and Robert A. Calvert, pp. ix–xxxv. College Station: Texas A & M Univ. Press, 1991.

Burbank, Garin. *When Farmers Voted Red: The Gospel of Socialism in the Oklahoma Countryside, 1910–1924*. Westport, Conn.: Greenwood Press, 1976.

Carr, Barry. *Marxism and Communism in Twentieth-Century Mexico*. Lincoln: Univ. of Nebraska Press, 1992.

"Celebrated Writer Assigned Guardian." *Prince George's Journal*, October 5, 1977, A8.

Ceplair, Larry, and Steven Englund. *The Inquisition in Hollywood: Politics in the Film Community, 1930–1960*. Berkeley: Univ. of California Press, 1983.

Charlot, Jean. *The Mexican Mural Renaissance, 1920–1925*. New Haven: Yale Univ. Press, 1963.

Chatfield, Charles. *For Peace and Justice: Pacifism in America, 1914–1941*. Knoxville: Univ. of Tennessee Press, 1971.

Chauncey, George, Jr. "The Way We Were." *Village Voice*, July 1, 1986: 29–30, 32.

Coles, Robert. *Dorothy Day: A Radical Devotion*. Reading, Mass.: Addison-Wesley, 1987.

Conger, Amy. *Edward Weston in Mexico, 1923–1926*. Albuquerque: Univ. of New Mexico Press, 1983.

Conkin, Paul K. "The South in Southern Agrarianism." In *The Evolution of Southern Culture*, ed. Numan V. Bartley, pp. 131–45. Athens: Univ. of Georgia Press, 1988.

Constantine, Mildred. *Tina Modotti: A Fragile Life*. New York: Rizzoli, 1983.

Core, George. "Lives Fugitive and Unwritten." In *Located Lives: Place and Idea in Southern Autobiography*, ed. J. Bill Berry, pp. 52–65. Athens: Univ. of Georgia Press, 1990.

Crosby, Alfred W., Jr. *Epidemic and Peace, 1918*. Westport, Conn.: Greenwood Press, 1976.

Dabney, Virginius. *Liberalism in the South*. Chapel Hill: Univ. of North Carolina Press, 1932.

DeLeon, David. *The American as Anarchist: Reflections on Indigenous Radicalism*. Baltimore: Johns Hopkins Univ. Press, 1978.

Delpar, Helen. *The Enormous Vogue of Things Mexican: Cultural Relations between the United States and Mexico, 1920–1935*. Tuscaloosa: Univ. of Alabama Press, 1992.

del Rio, Eduardo, ed. *Un Siglo de Caricatura en Mexico*. 2d ed. Mexico City: Grijalbo, 1984.

DeMouy, Jane Krause. *Katherine Anne Porter's Women: The Eye of Her Fiction*. Austin: Univ. of Texas Press, 1983.

Dodd, William E., Jr., and Martha Dodd, eds. *Ambassador Dodd's Diary, 1933–1938*. New York: Harcourt Brace, 1941.

Dulles, John W. F. *Yesterday in Mexico: A Chronicle of the Revolution, 1919–1936*. Austin: Univ. of Texas Press, 1961.

Duroselle, Jean-Baptiste. *From Wilson to Roosevelt: Foreign Policy of the United States, 1913–1945*. Translated by Nancy Lyman Roelker. New York: Harper and Row, 1963.

Emmons, Winfred S. *Katherine Anne Porter: The Regional Stories*. Austin: Steck-Vaughn, 1967.

Fain, John Tyree, and Thomas Daniel Young, eds. *The Literary Correspondence of Donald Davidson and Allen Tate*. Athens: Univ. of Georgia Press, 1974.

Featherstone, Joseph. "Katherine Anne Porter's Stories." *New Republic* 153 (4 Sept. 1965): 23–26.

Felix, David. *Protest: Sacco-Vanzetti and the Intellectuals.* Bloomington: Indiana Univ. Press, 1965.

Fischer, Conan. *The German Communists and the Rise of Nazism.* New York: St. Martin's Press, 1991.

Fitzgerald, Sally, ed. *The Habit of Being: Letters of Flannery O'Connor.* New York: Farrar, Straus, Giroux, 1979.

Flanders, Jane. "Katherine Anne Porter and the Ordeal of Southern Womanhood." *Southern Literary Journal* 9 (1976): 47–60.

——. "Katherine Anne Porter's Feminist Criticism: Book Reviews from the 1920's." *Frontiers* 4 (1979): 44–48.

Forkner, Ben, and Patrick Samway, S.J., eds. *A Modern Southern Reader: Major Stories, Drama, Poetry, Essays, Interviews and Reminiscences from the Twentieth-Century South.* Atlanta: Peachtree Publishers, 1986.

Fosado, Victor. "Death in Mexico." Translated by Maurice Harrah. In *Images of Mexico: The Contribution of Mexico to 20th Century Art,* ed. Erika Billeter, pp. 431–32. Dallas: Dallas Museum of Art, 1987.

Foster, William Z. *History of the Communist Party of the United States.* New York: Greenwood Press, 1968.

Fox Genovese, Elizabeth. "Between Individualism and Community: Autobiographies of Southern Women." In *Located Lives: Place and Idea in Southern Autobiography,* ed. J. Bill Berry, pp. 20–38. Athens: Univ. of Georgia Press, 1990.

Friedman, Jefferson. "Introduction." In *Southern Literature and Literary Theory,* ed. Jefferson Friedman, pp. vii–xvii. Athens: Univ. of Georgia Press, 1990.

Friedman, Susan Stanford. *Penelope's Web: Gender, Modernity, H.D.'s Fiction.* Cambridge: Cambridge Univ. Press, 1990.

Gaston, Edwin W., Jr. "The Mythic South of Katherine Anne Porter." *Southwestern American Literature* 3 (1973): 81–85.

Geduld, Harry M., and Ronald Gottesman, eds. *Sergei Eisenstein and Upton Sinclair: The Making and Unmaking of Qué Viva México!* Bloomington: Indiana Univ. Press, 1970.

Gibbons, Reginald. *William Goyen: A Study of the Short Fiction.* Boston: Twayne Publishers, 1991.

Gibson, Margaret. *Memories of the Future: The Daybooks of Tina Modotti, Poems.* Baton Rouge: Louisiana State Univ. Press, 1986.

Gide, André. "Second Thoughts on the U.S.S.R." *Partisan Review* 4 (Jan. 1938): 21–28.

Gilbert, Sandra M., and Susan Gubar. *No Man's Land: The Place of the Woman Writer in the Twentieth Century: Vol. II, Sexchanges.* New Haven: Yale Univ. Press, 1989.

——. *No Man's Land: The Place of the Woman Writer in the Twentieth Century; Vol. I, The War of the Words.* New Haven: Yale Univ. Press, 1988.

Givner, Joan. *Katherine Anne Porter: A Life.* 1982. Rev. ed. Athens: Univ. of Georgia Press, 1991.

——. "Problems of Personal Identity in Texas' 'First Writer.'" In *Katherine Anne Porter and Texas: An Uneasy Relationship,* ed. Clinton Machann and William Bedford Clark, pp. 41–57. College Station: Texas A & M Univ. Press, 1990.

——. *The Self-Portrait of a Literary Biographer.* Athens: Univ. of Georgia Press, 1993.

——, ed. *Katherine Anne Porter: Conversations.* Jackson: Univ. Press of Mississippi, 1987.

Golsan, Richard J. "Introduction" in *Fascism, Aesthetics, and Culture,* ed. Richard J. Golsan, pp. ix–xviii. Hanover, N.H.: Univ. Press of New England, 1992.

Gould, Lewis L. *Progressives and Prohibitionists: Texas Democrats in the Wilson Era.* Austin: Univ. of Texas Press, 1973.

Goyen, William. "At Lady A's." Unpublished manuscript, Harry Ransom Humanities Research Center, University of Texas.

Graham, Don. "A Southern Writer in Texas: Porter and the Texas Literary Tradition." In *Katherine Anne Porter and Texas: An Uneasy Relationship,* ed. Clinton Machann and William Bedford Clark, pp. 58–71. College Station: Texas A & M Univ. Press, 1990.

Graves, John. "The Old Guard: Dobie, Webb, and Bedichek." In *The Texas Literary Tradition: Fiction, Folklore, History,* ed. Don Graham, James W. Lee, and William T. Pilkingham, pp. 16–25. Austin: College of Liberal Arts, Univ. of Texas, and the Texas State Historical Association, 1983.

——. "The Southwest as the Cradle of the Writer." In *The American Southwest: Cradle of Literary Art,* ed. Robert W. Walts. San Marcos: Southwest Texas State Univ., 1981.

Gray, Richard. *The Literature of Memory: Modern Writers of the American South.* London: Edward Arnold, 1977.

——. *Writing the South: Ideas of an American Region.* Cambridge: Cambridge Univ. Press, 1986.

Green, James Robert. *Grass-Roots Socialism: Radical Movements in the Southwest, 1895–1943.* Baton Rouge: Louisiana State Univ. Press, 1978.

Gretlund, Jan Nordby. "'The Man in the Tree': Katherine Anne Porter's Unfinished Lynching Story." *Southern Quarterly* 31 (1993): 7–16.

Groff, Edward. "'Noon Wine': A Texas Tragedy." *Descant* 22 (1977): 39–47.

Gubar, Susan. "'This Is My Rifle, This Is My Gun': World War II and the Blitz on Women." In *Behind the Lines: Gender and the Two World Wars,* ed. Margaret Randolph Higonnet et al., pp. 227–59. New Haven: Yale Univ. Press, 1987.

Hall, Linda B. *Alvaro Obregón: Power and Revolution in Mexico, 1911–1920.* College Station: Texas A & M Univ. Press, 1981.

Hammer, Langdon. *Hart Crane and Allen Tate: Janus-Faced Modernism.* Princeton: Princeton Univ. Press, 1993.

Hardy, John Edward. *Katherine Anne Porter.* New York: Ungar, 1973.

Harris, Richard L. *Marxism, Socialism, and Democracy in Latin America.* Boulder, Colo.: Westview Press, 1992.

Hassan, Ihab. *Selves at Risk: Patterns of Quest in Contemporary American Letters.* Madison: Univ. of Wisconsin Press, 1990.

Heilman, Robert. "*Ship of Fools:* Notes on Style." *Four Quarters,* 1962. Reprinted in *Katherine Anne Porter: A Critical Symposium,* ed. Lodwick Hartley and George Core, pp. 197–210. Athens: Univ. of Georgia Press, 1969.

Helms, Cynthia Newman, ed. *Diego Rivera: A Retrospective.* Detroit: Founders Society, Detroit Institute of the Arts, in association with W. W. Norton, 1986.

Hendrick, George. *Katherine Anne Porter.* 1965. Rev. ed., with Willene Hendrick. Boston: Twayne, 1988.

Herbst, Josephine. "Miss Porter and Miss Stein." *Partisan Review* 15 (1948): 568–72.

Hill, Larry D. "Texas Progressivism: A Search for Definition." In *Texas through Time: Evolving Interpretations,* ed. Walter L. Buenger and Robert A. Calvert. pp. 229–50. College Station: Texas A & M Univ. Press, 1991.

Hilt, Kathryn, and Ruth M. Alvarez. *Katherine Anne Porter: An Annotated Bibliography.* New York: Garland Publishing, 1990.

Hobson, Fred. *Tell About the South: The Southern Rage to Explain.* Baton Rouge: Louisiana State Univ. Press, 1983.

Holman, C. Hugh. "Introduction" in *Southern Fiction Today: Renascence and Beyond,* ed. George Core. Athens: University of Georgia Press, 1969.

Hooks, Margaret. *Tina Modotti: Photographer and Revolutionary.* London: Pandora, 1993.

Horton, Philip. *Hart Crane: The Life of an American Poet.* New York: W. W. Norton, 1937.

Howarth, William. "Writing Upside Down: Voice and Place in Southern Autobiography." In *Located Lives: Place and Idea in Southern Autobiography,* ed. J. Bill Berry, pp. 13–19. Athens: Univ. of Georgia Press, 1990.

Howell, Elmo. "Katherine Anne Porter and the Southern Myth: A Note on 'Noon Wine.'" *Louisiana Studies* 11 (1972): 252–59.

Humphries, Jefferson. *Southern Literature and Literary Theory.* Athens: Univ. of Georgia Press, 1990.

Jameson, Fredric. *Fables of Aggression: Wyndham Lewis, the Modernist as Fascist.* Berkeley: Univ. of California Press, 1979.

Johnson, James William. "Another Look at Katherine Anne Porter." *Virginia Quarterly Review* 36 (1960): 598–613.

Jones, Anne Goodwyn. *Tomorrow Is Another Day: The Woman Writer in the South, 1859–1936*. Baton Rouge: Louisiana State Univ. Press, 1981.

Jones, Suzanne W. "Reading the Endings in Katherine Anne Porter's 'Old Mortality.'" *Southern Quarterly* 31 (1993): 29–44.

Joseph, G. M. *Revolution from Without: Yucatán, Mexico, and the United States, 1880–1924*. Cambridge: Cambridge Univ. Press, 1982.

"Joseph Retinger, Polish Diplomat." *New York Times,* June 24, 1960.

Kennedy, David M. *Over Here: The First World War and American Society*. New York: Oxford Univ. Press, 1980.

King, Richard H. *A Southern Renaissance: The Cultural Awakening of the American South, 1930–1955*. New York: Oxford Univ. Press, 1980.

Knowles, Sebastian D. G. *A Purgatorial Flame: Seven British Writers in the Second World War*. Philadelphia: Univ. of Pennsylvania Press, 1990.

Langer, Elinor. *Josephine Herbst*. Boston: Little, Brown, 1984.

Leiter, Louis. "The Expense of Spirit in a Waste of Shame: Motif, Montage, and Structure in *Noon Wine*." In *Seven Contemporary Short Novels,* ed. Charles Clerc and Louis Leiter, pp. 185–219. Glenview, Ill: Scott, Foresman, 1969.

Leonard, Thomas M. *Central America and the United States: The Search for Stability*. Athens: Univ. of Georgia Press, 1991.

Levenstein, Harvey A. *Labor Organizations in the United States and Mexico: A History of Their Relations*. Westport, Conn.: Greenwood Publishing, 1971.

Levy, Helen Fiddyment. *Fiction of the Home Place: Jewett, Cather, Glasgow, Porter, Welty, and Naylor*. Jackson: Univ. Press of Mississippi, 1992.

Liberman, Myron M. *Katherine Anne Porter's Fiction*. Detroit: Wayne State Univ. Press, 1971.

Lopez, Hank. "A Country and Some People I Love" [interview with Porter]. *Harper's,* September 1965. Reprinted in *Katherine Anne Porter: Conversations,* ed. Joan Givner, pp. 120–34. Jackson: Univ. Press of Mississippi, 1987.

MacKinnon, Janice R., and Stephen R. MacKinnon. *Agnes Smedley: The Life and Times of an American Radical*. Berkeley: Univ. of California Press, 1988.

Makowsky, Veronica A. *Caroline Gordon: A Biography*. New York: Oxford Univ. Press, 1989.

Male, Roy R. "The Short Story of the Mysterious Stranger in American Fiction." *Criticism* 3 (1961): 281–94.

Manning, Carol S. "Introduction: On Defining Themes and (Mis)Placing Women Writers." In *The Female Tradition in Southern Literature,* ed. Carol S. Manning, pp. 1–12. Urbana: Univ. of Illinois Press, 1993.

Martinez Penaloza, Porfirio. "Folk Art in Mexico." In *Images of Mexico: The Con-*

tribution of Mexico to 20th Century Art, ed. Erika Billeter, pp. 422–30. Dallas: Dallas Museum of Art, 1987.

McAlmon, Robert. *Being Geniuses Together, 1920–1930.* Revised and with supplementary chapters by Kay Boyle. London: Michael Joseph, 1970.

Morganthau, Henry, Jr. *Germany Is Our Problem.* New York: Harper, 1945.

Murphy, James F. *The Proletarian Moment: The Controversy over Leftism in Literature.* Urbana: Univ. of Illinois Press, 1991.

Murray, Robert K. *Red Scare: A Study in National Hysteria, 1919–1920.* Minneapolis: Univ. of Minnesota Press, 1955.

Nance, William. *Katherine Anne Porter and the Art of Rejection.* Chapel Hill: Univ. of North Carolina Press, 1963.

Newhall, Nancy, ed. *The Daybooks of Edward Weston; Volume I, Mexico.* New York: Aperture, 1961.

Nielsen, Aldon Lynn. *Reading Race: White American Poets and the Racial Discourse in the Twentieth Century.* Athens: Univ. of Georgia Press, 1988.

O'Connor, Flannery. *Mystery and Manners: Original Prose.* Edited by Sally Fitzgerald and Robert Fitzgerald. New York: Farrar, Straus and Giroux, 1969.

Olsen, Tillie. *Silences.* New York: Dell, 1965.

Orozco, José Clemente. *An Autobiography.* Translated by Robert C. Stephenson. Austin: Univ. of Texas Press, 1962.

Pells, Richard H. *The Liberal Mind in a Conservative Age: American Intellectuals in the 1940s and 1950s.* 1985. 2d ed. Middletown, Conn.: Wesleyan Univ. Press, 1989.

———. *Radical Visions and American Dreams: Culture and Social Thought in the Depression Years.* 1973. 2d ed. Middletown, Conn.: Wesleyan Univ. Press, 1984.

Pomian, John, ed. *Joseph Retinger: Memoirs of an Eminence Grise.* Sussex, Eng.: [Sussex] Univ. Press, 1972.

Porter, Paul. "Remembering Aunt Katherine." In *Katherine Anne Porter and Texas: An Uneasy Relationship,* ed. Clinton Machann and William Bedford Clark, pp. 25–37. College Station: Texas A & M Univ. Press, 1990.

Prenshaw, Peggy Whitman. "Southern Ladies and the Southern Literary Renaissance." In *The Female Tradition in Southern Literature,* ed. Carol S. Manning, pp. 73–88. Urbana: Univ. of Illinois Press, 1993.

Reed, John Shelton. *Southerners: The Social Psychology of Sectionalism.* Chapel Hill: Univ. of North Carolina Press, 1983.

———. *Southern Folk, Plain and Fancy: Native White Social Types.* Athens: Univ. of Georgia Press, 1986.

Retinger, J. H. *The Rise of the Mexican Labor Movement.* Reprint of *Morones of Mexico,* 1926. Washington, D.C.: Documentary Publications, 1976.

Reyes Palma, Francisco. "Workshop of Popular Graphics during the Times of Cardenas." Translated by Kenneth W. Johnson. In *Images of Mexico: The Contribution of Mexico to 20th Century Art,* ed. Erika Billeter, pp. 111–14. Dallas: Dallas Museum of Art, 1987.

Rivera, Diego. *My Art, My Life.* New York: The Citadel Press, 1960.

Romines, Ann. *The Home Plot: Women, Writing and Domestic Ritual.* Amherst: Univ. of Massachusetts Press, 1992.

Ruíz, Ramón Eduardo. *The Great Rebellion: Mexico, 1905–1924.* New York: W. W. Norton, 1980.

Rupp, Leila J. *Mobilizing Women for War: German and American Propaganda, 1939–1945.* Princeton: Princeton Univ. Press, 1978.

Ruppersburg, Hugh. *Robert Penn Warren and the American Imagination.* Athens: Univ. of Georgia Press, 1990.

Schmidt, Henry C. "The American Intellectual Discovery of Mexico in the 1920's." *South Atlantic Quarterly* 77 (1978): 335–51.

——. *The Roots of Lo Mexicano: Self and Society in Mexican Thought, 1900–1934.* College Station: Texas A & M Univ. Press, 1978.

Scholes, Robert, and Robert Kellogg. *The Nature of Narrative.* New York: Oxford Univ. Press, 1966.

Schultz, Sigrid. *Germany Will Try It Again.* New York: Reynal and Hitchcock, 1944.

Schulz, Joan. "Orphaning as Resistance." In *The Female Tradition in Southern Literature,* ed. Carol S. Manning, pp. 89–109. Urbana: Univ. of Illinois Press, 1993.

Schwartz, Edward G. "The Fictions of Memory." *Southwest Review* 1960. Reprinted in *Katherine Anne Porter: A Critical Symposium,* ed. Lodwick Hartley and George Core, pp. 67–82. Athens: Univ. of Georgia Press, 1969.

Seidel, Kathryn Lee. *The Southern Belle in the American Novel.* Tampa: Univ. of South Florida Press, 1985.

Seideman, David. *The New Republic: A Voice of Modern Liberalism.* Westport, Conn.: Praeger, 1986.

Seton, Mary. *Sergei M. Eisenstein: A Biography.* London: Bodley Head, 1952.

Shi, David. *Matthew Josephson, Bourgeois Bohemian.* New Haven: Yale Univ. Press, 1981.

Shouse, Sarah N. "Introduction" in *Lower Piedmont Country: The Uplands of the Deep South,* by H. C. Nixon [1946]. Tuscaloosa: Univ. of Alabama Press, 1974.

Singal, Daniel Joseph. *The War Within: From Victorian to Modernist Thought in the South, 1919–1945.* Chapel Hill: Univ. of North Carolina Press, 1982.

Smaller, Sanford J. *Adrift among Geniuses: Robert McAlmon, Writer and Publisher of the Twenties.* University Park: Pennsylvania State Univ. Press, 1975.

Smith, J. Oates. "Porter's *Noon Wine:* A Stifled Tragedy." *Renascence* 17 (1965): 157–62.

Smith, Sidonie. *A Poetics of Women's Autobiography: Marginality and the Fictions of Self-Representation.* Bloomington: Indiana Univ. Press, 1987.

Sontag, Susan. "Fascinating Fascism." In *Women and the Cinema: A Critical Anthology,* ed. Karyn Kay and Gerald Peary, pp. 352–76. New York: E. P. Dutton, 1977.

Spratling, William. *File on Spratling: An Autobiography.* Boston: Little, Brown, 1967.

Squires, Radcliffe. *Allen Tate: A Literary Biography.* New York: Pegasus, 1971.

Stout, Janis P. "Estranging Texas: Porter and the Distance from Home." In *Katherine Anne Porter and Texas: An Uneasy Relationship,* ed. Clinton Machann and William Bedford Clark, pp. 86–101. College Station: Texas A & M Univ. Press, 1990.

——. *The Journey Narrative in American Literature: Patterns and Departures.* Westport, Conn.: Greenwood Press, 1983.

——. *Strategies of Reticence: Silence and Meaning in the Works of Jane Austen, Willa Cather, Katherine Anne Porter, and Joan Didion.* Charlottesville: Univ. Press of Virginia, 1991.

Tannenbaum, Frank. *Mexico: The Struggle for Peace and Bread.* New York: Alfred A. Knopf, 1950.

Tate, Allen. "A Southern Mode of the Imagination." In *Essays of Four Decades.* Chicago: Swallow Press, 1968.

Thomas, M. Wynn. "Strangers in a Strange Land: A Reading of 'Noon Wine.'" *American Literature* 47 (1975): 230–46.

Thompson, Barbara. "Katherine Anne Porter: An Interview." *Paris Review* 1963. Reprinted in *Katherine Anne Porter: Conversations,* ed. Joan Givner. Jackson: Univ. Press of Mississippi, 1987.

Titus, Mary. "The Agrarian Myth and Southern Womanhood." In *Redefining Autobiography in Twentieth-Century Women's Fiction: An Essay Collection,* ed. Janice Morgan and Colette T. Hall. New York: Garland Publishing, 1991.

"Twelve Southerners." *I'll Take My Stand: The South and the Agrarian Tradition.* New York: Harper, 1930.

Unrue, Darlene Harbour. "Katherine Anne Porter and Henry James: A Study in Influence." *Southern Quarterly* 31 (1993): 17–28.

——. "Katherine Anne Porter, Politics, and Another Reading of 'Theft.'" *Studies in Short Fiction* 30 (1993): 119–26.

——. *Truth and Vision in Katherine Anne Porter's Fiction.* Athens: Univ. of Georgia Press, 1985.

——. *Understanding Katherine Anne Porter.* Columbia: Univ. of South Carolina Press, 1988.

Vande Kieft, Ruth M. "The Love Ethos of Porter, Welty, and McCullers." In *The*

Female Tradition in Southern Literature, ed. Carol S. Manning, pp. 236–58. Urbana: Univ. of Illinois Press, 1993.

Waldron, Ann. *Close Connections: Caroline Gordon and the Southern Renaissance.* Knoxville: Univ. of Tennessee Press, 1989.

Walsh, Thomas F. "Deep Similarities in 'Noon Wine.'" *Mosaic* 9 (1975): 83–91.

——. "From Texas to Mexico to Texas." In *Katherine Anne Porter and Texas: An Uneasy Relationship,* ed. Clinton Machann and William Bedford Clark, pp. 72–85. College Station: Texas A & M Univ. Press, 1990.

——. *Katherine Anne Porter and Mexico: The Illusion of Eden.* Austin: Univ. of Texas Press, 1992.

——. "The 'Noon Wine' Devils." *Georgia Review* 22 (1968): 90–96.

Warren, Robert Penn. "Introduction" in Edward Schwartz, *Katherine Anne Porter: A Critical Bibliography.* New York: New York Public Library, 1953.

——. "Irony with a Center." In *Selected Essays.* New York: Random House, 1941.

——. *Segregation: The Inner Conflict in the South.* New York: Random House, 1956.

——. "Uncorrupted Consciousness: The Stories of Katherine Anne Porter." *Yale Review* 55 (1965): 280–90.

——. *Who Speaks for the Negro?* New York: Random House, 1965.

——, ed. *A Southern Harvest: Short Stories by Southern Writers.* Boston: Houghton Mifflin, 1937.

Watkins, Floyd C., and John T. Hiers, eds. *Robert Penn Warren Talking: Interviews, 1950–1978.* New York: Random House, 1980.

Welty, Eudora. "The Eye of the Story." *Yale Review* 55 (1966): 265–74.

Wescott, Glenway. *Continual Lessons: The Journals of Glenway Wescott, 1937–1955,* ed. Robert Phelps, with Jerry Rosco. New York: Farrar Straus Giroux, 1990.

——. *Fear and Trembling.* New York: Harper and Brothers, 1932.

——. *Images of Truth: Remembrances and Criticism.* New York: Harper and Row, 1962.

Windham, Donald, ed. *Tennessee Williams' Letters to Donald Windham, 1940–1965.* Verona, Italy: Sandy Campbell, 1976.

Winslow, Marcella Comès. *Brushes with the Literary: Letters of a Washington Artist, 1943–1959.* Baton Rouge: Louisiana State Univ. Press, 1993.

Wolfe, Bertram D. *The Fabulous Life of Diego Rivera.* New York: Stein and Day, 1963.

Womack, John, Jr. *Zapata and the Mexican Revolution.* New York: Alfred A. Knopf, 1969.

Wood, Sally, ed. *The Southern Mandarins: Letters of Caroline Gordon to Sally Wood, 1924–1937.* With a foreword by Andrew Lytle. Baton Rouge: Louisiana State Univ. Press, 1984.

Woodward, C. Vann. *The Burden of Southern History.* Baton Rouge: Louisiana State Univ. Press, 1960.

Young, Thomas Daniel, and John J. Hindle, eds. *The Republic of Letters in America: The Correspondence of John Peale Bishop and Allen Tate.* Lexington: Univ. Press of Kentucky, 1981.

Young, Thomas Daniel, and Elizabeth Sarcone, eds. *The Lytle-Tate Letters: The Correspondence of Andrew Lytle and Allen Tate.* Jackson: Univ. Press of Mississippi, 1987.

INDEX

Aaron, Daniel, 121, 142–43, 267
Abels, Cyrilly, 101, 142, 211, 214, 289
"Act of Faith," 154
Adam (character), 28–31
African Americans, 3, 125; in KAP's fiction, 134–36; and southern history, 118, 130–31
"After a Long Journey," 104, 111
Agrarianism, 124–25, 141
Agrarians, 115, 119, 121–23, 140–41; Porter and, 117, 119, 123, 129–30, 141, 147, 268; racial views of, 122–23, 130–32
Aguilera, Francisco, 19, 173, 185
Alexandrov, Grigori, 81, 87
Allen, Liza, *see* Dallett, Liza
Alvarado, Salvador, 47, 302 n. 33
American Academy of Arts and Sciences, Gold Medal, 226
American Civil Liberties Union, 145
American Federation of Labor, 46–47, 49
Ames, Elizabeth, 158, 163, 237
Amy (character), 193–94
Anderson, Jane, 27, 49
Anderson, Sherwood, 190
"Anniversary in a Country Cemetery," 104–5
Anorexia, 176
Anti-Semitism, 160, 179; of Ezra Pound, 162
Appearance, problem of, 175, 176, 193
Art, social value of, 247, 261
Asia, 108, 166
Atl, Dr. (Gerardo Murillo), 51, 76
"At Lady A's" (Goyen), 12, 183
Atlantic Monthly, 213
"Audubon's Happy Land," 128–29
Aunt Amy, *see* Amy (character)
Austen, Jane, 229, 242, 250
Autobiographical mode, 14, 19, 192, 216–17, 248–49, 258, 260–61; in "Reflections on Willa Cather," 243–45
"Autumn Journal" (MacNeice), 149–50

Baker, Carlos, 174
Barber, Samuel, 107
Barron, Rosa, 62
Barzun, Jacques, 190, 231
Basel, 98
Baton Rouge, 128
Bayley, Isabel, 278, 285, 289, 309 n. 87
Beach, Robert A., Jr., 212
Beach, Sylvia, xvi, 99, 197, 236, 238
Beauvoir, Simone de, 168, 270
Becher, Johannes R., 143
Belgium, 99
Berlin, 93–94, 97–98, 101, 111, 143; *see also* "Leaning Tower, The"
Bermuda, 12, 61, 63–64, 96
Best-Maugard, Adolfo, 10, 42, 46, 52, 55, 56, 71, 92, 95; aesthetic theo-

Best-Maugard, Adolfo (*cont.*) ries of, 52, 76; in "Hacienda," 81, 84; *Method for Creative Design, A,* 52, 56–57, 81; and *Qué Viva Mexico!* 81
Betancourt (character), 84
Bishop, John Peale, 27, 190
Black, Helen, 63
Blasco Ibáñez, V., 47, 59, 308 n. 72
Bloom, Harold, 242
Bode, Winston, 226–27, 279
Bogan, Louise, 201–2, 250
Bollingen Prize, 159, 162–63
Boyle, Kay, 207, 225, 234, 282
Brace, Donald, 205
Braggioni (character), 80
Breit, Harvey, 231
Brenner, Anita, 53, 56, 69
Brinnin, John Malcolm, 107, 237
Brooks, Cleanth, 39, 109, 129–30, 192; on KAP's feminism, 187; on southern literature, 117–18
Brooks, Roger L., 286
Brooks, Tinkum, 23, 278
Brown v. Board of Education, 138
Burke, Kenneth, 282

Capitalism, opposition to, 45, 48, 51, 58–59, 124, 129, 269
Capote, Truman, 179, 225
Caricature, 56, 85, 86, 112, 214–15
Caricatures: KAP's drawing of, 86; political, in Mexico, 80
Carillo Puerto, Felipe, 47, 85, 169, 173, 302 n. 33
Carranza, Venustiano, 47, 48
Cash, W. J., 131
Cather, Willa, 5–6, 14, 242–45, 264; "Escapism," 242
Catholic Church: and fascism, 103, 160–61; KAP's distrust of, 160; in Mexico, 59, 75, 82, 88, 272
Catholicism, 74–75, 161
Century, 54, 60
Cheney, Brainard, 214
Cheney, Frances, 39
Chicago, 8
Childhood, 22, 85, 282; *see also* Porter, Katherine Anne, childhood of
"Children of Xochitl, The," 311 n. 16
Children's stories, 10, 64, 71, 73
Christian Science Monitor, 71
"Christmas Story, A," 33
"Circus, The," 103, 135
Clark, Eleanor, 139, 237, 275
Class conflict, theme of, 61, 74, 83–84, 269
Collected Essays and Occasional Writings, 58, 199, 211–12, 224, 227–28, 230, 232
Collected Stories, 13
Communism, 40, 103, 145–46, 151, 156, 162; in Mexico, 40; opposition to, 39, 103, 159; *see also* Porter, communist associates of; Communist party membership, and, communist sympathies of; Radicalism; Socialism
Communist party, 40, 62, 102, 156, 299 n. 4; and art, 39, 57–58, 143, 162, 164, 246, 267; and freedom of expression, 57, 139, 161; in Germany, 94, 102, 143, 148, 246; in Mexico, 40, 48, 53, 300 n. 6
Confessions of St. Augustine, The, 222, 271–72
Congress for Cultural Freedom, 164
"Conquistadora, La," 60
Core, George, 192, 212
Corpus Christi, Tex., 8

"Corridos," 56–57, 86
Coughlin, Father Charles E., 160
Cousin Eva, *see* Eva (character)
Covarrubias, Miguel, 10, 86, 112, 173
Cowley, Malcolm, 3, 10, 31, 124, 178, 189, 228, 279; *Exile's Return,* 77
Cowley, Peggy, 10, 66, 79, 99, 169, 178
"Cracked Looking Glass, The," 186, 282
Crane, Hart, 11, 65–66, 72, 97–98, 101, 162, 179
Crawford, Becky, 79, 172
Crawford, Kitty Barry, 8–9, 26–27, 51
CROM, 48, 67
Crosby, Caresse, 99
Curran, Father Edward L., 160

Dallas Morning News, 32, 286
Dallett, Liza, 54, 176, 178
Davidson, Donald, 115, 130
Day, Dorothy, 48, 160–61, 169, 282
Death, in Mexican culture, 80, 87, 90, 314 n. 34
Debs, Eugene V., 44–45, 49, 153
de la Selva, Salomón, 173
Democratic party, 15, 43, 165
DeMouy, Jane Krause, 279, 284
Denver, 9, 27, 32
Depression, Great, 109, 121, 149
Dewey, Thomas, 159
Díaz, Bishop Pascual, 69
Dicey (character), 135–36
Dillard, Richard, 140
Dobie, J. Frank, 206, 226–27
Dodd, William E., Jr., 149, 153
Doherty, Mary Louis, 40, 49, 51, 54, 55–56, 65, 94, 210; and "Flowering Judas," 80
Doña Julia (character), 84
Don Genaro (character), 84
"Dove of Chapacalco, The," 272
"Downward Path to Wisdom, The," 256, 348 n. 34
Doylestown, Pa., 104–6, 204, 258
Durant, Kenneth, 44, 63, 142, 199, 267

Eisenstein, Sergei, 67, 81–84, 87
Elder, Donald, 180, 289
Elías Calles, Plutarco, 48, 69
Eliot, T. S., 127, 179, 238–40, 262–64
Eliza (character), 191–92
Enciso, Jorge, 52
Erskine, Albert, 5, 12, 121, 126, 127–28, 139, 152
Espionage Act of 1917, 30, 45
Esquire, 166
Essays (Montaigne), 220
Eugenio (character), 80
Europe: KAP's interest in, 9, 71, 78, 94–95, 107, 210; and KAP's perspective, 93, 109
Eva (character), 175, 193–94
Evans, Ernestine, 41, 71, 169
"Everybody Is a Real One," 232
Everyland, 10, 71
Exhibition of Mexican Popular Art, 51–53, 76; see also *Outline of Mexican Arts and Crafts*
Exile's Return (Cowley), 77
Exoticism, 87–88
Expatriates, 77–78
"Eye of Memory, The" (film), 287

Family, 1–5; finances of, 1–2, 5; KAP's attitudes toward, 20, 22–23, 36, 116; and KAP's personal identity, 18, 24, 40; KAP's relations with, 21–22, 34, 36, 103, 109, 127, 149, 171
Farrell, James, 157; *Bernard Clare,* 231

Fascism, 39, 102–3, 216; in the U.S., 106, 151, 156–57, 159; *see also* Porter, antifascism of
Father, importance of, 20, 216; *see also* Porter, Harrison Boone
FBI, 157–58, 268, 288
Feely, Sister Kathleen, 271
Feminine Mystique, The (Friedan), 168
Feminism, 168–69; *see also* Porter, feminism, dislike of, *and* Porter, feminism of
Feminist criticism, 197, 251
Feminist themes, 73, 170, 174, 187, 191, 195
Festival of the Dead, 87
"Fiesta of Guadalupe, The," 6, 47, 58, 60, 61, 88
"Fig Tree, The," 134, 218, 252
Film industry, 8–10, 186, 205
Flanders, Jane, 174
Flanner, Janet, 149
Fletcher, John Gould, 122, 123
"Flowering Judas," 37, 57, 64, 70, 79–81, 85, 136, 256; autobiographical references in, 48, 80
Flowering Judas and Other Stories, 64, 119–20, 282
Ford, Ford Madox, 11, 99, 100, 120, 282; *Good Soldier, The,* 229
Forster, E. M., 179, 226, 241; *Passage to India, A,* 229, 241; *Two Cheers for Democracy,* 241
Fort Worth Star Telegram, 32
France, 99, 105, 107, 152; *see also* Paris
Freedom of expression, 39, 57, 147, 157, 159, 161, 164, 240, 246
French Song Book, 101, 283
Freud, Sigmund, 222–24, 270
Freudian criticism, 245
Friedan, Betty, 168, 269
Frost, Robert, 163, 226
Fugitives, 115
Fulbright appointment, 99

Gamio, Manuel, 10, 47, 54
Garrett, George, 140
Gender, 235; in discourse, 190; *see also* Porter, femininity of, gender issues, awareness of by, *and* gender conflicts of; Womanhood, ideals of
Gender stereotypes, 184, 191
Genre, 16, 70, 197; and gender, 197–98; KAP and the essay, 70, 198, 224; KAP and the novel, 16, 197, 199, 202, 215; KAP and the novella, 11, 197, 199, 248; KAP and poetry, 198–99; KAP and the short story, 198, 202, 244, 248
Germans, KAP's dislike of, 97–99, 155, 223
Germany, 93, 95; KAP's dislike of, 93, 95, 98, 111, 147–48, 152, 155; wartime atrocities of, 137, 212–13, 298 n. 35; *see also* Berlin
Germany Is Our Problem (Morgenthau), 155
Germany Will Try It Again (Schultz), 155
"Gertrude Stein: A Self Portrait," 232
Gide, André, 146–47
Gilbert, Sandra M., and Susan Gubar, 235, 262–63
Givens (character), 74
Givner, Joan, 13, 173, 185, 202, 235, 277; acquaintance with KAP, 286–87; biography by, 282, 284–89; emphasis on KAP's father by, 5, 16; on Herbst issue, 156–58; KAP's selection of, 286
Glasgow, Ellen, 242
Goering, Hermann, 102, 284, 293 n. 2

Gold, Michael, 41, 63, 102, 140, 143, 189
Goldman, Emma, 99
Gompers, Samuel, 49, 302 n. 29
Gordon, Caroline, 26, 41, 96–97, 126, 131, 161, 169, 201, 234, 268, 278, 282; and the Agrarians, 115, 120–21; KAP's quarrel with, 331 n. 60; on KAP's flirtatiousness, 177; and politics, 142, 145; as writer, 189, 242
Goyen, William, 12, 22, 185, 188, 280, 287; KAP's love affair with, 177–78, 179–83
Graham, Billy, 275
Grandmother (character), 134–35, 191
Grass, Günter, *The Tin Drum,* 225
"Grave, The," 6, 103, 256, 282
Graves, Robert, *Goodbye to All That,* 241
Great-Aunt Eliza, *see* Eliza (character)
Greenwich Village, 9, 11, 46, 178, 189, 300 n. 12
Guerrero, Xavier, 52–53, 69, 75, 90, 173
Guggenheim Fellowship, 7, 12, 67, 95, 97; William Goyen's, 177, 181
"Guild Spirit in Mexican Art, The," 57, 77

Haberman, Robert, 46–48, 49, 50, 54
Haberman, Thorberg, 46–48, 49
"Hacienda," 67, 70, 73, 81–85, 86, 103, 112, 113, 228, 249, 282; factual basis of, 81–84; theme of political disillusionment in, 69, 74, 81–85, 267
Hacienda, 83, 101
Hacienda Tetlapayec, 67, 81
Hanna, Paul, 49
Harcourt Brace, 64, 200, 202–3
Hardy, John Edward, 283–84
Hardy, Thomas, 151, 238–40, 241, 276; *Jude the Obscure,* 239
Harper's, 200, 232, 236
Harrison, Barbara, *see* Wescott, Barbara Harrison
Harrison of Paris, 83, 100
Hatch, Mr. (character), 254–56
"He," 61, 63, 64, 252, 256, 282; southern setting of, 26, 61, 90, 118, 121
Hearst, William Randolph, 69
Heilman, Robert, 214, 251
Heintze, Ann Holloway (niece), 23, 36, 109, 175, 189–90
Helton, Mr. (character), 254–55
Hemingway, Ernest, xvi, 225, 263; "Big Two-Hearted River," 229; *Sun Also Rises, The,* 262
Hendrick, George, 251, 283, 294 n. 4
Heraldo de México, El, 46–47
Herbst, Josephine, 35, 119, 137, 156; feminism of, 188–89; investigation of, by FBI, 158–59, 268, 288; KAP's friendship with, 3, 156, 238, 268; on KAP's writing, 214, 237–38, 250; radicalism of, 39, 41, 143–47, 162; as writer, 10, 201, 242
Herrmann, John, 86, 189; and Communist party, 15, 36, 41, 144; as writer, 10, 190, 253
Hidalgo, Luis, 86, 173
High Wind in Jamaica, A (Hughes), 229
Hill, Benjamín, 47
Hillendahl, Mary Alice Porter (sister), 6, 21, 23
"Hind Tit, The" (Lytle), 123–24
Hinojosa, Alvaro, 173
Hiss, Alger, 144

Hitler, Adolf, 93, 98, 105, 112–13, 148, 284
"Holiday," 90, 121, 218
Holloway, Gay Porter (sister), 6, 8, 21, 34, 70, 128, 160, 230; KAP's devotion to, 23–24, 36, 279; racial views of, 132–33
Holloway, Mary Alice (niece), 9, 27, 33–34, 160
Homosexuality: KAP's aversion to, 66, 101–2, 178–82, 235; and modernism, 178–79; *see also* Porter, homosexual friends of
Houghton Mifflin, 211–12
House of Breath (Goyen), 177, 181
"House of My Own, A," 109
House Un-American Activities Committee, 157–58, 159
Housework, problem of, 188–89
Houston, Tex., 104, 128
Houston Chronicle, 32
Howard Payne University, 286
Hughes, Richard: *High Wind in Jamaica,* 229
Humphrey, Hubert, 165, 266
Humphrey, William, 36, 212

I'll Take My Stand, 120–25, 130
Indian Creek, Tex., 3, 22, 104
Indians, 230; KAP's prejudice against, 134, 138, 325 n. 58; of Mexico, 50, 58–60, 72, 74–75, 82, 84, 228
Influenza, Spanish, of 1918, 27, 29, 297 nn. 25 and 27; *see also* Porter, influenza of
Institute of Texas Letters, 206
Invitation to Learning, 190
Irony, in modernism, 262; *see also* Style, KAP's *and* irony in
Isabel (character), 54
Italian-Americans, 329 n. 41
Italy, 107
Itching Parrot, The, 85, 96
"It Is Hard to Stand in the Middle," 162–63

"Jacqueline Kennedy," 165
James, Henry, 72, 221, 226, 282
Jeffers, Robinson, 225
"Jilting of Granny Weatherall, The," 64, 118, 251–52, 256
Jimbilly (character), 135
Johns, Erna Schlemmer, 5, 19, 95, 210, 286–87
Johnson, Lyndon, 165
Johnson, Rhea, 212
Jones, Anne Goodwyn, 170
Josephson, Matthew, 64, 173, 188
Journalism, by KAP, 59, 72; *see also* Porter, newspaper work of
"Journey, The," 103, 134–35
Journey motif, 192, 194, 215–18
Joyce, James, 72, 234, 236, 239, 245, 263; *Dubliners,* 229; *Portrait of the Artist as a Young Man,* 229

Kennedy, John F., 165
Kennerly (character), 81–84
King, Martin Luther, Jr., 133–34
Kirchwey, Freda, 40, 63, 93, 151
Klein, Herbert, 143
Knopf, Alfred A., 211
Koontz, John Henry, 7–9, 42, 121
Kyle, Tex., 4–5, 42

Labor unrest, 42, 74, 132; *see also* Porter, pro-labor views of
Lady Chatterley's Lover (Lawrence), 190, 231
Land redistribution, 57, 85, 269, 309 n. 91

Langer, Elinor, 39–40, 156, 288
language: as ethical measure, 31; and identity, 97–98; and modernism, 262–63; obscene, 231–32; patriotic, 31, 154–55; sexist, 174–75, 188
Language as Gesture (Blackmur), 221
Lanier, Lyle H., 122–23
"Last Leaf, The," 134–35
Laura (character), 19, 80, 83–84
Lawrence, D. H., 87, 89, 190, 229–32
Lawrence, Seymour, 12, 202, 206–12, 285
League of American Writers, 142, 267
"Leaning Tower, The," 11, 110–14, 196, 202, 261; factual basis of, 111–13
Leaning Tower and Other Stories, The, 205
"Legend and Memory," 249
Letter writing, *see* Porter, correspondence of
Lewis, Wyndham, 335 n. 35
Liberman, M. M., 251
Liberty Bonds, 30
Linkskurve, 143–44
Literary reputation: of KAP, 78, 206, 248–49, 249–51, 256, 264, 281–83; of women writers, 250
Little, Brown, 202, 208, 211
Liveright, Horace, 200
Locher, David, 276
Louisiana, 42, 106, 116, 128; KAP's reported childhood in, 26, 117; KAP's residence in, 8, 25
"Love and Hate," 172
Lowell, Robert, 126, 278
Löwenthal, Herr (character), 214
Loyalty oath, 159
Lynes, George Platt, 100–101, 148, 171, 203–4
Lynes, Russell, 100, 201, 236
Lytle, Andrew, 115, 120–21, 126, 145, 268, 282; "Hind Tit, The," 123–25

Macauley, 64
Machete, El, 53, 306 n. 53
MacLeish, Archibald, 145, 231
MacNeice, Louis: "Autumn Journal," 149–50
Mademoiselle, 111, 142, 168, 172, 243
Madrid, 97, 99
Magazine of Mexico, 47–48, 59, 71, 302 n. 32
"Magic," 61, 64, 269
Mailer, Norman, 226
Male dominance, 188, 190
"Man in the Tree, The," 136–39, 199, 258
Mansfield, Katherine, 190–91, 282
"Many Redeemers," 20, 68, 249
Marginalia, 220–21, 224
Maria (character), 136
"María Concepción," 10, 54, 60, 64, 70, 72–75, 79, 85, 282
María Concepción (character), 73–75
María Rosa (character), 73–75
Marín, Guadalupe, 54, 55, 86
Marriage, 172, 187
"Marriage Is Belonging," 172–73
"Martyr, The," 54, 64, 70, 75, 86
Mather, Cotton, projected book on, 12, 61, 63, 78, 96, 103–4, 199, 246
Maugham, Somerset, 179, 261
McAlmon, Robert, 64, 149, 282
McCarthy, Joseph, 110, 157
McCarthy, Mary, 225
McCarthyism, 158–59
McCullers, Carson, 225
Mella, Julio Antonio, 55–56
Memory, as source of fiction, 85, 89, 248–49, 260; *see also* Autobiographical mode

Méndez, Sidronio, 51, 80, 304 n. 44
Method for Creative Design, A (Best-Maugard), 52, 56–57, 81
Metro-Goldwyn-Mayer, 205
Mexican Femenist [*sic*] Council, 169
Mexican novel, projected, 78–79, 96, 105, 199–200
Mexican Revolution, 42, 46, 66–69, 269; KAP's disappointment in, 58, 60, 66–67, 68–69, 74, 82–85, 111
"Mexican Trinity, The," 58, 60
Mexico: art in, 52–53, 72, 75–76, 86, 90–91; effects on Porter's writing of, 61, 64, 68, 72, 78, 80, 85–87, 89–90, 93; father's venture in, 3–4; KAP's interest in, 43, 78, 119; KAP's presence in, 37, 46–47, 50–51, 54, 64–67, 70, 71–72, 79, 92; KAP's writings about, 67, 70, 91, 230; oil industry in, 59, 88, 272
"Midway of This Mortal Life," 249
Miranda (character), 27–31, 32, 154, 191–95; autobiographical nature of, 6, 19–21, 27–29, 68; name, 19, 185
Miranda stories, 19, 136, 216; *see also specific titles*
Modernism, 168, 179, 262–64; and gender, 235, 263
Modernist, KAP as, 253, 262–64, 277
Modern Poetry and the Tradition (Brooks), 221
Modotti, Tina, 55–56, 61, 69, 87, 306 n. 61
Monk, Liza, *see* Dallett, Liza
Montagu, Mary Wortley, Lady, 190
Morones, Luis, 10, 47, 48–50, 173, 303 n. 35, 303 n. 37; in "Flowering Judas," 80
"Most Lively Genius, A," 228
Mundt-Nixon Bill of 1948, 159
Mural movement, in Mexico, 53, 55, 69, 75, 86
Murry, John Middleton, 190
My Chinese Marriage, 10

Nacho, Tata (Ignacio Fernández Esperón), 42
Nance, William, 210, 270
Nannie (character), 134–35, 191
Nation, 151
National Book Award, 13
National Institute of Arts and Letters, Gold Medal, 133
National Socialist (Nazi) Party, 93–94, 98, 105, 147–48, 267
"Necessary Enemy, The," 172
"Negro Question, The" (notes), 137–39
Neutrality, U.S., 150
"Never-ending wrong," 232
"Never-Ending Wrong, The," 137
Never-Ending Wrong, The, 62, 145, 207, 279, 281
New Criticism, 129–30, 192, 241, 251
New Era, 43
"New Man and the New Order, The," 48
New Masses, 41, 58, 63, 121, 140, 143–44, 146
New Orleans, 26, 61, 119, 127, 284
New Republic, 143, 150, 188–89
New South, 122, 124
Newsweek, 168
New York, 9, 19, 61, 96, 126; KAP's associates in, 33, 41, 46, 71, 120, 169
New York Call, 48, 49
New York Herald Tribune, 200, 227, 232

New York Times Book Review, 177, 242
Nin, Anaïs, 225
Niven, William, 51, 52, 75
Nixon, Herman Clarence, 124
Nixon, Richard, 159, 165
Nobel Prize, 133–34
"Noon Wine," 6, 11, 26, 90, 114, 199, 216, 254–56; critical interpretations of, 256; writing of, 79, 103, 104–6, 258–59
" 'Noon Wine': The Sources," 35, 89–90, 119, 260
"No Plot, My Dear, No Story," 197
No Safe Harbour, 203
"Notes on Writing," 260

Obregón, Alvaro, 41, 47, 48, 56, 67, 68, 69, 80, 309–10 n. 91
O'Connor, Flannery, 25, 167, 172, 206, 231, 242, 275
O'Higgins, Pablo, 55, 56, 98, 144
"Old Mortality," 11, 114, 136, 199, 216, 256; autobiographical nature of, 19, 21, 192; gender issues in, 16, 170, 174–75, 187, 191–95; setting of, 26; writing of, 79, 103, 105–6, 258
"Old Order, The," 103, 134, 191, 192, 197
Olivet College Writers' Conference, 126
Olsen, Tillie, 187, 288–89
"On a Criticism of Thomas Hardy," 127, 151, 238–40
"On Communism in Hollywood," 157–58, 162
Orozco, José Clemente, 52, 75
Orwell, George, 149, 163
Outline of Mexican Arts and Crafts, 51–54, 72, 76–77
"Over Adornment," 227
Owsley, Frank Lawrence, 124, 130

Pacifism, 153; and Socialist party, 30, 150, 153; *see also* Porter, pacifism of
PAFL, 49
"Pale Horse, Pale Rider," 11, 27–33, 136, 154, 195, 210, 256, 297 n. 25; autobiographical elements in, 9, 27–29, 31–33, 127–28; gender issues in, 16; political background of, 29–30, 46, 151; writing of, 106, 127, 199, 258–59
Paris, 35, 99–100, 101, 102, 106–7
Paris Conference of Writers, 162, 164
Paris Review, 210
Partisan Review, 144, 145–46, 163, 246
"Paternalism and the Mexican Problem," 61
Paul (character), 6
Pecile, Jordan, 174, 287
Pells, Richard H., 121
Perry, George Sessions, 26
Peyser, Ethel R., 71
Phillips, William, 146
Politics and art, 31, 54–55, 58, 74, 86, 113, 163–64, 246
Populist party, 42, 45, 301 n. 15
Porter, Asbury (grandfather), 3
Porter, Catherine (grandmother), 3–6, 7, 119, 131
Porter, Gay, *see* Holloway, Gay Porter
Porter, Harrison Boone (father), 1–5, 12, 20, 216, 339 n. 76; and KAP's insecurities, 5, 16, 23, 170–71, 179, 184; library of, 2–3; in Mexico, 3–4, 70; political views

Porter, Harrison Boone (father) (*cont.*) of, 43–44, 301 n. 17; rationalism of, 4, 20–21, 34, 272; reading of, 34, 119; and southern history, 44, 118–19

Porter, Harrison Paul (brother), 21, 169

Porter, Katherine Anne: acquaintances of, 10–11, 41, 71–72; anticlericalism of, 47, 271–72; antifascism of, 15, 102, 110, 147, 151–52, 159–61; anti-Semitism of, 162, 214, 222; appearance a fixation of, 16, 167–68; appearance and beauty of, 7, 16, 171–72; artistic vocation of, 9, 19–20, 24, 33, 36–37, 69, 99; Catholicism, conversion to, 36, 272, 285; Catholicism of, 141, 271–72, 285; childhood of, 3–5, 22–24, 33, 117, 164, 170–71, 174; childhood, acquaintance with Mexico during, 70 (*see also* Louisiana, KAP's reported childhood in); childlessness of, 8, 33, 97, 185; class consciousness of, 4, 5–7, 15–16, 294 n. 13; communist associates of, 15, 38, 41, 55, 62–63, 94, 158; Communist party membership, and, 36, 39, 58, 139, 143–44, 299 n. 4; communist sympathies of, 15, 38–39, 41, 58, 102–3, 145–47; communist sympathies, waning of, 145–47, 156–57, 159, 164, 268; correspondence of, 11, 100–101, 206, 225, 257; death, acceptance of by, 280; death, fixation on by, 80, 87, 89; depression of, 12, 64–65, 71, 79, 97, 112, 184–86, 205, 257–58; domesticity of, 100, 127, 188, 201; drinking of, 100, 157, 186, 336–37 n. 52; education of, 2, 7, 13–14; emotional instability of, 12–13, 79, 93, 97–98, 100–101, 181–82, 186, 204; family origins of, 2–3, 5, 15, 21, 63–64, 117, 119; femininity of, 36, 167–68, 174, 184; feminism, dislike of by, 168–69, 174, 269; feminism of, 40, 168–69, 187, 190, 269–70 (*see also* Feminist themes); finances of, 1, 23, 36, 65, 71, 79, 109, 168, 186, 204, 210–11, 257 (*see also* Family, finances of); gender conflicts of, 174, 176–77, 201, 263; gender issues, awareness of by, 16, 77, 168–70, 175–76, 187, 190, 269–70; guardianship of, 220, 279; health of, 8–9, 12, 32, 61, 64, 79, 204, 224 (*see also* Influenza; Tuberculosis); historical sense of, 219, 289; homelessness, sense of by, 104–5, 108–9, 139, 211; home wanted by, 92, 106, 108–9, 203, 210–11; homosexual friends of, 101, 178–79 (*see also* Homosexuality); hysterectomy of, 185; inconsistency of, 2, 7, 17, 202, 266, 269–70; inconsistency of, regarding gender, 16, 168–70, 186–91, 269–70; inconsistency of, in politics, 15, 38, 102, 161, 164–65, 266, 269; inconsistency of, regarding regional origins, 15, 25–26, 34–36; inconsistency of, in religion, 4, 273, 276; influenza of, 9, 27, 29, 32–33, 80, 160; as intellectual, 2, 265–66, 281; internationalism of, 71, 93, 100, 107–8, 109, 114, 166; joie de vivre of, 12, 278, 287–88; liberalism of, 15, 143, 158, 161, 164, 240, 267, 296 n. 31; library of, 2, 219–21;

literary principles of, 229, 238, 246–47; love affairs of, 12, 16, 37, 62, 97, 141, 172–73, 176–84, 209; marriages of, 7–8, 96, 97, 105, 126, 128, 172–73, 285; misrepresentations by, 2–3, 117, 120, 145, 192, 205, 284–85, 289, 294 n. 4, 299 n. 4; name of, 1, 7; newspaper work of, 9, 26–27, 31–32, 51; old age of, 186, 219–20, 279–81, 287–88; pacifism of, 27, 110, 151–53, 161, 165; papers of, 11; patriotism of, 114, 154–55, 268; as performer, 7–8, 25, 51; pessimism of, 273, 277–78; political views of, 15, 38–39, 41, 50, 158, 161, 266–68 (*see also specific political movements*); prejudices of, 98–99, 102, 107, 108, 110, 132, 134, 138, 178–79; productivity of, 10–13, 65, 72, 78–79, 97, 200, 264 (*see also* Writer's block); pro-labor views of, 6–7, 15, 164, 269; publishers' advances to, 36, 65, 79, 105, 199, 200, 203, 207–8, 211; racial views of, 107, 110, 123, 125, 132–34, 136–39, 165, 269; rationalism of, 34, 271, 276–77, 298 n. 45; reading of, 8, 14, 219–21; residences of, 4–5, 7, 8, 10, 27, 51, 61, 108–9, 127, 202; restlessness of, 37, 62, 96, 107–10, 127; restlessness as an escape from Texas, 109, 164; retreats by, for writing, 101, 104, 203, 204, 206, 209–10; scholarly interest in, 283–85; sexuality of, 223; social consciousness of, 6, 63, 74, 78, 83; social consciousness in "Noon Wine," 250; southern origins of, 15, 117; speaking engagements of, 167, 209, 333 n. 2; suicidal impulses of, 12, 100; talkativeness of, 12; Texas origins of, 3–5, 9, 13, 18, 22, 25, 34–35, 46, 109, 117, 164; truthfulness, lack of, by, xvii, 266; tuberculosis of, 8–9, 26, 64, 79; wardrobe of, 1, 167, 171–72, 186, 235; working methods of, 256–59; writer's block of, 12, 66, 100, 105, 181, 201–2

Porter, Mary Alice (sister), *see* Hillendahl, Mary Alice

Porter, Mary Alice Jones (mother), 3–4, 80, 104–5

Porter, Paul (nephew), 23, 36, 101, 160, 165, 171, 186, 224, 236, 271, 278–79, 285, 287–88; as guardian, 212, 220

"Portrait: Old South," 118

Posey, Cora, 5

Pound, Ezra, 159, 162–63, 197

Pressly, Eugene, 12, 65, 85, 93, 96–100, 103–6, 126–27, 144, 148, 172, 177

Prettyman, E. Barrett, 173, 212, 279, 287

Primitivism, 76–77

Proletarian literature, 63, 140, 144, 162

"Promised Land," 128, 199–200, 258–59

Propaganda, KAP's writing of, 74

Protestant origins, 272

Pulitzer Prize, 13

Pulqueria frescos, 75–76, 86

Qué Viva México! 67, 81–82

Racial issues, 44, 45, 125, 130–32, 138; as theme, 134–37; *see also* Porter, racial views of; Agrarians, racial views of

Radicalism, 39, 40, 46, 62; *see also* Communism; Socialism

Rahv, Philip, 146
Ransom, Harry, 299 n. 47
Ransom, John Crowe, 115, 120, 226, 298 n. 44
Rebel, 43–44
Reconstruction, 44
"Reflections on Willa Cather," 233, 242–45
Regionalism, 25, 93, 116–17; KAP and, 85, 90, 109; *see also* South, the; Texas
Religious sense, 271–77; heterodoxy of, 273–75, 276–77
Republican party, 153, 159
Retinger, Joseph H., 47, 49, 50–52, 54, 94–95, 173, 200
Reviews: of *Ship of Fools,* 213–14, 261
Reviews, by KAP, 224, 227; *Captain's Death Bed, The* (Woolf), 241; *Character and Situation* (Sykes), 274–75; *Chinese Coat, The* (Lee), 227; *Ducdame* (Powys), 227; *Gringo in Mañanaland, A* (Foster), 227; *Idols Behind Altars* (Brenner), 53, 69; *Lady Chatterley's Lover* (Lawrence), 190, 230–31; *Making of Americans, The* (Stein), 232–33; *Mexico: A Study of Two Americas* (Chase), 228; *Mexico in Revolution* (Blasco Ibáñez), 47; *Plumed Serpent, The* (Lawrence), 87–88, 89, 188, 229–31; *Prince of Wales and Other Famous Americans, The* (Covarrubias), 86; *Short Novels of Colette,* 228; *Story of Woman, The* (George), 169; travel books, 227; *Two Cheers for Democracy* (Forster), 241; *Useful Knowledge* (Stein), 232, 234; *Willa Cather on Writing,* 242; *Wind That Swept Mexico, The* (Brenner), 56, 69
Ric and Rac (characters), 213–14, 215
Rivera, Diego, 10, 52, 54, 76–77, 86, 90, 165, 173; Communist party membership of, 53, 57–58; murals of, 55, 75
Robbins Wells, Amy Catherine, 190
Rocky Mountain News, 9, 27, 29, 227
Romantic love, myth of, 28, 184
Roosevelt, Franklin Delano, 153, 165
"Rope," 64, 86, 252
Roseliep, Fr. Raymond, 276, 335 n. 30
ROSTA, 63
Rote Fahne, Die, 143
Ruben (character), 54
Rukuyser, Muriel, 162
Russia, 41, 56, 98, 121, 143–44, 145–47; KAP's interest in, 15, 41, 58, 95, 112, 143–44

Sacco and Vanzetti, 37, 55, 62, 69, 145, 164, 207, 239
Salinger, J. D., 226
San Antonio, 7, 42, 70
Saturday Review of Literature, 144, 157
Schlemmer, Erna, *see* Johns, Erna Schlemmer
Schorer, Mark, 231
Schumann, Robert, 155
Second American Caravan, The, 64
Second Sex, The (Beauvoir), 168, 270
"Second Wind," 234
Sedition Act of 1918, 30
Seeger, Pete, 283
Seldes, Gilbert, 27, 49, 297 n. 22
Shannon, Charles, 173–74, 177, 205
Shapiro, Karl, 11, 163
Ship of Fools, 11, 16, 70, 107, 110, 111, 196–97, 212–18, 279; anti-Semitism in, 214; autobiographical elements in, 216–17; critical valuation of, 196–97, 214–15;

genesis of, 96, 199; income from, 1, 23, 140, 210–11, 279; reviews of, 213–14; writing of 12, 101, 200, 202–10, 257
Sibon, Marcelle, 170, 275
Signatures: Work in Progress, 259
Sinclair, Upton, 81–82
Siqueiros, David Alfaro, 52, 53, 305 n. 48
Slavery, apologists for, 130–31
Smedley, Agnes, 11
Socialism, 42–43, 45, 124, 266, 299–300 n. 4; *see also* Communism; Radicalism
Socialist party, 30, 46, 150; pacifism of, 30, 150–51, 298 n. 34; suppression of, 30; in Texas, 42–45
Socialist press, 42–43
Sontag, Susan, 94
Sophia Jane (character), *see* Grandmother (character)
"Source, The," 134
South, the 90, 107, 115–16, 120, 125; African Americans and history of, 118; and family, 35, 116; KAP's attitudes toward, 25, 35, 117, 119, 125–26, 139–40, 268; racial guilt of, 136–37; sense of defeat of, 118; as setting, 90, 120–21
Southern belle, 16, 140, 167–68, 170, 175, 193–94
Southern literature, 116, 117–18
Southern Review, 121, 127, 192, 268
Southern women writers, 170
Southern writer, KAP as, 26, 117–18
South Hill, 203
Soviet Union, *see* Russia
Spanish-American War, 153
Spanish Civil War, 149
Speech, as index to character, 31, 254–56
Spencer Carr, Virginia, 280
Spender, Stephen, 149, 181
Spiritualism and the occult, 34, 230
Spratling, William, 56
Stafford, Jean, 225
Stalin, Joseph, 145, 147, 152
St. Augustine, 222
"St. Augustine and the Bullfight," 14, 70, 71, 87–89, 195
Stein, Gertrude, 86, 178, 232–38; KAP's visit to, 234–35; Paul Porter's visit to, 236
Stevenson, Adlai, 165
Stock, Ernest, 61, 86, 172, 233, 284
"Striking the Lyric Note in Mexico," 74
Style, literary, 129–30, 216, 246, 251; compression in, 31, 85, 249, 251; as indicator of integrity, 253–54; irony in, 88–89, 251; KAP's, 13; visual clarity of, 69, 75, 85, 86–87; Welty on, 251–52; Wescott on, 252–53
Suffrage, *see* Woman suffrage
Sun Also Rises, The (Hemingway), 262
Survey Graphic, 54, 56, 77, 86, 200
Sutherland, Donald, 191, 234–37

Taggard, Genevieve, 11, 41, 198
TASS, 63, 143
Tate, Allen, 6, 41, 120, 126, 129–30, 142, 161, 163, 164, 174, 190, 234, 264, 276; Agrarians, and, 115, 122, 124, 268; on KAP's writing, 27–28, 119–20, 214, 250, 282; racial views of, 131–32; southern myth, and, 118, 120–21
Tate Wood, Nancy, 177–78, 293 n. 2
Tenney, Jack, Calif. State Senator, 158
Texas: artistic vocation and, 25, 35, 99, 164; KAP's attitudes toward, 9, 15, 22, 34–36, 104, 116–17, 126, 127, 240, 268; KAP's departure

Texas (*cont.*)
from, 9, 22, 36, 40, 96, 126; KAP's personal identity and, 18, 25–26, 35, 40, 99; literature of, 25; Mexican presence in, 70; politics in, 38, 42–46; regional divisions of, 25–26, 116–17, 119; as setting, 6, 26, 127–28, 260–61; southerners in, 45–46, 116; writers of, 297 n. 21; *see also* Porter, Texas origins of
Texas, University of, 35, 299 n. 47
"That Tree," 70
"Theft," 269, 282
Thomas, Dylan, 11
Thomas, Norman, 153
Thomas School, 244
Thompson Davis, Barbara, 210
Thompsons (characters), 6, 254–56, 261
Thunder over Mexico, 67
Tinkle, Lon, 226, 286
Toklas, Alice B., 234–35
Toledano, Vincente Lombardo, 52
Town and Country, 171
"Tradition and the Individual Talent" (Eliot), 179
Transition, 64, 188
Travel, value of, 108, 110
Travel books, 227–28
Travis Rifles, 44
Trotsky, Leon, 143, 146, 151
Truman, Harry S., 159, 165
Tuberculosis, disease, 8

Uncollected Early Prose, 228
Understanding Fiction (Brooks and Warren), 192
Union of Technical Workers, Painters, and Sculptors, 52, 57
Unrue, Darlene Harbour, 68–69, 214, 270; *Truth and Vision,* 284
Upton, Charles (character), 111–12
Uspensky (character), 84

Vanderbilt University, 115
Van Doren, Carl, 11, 60
Van Doren, Mark, 190
Vasconcelos, José, 47, 52
Vera, 217; see also *Werra*
Victoria, Texas, 7
Vietnam War, 165
Villa, Pancho, 43
Vindication of the Rights of Women, A (Wollstonecraft), 190
Virginia, University of, 140
"Virginia Woolf's Essays—A Great Art, a Sober Craft," 241
"Virgin Violeta," 64, 70
Vogue, 168, 171, 243

Waldron, Ann, 115, 120
Walsh, Thomas F., 63, 80, 87, 157, 214–15, 283
War and Peace (Tolstoy), 170
War effort, 156; writers and, 154
Ware Group, 144
Warren, Robert Penn, 26, 115, 118, 125–26, 225, 226, 268, 278, 285; *All the King's Men,* 238; on KAP's writing, 86, 114, 214, 251, 256, 277, 282–83; New Criticism and, 129–30, 192; racial views of, 122–23
Washington, D.C., 107
Washington and Lee University, 140
Water Wheel Tavern, *see* Doylestown, Pa.
Welty, Eudora, 197, 200, 242, 251; on KAP's writing, 251, 282–83
Werra, 96, 268
Wescott, Barbara Harrison, 83, 100, 143, 148, 205, 208, 283; financial assistance by, 100–101, 203–4

Wescott, Glenway, xvii, 101–2, 132, 173–74, 177, 184–85, 186, 212, 257, 268, 273–74, 281; correspondence with KAP, 11, 100–101, 206, 225; *Fear and Trembling,* 148–49; on KAP's writing, 70, 114, 214, 252–53, 282; and writing of *Ship of Fools,* 203–6
Weston, Edward, 55, 76, 87, 305 n. 52
Weston, Hattie, 195
Wheeler, Monroe, 83, 100–101, 127, 145, 148, 203, 268
"Where Presidents Have No Friends," 31, 58–59, 60, 82
Wilkins, William R., 279–80, 285
Williams, Sumner, 173, 185
Williams, Tennessee, 179
Williams, William Carlos, 146, 163, 190, 226
Wilson, Edmund, 189, 231
Winslow, Marcella Comés, 220, 224, 271
Winters, Janet, 190
Winters, Yvor, 79, 98, 122
"Witness, The," 135
Wolfe, Thomas, 190, 225–26
Wollstonecraft, Mary, 190
Womanhood, ideals of, 175–76, 190, 194
Woman's Home Companion, 168
Woman suffrage, 40, 169, 335 n. 26
Women: composers, 191; status of, 77, 187, 195, 289; writers, 170, 187, 189, 190–91, 242
"Wooden Umbrella, The," 232–38
Woodward, C. Vann, 117–18
Woolf, Virginia, 240–42, 250; *Captain's Death Bed, The,* 241; *To the Lighthouse,* 229; *Waves, The,* 240
World War I, 29–30, 154–55, 223, 262; and civil liberties, 30, 304 n. 45; KAP's dissent from chauvinism of, 27, 46, 151; in "Pale Horse, Pale Rider," 9; results of, 113, 140, 179, 316 n. 4
World War II, 27, 93, 102, 105, 113, 148–57, 196, 273; and civil liberties, 156–57; KAP's support of, 110, 151–54, 268; and shift in KAP's politics, 15, 27, 39, 268
"Wreath for the Gamekeeper, A," 231–32
Writer's block, 184; *see also* Porter, writer's block of
Writers Take Sides, 142

Yaddo Artists' Colony, 128, 158, 177, 179–80, 279
Yeats, W. B., 226
Young, Stark, 123
Yúdico, Samuel, 80

Zapata, Emiliano, 43, 57, 69